Introduction to Legal Research and Writing

Carol M. Bast

Professor in the Department of Legal Studies
University of Central Florida

Carolina Academic Press
Durham, North Carolina

Library of Congress Cataloging-in-Publication Data
Names: Bast, Carol M., author.
Title: Introduction to legal research and writing / by Carol M. Bast.
Description: Durham, North Carolina : Carolina Academic Press, LLC, [2020]
Identifiers: LCCN 2020036429 (print) | LCCN 2020036430 (ebook) | ISBN 9781531020255 (paperback) | ISBN 9781531020262 (ebook)
Subjects: LCSH: Legal composition. | Legal research--United States. | Law--Methodology.
Classification: LCC KF250 .B3787 2020 (print) | LCC KF250 (ebook) | DDC 808.06/634--dc23
LC record available at https://lccn.loc.gov/2020036429
LC ebook record available at https://lccn.loc.gov/2020036430

Carolina Academic Press
700 Kent Street
Durham, North Carolina 27701
Telephone (919) 489-7486
Fax (919) 493-5668
www.cap-press.com

Printed in the United States of America

Contents

Preface

This text is designed to provide:

a) a clear explanation of basic information;
b) exercises to give the student the necessary practice in researching and writing; and
c) sample legal writing documents.

The ideal text should be "user-friendly" and readable while balancing the need for detail. Each chapter would cover only a manageable amount of material for someone who has not been previously exposed to the law. This book attempts to fill that need for the legal studies student and professor.

The objectives of the legal research portion of the book are to teach the student how:

1. to competently perform legal research in the law library and on the computer;
2. to use correct citation form; and
3. to understand the fundamentals of legal research.

The objectives of the legal writing portion of the book are:

1. to explain the fundamentals of legal analysis and writing;
2. to teach the student how to communicate clearly; and
3. to explain how to eliminate mechanical errors.

Organization of the Text

The legal research portion of the book and Appendix B contain basic citation rules and research exercises. To facilitate the student's participation, this portion emphasizes the process of finding and using primary sources and gives the student "hands-on" experience by completing legal research exercises. Chapters 1 and 2 give an important overview of the legal system and legal reasoning. Chapters 3 through 6 introduce legal encyclopedias, digests, *American Law Reports*, cases, constitutions, statutes, court rules, administrative law, and citators. The chapters also contain lengthy research assignments, allowing the professor to assign certain of the exercises one term and a different set of exercises another term. Chapter 7 gives an overview of the research process and explains how the various legal sources studied relate to each other. Chapter 8 introduces computer-assisted legal research and explores the Internet as a legal research tool.

Primary and secondary sources are covered in separate chapters in the text. This organization allows the professor the freedom to choose which type of source to cover first. The chapter on secondary sources precedes the chapters on primary sources because many legal research professors cover secondary sources before primary sources.

The sequence chosen for these chapters tracks the order in which a researcher who is unfamiliar with a particular area of the law commences a research assignment. Unless the legal researcher has somehow already found a primary source on point, the researcher will most likely begin research by referring to a secondary source first.

The legal writing portion of the book explains how to write legal documents and includes samples of various types of legal documents. Chapters 9 and 10 give an introduction to legal writing and legal writing fundamentals. Chapters 11 through 15 are each devoted to a different type of legal document, starting with the transmittal letter and the client opinion letter and continuing through pleadings and motions, the office memo, the memorandum of law, and the appellate brief.

The various types of legal documents are explained in separate chapters, again to allow the professor to choose which chapters are to be covered, time permitting. A professor who does not usually cover a particular type of document may enjoy the challenge of teaching something a little different. In addition, the book is a good reference for the student who is later asked to write a type of legal document not studied in legal writing class.

The appendices contain additional material that could be profitably used in either legal research or legal writing. They provide the student with an explanation of and necessary practice in eliminating mechanical errors, quoting correctly, and writing short- and long-form citations correctly. The rules for quotations and short-form citations are not covered in many other texts but are something the student should master. Appendix E contains four fact patterns. These fact patterns can serve as the subject of a legal research assignment and then later as the subject of a client opinion letter, office memo, memorandum of law, or appellate brief.

Making the Book "User Friendly" by Including a Search and Seizure Problem

A legal research and writing book could easily be the most boring textbook in the entire bookstore. My challenge was to write a book that would spark student interest and involve the student in the research and writing process. Students learn more if they are involved in the course materials. I found that students are keenly interested in "search and seizure" because the topic is easy to "picture" and understand. I decided to use the topic to make the book student friendly.

The text entices the student to participate in the learning process by discussing primary sources and documents relating to the search-and-seizure topic. The search-and-seizure materials are fairly easy to understand, contain interesting and easy-to-grasp facts, and can be a basis for a number of class discussions. References throughout the book to the search-and-seizure topic involve the students in the course materials and provide continuity. The search-and-seizure topic also lends itself to some great class discussions. By using this important topic, students will learn legal research and writing and some substantive law at the same time. Where the search-and-seizure topic is not used, other topics appear several times in the text and in the exercises.

Appendix A expands the student's involvement with Joshua, who was first introduced in Chapter 2. That appendix cites suggested primary authorities to use in answering the issues raised in *Smeek*. These materials can profitably be used when completing the writing exercises found at the end of the appendix.

Decreasing Professor Preparation Time

Legal research and legal writing are typically very time-consuming courses in a legal studies curriculum. Many professors shy away from teaching these courses because of the time commitment. Just keeping up with grading assignments leaves very little time for outside preparation of material. A "professor friendly" book is self-contained and eliminates the need for a great deal of professor-prepared materials.

This book is designed to be the only one the student and the professor need for legal research and legal writing. Basic citation rules are included in Chapters 3 and 5 and Appendix B, thus eliminating the need for a separate citation manual. However, some professors may require students to purchase a citation manual, such as the *Bluebook*, for reference. The citation rules are consistent with *Bluebook* form so that the advanced student can later refer to the *Bluebook* or other citation manual when necessary. As explained, the legal research portion of the book contains sample pages from the various authorities and research exercises. The legal writing portion of the book contains sample documents, heavily footnoted to offer the student guidance on the writing process.

Key Features of *Introduction to Legal Research and Writing*

This book the following features:

- the writing style is student-friendly;
- key terms are bolded on first use, are defined in text boxes, and are included in the glossary;

- the "Research Tip" feature highlights important legal research procedures;
- the "Legal Analysis Tip" feature highlights information crucial to legal analysis;
- students can use the "You Be the Judge" feature to enhance their critical thinking skills, and the instructor can use this feature to spark classroom discussion;
- the "Writing Tip" feature highlights writing advice that otherwise might be overlooked;
- Chapters 1 through 7 contain a lengthy discussion of sources of law and law library resources;
- Chapter 2 provides a detailed explanation of legal analysis and legal reasoning;
- Chapter 6 contains an explanation of the use of online citators;
- Chapter 8 provides a comprehensive, but not overly detailed, discussion of computer-assisted legal research;
- Chapter 9 introduces legal writing and discusses ethical obligations in writing legal documents with examples from recent cases;
- Chapter 10 discusses writing basics, including the writing process, avoidance of mechanical errors, and editing and proofing;
- Chapters 11 through 15 contain sample legal writing documents, with the documents in Chapters 11 through 14 heavily annotated by footnotes to provide writing assistance to students;
- Appendix B explains how to locate and cite to cases;
- Appendix F contains the text of wiretapping statutes discussed in Chapter 5;
- many chapters provide discussion points to spark classroom discussion; and
- many chapters include cyberlaw exercises that can be assigned to further explore relevant information online.

Acknowledgments

I could not have written this book without the help of my husband, Richard Firth. He gave me the emotional support I needed (as well as the technological support).

Carol M. Bast

Introduction

If you are just starting your study of law, you may be wondering what legal research and legal writing have to do with law. After all, you do not see television and movie lawyers performing legal research or writing legal documents. They are usually portrayed arguing eloquently to the judge and jury. What television and movies do not show is all the legal research and writing that took place before the lawyer entered the courtroom.

The job of the lawyer and those working with the lawyer is to competently deal with the client's problem. The client may need the lawyer to either help the client avoid a problem or help the client solve a problem. A client may ask the lawyer to write a will or contract or represent the client in a real estate closing. In these types of transactions, the lawyer helps the client avoid problems by advising the client of the client's rights and responsibilities, by helping the client plan the best course of action, and by drafting any necessary legal documents. Where a problem exists, the client may ask the lawyer to file a lawsuit on the client's behalf or defend the client in a lawsuit. In dealing with a litigation matter, the lawyer advises the client, drafts any necessary legal documents, and represents the client in court.

Legal research and writing are the basic skills necessary for avoiding and solving legal problems. To deal with a problem, the lawyer first has to know the relevant law. Discovering what the law is requires legal research. Inadequate knowledge of relevant law may cause the client to lose money or lose a lawsuit. Once the lawyer knows the relevant law, the lawyer avoids or solves problems by communicating—with the client, another lawyer, the court, the jury, and others. Many times the communication is oral, but the lawyer often must communicate using the lawyer's legal writing skills.

Besides causing the client problems, inadequate legal research or mistakes in written communication may cause the lawyer to be disciplined or disbarred because state lawyer ethics rules also govern lawyer legal research and communication.

The provisions of a number of lawyer ethics rules are discussed in Chapters 7 and 9. The attorney must perform legal tasks in a timely manner. The lawyer generally may not reveal client confidential information. The lawyer has a duty to give the client honest advice. The lawyer may not represent the client if the claim or defense is frivolous. The lawyer must be truthful in dealing with the court and others and has a duty to explain the law to the court. The lawyer must respect the legal rights of others and not cause undue "embarrass[ment], delay or burden." The lawyer must supervise nonlawyer assistants and may be held responsible for the actions of the nonlawyer assistants. A lawyer may not falsely attack the reputation of a judge, a juror, or a legal official. A lawyer may not engage in conduct that violates an ethics rule or that is dishonest, fraudulent, or deceitful.

In today's competitive legal job market, you need to know how to competently research and write. Potential employers and colleagues are looking for someone who has these skills. Once on the job, those you come in contact with will assume that you know how to perform legal research and write legal documents. They may not have enough time to teach you those skills if you do not already have them. You will have to work hard to build credibility. You may easily lose this credibility if your colleagues sense you lack basic skills.

The legal researcher must find all law relevant to the legal question being researched, must apply the law to the legal question, and must reach an answer. An answer to a legal question is inadequate if it is not supported by legal principles, if it is not based on current law, or if it is based on incomplete legal research. A lawyer's competency is immediately in question if the lawyer's argument does not take into account recent changes in the law or applicable legal principles.

The legal writer has the challenge of representing the best interests of the client while often facing a hostile audience. A court document will be closely scrutinized by the judge and opposing counsel. The details of a will are studied when the decedent's estate is administered and may be challenged by relatives omitted from the will. The wording of a contract will be analyzed as the contract is performed, especially if a problem arises. Drafting legal documents is an important part of a lawyer's role; the reader judges the competency of the writer by the clarity and effectiveness of the legal document. Poor writing will deter and prejudice the reader and may cause problems if the writing is misunderstood; inept writing may cause litigation; unclear writing obscures the message the writer is attempting to communicate.

Legal research and legal writing are skills learned with practice. This book is written to give you basic information on legal research and legal writing; it contains research and writing exercises to help you learn how to perform legal research and write legal documents. The first half of the book describes basic legal research materials found in the law library and online. You will be searching these materials to find relevant legal principles. You will apply the legal principles you discover to answer legal research exercises. The second half of the book first helps you improve your basic writing skills by avoiding common errors, writing in plain English, and organizing. The book then introduces the traditional format of common legal documents—letters, office memos, pleadings, memoranda of law, and appellate briefs. Now that you know why legal research and legal writing are important to someone dealing with the law, it is time for you to learn how to perform legal research and write legal documents.

About the Author

Carol M. Bast, J.D., LL.M., is a professor in the Department of Legal Studies at the University of Central Florida, where she has taught for the past thirty years. She teaches Legal Research and Legal Writing and authored an undergraduate textbook on those topics. She teaches the survey course, Law and the Legal System, and co-authored an undergraduate textbook used in the course. Her areas of research and writing include eavesdropping and wiretapping, plagiarism, legal ethics, legal research, legal writing, and international trade agreements. She served as editor-in-chief of the *Journal of Legal Studies in Business*, November 2008–November 2010; she served as editor-in-chief of the *Journal of Legal Studies Education*, August 2006–August 2008. Prior to becoming a professor, Bast clerked for a federal district judge and practiced corporate, securities, and real estate law. She received her LL.M. in International Economic Law and Policy from the University of Barcelona in 2016, her J.D. magna cum laude from New York Law School in 1982, and her B.A. from Kalamazoo College in 1974.

Introduction to Legal Research and Writing

Chapter 1

Law and Sources of Law

Introduction

The material in Chapters 2 through 7 will teach you basic legal research skills. This chapter is designed to provide you with an understanding of:

- the American system of law,
- our tripartite system of government, and
- sources of law.

The first portion of the chapter introduces you to basic terminology such as *common law*, *civil law*, and *federalism*. The second portion of the chapter discusses the roles of the three branches of government and the interplay among the three branches in lawmaking. The final portion of the chapter introduces you to the terms *primary sources*, *secondary sources*, and *finding tools*.

The information in this chapter may be a review for those of you who have completed an introductory law course; for others, the chapter may contain new information. The chapter provides you with basic information needed to better understand subsequent chapters concerning legal research; thus, the chapter describes a framework into which you can fit the pieces of the legal research puzzle. You may find yourself referring to this chapter as you learn to perform legal research. You will be amazed at how much better you understand the material in this chapter after you have covered subsequent chapters.

The American System of Law

Our Common Law Heritage

Common law and civil law systems rely on different sources of law. **Common law** is the system of law developed in England and transferred to most of the English-speaking world. A traditional common law system emphasizes case law or common law over legislation.

Common Law
1. Either all caselaw or the caselaw that is made by judges in the absence of statutes.
2. The legal system that originated in England and is composed of caselaw and statutes that grow and change, influenced by ever-changing custom and tradition.

Many other countries are civil law jurisdictions. The **civil law** system traditionally emphasizes a comprehensive statutory code over case law. Louisiana is the only state in the United States that is a civil law jurisdiction and whose law is based on both common and civil law systems. Because of the state's French and Spanish heritage, Louisiana's civil code is based on the French Code Napoléan and the Spanish Fuero Real.

Civil Law
1. Law handed down by the Romans. Law that is based on one elaborate document or "code," rather than a combination of many laws and judicial opinions.
2. "Noncriminal law."

Common law is law developed case-by-case from court decisions. Legal principles are developed over time as cases are decided. Judges decide cases after examining what other courts have done in similar cases in the past. Judges may have to examine many cases before reaching a decision. Common law combines stability and flexibility. It is predictable, yet it allows legal principles either to be expanded to fit new situations or to be replaced with a new legal principle that better accommodates current or changing social and economic conditions. The common law system considers prior case law to be a very high source of authority and follows the **doctrine of stare decisis**. Stare decisis means "let the decision stand." Under the doctrine of stare decisis, a court should follow the legal principle decided by that court or a higher court in a prior case where the facts of the prior case are substantially the same as the facts in the present case.

Doctrine of Stare Decisis (Latin) "Let the decision stand." The rule that when a court has decided a case by applying a legal principle to a set of facts, the court should stick to the principle and apply it to all later cases with clearly similar facts, unless there is a strong reason not to, and that inferior courts must apply the principle in similar cases.

At the founding of this country, common law was the primary source of law, except in Louisiana. There was no important body of United States statutory law until the late nineteenth century. Until the turn of the twentieth century, courts were more active than legislatures in developing the law. Congress and the state legislatures played a subsidiary role to the courts until the late nineteenth and early twentieth centuries. Congress and the state legislatures began to be very active at the beginning of the twentieth century with the advent of the industrial revolution. Federal and state legislatures became more active with the increase in population, the change from a rural to an urban economy, and the increase in industrial accidents following the industrial revolution. The legislatures felt the need to provide broad and detailed solutions to the problems of an increasingly industrialized society. Legislation could provide resolution to commonly occurring disputes without waiting for the courts to decide on a case-by-case basis. Statutory law changed many common law principles to reflect societal changes. The increasing legislative activity shifted the focus of lawmaking from the courts to federal and state legislatures. Legislatures were better able to deal with problems inherent in a rapidly growing, increasingly industrialized country. The federal and state legislatures began to pass statutes to safeguard the welfare of an increasingly industrialized workforce and to guarantee the safety of mass-produced products to the consumer. As federal and state legislatures became more active, statutory law increased in importance. Statutes have replaced common law as the primary source of law.

Civil Law

Civil law is based on a civil code, a systematic and comprehensive written set of rules of law. Judges look to the civil code to settle disputes, rather than rely on precedent. The civil law system considers the legislative code of laws to be a very high source of authority. The legislative code provides comprehensive coverage of all of the basic law of the country. In deciding a legal problem, the code must be reviewed to find the appropriate code provision, and the provision must be applied to solve the legal problem. In applying code provisions, judges rely primarily on scholarly articles and books written by professors rather than on prior case law. Cases may also be reviewed, but prior case law is not binding as it is in a common law system. Judges also consult the interpretive notes following court decisions. The professors writing the interpretive notes discuss the relationship of the court decision to applicable code provisions and legal principles.

For example, the Louisiana civil code is comprised of articles; the articles contain short, declarative sentences without subparagraphs or internal definitions. Attorneys and judges faced with a legal problem consult the detailed rules of the code, which contains a mixture of general legal principles and answers to specific legal problems. The code governs wills, estates, succession law and marital property, sales, real property transactions, mortgages, conflicts of laws, statutes of limitation, co-ownership, contract formation and interpretation, tort liability, and allocation of loss. Louisiana follows the doctrine of **jurisprudence constante** rather than the doctrine of stare decisis. As explained earlier, courts following the doctrine of stare decisis are bound to follow a decision of the same court or a higher court when the facts in the prior decision are substantially the same as the facts in the present case. Under jurisprudence constante, a court respects a prior decision but is not bound to follow even the decision of a higher court where the higher court decision differs from the language of the code.

Jurisprudence Constante In deciding a legal problem, the code must be reviewed to find the appropriate code provision, and the provision must be applied to solve the legal problem. In applying the code provisions, judges rely primarily on scholarly articles and books written by professors rather than on prior case law. Cases may also be reviewed, but prior case law is not binding as it is in a common-law system.

In applying a provision of the Louisiana civil code that is similar to a Code Napoléon provision, state courts might consult scholarly treatises interpreting the Code Napoléon.

Federalism

The United States **Constitution** is perhaps the most important legal document for our country because it both establishes the federal tripartite system of government and contains our country's fundamental principles of law.

Constitution

1. A document that sets out the basic principles and most general laws of a country, state, or organization.
2. The United States Constitution is the basic law of the country on which most other laws are based and to which all other laws must yield.

In addition, the Constitution divides governing and lawmaking power between federal and state governments, with this division of power referred to as **federalism**.

Federalism A system of political organizations with several different levels of government (e.g., city, state, and national) coexisting in the same area with the lower levels having some interdependent powers.

As more fully explained below, the Constitution grants the federal government certain powers on an exclusive basis, meaning that the states are prohibited from exercising power in those areas. The Constitution grants the federal government other powers on a nonexclusive basis, meaning that the federal and state governments can exercise their powers in those areas concurrently. For example, both federal and state governments criminalize possession and distribution of certain substances, such as narcotics, deemed to be dangerous.

The Constitution sets forth the powers of Congress in Article I. Article I, section 8 specifically lists certain powers granted to Congress, and Article I, section 10 prohibits the states from exercising certain powers granted to Congress. Powers exclusively granted to Congress include regulating interstate and foreign commerce, establishing immigration and bankruptcy law, coining money, issuing patents, declaring war, establishing an army and a navy, making treaties, conducting foreign diplomacy, and imposing import and export taxes. The Tenth Amendment to the United States Constitution reserves the powers not granted to the federal government to the states.

Article I, section 8 of the United States Constitution provides:

> The Congress shall have Power To lay and collect Taxes, Duties, Imposts and Excises, to pay the Debts and provide for the common Defence and general Welfare of the United States; but all Duties, Imposts and Excises shall be uniform throughout the United States;
>
> To borrow Money on the credit of the United States;
>
> To regulate Commerce with foreign Nations, and among the several States, and with the Indian Tribes;
>
> To establish an uniform Rule of Naturalization, and uniform Laws on the subject of Bankruptcies throughout the United States;
>
> To coin Money, regulate the Value thereof, and of foreign Coin, and fix the Standard of Weights and Measures;
>
> To provide for the Punishment of counterfeiting the Securities and current Coin of the United States;
>
> To establish Post Offices and post Roads;
>
> To promote the Progress of Science and useful Arts, by securing for limited Times to Authors and Inventors the exclusive Right to their respective Writings and Discoveries;
>
> To constitute Tribunals inferior to the supreme Court;
>
> To define and punish Piracies and Felonies committed on the high Seas, and Offences against the Law of Nations;
>
> To declare War, grant Letters of Marque and Reprisal, and make Rules concerning Captures on Land and Water;
>
> To raise and support Armies, but no Appropriation of Money to that Use shall be for a longer Term than two Years;
>
> To provide and maintain a Navy;
>
> To make Rules for the Government and Regulation of the land and naval Forces;
>
> To provide for calling forth the Militia to execute the Laws of the Union, suppress Insurrections and repel Invasions;
>
> To provide for organizing, arming, and disciplining, the Militia, and for governing such Part of them as may be employed in the Service of the United States, reserving to the States

respectively, the Appointment of the Officers, and the Authority of training the Militia according to the discipline prescribed by Congress;

To exercise exclusive Legislation in all Cases whatsoever, over such District (not exceeding ten Miles square) as may, by Cession of particular States, and the Acceptance of Congress, become the Seat of the Government of the United States, and to exercise like Authority over all Places purchased by the Consent of the Legislature of the State in which the Same shall be, for the Erection of Forts, Magazines, Arsenals, dock-Yards, and other needful Buildings; — And

To make all Laws which shall be necessary and proper for carrying into Execution the foregoing Powers, and all other Powers vested by this Constitution in the Government of the United States, or in any Department or Officer thereof.

Article I, section 10 of the United States Constitution provides:

No State shall enter into any Treaty, Alliance, or Confederation; grant Letters of Marque and Reprisal; coin Money; emit Bills of Credit; make any Thing but gold and silver Coin a Tender in Payment of Debts; pass any Bill of Attainder, ex post facto Law, or Law impairing the Obligation of Contracts, or grant any Title of Nobility.

No State shall, without the Consent of the Congress, lay any Imposts or Duties on Imports or Exports, except what may be absolutely necessary for executing its inspection Laws: and the net Produce of all Duties and Imposts, laid by any State on Imports or Exports, shall be for the Use of the Treasury of the United States; and all such Laws shall be subject to the Revision and Controul of the Congress.

No State shall, without the Consent of Congress, lay any Duty of Tonnage, keep Troops, or Ships of War in time of Peace, enter into any Agreement or Compact with another State, or with a foreign Power, or engage in War, unless actually invaded, or in such imminent Danger as will not admit of delay.

The Tenth Amendment to the United States Constitution provides:

The powers not delegated to the United States by the Constitution, nor prohibited by it to the States, are reserved to the States respectively, or to the people.

The United States has a legal system for the federal government and a legal system for each state and the District of Columbia. A state constitution provides a legal foundation for the state in a way similar to that provided for by the United States Constitution. A state constitution typically establishes the state branches of government and contains basic principles of law. In addition, local governments, such as counties, cities, and towns, can enact local laws, including **charters** and **ordinances**.

Charter An organization's basic starting document.

Ordinance A local or city law, rule, or regulation.

The Supremacy Clause

One of the basic principles of this country's law is the **supremacy clause** that is found in Article VI of the United States Constitution:

> This Constitution, and the Laws of the United States which shall be made in Pursuance thereof... shall be the supreme Law of the Land; and the Judges in every State shall be bound thereby, any Thing in the Constitution or Laws of any State to the contrary notwithstanding.

Supremacy Clause The provision in Article VI of the United States Constitution that the Constitution, laws, and treaties take precedence over conflicting state constitutions or laws.

This provision makes the United States Constitution the supreme law of the land and prohibits any federal statute, state constitution, or state statute from conflicting with it. A perceived conflict can be subject to a court challenge; the issue in such a case is typically whether the federal government has **preempted** state action.

Preempted Foreclosed, prevailed over, took precedence over.

If a court finds a conflict, the court would hold the offending provision as unconstitutional and unenforceable.

Under the **preemption doctrine**, the action of the federal government reigns over any state action if (1) Congress declared its intention to exclusively govern (express preemption); (2) federal law, by its substance and purpose, disallows application of state action (implied preemption); or (3) an actual conflict exists between current federal and state law (conflict preemption).

Preemption Doctrine Describes the first right to do anything. For example, when the federal government preempts the field by passing laws in a subject area, the states may not pass conflicting laws and sometimes may not pass laws on the subject at all.

An example of conflict preemption would be a state attempting to set a minimum wage less than the minimum wage required to be paid under the federal Fair Labor Standards Act. When challenged, a court would hold the state statute unconstitutional and unenforceable.

Our Tripartite System

The United States Constitution divides federal power among the **legislative, judicial**, and **executive branches** of government, each with a crucial role in lawmaking. This chapter provides basic information on the three branches of the federal government and the interplay among the three branches.

Legislative Branch Lawmaking, as opposed to "executive" (carrying out or enforcing laws) or "judicial" (interpreting or applying laws). Concerning a legislature.

Judicial Branch Describes the branch of government that interprets the law and that resolves legal disputes.

Executive Branch The branch of government that carries out the laws (as opposed to the judicial and legislative branches). The administrative branch.

The distribution of powers among the three branches requires each branch to interact with the other two in significant ways; this required interaction has inherent in it certain checks and balances, such that no one branch is more powerful than the other two. State constitutions establish similar frameworks for the states. Legislatures pass statutes setting forth broad public policies. The legislative branch is discussed more fully later in this chapter and in Chapter 5. The president is responsible for administering and enforcing the nation's laws, conducting foreign affairs, negotiating treaties, and is the commander in chief of the military.

Administrative agencies, often considered a part of the executive branch, promulgate detailed administrative rules and regulations that have the force of law.

Administrative Agency A subbranch of the government set up to carry out the laws. For example, the police department is a local administrative agency, and the IRS is a national one.

The executive branch is discussed more fully in this chapter. The courts make law; interpret constitutions, statutes, and administrative regulations; and settle disputes based on the law. The judicial branch is discussed more fully in this chapter and in Chapter 4.

Administrative Law Rules, regulations, and orders written by administrative agencies.

Interplay among the Three Branches of Government in Lawmaking

The three branches of government have different roles in the lawmaking process. These roles and the interplay among the three branches balance the lawmaking power, with each branch checking the lawmaking power of the other two.

Interplay between the Legislative and Judicial Branches

Look first at the interplay between the legislative and judicial branches. Legislatures pass statutes to address a public problem. Where statutory language is very general, the courts have a lot of freedom to interpret statutes through cases in which the courts decide if and how a statute applies to a problem. Even where statutory language is much more specific, a court may be called upon to interpret particular statutory language or to decide if a statute applies to the problem before the court.

Legislatures enact statutes governing many different types of matters. However, statutes do not cover all legal problems that arise. When a legal problem is not covered by a statute, attorneys and judges consult case law (common law). Judges make common law principles. Common law principles emerge as cases are decided.

The founders of the American legal system chose to adopt the common law system as the basis of our country's law. Common law is based on the doctrine of precedent. Precedent lends fairness, coherence, predictability, and reliability to the common law. The common law is stable, yet flexible, changing to meet the needs of a dynamic society. Historically, case law was emphasized over legislation, but this has changed with the rapid growth of and importance of legislation. Today, some areas of the law, such as torts, continue to be governed almost exclusively by case law; some areas are governed by statutes (as interpreted by the courts and administrative agencies); other areas are governed partly by case law and partly by statutes.

In *Marbury v. Madison*, Chief Justice John Marshall wrote that federal courts could determine if a statute were invalid because it was in conflict with the United States Constitution. Judicial review of the constitutionality of a statute is grounded in the supremacy clause and the clause giving federal courts jurisdiction over cases "arising under this Constitution." Federal courts in the United States can declare a statute invalid if it conflicts with the United States Constitution. State courts can declare a statute invalid if it conflicts with the United States Constitution or the state constitution. This is commonly known as the **doctrine of judicial review.**

Doctrine of Judicial Review Principle that a higher court examines a lower court decision.

The legislature can change common law by passing statutes that supersede the common law. One reason to change the prior common law is because the legislature recognizes a need to systematically regulate an area of the law previously governed by case law. An example of this is the Uniform Commercial Code, a portion of which, in some form, has been adopted by all 50 states. Another reason to change the prior common law is to "overrule" unpopular court decisions. In 1989, the United States Supreme Court ruled that burning the United States flag was constitutionally protected as an expression of free speech. In response, several members of Congress proposed amending the United States Constitution to outlaw flag burning. Because it generally takes such a long time to amend the Constitution, the members suggested passing a federal statute prohibiting flag burning in the meantime. Congress enacted a federal statute criminalizing this conduct, in obvious contravention of the First Amendment. That statute might have been enforced until challenged in court. After the statute was challenged in court, the United States Supreme Court declared it unconstitutional in 1990.

Once enacted, constitutions, statutes, and regulations are then interpreted by the courts. In applying constitutions, statutes, and regulations to a particular case, a court in effect explains what a provision means. The court's interpretative role is such a significant one that constitutions, statutes, and regulations must be read in light of the case law application of them. Sometimes a court is asked to determine the constitutionality of a statute or regulation. For example, in *Roe v. Wade*, 410 U.S. 113 (1973), the United States Supreme Court based its decision on an implied constitutional right to privacy. Although this right is not explicitly stated in the Constitution, the United States Supreme Court interpreted the Bill of Rights to require the existence of this unstated right under the theory that other important rights, such as the right against unreasonable search and seizure, would be meaningless without an implied right to privacy. The Court thus struck down Texas antiabortion statutes because they conflicted with the constitutional right to privacy.

Congress possesses considerable authority over the jurisdiction of the federal courts. Political concerns could, therefore, cause legislators to limit the jurisdiction of the judiciary over certain issues. Congress has the authority to remove cases from the appellate jurisdiction of the United States Supreme Court and, presumably, could limit the jurisdiction of lower courts. Also, because the courts inferior to the United States Supreme Court were created by Congress, they could be abolished by Congress.

The Chief Executive

The primary role of the **chief executive** is to enforce the law.

> **Chief Executive** The head of the executive branch of government. For a state, the chief executive is the governor and, for the federal government, the chief executive is the president.

Article II, section 1 of the United States Constitution provides:

> The executive Power shall be vested in a President of the United States of America.

Article II, section 2, clause 2 of the United States Constitution gives the president the following powers:

> He shall have Power, by and with the Advice and Consent of the Senate, to make Treaties, provided two thirds of the Senators present concur; and he shall nominate, and by and with the Advice and Consent of the Senate, shall appoint Ambassadors, other public Ministers and Consuls, Judges of the supreme Court, and all other Officers of the United States, whose Appointments are not herein otherwise provided for, and which shall be established by Law: but the Congress may by Law vest the Appointment of such inferior Officers, as they think proper, in the President alone, in the Courts of Law, or in the Heads of Departments.

Several of the president's official roles, including that of a United States military commander, give the president the power to issue proclamations and executive orders. These documents have the force of law, similar to case law or statutory law.

The executive branch affects and is affected by the other two branches in a number of ways. The chief executive may veto legislation. Vetoed legislation can be enacted only if the legislature has sufficient votes to override the veto. The chief executive also greatly influences the enforcement of legislation, in part through funding and publicity. Usually there is insufficient personnel and money to enforce all legislation, so the executive may direct that special attention be paid to certain laws. A priority in recent years has been the enforcement of criminal statutes prohibiting illegal drug trade. The most lasting effect a president has may be from the constitutional mandate to nominate federal judges. Once confirmed by the Senate, such an appointment is for life, unless the judge resigns or is impeached.

The president conducts foreign affairs and negotiates treaties. Congress, the Senate in particular, must ratify treaties. The president is the commander in chief of the military, but Congress possesses significant authority over the military as well. It is charged with making rules regulating the military and is responsible for declaring war. The president has been delegated the authority to nominate federal judges and other governmental officers, but the appointments are final only after Senate confirmation. As a check on both the president and the judiciary, Congress holds the power of impeachment.

The Judicial Branch

The Constitution delegates to the president the power to nominate, and the Senate to confirm, all federal court judges and justices. Once appointed, a federal judge serves until retirement, death, or **impeachment**. Congress has the power to impeach a federal judge for high crimes and misdemeanors.

Impeachment	The first step in the removal from public office of a high public official.

To impeach the United States president, the House of Representatives drafts articles of impeachment, votes on them, and presents them to the Senate. But impeachment is popularly thought to include the process that may take place after the impeachment: the trial of the president in the Senate.

Administrative Agencies

By statute, federal and state legislatures can establish administrative agencies and delegate the power to promulgate **administrative regulations** to those agencies. Administrative regulations make up **administrative law**, a source of law similar to statutes and cases.

Administrative Regulations	Law written by administrative agencies.

Some consider these agencies a "fourth branch" of government; however, they are usually placed under the executive branch because the heads of administrative agencies may be nominated by the chief executive (president or governor). In promulgating administrative regulations, an agency is performing a quasi-legislative function. In addition, the agency is usually given the quasi-executive power to enforce the regulations and the quasi-judicial power for administrative law judges to decide disputes concerning the administrative regulations and impose sanctions.

Federal agencies include the Federal Trade Commission, the Environmental Protection Agency, the Internal Revenue Service, and the Food and Drug Administration. States have state administrative agencies. For example, Florida has the Department of Natural Resources, the Department of Business and Professional Regulation, and the Department of Children and Families.

Now that you know something about the law produced by the three branches of our government, you need to know where to look to find it. The next section briefly introduces primary sources, secondary sources, and finding tools. Chapters 3 through 6 contain an in-depth discussion of primary sources, secondary sources, and finding tools.

Sources of Law

Your first trip through the law library may seem overwhelming. The law library contains all kinds of sources you need to consult when researching a legal question. By the end of your legal research class, you will be familiar with many of these sources. Primary sources, secondary sources, and finding tools are all sources of law, but they are used in different ways. Their use depends on the information they contain and how authoritative they are. **Primary sources** contain the law itself and may be mandatory authority, **secondary sources** contain commentary on the law, and **finding tools**, as the name implies, are used to find primary and secondary sources.

> **Primary Sources** Contain the actual law itself and are given the most weight by courts.
>
> **Secondary Sources** Are designed to explain legal concepts and can be used to understand basic legal terms and general concepts.
>
> **Finding Tools** Those sources in a law library used to locate primary and secondary authority.

Examples of primary law include cases, constitutions, statutes, administrative regulations, municipal codes and ordinances, and court rules. Secondary sources provide the researcher with background information and a framework for an area of the law, arranging legal principles in an orderly fashion. In contrast to primary authority (constitutions, cases, statutes, court rules, and administrative regulations), secondary sources do not have the force and effect of law.

Chapter 2 contains a discussion of mandatory authority and persuasive authority. Primary sources are given the most weight, but secondary sources are considered persuasive and may be used if no primary sources are available. Finding tools are not authoritative and may not be quoted or cited. Nevertheless, finding tools are an important part of legal research. You may be able to locate relevant primary and secondary sources only by using finding tools.

The following charts show the judicial, legislative, and executive branches for the federal government and the state government of Florida as an example of a state government; these exhibits give the names of the various entities within those branches and the reference materials containing the law made by each entity. To learn about legal research for your state, you should compile a similar chart containing the information for your state.

Federal Government

Judicial Branch	Legislative Branch	Executive Branch
United States Supreme Court	Congress	President
• *slip opinions* • *loose-leaf services* • *reporters* • *United States Reports* (U.S.) • *Supreme Court Reporter* (S.Ct.) • *United States Supreme Court Reports, Lawyers' Edition* (L. Ed.)	• *slip laws* • *advance session law service* • *United States Code Congressional and Administrative News* • *session laws* • *United States Statutes at Large*	• *presidential documents*
United States Courts of Appeals	• *code* • United States Code (U.S.C.)	Administrative Agencies
• *reporters* • *Federal Reporter* (F.) • *Federal Appendix* (F. App'x)	• *annotated codes* • *United States Code Annotated* (U.S.C.A.)	• *daily publication* • *Federal Register* • *code* • *Code of Federal Regulations*
United States District Courts	• *United States Code Service* (U.S.C.S.)	
• *reporters* • *Federal Supplement*		

Florida State Government

Judicial Branch	Legislative Branch	Executive Branch
Florida Supreme Court and District Courts of Appeal	Florida Legislature	Governor
Southern Reporter *Florida Law Weekly*	*Florida Statutes* *Florida Statutes Annotated*	Administrative Agencies
Circuit and County Courts	*Florida Session Law Service*	*Florida Administrative Code*
Florida Law Weekly Supplement	*Laws of Florida*	

Primary Sources and Secondary Sources

The difference between primary sources and secondary sources is critical when working with the law. The following chart lists common and frequently used primary and secondary sources and finding tools. These sources are covered in greater depth in later chapters.

Primary Sources	Secondary Sources	Finding Tools
• constitutions • statutes • court rules • administrative regulations • cases	• treatises • law review articles • legal periodicals • restatements • *American Law Reports* • legal encyclopedias	• digests • citators

Primary sources are law. The chart above lists constitutions, cases (common law), statutes, administrative regulations, ordinances, and court rules as primary sources. Secondary sources, containing a commentary on the law, include treatises, legal periodicals, law review articles, legal encyclopedias, *American Law Reports* annotations, and restatements. Finding tools are reference publications used to find primary and secondary sources. They include digests and citators.

A major goal in legal research is to locate the primary sources relevant to the problem you are researching. Secondary sources are often used to find primary sources. Another reason for consulting a secondary source is to gain a basic understanding of the subject matter being researched.

Secondary sources used in researching Florida Law include *Florida Jurisprudence*, the state-specific legal encyclopedia, as shown in the following chart. To learn about legal research for your state, you should compile a similar chart containing the information for your state.

Secondary Sources
• *Florida Jurisprudence, Second Series* • law reviews • treatises
Finding tools
• *Florida Digest* • citators

Citation to Legal Sources

In legal writing, always **cite** the relevant primary source. We will be using the *Bluebook* to determine correct citation.

Cite Refers to specific legal references or authorities; short for "citation."

Determining which primary sources are relevant and then deciding which of those sources to cite requires an understanding of legal reasoning and the performance of legal analysis. (Legal reasoning and legal analysis are discussed in Chapter 2.) If you have found few or no relevant primary sources, you may cite certain types of secondary sources. The preferred secondary sources are treatises, legal periodicals, law review articles, law dictionaries, legal thesauruses, restatements, and continuing legal education publications. Digests should never be cited. Although you may cite legal encyclopedias and *American Law Reports* annotations, they are not a preferred citation source, and you should do so with caution. It is always better to find ("pull") the primary authority referred to in the legal encyclopedia or annotation and cite that as a primary authority rather than a secondary authority.

Summary

- Federal and state governments are each made up of three branches: legislative, judicial, and executive.
- The judicial branch (the courts) produces what is called common law, case law, or judge-made law.
- Common law is law developed case-by-case from court decisions.
- The legislative branch (elected representatives) passes statutes.
- Administrative agencies (often considered part of the executive branch) promulgate administrative rules and regulations.
- The chief executive (the president or governor) issues proclamations and executive orders.
- Federal and state laws are a product of an important interplay among the three branches of government.
- A legislature can pass statutes that supersede common law.
- The courts interpret and apply constitutions, statutes, and administrative regulations.
- The chief executive may veto legislation, set priorities in law enforcement, and appoint judges.
- The supremacy clause of the United States Constitution makes the United States Constitution the supreme law of the land. No federal or state statute or state constitution may conflict with it.
- In the law library, primary sources contain the law itself while secondary sources and finding tools are used to locate relevant primary sources.
- In addition to books from the law library, many legal researchers use computers to assist them in legal research.

Key Terms

administrative agencies
administrative law
administrative regulations
charters
chief executive
cite
civil law
common law
constitution
doctrine of judicial review
doctrine of stare decisis
executive branch
federalism
finding tools
impeachment
judicial branch
jurisprudence constante
legislative branch
ordinances
preempted
preemption doctrine
primary sources
secondary sources
supremacy clause

Exercises

1. The chart shown in this chapter uses Florida as an example of a state government. Research and create a similar chart for your state government.
2. The chart shown in this chapter containing the names of secondary sources and finding tools contains information for researching Florida law. Research and create a similar chart for your state.
3. Visit the law library you will be using and identify the federal and state primary sources, secondary sources, and finding tools you will be using in your research.
4. Find out what types of computer-assisted research are available to you.

Cyberlaw Exercises

1. Go to the website https://www.usa.gov and, from there, access a chart showing the three branches of the federal government. At the website, read about the interplay among the three branches of government.
2. For a lighthearted look at print research, go to https://www.youtube.com and watch the video "medieval helpdesk."
3. The federal judiciary homepage is located at https://www.uscourts.gov/. Using the homepage, locate your federal district court and federal court of appeals.
4. The United States Supreme Court's webpage is located at https://www.supremecourt.gov/. Using the homepage, read some of the information accessible from "Visiting the Court."
5. Congress' homepage is located at https://www.congress.gov/. Using the website, find the names of the senators and representatives from your state in the House and Senate directories.
6. The White House homepage is located at https://www.whitehouse.gov/. Using the homepage, go into the news portion of the website and read several of the recent statements and releases.
7. The homepage of the National Center for State Courts links you to websites for the courts of your state. The homepage is located at https://www.ncsc.org/. Use the page to locate information on the courts of your state.

Chapter 2

Legal Reasoning and Analysis

> When a legal distinction is determined, as no one doubts that it may be, between night and day, childhood and maturity, or any other extremes, a point has to be fixed or a line has to be drawn, or gradually picked out by successive decisions, to mark where the change takes place. Looked at by itself without regard to the necessity behind it the line or point seems arbitrary. It might as well or nearly as well be a little more to one side or the other. But when it is seen that a line or point there must be, and that there is no mathematical or logical way of fixing it precisely, the decision of the legislature must be accepted unless we can say that it is very wide of any reasonable mark.

Louisville Gas. Co. v. Coleman, 277 U.S. 32, 41 (1928) (Holmes, J., dissenting).

Introduction

Attorneys and judges use the process of legal reasoning and analysis to plan transactions and to solve legal problems by applying cases and rules (constitutions, statutes, court rules, and administrative regulations). When you research a legal problem, you are looking for primary sources that will be applicable to your problem. You must use legal reasoning and analysis to determine whether a source is in fact applicable and how it applies. This chapter begins with a quotation by Justice Oliver Wendell Holmes in which Justice Holmes talks of making legal distinctions. In performing legal reasoning analysis, you first are making a legal distinction between whether a legal source applies or does not apply. If you determine that a legal source applies, you then must determine how it applies.

This chapter is designed to provide you with an understanding of:

- the doctrine of stare decisis,
- judicial opinions,
- reasoning by analogy, and
- statutory analysis.

LEGAL ANALYSIS TIP

The Case Law Citation

The text of this chapter contains citations to a number of cases and an explanation of the information central to the citation might be helpful to the reader. For example, the first case cited is *Griswold v. Connecticut*, 381 U.S. 479 (1965). In this citation, the volume number (381) is followed by an abbreviation of the set of books containing the opinion (U.S., which stands for United States Reports). The abbreviation is followed by the number of the first page of the case (479). The year in parentheses is the year in which the case was decided.

The first portion of this chapter discusses the doctrine of stare decisis, a term central to understanding cases, and provides an example of the term. The second portion of the chapter discusses the types of judicial opinions and the terms *mandatory authority*, *persuasive authority*, and *obiter dictum* as well as reasoning by analogy. The final portion of the chapter discusses statutory analysis.

Doctrine of *Stare Decisis*

The doctrine of stare decisis states that when a court has set forth a legal principle, that court and all lower courts under it will apply that principle in future cases where the facts are substantially the same.

The doctrine of stare decisis can be illustrated with an example:

Griswold v. Connecticut, 381 U.S. 479 (1965) was a **landmark case** in which the United States Supreme Court first recognized an implied right to privacy under the United States Constitution. A landmark case is a case that establishes a new and important legal principle and is regularly cited by the courts when referring to the principle.

Landmark Case A court case that makes major changes in the law, especially a United States Supreme Court case that resolves a major issue and has substantial practical impact.

Griswold involved a Connecticut statute that banned the use of contraceptives, even between husband and wife. The constitutionality of the statute was first challenged in the Connecticut state courts. After the Supreme Court of Errors of Connecticut (the highest state court) affirmed the lower state court's enforcement of the state statute, the United States Supreme Court reviewed the case. The United States Supreme Court has jurisdiction to review final decisions of the highest state court, rejecting claims based on federal constitutional law. Thus, the United States Supreme Court makes the final interpretation of the meaning of the United States Constitution.

The Court found that "specific guarantees in the Bill of Rights have **penumbras**, formed by emanations from those guarantees that help give them life and substance.... Various guarantees create zones of privacy." The Court then determined that the Connecticut ban on the use of contraceptives "concerns a relationship lying within the zone of privacy created by several fundamental constitutional guarantees" and held the Connecticut statute unconstitutional.

Look again at the definition of the doctrine of stare decisis: "when a court has set forth a legal principle, that court and all lower courts under it will apply that principle in future cases where the facts are substantially the same." Consider the definition in light of the explanation of *Griswold*. Applying the definition to *Griswold*, "a court" and "that court" refer to the United States Supreme Court, the highest court that decided *Griswold*. In *Griswold*, the "legal principle" is that there is a constitutionally protected right to privacy. "Lower courts" to the United States Supreme Court are all federal courts and all levels of state courts in all fifty states. (See Chapter 4 for a discussion of the hierarchical structure of the federal and state courts.) Because the Court has established this principle, it and all lower courts should reach the same decision in future cases, but they only need to do so if "the facts are substantially the same."

LEGAL ANALYSIS TIP

Terms Helpful in Understanding the Discussion of Legal Analysis

Penumbra: a partially lighted area around an area of full shadow (e.g., the moon's penumbra during an eclipse)

Penumbra Doctrine: the doctrine of constitutional law that the rights specifically guaranteed in the Bill of Rights have "penumbras" creating other rights that are not specifically enumerated

Privacy: an example of a penumbra right

Legal reasoning involves determining what the legal principle is and when the facts of the present case are "substantially the same" as the prior case so that the prior case would be used as **precedent**.

Precedent A court decision that sets forth a legal principal followed in later cases.

A precedent-setting case is a case that sets forth a legal principal followed in later cases. This is sometimes called **reasoning by analogy** or **reasoning by example** because similar past cases are reviewed to determine the outcome of the present case. The terms reasoning by analogy and reasoning by example are more fully discussed in the final portion of this chapter.

> **Reasoning by Analogy** or **Reasoning by Example** Is reasoning by applying the doctrine of stare decisis: the researcher identifies case law relevant to the legal problem being researched, compares the similarities and differences among the legal problem and relevant case law, and reviews the significance of the various similarities and differences to determine if and how prior case law will control the answer to the legal problem being researched.

Griswold itself was binding only on the parties to the case. The doctrine of stare decisis makes the legal principle set forth in *Griswold* applicable to future cases. Although no two cases have material facts that are exactly the same, the facts of two cases may be similar.

Roe v. Wade *and the Doctrine of* Stare Decisis

The United States Supreme Court decided *Roe v. Wade* eight years after *Griswold*. *Roe v. Wade* was brought by a pregnant woman ("Jane Roe" was a pseudonym) challenging the constitutionality of Texas abortion laws. The laws made abortion a crime, except to save the mother's life. Before the case reached the United States Supreme Court, the federal district court had held the laws unconstitutional.

In *Roe*, the issue before the United States Supreme Court was whether the Texas laws were constitutional. Roe argued that a "woman's right [to an abortion] is absolute and that she is entitled to terminate her pregnancy at whatever time, in whatever way and for whatever reason she alone chooses." Texas argued that "life begins at conception and is present throughout pregnancy, and that therefore, the State has a compelling interest in protecting that life from and after conception."

In deciding *Roe*, the United States Supreme Court was bound by the doctrine of stare decisis to use *Griswold* as precedent if the facts in *Griswold* were "substantially the same" as the facts in *Roe*. The Court apparently decided that the facts in *Griswold* and *Roe* were similar and found that the "right of privacy ... is broad enough to encompass a woman's decision whether or not to terminate her pregnancy." The Court held that "the right of personal privacy includes the abortion decision, but that this right is not unqualified and must be considered against important state interests in regulation." The Court also held that the Texas statute was unconstitutional, but that the state could regulate the right to an abortion during the second trimester and prohibit it during the third trimester.

Application of Roe v. Wade *to a Later Case*

Would a state abortion statute requiring a twenty-four-hour wait and spousal consent be constitutional? That was the issue in *Planned Parenthood of Southeastern Pennsylvania v. Casey*, 505 U.S. 833 (1992) after the Pennsylvania abortion statute containing these provisions was challenged in federal court.

The attorney for plaintiffs who challenged the statute might have characterized *Roe* by saying that it was "**on point**" with *Casey*.

> **On Point** A term meaning that facts and the applicable law in two cases being examined are similar but not as similar as two cases on all fours.

Because of the similarity, the earlier-decided case may serve as precedent for the case under consideration. If a case is on point with a second case, the facts and the applicable law are similar but not as similar as two cases **on all fours**. If a case is on all fours with a second case, facts and the applicable law in the two cases are very similar.

> **On All Fours** A term meaning that facts and the applicable law in two cases being examined are very similar.

The plaintiffs' attorney probably urged the Court to apply the doctrine of stare decisis and hold the Pennsylvania statute unconstitutional. The attorney would have argued that the facts in *Casey* were substantially the same as those in *Roe* because the waiting period and consent requirements effectively denied the right to an abortion to a woman who could not obtain her spouse's consent, or had to travel a great distance, or could not afford to stay overnight.

In *Casey*, the attorney for the defendant—the state of Pennsylvania—might have argued that the facts in *Casey* were different from the facts in *Roe*. The state might have claimed the difference was that the Pennsylvania statute did not criminalize almost all abortions, as did the statute in *Roe*, and would have argued that the waiting period and consent requirements made sure the woman did not make hasty or ill-informed decisions. The state would thus be **distinguishing** *Casey* from *Roe* on the facts.

> **Distinguishing** Point out basic differences.

To distinguish a case is to show why it is irrelevant (or not very relevant) to the lawsuit being decided. The state might have then argued that, because the two statutes were not substantially the same, holding the statute constitutional would not violate the doctrine of stare decisis.

In *Casey*, the United States Supreme Court reaffirmed that *Roe* was still good law and applied the holding of *Roe* to *Casey*. The United States Supreme Court ruled that the twenty-four-hour wait was constitutional, but the spousal consent requirement was unconstitutional. The decision was a plurality opinion. Justices O'Connor, Kennedy, and Souter announced the judgment of the Court. Justices Stevens, Blackmun, and Scalia, and Chief Justice Rehnquist, each wrote separate opinions concurring in part and dissenting in part. Justices White, Scalia, and Thomas joined in the separate opinion by Chief Justice Rehnquist, and Justices White and Thomas and Chief Justice Rehnquist joined in the separate opinion by Justice Scalia. In deciding *Casey*, the Court explicitly reaffirmed *Roe* and restated *Roe*'s holding:

> It must be stated at the outset and with clarity that Roe's essential holding, the holding we reaffirm, has three parts. First is the recognition of the right of the woman to choose to have an abortion before viability and to obtain it without undue interference from the State. Before viability, the State's interests are not strong enough to support a prohibition of abortion or the imposition of a substantial obstacle to the woman's effective right to elect the procedure. Second is a confirmation of the State's power to restrict abortion after fetal viability, if the law contains exceptions for pregnancies which endanger a woman's life or health. And third is the principle that the State has legitimate interests from the outset of the pregnancy in protecting the health of the woman and the life of the fetus that may become a child. These principles do not contradict one another; and we adhere to each.

At Least Two Sides to Every Problem

In *Casey*, the state and the plaintiffs' attorneys reached opposite conclusions about the applicability of *Roe*. The state urged the Court to hold the Pennsylvania statute constitutional, while the plaintiffs' attorney urged the Court to hold the statute unconstitutional. They were pressing opposite decisions because their legal analysis of the effect of *Roe* on *Casey* was different. The state emphasized the differences between *Roe* and *Casey*, while the plaintiffs' attorney emphasized the similarity between *Roe* and *Casey*.

Every legal problem has at least two sides. The job of each attorney is to represent the client's best interest. An attorney represents the client's best interest by explaining to the court which primary sources apply to the problem, why certain primary sources apply, and what decision the court should reach based on applicable primary sources. Assuming that both attorneys have competently performed their legal research of a problem, they both have the same primary sources on which to base their arguments. Although the attorneys are relying on the same primary sources, their answers will be much different because of the way they have applied the primary sources to the problem. Each attorney will argue that the primary authority favorable to the client's case is substantially similar to the problem and should control. In contrast, each attorney will argue that primary authority unfavorable to the client's case is readily distinguishable from the problem, or they argue that the court should change the law.

The doctrine of stare decisis has worked well over the centuries because it gives case law stability and predictability, while at the same time allowing for gradual change.

There is stability and predictability because courts are bound to look to prior cases in deciding present cases. Much of what an attorney does is research the law to find cases on point and then predict how a court will decide—or try to convince the court to decide—based on those prior cases. Although the United States Supreme Court and the highest courts of the state have the power to **overrule** prior decisions, they hesitate to do so. A chronic practice of overruling prior decisions undermines the stability and predictability of the legal system.

Overrule To reject or supersede.

For example, a case is overruled when the same court, or a higher court in the same system, rejects the legal principles on which the case was based. This ends the case's value as a precedent.

Courts rarely state explicitly that they are overruling a prior case. Decades may pass between a precedent-setting case and a later case that overrules it. In *Plessy v. Ferguson*, 163 U.S. 537 (1896), the United States Supreme Court held that separate but equal accommodations for black and white railway passengers were constitutional. Over the years, *Plessy* was used to justify separate but equal public schools. It was not until over fifty years later that the Court overruled *Plessy*. In *Brown v. Board of Education of Topeka*, 347 U.S. 483 (1954), the Court held that separate but equal public school accommodations violated the equal protection clause of the United States Constitution.

LEGAL ANALYSIS TIP

Overrule and Reverse

When a court overrules a case, the court nullifies a prior decision as precedent. It usually occurs when the same court in a later case establishes a different rule on the same point of law involved in the earlier case. You might think of overruling as horizontal in effect because a court is announcing that it is nullifying one of the cases it previously decided.

When a court reverses a case, an appellate court sets aside (reverses) the decision of the lower court. You might think of reversing as vertical in effect, because a higher court reverses the decision of a lower court.

Instead of explicitly overruling a prior case, courts may limit its effect. The effect of a landmark case like *Roe* is unclear until the United States Supreme Court applies it in later cases. Many have argued that *Roe* was not the correct interpretation of the Constitution. In *Casey*, the Court was under great pressure to overrule *Roe*. The Court ruled only that the states may place certain limits, such as a twenty-four-hour waiting period, on the abortion right.

The *Casey* plurality opinion contained some interesting comments on the Court's apparent struggle to decide whether *Roe* should be overturned and how it applied to *Casey*:

> [I]t is common wisdom that the rule of stare decisis is not an "inexorable command," .... Rather, when this Court reexamines a prior holding, its judgment is customarily informed by a series of prudential and pragmatic considerations designed to test the consistency of overruling a prior decision with the ideal of the rule of law, and to gauge the respective costs of reaffirming and overruling a prior case. Thus, for example, we may ask whether the rule has proved to be intolerable simply in defying practical workability...; whether the rule is subject to a kind of reliance that would lend a special hardship to the consequences of overruling and add inequity to the cost of repudiation...; whether related principles of law have so far developed as to have left the old rule no more than a remnant of abandoned doctrine...; or whether facts have so changed or come to be seen so differently, as to have robbed the old rule of significant application or justification....
>
> ....
>
> Within the bounds of normal stare decisis analysis, ... the stronger argument is for affirming *Roe*'s central holding, with whatever degree of personal reluctance any of us may have, not for overruling it.

Judicial Opinions

The type of opinion (majority, plurality, concurring, dissenting, per curiam, or en banc opinion) in a case is important.

Majority Opinion

A **majority opinion** is an opinion agreed upon by at least a majority of the judges deciding the case. Usually one judge writes the opinion and other judges who agree with the opinion join in it.

> **Majority Opinion** A case decision agreed upon by at least a majority of the judges deciding the case.

Plurality Opinion

A **plurality opinion** is an opinion agreed upon by more judges than any other opinion, although less than a majority.

> **Plurality Opinion** A case decision agreed upon by more judges than any other opinion, although less than a majority.

Casey is an example of a plurality opinion. In *Casey*, only three Justices agreed upon the opinion. The only courts issuing plurality opinions are the United States Supreme Court, the highest court of the state, and intermediate appellate courts sitting en banc, because they are the only courts with enough members to have a plurality opinion.

Concurring Opinion

A **concurring opinion** is one agreeing with the result reached in the majority opinion but for different reasons.

> **Concurring Opinion** An opinion in which a judge agrees with the result reached in an opinion by another judge in the same case but not necessarily with the reasoning that the other judge used to reach the conclusion.

In *Casey*, a number of Justices agreed with (concurred in) the result but wrote separate concurring opinions to explain how their reasoning differed from the reasoning of the plurality opinion.

Dissenting Opinion

A **dissenting opinion** is written by a judge who disagrees with the result reached by the majority opinion; it expresses the judge's reasons for the disagreement.

> **Dissenting Opinion** A judge's formal disagreement with the decision of the majority of the judges in a lawsuit.

One or more judges may join in a concurring or dissenting opinion. A judge may join in any part of any decision. For example, a judge may join in part of the majority opinion, write his or her own concurring opinion as to another part of the majority opinion, and join in part of another judge's dissenting opinion.

Per Curiam Opinion

A **per curiam opinion** is written by the whole court rather than by one particular judge. Usually you will see a per curiam opinion in a relatively unimportant case.

> **Per Curiam Opinion** (Latin) "By the court." Describes an opinion backed by all the judges in a particular court and usually with no one judge's name on it.

In contrast, an **en banc opinion** is usually reserved for the most important or controversial cases, decided by the entire membership of the intermediate appellate court rather than by a three-judge panel.

En Banc Opinion (French) All the judges of a court participating in a case all together, rather than individually or in panels of a few.

Court Membership

Except for en banc decisions, intermediate appellate courts sit in panels to decide cases. The panels are made up of three judges selected at random from the membership of the intermediate appellate court. Sometimes one of the judges on the panel may be a lower court judge specially designated to hear an intermediate appellate case. After the three judges review the appellate briefs and hear any oral argument, they meet to decide the case. One of the two or three judges agreeing on how the case should be decided is assigned to write the majority opinion. Any judge disagreeing may choose to write a concurring or dissenting opinion. Before the opinion is announced, it is circulated to the other judges. A judge disagreeing with the opinion may either negotiate with the judge who wrote the opinion, to attempt to change certain language or to decide not to join in the opinion after all. A judge who originally intended to concur or dissent may decide to join in the majority opinion instead.

The entire membership of the United States Supreme Court and the highest state court in the state usually sit to decide a case. Each member of the United States Supreme Court is referred to as a "Justice" rather than a "judge," with the leader of the Court called the "Chief Justice." The members of the highest court in your state may also be referred to as "Justices."

A judge may be excused from hearing a case because of illness or because the judge **recuses** him- or herself.

Recusal The process by which a judge is disqualified (or disqualifies him- or herself) from hearing a lawsuit because of prejudice or because the judge has a conflict of interest.

A judge may recuse him- or herself because of a conflict of interest. For example, a judge may have had prior dealings with or have represented one of the parties to the case, which would lead the judge to believe that he or she could not be entirely impartial in deciding the case. A party also may request that a judge be recused because of a real or perceived conflict of interest.

The procedure for deciding a case in the United States Supreme Court or in the highest court of a state is similar to that described for intermediate appellate courts. Decisions of the United States Supreme Court and the highest state courts, sometimes referred to as **courts of last resort**, are not called *en banc* decisions, though, because the standard procedure is for the entire membership of the court to hear cases.

> **Court of Last Resort** The highest tier in the federal court system and the state court system, which usually contains one court, referred to as the court of last resort.

Most of the opinions you will use in research are published opinions of **appellate courts**, but not all opinions are published.

> **Appellate Court** Refers to a higher court that can hear appeals from a lower court.

The role of the appellate court is to determine whether the lower court applied the law correctly. If you learn of an unpublished opinion you would like to use as authority, the opinion may be available through computer-assisted legal research, or you may obtain a copy of the opinion from the clerk of the court issuing the opinion, usually for a nominal fee. Before citing an unpublished opinion, check applicable court rules to determine whether this is permitted; some states place limits on the use of unpublished opinions. You very rarely see published opinions of trial courts in researching state case law of certain states. Perhaps this is because it is not customary to publish them because they are only persuasive authority for other courts. Published opinions of federal district courts are easily accessible in the Federal Supplement.

Mandatory and Persuasive Authority

A **mandatory authority** is a case that must be followed under the doctrine of stare decisis.

> **Mandatory Authority** Binding authority.
>
> **Binding Authority** Sources of law that must be taken into account by a judge deciding a case.

Mandatory authority is also referred to as **binding authority**; for example, statutes from the same state or decisions by a higher court of the same state; a case that is mandatory or binding authority might be referred to as a **controlling case**. More precisely, the part of the case that is mandatory authority and therefore binding on other courts is the **holding** of the majority opinion.

> **Controlling Case** A court decision on a question of law (how the law affects the case) that is binding authority on lower courts in the same court system for cases in which those courts must decide a similar question of law involving similar facts.

A **persuasive authority**, just as the term implies, is a case that is only persuasive and is not required to be followed.

> **Persuasive Authority** All sources of law that a judge might use, but is not required to use, in making up his or her mind about a case, for example, legal encyclopedias or related cases from other states.

Brown v. Board of Education is mandatory authority for the United States Supreme Court, unless the Court overrules it, and for all lower courts. (See Chapter 4 for a discussion of the hierarchical structure of federal and state courts.) This means that *Brown* must be followed; it is binding on all federal and all state courts because it is the most current interpretation of the United States Constitution.

A decision of a United States Court of Appeals is binding on that circuit and all federal district courts within that circuit. (See Chapter 4 for a discussion of the hierarchical structure of federal and state courts.) The decision of a United States Court of Appeals is not mandatory authority for another circuit because all circuits are on the same level. For example, the United States Court of Appeals for the Eleventh Circuit covers Alabama, Georgia, and Florida. The United States Court of Appeals for the Fifth Circuit covers Texas, Louisiana, and Mississippi. A decision of one three-judge panel of the Eleventh Circuit would be mandatory authority for any future Eleventh Circuit case and for any federal district court in Alabama, Georgia, and Florida. That decision would only be persuasive authority, however, for the Court of Appeals for the Fifth Circuit and federal district courts within Texas, Louisiana, and Mississippi. Interestingly enough, a decision of a United States district or circuit court is considered persuasive rather than mandatory authority for state courts, even state courts geographically located within the district or circuit. This is because a case that is appealed through the various state courts up to the highest court in the state would go up to the United States Supreme Court rather than to a United States circuit or district court. In practice, though, a state court may give great weight to decisions of United States district and circuit courts covering the same geographical area when the federal court decisions deal with constitutional issues.

Plurality, concurring, and dissenting opinions are considered persuasive authority, as are all secondary sources. A decision of a court in one state is persuasive authority on the courts of another state. Although not binding, persuasive authority may be cited if there is no mandatory authority on point, or it may be cited to back up one's argument that the court should change the law by overruling a precedent.

Before becoming a United States Supreme Court Justice, Thurgood Marshall was one of the attorneys who argued *Brown* before the Court, claiming that *Plessy v. Ferguson* should be overruled. Marshall had only persuasive authority to rely on in his argument because the only way the Court could rule in favor of his client was to overrule *Plessy v. Ferguson*. The Court accepted his argument that the law should be changed and did overrule *Plessy v. Ferguson*.

A decision of the highest court in the state is binding on all courts within the state. A decision of an intermediate appellate court is binding on the trial-level courts within the geographical area covered by the intermediate appellate court. If the intermediate appellate court in your state is divided into districts or circuits, it would be interesting for you to research whether the decision of one district or circuit is mandatory or persuasive authority for other districts or circuits. You will very likely find that the relationship between different intermediate appellate courts in your state is that of "sister courts," with the decision of one intermediate appellate court considered persuasive rather than mandatory. The United States Courts of Appeals have this same relationship.

Another question is what effect a decision of an intermediate appellate court has on the trial-level court geographically located outside the area covered by the intermediate appellate court. The decision of the intermediate appellate court could be considered either mandatory or persuasive authority.

An example shows the difference between mandatory and persuasive authority. In *Johnson v. Davis*, 480 So. 2d 625 (Fla. 1985), the Florida Supreme Court held that "where the seller of a home knows of facts materially affecting the value of the property which are not readily observable and are not known to the buyer, the seller is under a duty to disclose them to the buyer." In *Johnson*, the homeowner knew that the roof leaked but failed to disclose this to the buyer. The court ruled that the seller's "fraudulent concealment" entitled the buyer to the return of the buyer's deposit plus interest, costs, and attorneys' fees. *Johnson* was a landmark case because the law in Florida had previously been that the **doctrine of caveat emptor** ("let the buyer beware") applied to home sales.

> **Doctrine of Caveat Emptor** (Latin) "Beware"; warning. Caveat emptor means "let the buyer beware."

The *Johnson* court cited decisions from California, Illinois, Nebraska, West Virginia, Louisiana, New Jersey, and Colorado in announcing its decision that the doctrine of caveat emptor would no longer apply to the sale of homes in Florida. These other state decisions constituted persuasive authority for the Florida court. After *Johnson*, a Florida trial court considering a similar case would have to follow *Johnson* and hold the home seller liable for fraud if the home seller knew the home had a leaky roof but failed to disclose it to the buyer. *Johnson* is mandatory authority in Florida for cases concerning material home defects undisclosed to the buyer.

Obiter Dictum

A court may raise and answer a hypothetical question in an opinion. The answer to the hypothetical question would not be mandatory authority for judges deciding later cases because the facts comprising the hypothetical question were not facts under consideration in the case being decided, and the answer to the hypothetical question is not part of the holding of the case.

> **LEGAL ANALYSIS TIP**
>
> ***Holding and Obiter Dictum***
>
> The holding of a case is the court's decision and the significant or material facts upon which the court relied in arriving at its determination. This is the binding portion of the case.
>
> Obiter dictum is everything else in the decision.

Obiter dictum is illustrated in *Sweet v. Josephson*, 173 So. 2d 444 (Fla. 1965). In *Sweet*, Josephson was injured when Sweet's dog knocked Josephson down. The dog did not bite Josephson.

In *Sweet*, the trial court relied on a Florida Supreme Court case from 1951, *Romfh v. Berman*, 56 So. 2d 127 (Fla. 1951). In *Romfh*, Berman was bitten by two bull dogs owned by Romfh. Romfh had displayed a "Beware of Dogs" sign in the yard. The Florida Supreme Court ruled that Romfh was not liable under Florida Statute § 767.04, a statute that relieves a dog owner from liability if the owner has a sign posted putting one entering the property on notice of the presence of a "Bad Dog."

Although not at issue, the Florida Supreme Court in *Romfh* considered Florida Statute § 767.01. Section 767.01 made a dog owner liable for injuries caused by the owner's dog; § 767.01 was a change from the common law, which had made the dog owner liable only if the owner had knowledge (scienter) of the dangerous propensities of the dog. In *Romfh*, the Florida Supreme Court ruled that § 767.04 had repealed and superseded § 767.01.

In *Sweet*, the intermediate appellate court examined *Romfh* and decided that the *Romfh* court's statement that § 767.04 had repealed and superseded § 767.01 was obiter dictum. The Florida Supreme Court agreed with the intermediate appellate court and stated:

> [T]he expression was obiter dictum inasmuch as the court was dealing with a case in which damage had resulted from the bite of a vicious dog and an element of the case was the owner's knowledge or ignorance of the dog's propensities. There was no occasion for the court to pass upon the effect of one statute upon the other. There is a field of operation for each.

Thus, the court's statement in *Romfh* was obiter dictum because it was unnecessary to the holding in the case.

Judicial Restraint and Judicial Activism

The judiciary and the legislature are co-equal branches of government. As more fully explained below, the judiciary is tasked with applying the plain language of the statute and, where the statute is ambiguous, the judiciary looks to legislative intent and legislative history. The judiciary is always tasked with interpreting whether a statute applies to a given set of facts. At times a court may be accused of judicial activism where the court decision seems, to its critics, to be too far-ranging from the language or intent of the statute by delving into the realm of making policy. Those critics would advocate that the court exercise judicial restraint in not making law or delving into matters reserved for the legislature. At other times, a court may be criticized for using excessive judicial restraint in refraining from taking action.

The federal judiciary also interprets the United States Constitution. *Roe v. Wade*, the abortion case discussed earlier in this chapter, has been roundly criticized for what many saw as judicial activism in ruling that the right to abortion falls within the right to privacy. Many critics have said that the United States Supreme Court should have exercised judicial restraint and should not have expanded the right to privacy, a right not explicitly stated in the United States Constitution, to the right to abortion.

Statutory Analysis

In a case, a court may have to determine whether a particular statute applies to the facts. The legislature may have had a particular situation in mind that needed to be remedied. Later, something slightly different occurred, and it might be slightly more ambiguous as to whether the statute applies to the new set of facts. The question is how a court should determine whether the statute applies to the new set of facts.

Statutory interpretation may occur in a criminal case. A bedrock principle in criminal cases is that a court must strictly construe a criminal statute. One could think of the possible application of a criminal statute as a ring of concentric circles drawn over incidents that potentially carry a criminal penalty. The statute would apply to the most heinous of acts, those falling within the smallest of the concentric rings. The less heinous activities fall within the larger rings. The public generally accepts that the government is justified in convicting someone who has committed a heinous act falling within the smallest of the concentric rings. One of the purposes of a criminal statute is to put the public on notice of what action is prohibited under the statute. One might argue that the statutory language is not sufficiently clear to convict someone whose activity falls within the outermost of the concentric rings.

To put the public on notice of prohibited conduct, a criminal statute is strictly construed, meaning that the language of a criminal statute should be read fairly narrowly. "[P]enal statutes are to be strictly construed, and all doubts are to be resolved in favor of the defendant." *Torres v. State*, 571 S.W.3d 456, 462 (Ark. 2019). The idea behind strict construction is to make the application of the statute fair to the defendant. Obviously, there is a limit to the narrowing of the circumstances to which the statute applies. "However, even a penal statute must not be construed so strictly as to defeat the obvious intent of the legislature." *Id.*

In determining the meaning of a statute, the first step is to review the plain language of the statute. Reviewing the plain language of the statute includes examining the context of the statute, especially if the statute was part of a number of statutes passed as an act. When a legislature passes an Act, the legislature typically has an overall scheme in mind; the Act may include a statement of the purpose of the Act and a set of definitions used when applying a statute falling within the Act. "[I]n construing any statute, we place it beside other statutes relevant to the subject matter in question and ascribe meaning and effect to be derived from the whole." *Id.*

In *Torres*, the state of Arkansas charged Torres with felony murder for the rape and death of his young son. The alleged rape occurred in Missouri and the death occurred in Arkansas. The idea of a felony murder is that an underlying felony is attempted or committed and the felony results in death. The court strictly construed the statute, the court finding that Torres could not be convicted of felony murder, although Torres might be convicted of another crime, because the underlying felony did not occur in Arkansas. "[B]ased on the plain language of the statute, extraterritorial jurisdiction does not extend to the alleged rape that occurred in Missouri." *Id.* at 464. The dissent would have read the statute more broadly to permit the felony murder statute to apply to Torres. *Id.* at 468–69 (Womack, J., dissenting).

Besides reviewing the plain language of the statute, a court must consider legislative intent. "The primary objective of statutory construction is to ascertain and give effect to the true intent of the legislature.... The most reliable indicator of legislative intent is the language of the statute, given its plain and ordinary meaning." *People v. Clark* 135 N.E.3d 21, 26 (Ill. 2019). The court in *Clark* included language that more fully explained what a court might consider in determining legislative intent. "The court may consider the reason for the law, the problems sought to be remedied, the purposes to be achieved, and the consequences of construing the statute one way or another. Also, a court presumes that the General Assembly did not intend absurdity, inconvenience, or injustice in enacting legislation." A court might also take into account legislative history, especially if the legislature amended a statute over time. *Id.* at 28–29.

Reasoning by Analogy and Deductive Reasoning

Legal analysis involves reasoning by analogy and deductive reasoning. The following section describes a hypothetical fact pattern. The fact pattern will be used in this portion of the chapter to explain legal analysis, reasoning by analogy, and deductive reasoning.

Joshua Smeek Illustrative Fact Pattern

Joshua was riding with two other college students, Mike and Charles Cooper, returning to college after a weekend at home. Joshua and the two brothers lived within a few blocks of one another, and a family friend suggested that Joshua catch a ride with them. Even though they lived close and attended the same college, Joshua had never met the brothers before. Mike was driving south on I-95 toward Daytona Beach, with Charles in the front seat and Joshua in the back, when a police officer pulled over Mike's car.

The officer said he had stopped the car because the driver's window was excessively tinted, making it impossible for the officer to see inside the car. The officer stood at the window on the driver's side and asked for Mike's license and car registration. In addition, the officer asked Charles and Joshua for their names and birth dates. While Mike was retrieving the documents, the officer used a tint meter to measure whether the tint on the driver's window complied with Florida statutes. The officer announced that if the window tinting were any darker, it would have been illegal; he claimed that the bright sun and the difference in color between the driver's window and the windshield made him think that the tinting was excessively dark.

The officer returned Mike's license and car registration, wished them a nice day, and walked toward the patrol car. After a few steps, the officer turned back to Mike's car and said, "You don't mind if I search your car and all containers therein, do you?" Mike stated, "I guess not." The officer asked the three students to wait in the patrol car while he searched Mike's car. Once in the back seat of the patrol car, Joshua said, "Do you think it was a good idea to let him search the car?" Charles told Mike, "Why did you do that? He'll find our stuff." Charles was referencing a number of small plastic bags containing white chunks of a non-crack cocaine nicknamed "hail," the result of a new production method designed to avoid the minimum sentences under the federal statutes for crack cocaine. When smoked, the smoker experiences a more intense high than that produced from smoking crack.

The officer found 300 grams of hail, half in the console between the front seats and half in a panel of the front seat passenger's door, with the packaging leading the officer to believe the hail was packaged for distribution. Using names and birth dates, the officer used his handheld radio to run a check on the three students. The officer discovered an outstanding arrest warrant for Mike and Charles on cocaine distribution charges, but nothing on Joshua. When the officer announced that he was arresting the three students, Joshua protested, explaining that he barely knew Mike and Charles and had no idea that the drugs were in the car. Joshua pointed out that neither the console, which opened from the front, nor the front door panel was accessible to a backseat passenger.

After the three were arrested, they discovered that the police officer had tape-recorded their conversation in the back of the patrol car. Joshua is worried because his innocent remark in the patrol car, "Do you think it was a good idea to let him search the car?" could make someone believe that Joshua knew about the illegal drugs. The three are facing criminal charges for possession of illegal drugs with the intent to distribute in the United States District Court for the Middle District of Florida.

Legal Analysis

Legal analysis is a sequential process. First, one must find all authority relevant to the problem. Some areas of the law are governed wholly by case law; other areas are governed by constitutions, statutes, court rules, or administrative regulations, as applied and interpreted by the courts. When researching case law, one must search for a prior case decided by the highest possible court in the jurisdiction with the same issue as presented in the legal problem you are researching and with as similar as possible material facts. Any case found should be further researched to make sure it has not been later heard and decided by a higher court or overruled or that there is not a more recent case from the same or a higher court. When researching constitutions, statutes, court rules, and administrative regulations, one must search for an applicable primary source and any case law applying or interpreting the primary source. A statute should be further researched to make sure it has not been amended, repealed, or held unconstitutional. Constitutions, court rules, and administrative regulations should be further researched to make sure they have not been amended.

Steps in Legal Analysis

Review Relevant Authority

⬇

Synthesize Cases

⬇

Formulate Rule of Law

⬇

Apply Rule of Law to Facts

⬇

Reach Legal Conclusion

In the *Smeek* problem, included in the preceding section, Joshua Smeek was arrested on federal criminal charges for drug possession with intent to distribute. Because Joshua's comment on the tape recording makes it appear Joshua knew the car in which he was a passenger contained illegal drugs, Joshua would like to have the tape suppressed. Federal eavesdropping statutes may apply and are discussed in the following section.

Deductive Reasoning

Deductive reasoning involves reasoning from the general (rule) to the specific (the impact of the rule on a particular fact pattern).

> **Deductive Reasoning** Legal rules (constitutions, statutes, court rules, and administrative regulations) are general statements of what the law permits, requires, and prohibits; therefore, it may not be clear whether a particular rule applies to a given factual situation. Deductive reasoning is used to determine if the rule applies; it involves reasoning from the general (rule) to the specific (the impact of the rule on a particular fact pattern).

The principle of deductive reasoning will be illustrated by using *Smeek* and the federal wiretapping and eavesdropping statutes.

The first step in deductive reasoning is identifying the rules that may apply to a particular fact pattern. A rule that may apply is referred to as the **major premise.**

> **Major Premise** The basis for a logical deduction. The facts or arguments upon which a conclusion is based.

The second step is to state the facts in terms of the rule. This statement is called the **minor premise.**

> **Minor Premise** The basis for a logical deduction weighed in light of the major premise. The facts or arguments upon which a conclusion is based.

The facts must be weighed in light of the language of the rule to formulate the minor premise. In other words, should the language of the rule be interpreted to include the facts of the fact pattern? The last step is to reach a conclusion, after analyzing the relationship between the major premise and the minor premise.

Federal wiretapping and eavesdropping statutes may apply to *Smeek*. Federal statutes prohibit secretly tape-recording an "oral communication." An oral communication is defined as "any oral communication uttered by a person exhibiting an expectation that such communication is not subject to interception under circumstances justifying such expectation." A penalty for tape-recording an oral communication is that the tape recording may not be used in court.

For *Smeek*, a major premise is: If an oral communication is secretly tape-recorded, the taped information can be suppressed.

It might be helpful to state two alternative minor premises:

1. Joshua will be successful in having his side of the conversation in the patrol car suppressed because he had a reasonable expectation that the police officer would not tape-record his conversation while he sat in the back of the patrol car.

2. Joshua will not be successful in having the conversation in the patrol car suppressed because it was not reasonable to expect that the police officer would not tape-record Joshua's conversation while he sat in the back of the patrol car.

The following are two alternative conclusions:

1. Because the conversation in the backseat of a patrol car was an oral communication, it should be suppressed.
2. Because the conversation in the backseat of a patrol car was not an oral communication, it should not be suppressed.

The researcher would have to determine which minor premise and which conclusion is the most likely to be employed by the court deciding *Smeek*. The determination hinges on the meaning of "reasonable" in "reasonable expectation of privacy." If Joshua's expectation of privacy in the rear seat of the patrol car was reasonable, then the tape should be suppressed; if not, then the tape would not be suppressed under the federal statute. If the facts were at one end or the other of the spectrum, formulation of the minor premise would be easy. An individual probably would have a reasonable expectation of privacy when conversing in the individual's home with the doors and windows closed; an individual probably would not have an expectation of privacy if conversing on a street corner in a loud voice. Were the facts toward the middle of the spectrum, it would be more difficult to determine whether an individual has a reasonable expectation of privacy.

The word "reasonable" is vague when we attempt to determine whether Joshua has a reasonable expectation of privacy when conversing in the back of a patrol car. Case law interpretation of the statute may help make the determination.

The following section discusses cases in which a police officer secretly taped a conversation of suspects while the suspects were seated in the officer's patrol car.

Reasoning by Analogy

Because we have a common law system, cases are central to legal analysis. Although a case settles a particular dispute as to the parties to the case, the case may be applicable to future cases through the doctrine of stare decisis. Determining whether a past case should apply to a case presently before a court and what impact the earlier case has on the later cases involves reasoning by analogy.

Reasoning by analogy first involves finding a past case with facts that appear to be similar to the case presently being decided. No two fact patterns are identical, even if they involve similarly situated parties or what appears to be the same issue. Therefore, there will always be similarities and differences between the two fact patterns. The second step is to compare the facts of the two cases to determine which facts are similar and which facts are different. The third step is to determine whether the facts of the two cases are so substantially similar that the past case should determine the result in the present case. If the facts in the two cases are substantially different, then the result in the present case might differ from the result in the past case. In examining factual differences and similarities, one must determine whether the similarities or differences are more significant. A few similarities between crucial facts in the two cases may outweigh numerous differences in unimportant facts.

Because Joshua Smeek is facing criminal drug charges in the United States District Court for the Middle District of Florida, a researcher would look for the mandatory authority of case law from the United States Supreme Court or from the Court of Appeals for the Eleventh Circuit. The next step in legal analysis is to synthesize cases.

The United States Supreme Court has never discussed whether it is permissible for police officers to tape such conversations; however, case law research has located two cases from the Eleventh Circuit that may be relevant. The cases are *United States v. Gilley*, 43 F.3d 1440 (11th Cir. 1995), and *United States v. McKinnon*, 985 F.2d 525 (11th Cir. 1993). In *Gilley* and *McKinnon*, the courts held that someone seated in a patrol car does not have a reasonable expectation of privacy. *Gilley* and *McKinnon* may apply because the facts in those two cases seem to be similar to the facts in *Smeek*.

The next step in legal analysis is to formulate a rule of law. In the deductive reasoning section of this chapter, we determined that it was unclear whether the federal eavesdropping statutes would apply to *Smeek*. In *Gilley* and *McKinnon*, the Eleventh Circuit decided that the federal eavesdropping statutes did not apply to the tape recorded conversation because the suspects had no reasonable expectation of privacy while seated in a patrol car. This is the rule of law from the two cases.

The next step in legal analysis is to apply the rule of law to the facts of the problem. Application of law to facts requires one to determine how the rule of law and the authority backing it up is similar to or different from the facts in the problem. If the facts in prior cases are substantially the same, then the result in the problem should be the same as the result in the prior cases. This is the step sometimes overlooked when students perform legal analysis. Students tend to carefully explain the rule of law and then skip directly from the rule of law to the conclusion. Instead, the reasoning followed must be explained. Legal analysis should lead step by step from the rule of law through the application of the rule of law to the facts in the problem to the conclusion.

In comparing *Gilley* and *McKinnon* to *Smeek*, there are many similarities. The *McKinnon* and *Smeek* cars were stopped for alleged traffic violations. In all three cases, the cars contained two occupants. In all three cases, the occupants were seated in the patrol car while their car was searched. In all three cases, the officers recorded the suspects while seated in the rear seat of the patrol car. All the tapes contained incriminating statements. The suspects were not under arrest when their conversations were recorded. There are also some differences. The reason the *Gilley* car was stopped is unknown and the alleged traffic violations in *McKinnon* and *Smeek* were different. In

Gilley, *McKinnon*, and *Smeek*, the occupants of the car were males. In *McKinnon* and *Smeek*, the driver consented to the search; in *Gilley*, the legal basis for the search is unknown.

The last step in legal analysis is to reach a conclusion by tying together the rule of law and the application of law to facts. The conclusion is the solution to the problem and must be thoroughly supported by the rule of law and the application of the rule of law to the facts in the problem. The conclusion is also a prediction of what a court will do based on relevant authority.

Federal eavesdropping statutes could be used to suppress the tape-recorded conversation if there was a reasonable expectation of privacy. *Gilley* and *McKinnon* can be used to determine if suspects have a reasonable expectation of privacy while seated in a patrol car. The *Gilley* and *McKinnon* courts held that there was no reasonable expectation of privacy under the facts presented in those cases. Using the doctrine of stare decisis, *Gilley* and *McKinnon* are binding on *Smeek* if the facts in the three cases are substantially similar. Although there are some factual differences among the three cases, the facts concerning the taping in the patrol car are virtually identical. While the police officers were conducting a car search, the car occupants were asked to sit in the patrol car. While in the patrol car, they made incriminating statements that were tape recorded. Because the facts in the three cases were substantially similar, the court deciding *Smeek* should decide that the taped information may not be suppressed under the federal eavesdropping statutes.

Summary

- The doctrine of stare decisis states that when a court has set forth a legal principle, that court and all lower courts under it will apply that principle in future cases where the facts are substantially the same.
- *Roe v. Wade* illustrates the doctrine of stare decisis:
    - In *Roe v. Wade*, the United States Supreme Court held that a Texas statute making abortion a crime was unconstitutional but that the state could regulate the right to an abortion during the second trimester and prohibit it during the third trimester.
    - Applying the doctrine of stare decisis, *Roe v. Wade* is used as precedent in later cases where the facts are "substantially the same."
    - If the facts in a later abortion case in which a state abortion statute is challenged are substantially the same as the facts in *Roe v. Wade*, then the court in the later case should hold the challenged abortion statute unconstitutional.
    - However, if the challenged abortion statute in the later case is distinguishable from the *Roe* statute, a court may uphold the constitutionality of the challenged statute.

- The doctrine of stare decisis gives case law predictability while allowing gradual change.
- There are at least two sides to every problem, and the attorney represents the client's best interest by arguing that authority favorable to the client's case should be applied and that unfavorable authority is distinguishable.
- When reading a court decision, note what type of opinion it is: majority, plurality, concurring, dissenting, per curiam, or en banc.
- A case may be mandatory authority, which must be followed under the doctrine of stare decisis, or a case may be persuasive authority, which may, but is not required, to be followed.
- In interpreting statutes, the legal researcher may consider legislative intent, the plain meaning of the statutory language, the immediate statutory context, strict construction of the statutory language, and legislative history.
- Legal analysis involves three steps: (1) reading and synthesizing all relevant authority to extract a rule of law; (2) applying the rule of law to the facts of the problem; and (3) reaching a conclusion.

Key Terms

appellate courts
binding authority
concurring opinion
controlling case
courts of last resort
dictum (plural, dicta)
dissenting opinion
distinguishing
doctrine of caveat emptor
en banc opinion
holding
landmark case
majority opinion
mandatory authority
obiter dictum
on all fours
on point
overrule
penumbras
per curiam opinion
persuasive authority
plain meaning rule
plurality opinion

preamble
precedent
recuses

Exercises

1. What was the holding (the central decision) of *Griswold v. Connecticut*?
2. What were the arguments of the two attorneys in *Roe v. Wade*?
3. Was *Griswold* used as precedent in *Roe*?
4. What was the issue (legal question before the court) in *Planned Parenthood of Southeastern Pennsylvania v. Casey*?
5. What were the arguments of the two attorneys in *Casey*?
6. Was *Roe* used as precedent in *Casey*?
7. What are the differences among majority, plurality, concurring, dissenting, per curiam, and en banc court decisions?
8. What is a "court of last resort"?
9. Give an example of mandatory authority for federal courts and for the courts of your state.
10. Give an example of persuasive authority for federal courts and for the courts of your state.
11. One of the issues before the court in *U.S. Fidelity and Guar. Co. v. Braspetro Oil Services Co.*, 369 F.3d 34 (2d Cir. 2004) was whether the sureties were liable for $36,700,000 in attorneys' fees under the contract provision obligating the sureties to pay "legal costs." According to the court, did the contract term legal costs include attorneys' fees? What was the court's reasoning?
12. *Muscarello v. United States*, 524 U.S. 125 (1998) consolidated two cases that involved a federal statute imposing a mandatory five-year prison term for anyone who "uses or carries a firearm" during an illegal drug offense. In one case, the firearm was in a locked glove compartment and in the other case the firearm was in the trunk of a car. What was the issue, and what was the holding? What was the court's reasoning?

Cyberlaw Exercises

1. A well-known legal research site where you can start your legal research is https://www.findlaw.com/. Use this site to find the full opinions of *Griswold v. Connecticut*, *Roe v. Wade*, and *Planned Parenthood of Southeastern Pennsylvania v. Casey* by using the volume and first page numbers of the cases. In a

case citation, the first number is the volume number. The volume number is followed by an abbreviation of the set of books containing the opinion. The abbreviation is followed by the number of the first page of the case.

2. The Library of Congress website is located at http://www.loc.gov. A portion of the website is designed for law researchers. Review the offerings accessible through the site.
3. A comprehensive legal research site is American Law Sources Online, http://www.lawsource.com/also/. Review the offerings accessible through the site.
4. Another good starting point is Cornell Law School's Legal Information Institute, https://www.law.cornell.edu/. Review the offerings accessible through the site.

Discussion Points

1. Was the United States Supreme Court bound by the doctrine of stare decisis to decide *Roe v. Wade* the way it did?
2. Does every legal problem have two sides?
3. Review some recent decisions of the United States Supreme Court. How many were unanimous? How many of the decisions contained a concurring or dissenting opinion? Did you note any plurality decisions?
4. Review a decision of the United States Supreme Court in which the Court interpreted a statute. Which rules of construction did the Court use in interpreting the statute?
5. Have you noted any examples of judicial restraint or judicial activism in the news lately? If so, what are they?

Chapter 3

Secondary Sources and Finding Tools

Introduction

This chapter introduces secondary sources and finding tools. It includes explanations of:

- legal encyclopedias
- American Law Reports
- digests

Other secondary sources include treatises, legal dictionaries, legal directories, formbooks, legal periodicals, law review articles, legal thesauri, continuing education publications, and restatements. Secondary sources are designed to explain legal concepts. They can be used to understand basic legal terms and general concepts. They provide the researcher with background information and a framework of an area of the law, arranging legal principles in an orderly fashion. In contrast to primary authority (constitutions, cases, statutes, court rules, and administrative regulations), secondary sources do not have the force and effect of law. They function as citation finders, leading the researcher to relevant primary sources. It is preferable to cite the primary authority found through secondary sources rather than citing the secondary sources themselves.

Finding tools are used to find primary sources. Secondary sources can also be classified as finding tools because the legal researcher often uses citations found in secondary sources to find relevant primary sources. However, several legal publications function solely as finding tools; these include digests and citators. Citators are covered in Chapter 6. Digests and citators are neither primary nor secondary authority and are never cited.

Encyclopedias

Legal encyclopedias offer a useful commentary on the law as it is and serve as a case finder to locate cases with which one can begin the research process. The legal encyclopedia is one of the many tools in the law library and should generally be used in combination with other legal research tools.

> **Legal Encyclopedias** Legal encyclopedias are a secondary source that offer a useful commentary on the law as it is and serve as a case finder to locate cases with which one can begin the research process.

In organization, legal encyclopedias have much in common with general encyclopedias. Legal encyclopedias are organized like the multivolume encyclopedias found in schools and public libraries. They are multivolume sets covering broad topics arranged in alphabetical order, with the topics divided into sections. Each topic gives a textual explanation of the law relating to that topic. Topic coverage serves as a valuable frame of reference for more in-depth research in other sources. Index volumes are located at the end of the set.

The two widely used national legal encyclopedias are ***Corpus Juris Secundum*** and ***American Jurisprudence 2d***. They are designed to systematically explain the law as it exists in the United States; they may be consulted to gain an overview of the law from a national perspective. Each contains over 400 topics.

> **Corpus Juris Secundum** A multivolume national legal encyclopedia.
>
> **American Jurisprudence 2d** A multivolume national legal encyclopedia.

The researcher may begin to access the legal encyclopedia either in an index (the general index or the volume index) or in a topic table of contents. Detailed subject index volumes are located at the end of the set, allowing the researcher to locate relevant material by looking up key terms. In addition, each volume is separately indexed and may contain more detailed information concerning the topics covered in that particular volume than the general index. Each legal encyclopedia topic is preceded by two tables of contents, the first listing major topic sections and the second listing topic sections and subsections in detail.

Legal encyclopedias can be used as a starting point for a researcher. They serve to educate the reader on the basic aspects of a topic with which the reader is unfamiliar; a more knowledgeable reader can refresh his or her understanding of the topic. The first sections of a topic in a legal encyclopedia give the reader a general basic statement of the law. Those sections are followed by a more detailed description of all aspects of the substantive law. The final sections generally describe available remedies.

In contrast to general encyclopedias, legal encyclopedias are heavily footnoted. The footnotes are a valuable feature of the legal encyclopedia, furnishing the legal researcher with primary source citations useful in the research process. Legal encyclopedias were first published at a time when the emphasis of the law was on case law rather than statutes or regulations. Legal encyclopedias still tend to emphasize case law over statutes and regulations. A researcher should carefully search for relevant statutes and regulations; legal encyclopedias may not reference highly relevant statutes and regulations.

> **Pocket Part** An addition to a lawbook that updates it until a bound supplement or a new edition comes out. It is found inside the back (or occasionally, front) cover, secured in a "pocket," and should always be referred to when doing legal research.

Each volume of the legal encyclopedia is annually updated with a cumulative pamphlet, generally referred to as a "pocket part." A **pocket part** is a paperbound "booklet" containing recent legal information. When researching, it is essential to check the pocket part for updated material. Pocket parts are usually reprinted annually and contain more recent information than the hardbound volume. The pocket part is inserted inside the back cover of the volume for easy reference, and the pamphlet from the prior year is discarded; the pocket part contains textual material and citations, new since the copyright date of the hardbound volume. Over time, the information for the annual pocket part supplement becomes too voluminous to be easily stored inside the volume's back cover. When this happens, the information is printed either in a separate paperbound volume, shelved next to the hardbound volume, or absorbed into the reprinted hardbound volume. The researcher should consult both the hardbound volume and the supplement.

When researching, note the copyright date of the hardbound volume and then the date on the front of the pocket part. Also note the date of coverage for the pocket part (this currency date tells the date on which research and updates for that pocket part was cut off). This information is found in the first few pages of the pocket part. Because of its inherent datedness, a pocket part dated May of the current calendar year may only cover material through December of the preceding year.

The copyright date of the hardbound volumes varies greatly. As just stated, volumes are recompiled and reprinted from time to time when the supplementary material becomes unwieldy. A recompiled volume incorporates new material and eliminates out-of-date information; volumes relating to more rapidly changing areas of the law are reprinted more frequently than other volumes. There may be no pocket part published in the year in which the reprinted volume is published because the material in the hardbound volume would be current without reference to a pocket part.

Many states have state legal encyclopedias; they cover the law in a similar fashion, although from a state perspective, and are arranged similarly to the national legal encyclopedias. The state legal encyclopedia attempts to explain the law as it exists in that particular state. State legal encyclopedias generally provide more extensive treatment of state-specific topics, such as community property, homestead, and oil and gas law, and provide more state-specific citations. For example, Florida law is covered in *Florida Jurisprudence 2d* (Fla. Jur. 2d). If you were researching Florida law, *Florida Jurisprudence* would be your first choice. If your research did not locate any primary sources from Florida, you could consult the national encyclopedias to find authority from other states. You could use this authority as persuasive authority to answer your legal question.

Caveat on the Use of Legal Encyclopedias

Use legal encyclopedias while keeping in mind their limitations. The text provides a short summary of the law, without detail, giving some background but usually not specific enough to answer a legal question. You must look up a case cited in the legal encyclopedia. Do not rely on what the legal encyclopedia says about a case, because it may not be completely accurate. Researchers generally do not quote from legal encyclopedias. Because a legal encyclopedia only contains the publisher's interpretation of the law at the time it was written, it is preferable to use the primary source itself. Do not omit statutory research. Legal encyclopedias emphasize case law rather than statutory law and may not reference applicable statutes.

> **RESEARCH TIP**
>
> ***Use of Hardbound Volumes and Pocket Parts***
>
> When researching in print sources, the researcher must make it a practice to check both the hardbound volume and the pocket part to obtain complete information.

Tips on Using Legal Encyclopedias

Do:

1. Use footnotes to locate relevant primary authority.
2. Pull and read primary authority.
3. Check pocket parts for recent information.
4. Update information found.

Do not:

1. Rely on a legal encyclopedia alone as an accurate statement of the law.
2. Generally cite a legal encyclopedia.

Once considered persuasive authority, legal encyclopedias are now considered a research tool, helpful in gaining a general understanding of a topic and locating case citations that would be useful as a basis for further research. Because of the exponential growth of the law and the limits of the legal encyclopedia, topic coverage tends to be general, elemental, and oversimplified. Legal encyclopedias are not designed to put the law into a historical or sociological perspective. An exhaustive and complex treatment of the law would require a much larger set of books. Even with annual supplements, the information in the legal encyclopedia quickly becomes outdated, and the cases cited may be a representative rather than an exhaustive reference to all relevant cases.

No longer considered persuasive authority, legal encyclopedias are generally not cited as authority in legal documents. Information gleaned from the legal encyclopedia may be the starting point in the research of a legal problem, but certainly not the conclusion to the research process. A solution offered by the legal encyclopedia may be inapplicable because of the peculiar fact pattern, more recent case law, or applicable statutes or regulations not discussed in the legal encyclopedia.

Use of Legal Encyclopedias

In summary, legal encyclopedias are best used:

1. To find primary authority; and
2. To give the researcher general background information.

For information on how to make legal encyclopedias a part of your research strategy, see Chapter 7.

Citation to Legal Encyclopedias

Although legal encyclopedias are not usually cited in documents submitted to court or opposing counsel, you will need to cite legal encyclopedias for assignments and more informal documents such as office memos. (See Chapter 13 for an explanation of the purpose and use of office memos.) The following are template examples of citations to *American Jurisprudence* and *Corpus Juris Secundum*.

CITATION TIP

Check for Correct Citation Form

Do not assume that the legal citations found when researching are in correct citation form. Citations, even those included in cases, may or may not comply with Bluebook. Always check your citations against the appropriate citation rule for correct form.

68 Am. Jur. 2d *Searches and Seizures* §§338–447 (_____ & Supp. ___).
86 C.J.S. *Telecommunications* §§215–254 (_____ & Supp. ___).

In each of the template examples, the first number is the volume number. The volume number is followed by the abbreviation of the legal encyclopedia, the legal encyclopedia topic, and the pertinent sections of the topic. Notice that the topic is italicized or underlined, and the citation includes two section symbols because the citation references more than one section. The citation would include a single section symbol if the citation were to reference a single section. The first blank within the parentheses would contain the copyright year of the hardbound volume and the second blank contains the year of the pocket part supplement. The reference to the supplement would be omitted if the hardbound volume is so recent that there is no pocket part supplement.

American Law Reports

The first major attempt at case reporting as a commercial venture began in the late 1800s. The two major approaches to case reporting were the exhaustive approach and the selective approach. As the names imply, the exhaustive approach undertook to publish all case opinions, from the most significant landmark decisions to the short, and often relatively unimportant, decisions. The selective approach published a limited number of cases selected by the publisher as "leading cases," because of their landmark status or their treatment of a novel or interesting legal issue, accompanying each of the selected cases was a commentary, called an "annotation." The **annotation** explored a particular legal issue in depth and referenced other cases concerning the same issue. The West Publishing Company followed the exhaustive approach. The **American Law Reports Series** ("ALR") typifies the selective approach. The exhaustive approach to case reporting won out over the selective approach, but ALR survived as a valuable research tool.

Annotation A note or commentary intended to explain the meaning of a legal issue (as in ALR) or a statutory passage (as in an annotated code), with textual explanations (called annotations) of the law, including lengthy footnotes to relevant cases.

American Law Reports Series A secondary source that offers useful commentary on selected legal issues and serves as a case finder to locate cases with which one can begin the research process.

While legal encyclopedias are designed to provide a comprehensive general treatment of the law, ALR provides a much more detailed and complex treatment of a particular legal issue. An ALR annotation provides a detailed discussion of cases concerning that legal issue from jurisdictions across the country. The cases are analyzed, and the annotation is organized to provide a framework for further research of the issue. The researcher should consult the opening sections of the annotation to determine the often-narrow scope of the annotation. Those sections conveniently reference other annotations concerning related issues.

Because its coverage is not comprehensive, the researcher will not always be lucky enough to find an ALR annotation concerning the issue being researched. In those instances when a relevant ALR annotation exists, the annotation can significantly speed one's research by providing an extensive discussion of relevant legal principles, majority and minority rules, and a synthesis of relevant case law. Each annotation represents an extensive study of the development and treatment of a particular issue across the jurisdictions. Where there is no case law from the researcher's jurisdiction, case law from other jurisdictions furnishes persuasive authority.

In addition, the ALR annotation functions as a case-finder, giving citations to cases with which the researcher can start researching to find more cases from a particular jurisdiction.

Use the index volumes of American Law Reports to find relevant annotations. The legal issues covered by annotations grow with developing case law. An annotation that supplements an earlier annotation should be read together with the earlier annotation. Extensive changes in case law may require a new "superseding" annotation. When an annotation supersedes an earlier annotation, only the later annotation should be read.

Unlike the topical arrangement of legal encyclopedias, annotations are published in the order they are written. The current series of ALR is *ALR, 7th*. Annotations from one of the earlier series may be consulted for topics with little change. The major organizational changes in *ALR, 7th* from earlier series are that illustrative cases are no longer printed in the volume and the citation references the article number within the volume rather than the first page of the annotation.

The organization of each annotation is fairly standard. The title and author of the annotation are followed by an abstract of the annotation. The following are the parts of the annotation:

Table of Contents
Article Outline
Article Body
Research References
Table of Cases, Laws, and Rules

The Table of Contents, Article Outline, and Table of Cases, Laws, and Rules help the researcher identify and locate relevant sections of the annotation, as they identify relevant sections by section number. The Research References aid the researcher in further research by cross-referencing parts of other sources in the law library that could profitably be consulted in further research.

The first two sections of the body of the annotation contain introductory material. Section 1, *Scope*, identifies the issue covered in the annotation. Section 2, *Background and summary*, briefly summarizes the information covered in the remainder of the annotation. The remainder of the annotation reviews cases concerning the issue that is the subject of the annotation, with the cases being organized around their facts and holdings.

Use of American Law Reports

The same cautions given about legal encyclopedias apply to American Law Reports. An annotation is a summary of the law and may not contain enough detail for your research. Be sure to review the cases cited in the annotation rather than relying on the annotation. The emphasis in the annotation is on case law, so do not omit statutory research. Never assume that the cases cited in the annotation—even in the pocket part to the annotation—are the most recent available. Use the cases cited in the annotation as starting points and use citators to locate more recent ones (see Chapter 6). Do not rely on the annotation as an accurate explanation of the law. The law may have changed since the annotation was written.

Generally, in legal writing, you would not quote from or refer to an ALR annotation because ALR annotations are not the law. They contain only the publisher's interpretation of the law. It is preferable to refer to the primary source itself.

In summary, American Law Reports are best used:

1. To find primary authority; and
2. To give the researcher general background information.

For information on how to make American Law Reports a part of your research strategy, see Chapter 7.

CITATION TIP

Check for Correct Citation Form

Do not assume that the legal citations found when researching are in correct citation form. Citations, even those included in cases, may or may not comply with Bluebook. Always check your citations against the appropriate citation rule for correct form.

Citation to American Law Reports

Although American Law Reports are not usually cited in documents submitted to court or opposing counsel, you will need to cite American Law Reports annotations for assignments and more informal documents such as office memos. (See Chapter 13 for an explanation of the purpose and use of office memos.) The following is a sample citation to an American Law Reports annotation.

George L. Blum, Annotation, *Liability in Negligence for Death or Injury Related to Rented Bicycle, Scooter, or Segway*, 48 A.L.R.7th Art. 3 (2020).

Notice that the citation begins with the author's name (but omitting J.D.), the word "Annotation," followed by the annotation title (either in italics or underlined), followed by the volume, "A.L.R.7th," followed by the identification of the article number, followed by the copyright year (in parentheses). When citing to an earlier series of American Law Reports, replace the article number with the first page of the annotation.

Tips on Using American Law Reports

Do:

1. Use footnotes to locate relevant primary authority.
2. Pull and read primary authority.
3. Check pocket parts for recent information.
4. Update information found.

Do not:

1. Rely on an American Law Reports annotation alone as an accurate statement of the law.
2. Generally cite American Law Reports.

Digests

The researcher is usually searching for cases containing facts and issues similar to those contained in the legal problem being researched. Digests contain summaries of cases and references to other research materials, with the case summaries arranged by topic, allowing one to find cases related to a particular legal principle. Finding similar cases would be almost impossible without **digests** or the ability to perform computer-assisted legal research. Digests have an essential role in the research process because of the manner in which cases are published. Cases are printed in rough chronological order in **reporters**, unorganized by subject matter, facts, or issues. A set of reporters contains no index volume. The case digest is a multivolume set of books that functions as an index, allowing the researcher to locate cases with similar subject matter, facts, and issues as that of the legal problem being researched. Digests contain summaries of cases and references to other research materials. The summaries are called "annotations." The case summaries are arranged by topic and subtopic, allowing researchers to find cases related to a particular legal principle.

Digests A multivolume set of books that functions as an index, allowing the researcher to locate cases with similar subject matter, facts, and issues as that of the legal problem being researched.

Reporters Sets of books containing judicial opinions.

Your law library probably contains several sets of digests. Usually, a digest set is shelved near the set of reporters with which it is used. There are two digests covering cases from the United States Supreme Court. The West federal digest series covers cases from various federal courts, including the district courts, courts of appeals, and the United States Supreme Court. Separate sets of digests accompany five of the seven regional reporters. State digests are published for most states. A state digest covers cases from the state courts of a particular state.

Digests are organized by topics, with the topics arranged in alphabetical sequence. The West Key Number System, the most commonly used arrangement of topics, contains over 400 topics. Other publishers use a similar alphabetical sequencing of topics in their digests. Each topic is further divided into subtopics, with some subtopics divided into sub-subtopics. Each subtopic and sub-subtopic represents a single point of law. Each subtopic and sub-subtopic receives a corresponding number, with a separate number sequence used for each topic. Thus, a topic and a number identify a single point of law. In a West publication, this is commonly referred to as the topic and "Key Number" because of the key outline preceding the number.

Digests have a number of advantages as well as limiting characteristics. The extensive number of digest topics makes the digest comprehensive in scope; digests are an essential case-finding tool. The identical West Key Number System is used throughout all West publications. The digest is devoid of the case commentary and analysis found in secondary sources; case law analysis and synthesis is left to the researcher. The digest summaries are not primary sources; the digest is a finding tool, and digest material should never be cited or quoted. The researcher relies on the summary alone at the researcher's peril. Instead, the researcher should read the case itself. The summary may be inaccurate, may take on a different meaning in the context of the entire case, or may have digested dictum rather than the holding of the case. Classification of a summary under a particular digest topic and number is an arbitrary decision made by the publisher; the text of the opinion supersedes any misleading digest classification. At the same time, an important point of law from a case may have been overlooked by the publisher and lack a corresponding headnote.

West Key Number System

The West Key Number System divides the law into over 400 topics and numerous subtopics within those topics. Each subtopic is assigned a Key Number. The topics comprising the West Key Number System are printed inside the cover of each West digest. A table of contents containing the Key Numbers and titles of subtopics appears at the beginning of each topic of the digest.

LexisNexis® publishes digests to accompany reporters such as *United States Supreme Court Reports, Lawyers' Edition*. LexisNexis publications use similar topics and subtopics, even though they are not referred to as "Key Numbers."

One of the topics in the West Key Number System is Searches and Seizures. The outline for the Searches and Seizures topic shows that there are 202 Key Numbers associated with the topic. *Byrd v. United States*, 138 S. Ct. 1518 (2018), is a case that is discussed in some detail in Chapter 4. *Byrd* involved a police officer stopping a rental car, and he and a fellow officer searching the car without consent when they found that the driver was not someone authorized to drive under the rental agreement. Because the driver was not authorized under the agreement, the officers assumed that the driver did not have an expectation of privacy in the vehicle. A good handful of the Key Numbers under the Searches and Seizures digest topic are related to *Byrd*. These Key Numbers include 23 (Fourth Amendment and reasonableness in general); 60 (Motor Vehicles); 61 (Expectation of privacy); 161 (Standing to Object); 162 (Privacy interest or expectation, in general); and 165 (Automobile searches).

Relationship between Digests and Reporters

Digests are closely related to case headnotes. Before a case is published in a reporter, an attorney on the publisher's staff prepares a number of short paragraphs, each of which summarizes an important legal principle from the case. Each summary is assigned a corresponding topic and number from the publisher's topic classification scheme. Some summaries that correspond to more than one topic or number can be assigned multiple topics and numbers or multiple numbers within a single topic, or both. The summaries, with their corresponding topics and numbers, are printed as "headnotes" at the beginning of the published opinion. The number of headnotes per case varies based on the length and complexity of the case. Some cases have a single headnote; other cases may have as many as several dozen.

The headnote summaries are reprinted in the digests under the appropriate topic and number. Each summary is followed by its case citation. Thus, in the digest, the topic number is followed by a collection of paragraphs, each relating to the same point of law. The digest is comprised entirely of topic number headings and summary paragraphs reprinted from case headnotes.

Headnote 24 from *Byrd* states:

> [24] **Searches and Seizures** Expectation of privacy
>
> The mere fact that a driver in lawful possession or control of a rental car is not listed as an authorized driver on the rental agreement will not defeat his or her otherwise reasonable expectation of privacy under the Fourth Amendment; ab-

rogating *U.S. v. Kennedy*, 638 F.3d 159, *U.S. v. Seeley*, 331 F.3d 471, *U.S. v. Wellons*, 32 F.3d 117, *U.S. v. Roper*, 918 F.2d 885. U.S.C.A. Const.Amend. 4.

The text of this headnote would be reprinted under Key Number 61 (Expectation of privacy) of the Searches and Seizures topic in the digest that contains cases from federal courts.

Using Digests to Find Cases

There are three basic approaches to finding cases using a digest. They are:

1. Using a digest topic and number from a known case;
2. Using the digest subject indexes; and
3. Using a digest topic outline.

The first approach allows you to use a known case and its headnotes to find other cases with similar facts or issues. You might have a case that contains facts or issues similar to those contained in the legal problem you are researching. To find more cases with similar facts or issues, look for the corresponding headnote. Use the topic and number from that headnote, and locate case summaries under the same topic and number in the digest. Once you find the case on point, determine the topic and Key Number from the case that are relevant to your search. Then look at the topic and Key Number in the digests. Cases concerning the same legal principle are grouped together under the same topic and Key Number.

The second approach requires you to use the digest's indexes, located at the end of the digest set. Identified as "Descriptive-Word Indexes" in West publications, these indexes are nothing more than subject indexes. The indexes supply a topic and Key Number when you look up key words in the indexes. Using key words from your legal problem, you can locate relevant digest topics and numbers.

The third approach requires you to use digest topic outlines. If you know a topic relevant to your problem, look at the table of contents at the beginning of the topic. From the titles of the subtopics, identify relevant Key Numbers to research. Each digest topic in the hardbound volumes begins with two outlines. The first is an abbreviated topic outline, and the second is a detailed topic outline. If you are fairly certain that a particular topic is relevant to the legal problem you are researching, you can review the topic outline for relevant topic numbers. Once you locate relevant topic numbers, review summaries following the relevant topic numbers.

Summary

- Legal encyclopedias can be used as secondary authority and as finding tools.
- *Corpus Juris Secundum* and *American Jurisprudence 2d* are the two most widely used national encyclopedias. There may also be a legal encyclopedia for the law of your state.

- Legal encyclopedias contain a textual explanation of hundreds of legal topics, with the explanation heavily footnoted to give citations to relevant primary authority.
- Legal encyclopedias are best used to find primary authority and to give the researcher general background information.
- Each *American Law Reports* annotation is a textual explanation of a legal issue with lengthy footnotes to relevant cases.
- *American Law Reports* are best used to find primary authority and to give the researcher general background information.
- Other secondary sources include treatises, legal dictionaries, legal directories, formbooks, legal periodicals, law review articles, legal thesauri, continuing education publications, and restatements.
- Digests are finding tools that contain case summaries and references to other research materials.
- Digests serve as indexes to cases and allow the researcher to locate relevant cases.
- When using digests, try to use the digest set that is most specific to the type of cases you are trying to find: a United States Supreme Court digest for cases from that court, a federal digest for cases from any of the federal courts, your state's digest for cases from your state, etc.
- Legal encyclopedias, digests, and other law books are updated by annual pocket parts and by paperbound supplementary pamphlets.

Key Terms

American Jurisprudence 2d
American Law Reports Series
annotations
Corpus Juris Secundum
digests
headnotes
legal encyclopedias
pocket part
reporters

QUESTIONS FOR LEGAL ENCYCLOPEDIA ASSIGNMENT

1. Using *Corpus Juris Secundum* or *American Jurisprudence*:

   a. How does the province of a jury differ from the province of the court?

b. What is the purpose of the jury in general and what is the additional purpose of the jury in a criminal case?

c. What is the correct citation for your answer?

2. Using *Corpus Juris Secundum* or *American Jurisprudence*:

a. Why must the president and Congress work together in the area of foreign commercial agreements (trade agreements)?

b. How is "fast track" legislation helpful in approving and implementing trade agreements?

c. What is the correct citation for your answer?

3. Using *Corpus Juris Secundum* or *American Jurisprudence*:

a. What are the names of four constitutional federal courts?

b. What makes legislative federal courts different from constitutional federal courts?

c. What are the names of four legislative federal courts?

d. What is the correct citation for your answer?

4. Using *Corpus Juris Secundum* or *American Jurisprudence*:

a. How is the United States Attorney General selected?

b. What are the limits on the removal of the United States Attorney General by the president?

c. What is the correct citation for your answer?

5. Using *Corpus Juris Secundum* or *American Jurisprudence*:

a. What is an "integrated bar"?

b. What provision of the United States Constitution protects the practice of law?

c. What is the correct citation for your answer?

6. Using *Corpus Juris Secundum* or *American Jurisprudence*:

   a. What are the elements of a legal malpractice claim?

   b. When can an attorney be liable to a third party for legal malpractice?

   c. What is the correct citation for your answer?

7. Using *Corpus Juris Secundum* or *American Jurisprudence*:

   a. What is the purpose of the intestate provisions of a probate code?

   b. How can an individual prevent the intestate provisions from applying to the individual's property?

   c. What is the correct citation for your answer?

8. Using *Corpus Juris Secundum* or *American Jurisprudence*:

   a. What is an expert witness?

   b. What are the general limitations on the admissibility of expert testimony?

   c. What is the correct citation for your answer?

9. Using *Corpus Juris Secundum* or *American Jurisprudence*:

   a. What are the essential elements of perjury?

   b. What are three defenses to a charge of perjury?

   c. What is the correct citation for your answer?

10. Using *Corpus Juris Secundum* or *American Jurisprudence*:

   a. What is a quiet title action?

   b. What must the plaintiff have to maintain a quiet title action?

c. What is the correct citation for your answer?

11. Using your state's legal encyclopedia:

a. What is a limited liability company?

b. How is a limited liability company formed?

c. What is the correct citation for your answer?

12. Using your state's legal encyclopedia:

a. What is defamation?

b. What is the difference between libel and slander?

c. What is the correct citation for your answer?

13. Using your state's legal encyclopedia:

a. What are the two theories pursuant to which a manufacturer may be held liable for a defective product?

b. What must a plaintiff show in asserting a claim for a defective product?

c. What is the correct citation for your answer?

14. Using your state's legal encyclopedia:

a. What are the qualifications for an out-of-state attorney to be licensed in your state?

b. What are the restrictions on the licensure of an out-of-state attorney who has been disciplined?

c. What is the correct citation for your answer?

15. Using your state's legal encyclopedia:

a. What is the purpose of recording a deed?

b. What determines the priority between two recorded documents affecting the same property?

c. What is the correct citation for your answer?

16. Using your state's legal encyclopedia:

a. What is contempt and what is an essential element of contempt?

b. What is the difference between criminal and civil contempt?

c. What is the correct citation for your answer?

17. Using your state's legal encyclopedia:

a. What are the requirements to establish a geographical area in which sales of alcoholic beverages is prohibited?

b. What types of entertainment and behavior may be regulated in an establishment licensed to sell alcoholic beverages?

c. What is the correct citation for your answer?

18. Using your state's legal encyclopedia:

a. What is the difference between venue and jurisdiction?

b. Does a court have the power to change venue and, if so, what are the restrictions on the power?

c. What is the correct citation for your answer?

QUESTIONS FOR AMERICAN LAW REPORTS ASSIGNMENT

1.

a. What is the citation to the annotation discussing the admissibility of expert testimony concerning extremist groups?

b. In a terrorism case, what are the competing rights of the government and the defendant that place them on a collision course?

c. What are the factors bearing on the reliability of expert opinion testimony concerning the structure, leadership, funding, and activities of foreign terrorist organizations?

d. What are the names of four extremist groups on which the government has sought to introduce expert opinion testimony?

2.

a. What is the citation to the annotation discussing when the courts will grant relief from a judgment in favor of the opposing party despite the fact that time limitations had lapsed because counsel had been careless or neglectful in accessing and dealing with the various e-filing requirements?

b. What are twelve specific mistakes that caused e-filing problems?

c. What are eight online-related reasons for an attorney's non-response?

3.

a. What is the citation to the annotation discussing the cases that have addressed the authentication of text messages?

b. What are the two components of authentication of text messages?

c. What are the four ways in which the identity of the purported sender may be established?

d. Which ten individuals have offered testimony to authenticate text messages?

4.

a. What is the citation to the annotation discussing the cases that have addressed the disqualification or recusal of a judge based upon the use or attributed use of social media?

b. What is the main concern with a judge using social media?

c. If the annotation contains a citation to a case from your state, what were the facts in the case and what was the holding of the case?

5.

a. What is the citation to the annotation discussing cases considering various challenges to the use of license plate recognition technology?

b. What are three concerns with the use of license plate recognition technology?

c. What level of proof is needed for an officer to conduct a traffic stop?

d. For the criminal defendant, what is the danger of not challenging aspects of a license plate reader system?

6.

a. What is the citation to the annotation discussing the cases that have addressed the use of cell-site simulators?

b. How does the cell-site simulator operate?

c. Why would officers use two devices in tandem?

d. What are three critical differences between a cell tower dump and use of a cell-site simulator?

7.

a. What is the citation to the annotation discussing the cases in which courts have considered the legal propriety of attorney website advertisements?

b. What four factors present when choosing attorney representation create a potential for consumer targeting?

c. What are four remedial grounds that may support a sanction or liability against an attorney?

d. If the annotation contains a citation to a case from your state, what were the facts in the case and what was the holding of the case?

8.

a. What is the citation to the annotation addressing state cases discussing the necessity and admissibility of evidence designated as expert testimony that concerns slang, lingo, code words, or jargon?

b. What four types of individuals have created language subcultures making it difficult for one with no familiarity with the terminology to comprehend?

c. If the annotation contains a citation to a case from your state, what were the facts in the case and what was the holding of the case?

9.

a. What is the citation to the annotation addressing state cases that have addressed opioid marketing, promoting, and distributing claims against opioid manufacturers and distributors?

b. What are some of the allegations against the defendants?

c. What are the three main types of litigation based on the identity of the plaintiff?

d. What are nine causes of action under which such litigation has been brought?

10.

a. What is the citation to the annotation discussing state cases discussing the admissibility of lay testimony that concerns slang, lingo, code words, or jargon?

b. What is the difference between lay opinion testimony and expert opinion testimony?

c. What are the exceptions to the rule that a lay witness is generally not permitted to give an opinion from facts observed?

d. What should an attorney do who wishes to challenge the admissibility of slang, jargon, or code?

e. If the annotation contains a citation to a case from your state, what were the facts in the case and what was the holding of the case?

11.

a. What is the citation to the annotation discussing the use of police-worn body camera footage in state criminal proceedings?

b. What is the reason for greater use of police-worn body cameras?

c. What are some of the concerns with the use of police-worn body cameras?

d. If the annotation contains a citation to a case from your state, what were the facts in the case and what was the holding of the case?

12.

a. What is the citation to the annotation discussing nondisclosure or confidentiality agreements in cases of sexual harassment, assault, or rape?

b. What are umbrella protective orders?

c. What are other ways to prevent information from being disclosed?

d. If the annotation contains a citation to a case from your state, what were the facts in the case and what was the holding of the case?

13.

a. What is the citation to the annotation discussing the admissibility of rap lyrics or videos in criminal prosecutions?

b. When are rap lyrics properly admitted?

c. If the annotation contains a citation to a case from your state, what were the facts in the case and what was the holding of the case?

14.

a. What is the citation to the annotation discussing the use of medical marijuana as a defense to a driving offense?

b. If one has approval to use marijuana for medical purposes, may one drive a vehicle?

c. What is the automobile exception?

d. Concerning marijuana, what generally establishes probable cause for a search?

e. If the annotation contains a citation to a case from your state, what were the facts in the case and what was the holding of the case?

15.

a. What is the citation to the annotation discussing the waiver or loss of protection of state attorney work product protection?

b. What is the work product doctrine?

c. If the annotation contains a citation to a case from your state, what were the facts in the case and what was the holding of the case?

16.

a. What is the citation to the annotation discussing issues arising from collaborative law practice?

b. What is collaborative law?

c. May the collaborative lawyers represent the parties in court?

d. What are the similarities between collaborative law and mediation?

e. What are the differences between collaborative law and mediation?

f. If the annotation contains a citation to a case from your state, what were the facts in the case and what was the holding of the case?

17.

a. What is the citation to the annotation discussing disclosure of video obtained by law enforcement from surveillance cameras?

b. What types of devices are used by law enforcement for recording or surveillance?

c. What types of state statutes may provide the public with information captured by these devices?

d. What are the reasons for exempting recorded information from disclosure?

e. If the annotation contains a citation to a case from your state, what were the facts in the case and what was the holding of the case?

18.

a. What is the citation to the annotation discussing validity under the First Amendment of limiting automatic dialing and announcing devices (ADAD) and robocalls?

b. What is the benefit derived from ADADs?

c. What are the problems with ADADs?

d. If the annotation contains a citation to a case from your state, what were the facts in the case and what was the holding of the case?

19.

a. What is the citation to the annotation discussing the regulation of online fantasy sports?

b. What is the legal status of gambling and online gambling?

c. What gives the states the right to regulate gambling?

d. How does a fantasy sport game operate?

e. If the annotation contains a citation to a case from your state, what were the facts in the case and what was the holding of the case?

QUESTIONS FOR DIGEST ASSIGNMENT

1. Give the citation to the 2019 United States Supreme Court case in which the Court found that the residual clause of the definition of violent felony in a federal statute providing mandatory minimum sentences for using or carrying a firearm during and in relation to a federal crime of violence, or possessing a firearm in furtherance of a federal crime of violence, which definition treats as a crime of violence a felony that by its nature involves a substantial risk that physical force against the person or property of another may be used in the course of committing the offense, is unconstitutionally vague under due process and separation of powers principles.

2. Give the citation to the 2019 United States Supreme Court case in which

the Court found that consumers who bought smartphone applications, or apps, from smartphone manufacturer's electronic retail store were "direct purchasers" who, pursuant to the Clayton Act, could sue the manufacturer for allegedly monopolizing the sale of the apps and charging higher-than-competitive prices; in the distribution chain at issue, there was no intermediary between the manufacturer and consumers, and thus consumers were not indirect purchasers but, instead, bought directly from the manufacturer, and so were the proper plaintiffs to sue the alleged monopolist, notwithstanding allegations that app developers, not manufacturer, set the retail price charged to consumers.

3. Give the citation to the 2019 United States Supreme Court case in which the Court found that a circuit judge who died before the United States Court of Appeals for the Ninth Circuit filed an en banc decision could not be counted as a member of the en banc majority, even though the en banc Ninth Circuit stated that the majority opinion and all concurrences were final, and voting had been completed by the en banc court, before the judge's death; counting the judge effectively allowed a deceased judge to exercise the judicial power of the United States after his death, but federal judges were "appointed for life, not for eternity."

4. Give the citation to the 2019 United States Supreme Court case in which the Court found that when police have probable cause to believe a person has committed a drunk-driving offense and the driver's unconsciousness or stupor requires him to be taken to the hospital or similar facility before police have a reasonable opportunity to administer a standard evidentiary breath test, they may almost always order a warrantless blood test to measure the driver's blood alcohol concentration (BAC) without offending the Fourth Amendment.

5. Give the citation to the 2018 United States Supreme Court case in which the Court found that the fact that defendant violated a rental car agreement signed by a third party, by driving the rental car while not listed as an authorized driver on the agreement, did not eliminate any reasonable expectation of privacy he had in the vehicle, which was protected by the Fourth Amendment at the time troopers conducted warrantless search of the vehicle; for Fourth Amendment purposes there was no meaningful difference between agreement's authorized-driver provision and other restrictions in rental car agreements, such as prohibitions on driving the car on unpaved roads or driving while using a handheld cellphone, all of which concerned risk allocation between private parties,

under which violators might pay additional fees, lose insurance coverage, or assume liability for damage resulting from the breach.

6. Give the citation to the 2018 United States Supreme Court case in which the Court found that the automobile exception to the Fourth Amendment's warrant requirement for searches did not justify police officer's invasion of curtilage of home, for warrantless search of motorcycle covered by tarp and parked in partially enclosed top portion of driveway of home, though officer had probable cause to believe that the motorcycle was the one that had eluded officer's attempted traffic stop; officer invaded not only defendant's interest in the item searched, i.e., the motorcycle, but also invaded defendant's Fourth Amendment interest in the curtilage of the home.

7. Give the citation to the 2018 United States Supreme Court case in which the Court held a provision of the federal Professional and Amateur Sports Protection Act that makes it unlawful for a state to authorize sports gambling to be unconstitutional because the provision violates the anti-commandeering doctrine.

8. Give the citation to the 2018 United States Supreme Court case in which the Court held that the government must generally obtain a search warrant supported by probable cause before acquiring cell-site location information from a wireless carrier.

9. Give the citation to the 2017 United States Supreme Court case in which the Court found that the district court applied the wrong standard in awarding sanctions under its inherent powers against tire manufacturer in products liability action for bad-faith conduct, when it specifically disclaimed the "usual" need to find a "causal link" between misconduct and fees when the sanctioned party's behavior "r[ose] to a truly egregious level," and thought that in such situation it could award "all" fees, including those that would have been incurred in absence of misconduct.

10. Give the citation to the 2015 United States Supreme Court case in which the Court found that town's sign code, which subjected ideological signs to certain restrictions, subjected political signs to greater restrictions, and subjected temporary directional signs relating to events to even greater restrictions, was content based on its face, and thus was subject to strict scrutiny in free speech challenge by a church seeking to place temporary signs announcing its services; any innocent motives on part of town did

not eliminate danger of censorship, sign code singled out specific subject matter for differential treatment even if it did not target viewpoints within that subject matter, and sign code singled out signs bearing a particular message, i.e., the time and location of a particular event.

11. Give the citation to the 2018 case of the United States Court of Appeals for the Federal Circuit in which the court found that the regulations creating presumption of service connection for listed diseases for veterans who served in "the Republic of Vietnam" or in "Vietnam" did not render subsequently enacted Agent Orange Act, which codified those regulations, ambiguous as to whether the act applied to those who served in the territorial sea of "the Republic of Vietnam," despite government's assertion that regulations created foot-on-land requirement; regulations covered everyone whose service included duty or visitation "in the Republic of Vietnam," which embraced the territorial sea.

12. Give the citation to the 2018 case of the United States Court of Appeals for the Ninth Circuit in which the court found that the consumer did not state a claim against a chocolate manufacturer for violation of California's Unfair Competition Law based on the manufacturer's failure to include information about child and forced labor practices of its suppliers on its product labels.

13. Give the citation to the 2018 case of the United States Court of Appeals for the Fifth Circuit in which the court found that Texas law, as predicted by federal court, would not have recognized a neurobiological compulsion induced by manufacturer's smartphone as a substantial factor in driver's tortious acts of reading a text while driving, and thus driver's smartphone could not have been a cause in fact of injuries arising from driver's fatal collision with another vehicle in which parents died and child was rendered paraplegic, and therefore manufacturer was not liable for negligence or products liability for failing to implement patent for lock-out mechanism on driver's phone, or for failing to warn drivers of dangers of distracted driving.

14. Give the citation to the 2018 case of the United States Court of Appeals for the Eleventh Circuit in which the court found that, under Alabama law, sum stipulated by liquidated-damages clause in cooperative cotton marketing agreement was not reasonable pre-breach estimate of probable loss, and thus clause was void as a penalty; liquidated-damages formula involved subtracting price of cotton on New York futures mar-

ket, such price being determined in part by "date of breach," which was not defined, from highest price per pound received by cooperative for cotton at any time during relevant crop year, no matter how small the amount, yielding liquidated-damages figure vastly exceeding anything cooperative could have possibly lost.

15. Give the citation to the 2018 case of the United States Court of Appeals for the Eleventh Circuit in which the court found that the Colombian flag painted on side of vessel, which was found to be transporting cocaine in international waters by United States Coast Guard, was not "flying" for purpose of making claim of nationality or registry under Maritime Drug Law Enforcement Act, and thus, absent documents evidencing vessel's nationality or verbal claim of nationality by master of vessel, vessel was without nationality and therefore subject to extraterritorial jurisdiction of United States pursuant to the act.

16. Give the citation to the 2018 case of the United States Court of Appeals for the Fifth Circuit in which the court found that the district court did not misapply an eight-level sentencing enhancement to defendant's sentence for possession of an unregistered silencer and possession of an unregistered destructive device, based on his attempt to purchase 144 live grenades, although he only received one live grenade and 143 inert grenades; whether defendant possessed inert grenades had no bearing on whether he unlawfully sought to obtain real ones, and what mattered under the applicable sentencing guideline was what was desired, not what was acquired.

17. Give the citation to the 2017 case of the United States Court of Appeals for the Seventh Circuit in which the court found that, while configuration of marked police van in which detainees were transported, with their hands handcuffed behind their backs, by agents of the Bureau of Alcohol, Tobacco, Firearms & Explosives (ATF) may have caused detainees to believe that what they said quietly in rear compartment of van, separated by two metal walls from compartment in which the ATF agents operating the van were seated, would not be overheard, any expectation of privacy was not one which society would recognize as reasonable, so that interception and recording of detainees' statements with hidden electronic equipment did not violate detainees' rights under either the Fourth Amendment or Title III of the Omnibus Crime Control and Safe Streets Act.

18. Give the citation to the 2018 case of the United States District Court for the District of Columbia in which the court found that files likely to contain requested pornographic materials collected during a military operation were exempt under the CIA Information Act from Freedom of Information Act disclosure as "operational files."

Chapter 4

The Judicial Branch and Cases

Introduction

As identified by the chapter title, this chapter provides information on the judicial branch and cases. The first portion of this chapter on the judicial branch discusses:

- jurisdiction
- trial courts
- appellate courts
- federal courts, and
- state courts

The balance of the chapter discusses how to:

- read a case, and
- brief a case.

The Judicial Branch

As we learned in Chapter 1, federal and state governments are divided into the judicial, legislative, and executive branches. The judicial branch of government is made up of a system of courts, with one court system of federal courts for the United States government and a court system for each state and the District of Columbia. The court systems have a hierarchical arrangement, with the courts organized into various levels, or tiers. A court system is typically comprised of three or four tiers; in a three-tier system, the lowest tier of courts are **trial courts** and in a four-tier system, the two lowest tiers are trial courts, with the lower tier comprised of inferior trial courts and the next tier comprised of superior trial courts. The level above the trial courts is typically comprised of the **intermediate appellate courts**. The upper-most tier is typically comprised of a single court, the **court of last resort**.

Court of Last Resort

The highest tier in the federal court system and the state court system, which usually contains one court. In a court of last resort, such as the United States Supreme Court or a state supreme court, all members of the court participate in deciding a case.

⬆

Intermediate Appellate Court

An appellate court that is subject to judicial review by a higher appellate court.

⬆

Trial Courts

In our adversarial system, the two parties present their evidence at the trial level. The evidence may be testimony, documents, or tangible evidence. The role of the trial court is to determine the facts and to apply the applicable law to the facts.

In our adversarial system, the two parties present their evidence at the trial level. The evidence may be testimony, documents, or tangible evidence. The role of a trial court is to determine the facts and to apply the applicable law to the facts. An intermediate appellate court is an appellate court that is subject to judicial review by a higher appellate court. The highest tier in the federal court system and the state court system usually contains one court: the court of last resort. In a court of last resort, such as the United States Supreme Court or a state supreme court, all members of the court participate in deciding a case.

Jurisdiction

A court must have the power, in other words **jurisdiction**, to decide a particular case before it. Jurisdiction assumes that the court has geographical jurisdiction, subject matter jurisdiction, and hierarchical jurisdiction. A court is limited to deciding cases within a particular geographical region and would have **geographical jurisdiction** to decide a case arising within this geographical region.

Jurisdiction The right and power of a court to make legally binding decisions in a particular geographical area over particular persons and subject matters.

Geographical Jurisdiction Geographical jurisdiction refers to the geographical area within which a court has the right and power to make decisions that are legally binding.

For example, the United States District Court for the Middle District of Florida (a trial-level court) is restricted to hearing cases arising within the district covering the middle of the state. A party appealing a case from that court would appeal to the United States Court of Appeals for the Eleventh Circuit. The Eleventh Circuit is restricted to hearing cases arising in Alabama, Florida, or Georgia.

Online research:

The website www.uscourts.gov contains a map showing the geographical arrangement of the federal circuits.

A court must have the power to decide the substance of a particular case before it; in other words, the court must have **subject matter jurisdiction.** A court may be a court of **limited jurisdiction**, restricted to hearing cases concerning certain substance, or of **general jurisdiction**, with the power to hear cases not heard by the courts of limited jurisdiction.

Subject Matter Jurisdiction The person about whom and the subject matters about which a court has the right and power to make decisions that are legally binding.

Limited Jurisdiction A court of limited jurisdiction is limited to hearing certain types of cases.

General Jurisdiction The power of a court to hear and decide a wide range of cases that arise within its geographic area.

For example, United States bankruptcy courts are restricted to hearing bankruptcy cases; therefore, they are courts of limited jurisdiction. United States district courts are considered courts of general jurisdiction, hearing civil and criminal cases not heard by specialized trial-level federal courts.

Subject matter jurisdiction also requires that the court have either **in personam jurisdiction**, in a case in which the court is to decide the rights of the defendant, or **in rem jurisdiction**, in a case in which the court is to decide the status of property.

In Personam Jurisdiction The authority of a court to determine the rights of the defendant.

In Rem Jurisdiction The authority of a court to determine the status of property.

The third type of jurisdiction necessary is **hierarchical jurisdiction**; in other words, the court deciding the case must be of the appropriate level in the hierarchy. A court may be a court that hears and decides a case at its initial stage, or a court with **appellate jurisdiction**, a court that hears and decides a case when the case is appealed after the initial decision. The court of original jurisdiction initially hears and decides a case. On appeal, the case is heard by a court with appellate jurisdiction.

> **Hierarchical Jurisdiction** Hierarchical jurisdiction refers to the level of court deciding a case.
>
> **Appellate Jurisdiction** The power and authority of a higher court to take up cases that have already been in a lower court and the power to make decisions about these cases.
>
> **Original Jurisdiction** The power of a court to take a case, try it, and decide it (as opposed to appellate jurisdiction, the power of a court to hear and decide an appeal).

A case typically begins in a trial-level court, a court of **original jurisdiction**, and is appealed to an intermediate appellate court or a court of last resort, both courts with appellate jurisdiction. In a three-tier court system, a court in the lowest tier, a trial court, is the court of original jurisdiction. In a four-tier court system, a case in which original jurisdiction is in an inferior trial court may be appealed to a superior trial court, meaning that the superior trial court has appellate jurisdiction of the case. For certain types of cases, original jurisdiction may be set in a court other than a trial court. For instance, Article III, section 2 of the United States Constitution dictates that the United States Supreme Court is a court of original jurisdiction for certain specified types of cases: "In all Cases affecting Ambassadors, other public Ministers and consuls, and those in which a State shall be a Party, the supreme Court shall have original jurisdiction."

The next two sections describe how trial courts and appellate courts function within the court system.

Trial Court

The American courts are based on an adversary system in which the attorney presents the facts and applicable law in the light most favorable to the client. An attorney may characterize the facts very differently than the opposing attorney and may argue that the court should decide the case relying on a different legal theory than that advocated by the opposing attorney. The evidence of the facts in a case, be it **testimony**, documents, or tangible evidence, is presented at the trial level typically presided over by a single judge. This evidence is "testimonial" and is different from demonstrative evidence. Because opposing parties may present differing versions of the facts, the role of the fact finder is to decide what the facts are after hearing testimony and reviewing documentary and tangible evidence. The jury is the fact finder in a jury trial, while the judge is the fact finder in a **bench trial**, a case tried without a jury. In a bench trial, the judge determines the facts and decides questions of law. If there is a jury, the jury determines the facts in conformity with the judge's instructions, in other words, the judge's **charge** to the jury.

> **Testimony** Evidence given by a witness under oath.
>
> **Bench Trial** A case tried without a jury.
>
> **Charge** The judge's final summary of a case and instructions to the jury.

The role of the judge is to decide **questions of law**. Examples of questions of law include whether evidence is **admissible**, which of conflicting legal theories applies, and whether to grant a **motion**, such as a **motion for a directed verdict** or a **motion for a summary judgment**.

> **Questions of Law** A point in dispute in a lawsuit; an issue for a decision by the judge.
>
> **Admissible** A judge must decide whether a piece of evidence may be considered by the fact finder in deciding a case.
>
> **Motion** A request that a judge make a ruling or take some other action. Motions are either granted or denied by the judge.
>
> **Motion for a Directed Verdict** A request that the judge take the decision out of the jury's hands. The judge does this by telling jurors what the jury must decide or by actually making the decision. The judge might do this when the person suing has presented facts that, even if believed by a jury, cannot add up to a successful case.
>
> **Motion for a Summary Judgment** A request that the judge enter a final judgment (victory) for one side in a lawsuit (or in one part of a lawsuit), without trial, when the judge finds that there is no genuine factual issue in the lawsuit (or in part of the lawsuit).

Appellate Court

The **appellate court** reviews what the lower court did, with its review of **questions of fact** quite distinct from its review of questions of law. Because the fact finder in the lower court was in the best position to decide what the facts were, the appellate court defers to the trial court's decision on the facts; therefore, the appellate court does not substitute its judgment for that of the trial court fact finder unless the jury's fact finding was not supported by substantial evidence or the judge's fact finding was clearly erroneous. With regard to questions of law, the trial court's ruling, such as admitting evidence, is treated as discretionary and the appellate court may reverse the ruling of the trial court if the trial court abused its discretion.

Thus, one of the primary functions of the appellate court is to correct any error made by the lower court if the appellate court determines that the ruling of the lower court in its application of the law was not correct. If the error by the lower court was greater than a harmless error, the appellate court would reverse the lower court decision; with a reversal, the appellate court may also **remand** the case to the lower court for further proceedings. For example, a higher court may remand (send back) a case to a lower court, directing the lower court to take some action. If the lower court ruling was correct or any error was harmless, the appellate court would affirm the ruling of the lower court. The appellate court may agree with the lower court on certain issues and disagree on other issues; in that instance, the appellate court would affirm the lower court as to the rulings of the lower court with which the appellate court agrees and reverse as to the rulings of the lower court with which the appellate court believes the lower court has erred.

Appellate Court Refers to a higher court that can hear appeals from a lower court.

Questions of Fact A point in dispute in a lawsuit; an issue for decision by judge or jury.

Remand Send back.

Typically, the party who loses the case at the trial level has the right to appeal the case to the intermediate appellate court. Perhaps because the losing party is guaranteed the right to one appeal, its appeal to the intermediate appellate court is mandatory, which means that the intermediate appellate court is required to hear the appeal.

In contrast to the trial court, where a single judge presides, the intermediate appellate-level case is usually decided by a three-judge **panel**. The members of the three-judge panel are randomly chosen from the approximately dozen judges who are members of the intermediate appellate court. The appellate court considers the record, materials designated by the attorneys to be included, commonly including documents and exhibits from the trial, a transcript of a portion or all of the trial activities, and **appellate briefs** filed by the parties. An appellate brief argues the facts of the case, supported by specific page references to the record, and the applicable law, supported by citations of authority. In contrast to the trial court, the evidence that the appellate court considers is limited to that presented at trial, and the appellate court proceeding does not include additional testimony or presentation of evidence. The appellate court may find it helpful to hear an **oral argument** presented by the attorneys representing the parties to the appeal. During oral argument each attorney has a specified amount of time to present the client's theory of the case and to field any questions from the judges. The presentation typically involves oral statements by a lawyer, interrupted by questions from the judges.

> **Panel** A group of judges (smaller than the entire court) that decides a case.
>
> **Appellate Brief** Written statement submitted to an appellate court to persuade the court of the correctness of one's position.
>
> **Oral Argument** The presentation of each side of a case before an appeals court.

Should the circumstances warrant it, the decision at the intermediate appellate level may be heard or reheard by the entire membership of the court rather than the usual three-judge panel. As explained in Chapter 2, an *en banc* decision means that all the members of the court sit to hear the case rather than the case being heard by a three-judge panel. For example, if the Seventh Circuit Court of Appeals decides to hear a case *en banc* and there are eleven judges who are members of the Seventh Circuit, all eleven judges would hear the case. Because an *en banc* decision is rare and typically concerns important legal issues, special attention should be paid to an *en banc* decision.

The party who loses at the intermediate appellate court level may request review by a higher court. Although the losing party at the trial level generally has the right to appeal, appeal to a court of last resort, the highest level state court or the United States Supreme Court, may be within the court's **discretionary jurisdiction**; a court exercising discretionary jurisdiction can decide which cases it reviews and the number of cases in which the court issues a full decision is a small percentage of those cases in which review is requested.

> **Discretionary Jurisdiction** A court with discretionary jurisdiction over a case can decide if the court should hear the case.

In a court of last resort, such as the United States Supreme Court or a state supreme court, all members of the court participate in deciding a case. In other words, a case in a court of last resort is heard *en banc*.

Because of time constraints and their non-precedential effect, trial court judges, especially state trial court judges, author few opinions, with most opinions authored by appellate court judges. With a number of judges participating in the decision of an appellate court, the majority opinion in the case could be written by any judge or justice in the **majority**; a particular court may have a method for designating which judge in the majority is to write the majority opinion. The tradition in the United States Supreme Court is for the Chief Justice, if in the majority, or the most senior Justice in the majority to assign the Justice who will write the majority opinion. A judge or justice who disagrees with the majority decision has the option of writing a **dissenting opinion** that explains the basis of the disagreement. A majority opinion is an opinion agreed upon by greater than half of the judges hearing the case.

Majority Greater than half of the judges hearing the case.

Dissenting Opinion A judge's formal disagreement with the decision of the majority of the judges in a lawsuit. If the judge puts it in writing, it is called a dissenting opinion.

Federal Courts

The United States Supreme Court, the highest court in the federal court system, is the sole court referenced by name in the United States Constitution, with the other lower federal courts to be established by statute. Article III, section 1 states: "the judicial Power of the United States shall be vested in one supreme Court, and in such inferior Courts as the Congress may from time to time ordain and establish." Congress created a federal court system below the United States Supreme Court that is hierarchical in structure with intermediate and trial levels of courts; in addition, Congress established a number of specialized courts. Federal intermediate appellate courts include the twelve regional United States courts of appeals and the United States Court of Appeals for the Federal Circuit. Federal trial courts include the 94 United States district courts; the United States Court of International Trade and the United States Court of Federal Claims are specialized courts also at the trial level.

The United States Supreme Court and those courts Congress created pursuant to Article III of the United States Constitution, including the United States courts of appeals and the United States district courts, are known as Article III, or constitutional, courts. The president nominates justices and judges of constitutional courts, who, after being confirmed by a majority vote of the Senate, receive a lifetime appointment and can only be removed by impeachment.

Federal Trial-Level Courts

The **United States district courts** are the principal federal trial-level courts of general jurisdiction. Each state has at least one district court, as does the District of Columbia and Puerto Rico, and each district has a bankruptcy court operating as a unit of the court.

United States District Courts The U.S. trial courts.

The jurisdiction of the courts in the state court systems is broader than that of the federal courts, and the majority of disputes in this country are decided in those courts; however, a given plaintiff may have grounds for filing a case in either state or federal court and would have to decide which would be the more appropriate forum. Certain categories of cases arising under the United States Constitution or federal statute, such as bankruptcy, copyright, and patent, may only be filed in federal court.

Generally, the jurisdiction of the United States district courts is limited to two categories of cases, federal question cases and diversity cases. **Federal question jurisdiction** gives the United States district court the power to decide a case involving the federal government or its officials, the United States Constitution, a United States statute, a treaty to which the United States is a party, or a controversy between states. **Diversity jurisdiction** gives the United States district court the power to decide a case with more than $75,000 in controversy where the litigants are citizens of different states or where one litigant is a citizen of the United States and the other litigant is a citizen of another country. The diversity requirement is met so long as no plaintiff is of the same state as any defendant; in other words, the diversity must be complete such that no one state's citizenship is represented on both the plaintiff and defendant sides of the lawsuit. This means that no plaintiff may be a citizen of the same state or foreign country as any defendant.

Federal Question Jurisdiction A legal issue directly involving the U.S. Constitution, statutes, or treaties. Federal courts have jurisdiction in cases involving a federal question.

Diversity Jurisdiction Federal courts have diversity jurisdiction as long as the amount in controversy is more than $75,000 and the parties are citizens from different states or one party is a citizen of a state and the other party is a citizen of a foreign country.

Federal Appellate Courts

The thirteen **United States courts of appeals** are the intermediate appellate courts within the federal court system. Because of their history, these courts are many times called "circuit" courts; in the early years of the country, the judges were obligated to hear cases traveling by horseback from location to location within a circuit. All but one of these courts, the United States courts of appeals for the First through the Eleventh Circuits and the District of Columbia, have jurisdiction of cases arising from the district courts and federal administrative agencies within a particular geographical region. The other court of appeals, the United States Court of Appeals for the Federal Circuit, has jurisdiction over patent cases and those cases appealed from the United States Court of International Trade and the United States Court of Federal Claims.

United States Courts of Appeals Hear appeals from lower federal courts and administrative agencies; there is one court for each of twelve geographical circuits plus the Federal Circuit, which hears appeals nationwide from specialized federal courts and other appeals such as patent cases.

United States Supreme Court

Nine **Justices** comprise the **Supreme Court of the United States**, with one Justice designated as the **Chief Justice**; besides this leadership role on the Supreme Court, the Chief Justice has various administrative duties concerning the Supreme Court and the federal court system. The Chief Justice of the United States Supreme Court presides over the Court and has additional administrative duties related both to the Supreme Court and to the entire federal court system.

Supreme Court of the United States The highest of the United States courts.

Justices A judge, especially an appellate judge such as a Justice of the United States Supreme Court.

Chief Justice The presiding Justice, usually of a court of last resort.

As described above, the jurisdiction of the United States Supreme Court is largely discretionary, with cases sought to be heard by the Supreme Court coming from a United States Court of Appeals or a state court of last resort. The usual procedure for seeking review of a case by the Supreme Court is for the litigant who lost below to file a **petition for writ of certiorari** with the Supreme Court. At least four Justices, the "rule of four," must vote to grant a petition for the case to be heard by the Supreme Court.

Petition for Writ of Certiorari (Latin) "To make sure." A request for certiorari (or "cert." for short) is like an appeal, but one which the higher court is not required to take for decision. It is literally a writ from the higher court asking the lower court for the record of the case.

The annual term of the United States Supreme Court starts with the first Monday in October and continues through June of the following calendar year, with each term distinguished from other terms by reference to the calendar year in which the term commences. Following that scheme, the Court term beginning in October 2019 and ending in June of 2020 is designated as the October 2019 term. Statistics for the last few years show as many as between 8,000 and 10,000 cases on the Supreme Court's docket, with most cases disposed of by a one-line decision that review is denied. During each term, the Supreme Court reaches a decision in 170 or so cases, with fewer than 100 decided with full opinions and many announced in June shortly prior to the start of the Supreme Court's summer recess.

State Courts

The organization of the courts within the judicial branch of the various states is not uniform; however, a typical organization is a simplified court structure, referred to as a **unified court structure**, with three or four levels or tiers. The organization of the judicial branch in states not following a unified court structure may be more complicated, with many levels of courts, some with overlapping jurisdiction. The judicial branch of the Florida State government has a simplified court structure with four levels. The following sections contain information on the Florida State courts as an example of a state court system with a unified court structure.

> **Unified Court Structure** A simplified state court structure with three or four tiers; the court structure of other states that do not have a unified court structure is more complex.

The Structure of the Florida State Court System

Court	Type of Court
Florida Supreme Court	state appellate court of last resort
District Courts of Appeal	intermediate appellate court
Circuit Courts	upper-level trial court
County Courts	lower-level trial court

As shown in the above chart, the Florida State court system has a unified court structure comprised of two appellate courts, the Florida Supreme Court and the district courts of appeal, and two trial courts.

Florida Supreme Court

The Florida Supreme Court is the appellate court of last resort in the system, and its review is largely discretionary. However, the Florida Supreme Court has mandatory jurisdiction over:

trial court decisions imposing the death penalty; and

decisions of district courts of appeal invalidating a state statute or a provision of the Florida Constitution.

The discretionary jurisdiction of the Florida Supreme Court includes review of:

A district court of appeal decision validating a state statute or interpreting the Florida Constitution or United States Constitution;

A district court of appeal decision directly conflicting with another district court of appeal decision or a decision of the Florida Supreme Court;

A district court of appeal decision containing a question certified to be of great public importance;

A trial court order or judgment that a district court of appeal certifies to be of great public importance or to have a great effect on the proper administration of justice; and

A question of law that the United States Supreme Court or a United States court of appeals certifies as determinative of a case and for which the Florida Court has announced no controlling precedent.

District Courts of Appeal

The district courts of appeal are intermediate appellate courts. There are five district courts of appeal with the geographical jurisdiction pictured below.

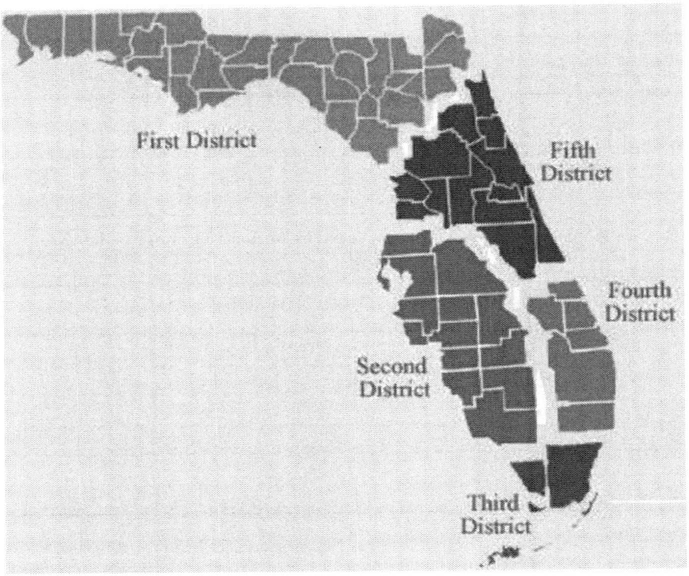

The jurisdiction of the district courts of appeal is broad because a party can appeal an order or final judgment not directly appealable to the Florida Supreme Court as a matter of right to a district court of appeal.

Circuit Courts

The upper-level trial courts, the circuit courts, are divided into twenty circuits with the geographical jurisdiction pictured above.

Whether a case is filed in circuit court or county court is largely dependent on the amount in controversy, the severity of the criminal charge, or the subject matter of a case.

The types of cases over which the circuit court has jurisdiction are listed below:

civil cases involving more than $15,000
felonies
family law cases
juvenile law cases
probate and guardianship cases

In addition, the circuit court functions as an appellate court for cases appealed from county court.

County Court

Each of Florida's sixty-seven counties has its own lower-level trial court, county court.

The types of cases over which the county court has jurisdiction are listed below:

civil cases other than small claims involving $15,000 and less
misdemeanors
traffic court cases
small claims cases

Using *Byrd v. United States* to Illustrate Reading and Briefing a Case

Now would be a good time to access *Byrd v. United States* so that you have it ready as you read the following two sections. *Byrd v. United States* is a United States Supreme Court case decided in 2018. At the time this book was being written, it had not yet been published in *United States Reports*, but it was available in *Supreme Court Reporter* at 138 S.Ct. 1518 and in *United States Supreme Court Reports, Lawyers' Edition, Second Series* at 200 L.Ed.2d 805.

Reading a Case

In glancing over the case, the first portion of the case you see is the case caption:

Supreme Court of the United States
Terrence BYRD, Petitioner
v.
UNITED STATES.
No. 16–1371.
Argued Jan. 9, 2018.
Decided May 14, 2018.

The case caption provides basic information, including the court deciding the case, the names of the parties, the case docket number, the date the case was argued, and the date on which it was decided. If you are viewing the case in *Supreme Court Reporter*, you will see a portion entitled "Synopsis," which is the case summary, often referred to as the syllabus. Following the syllabus are twenty-four headnotes. Each headnote is numbered and is associated with a topic and Key Number from the West digests. In *Byrd*, there is another, more detailed, syllabus following the headnotes. The asterisk accompanying this syllabus indicates that the syllabus was prepared by the Reporter of Decisions of the United States Supreme Court.

The Court opinion begins as follows:

Opinion

Justice Kennedy delivered the opinion of the Court.

Immediately preceding the opinion, the case provides the vote of the Justices and identifies the attorneys and law firms representing the parties. The reader learns that, although the opinion was unanimous, Justice Thomas wrote a concurring opinion, Justice Gorsuch joined in Justice Thomas' concurring opinion, and Justice Alito wrote a concurring opinion.

The bulk of the case is the court's opinion; however, the publisher generally enhances the reading experience by adding information that the reader may find helpful in understanding the opinion and in performing further research. The portions of the case added by the publisher include the case syllabus and headnotes. As stated above, the Reporter of Decisions added a second syllabus.

The syllabus is the case summary that follows the case caption. One may glance over the syllabus to gain an overall idea of the court's opinion. A common mistake made by the novice is to confuse the syllabus with the opinion and reference material from the syllabus rather than from the court opinion. Because the court did not prepare the syllabus, it is not authoritative and may not necessarily be an accurate summary of the court opinion. In your writing do not, under any circumstance, quote from or reference the case syllabus.

Byrd has twenty-four headnotes that precede the opinion and that are consecutively numbered. Each headnote states a legal principle discussed in *Byrd* and oftentimes are almost verbatim statements from the court opinion. A reader wishing to read the portion of the opinion concerning a particular headnote need only look for the bracketed headnote number inserted at the beginning of the corresponding paragraph. Bracketed headnote numbers in an opinion indicate that the information inside the brackets was added by the publisher. Each headnote contains a reference to a digest topic and Key Number. In your writing do not, under any circumstance, quote from or reference headnote material.

In glancing over the twenty-four headnotes, one notices that the digest topic of a majority of the headnotes is Searches and Seizures and half of the headnotes reference the same Key Number within the Searches and Seizures topic, Expectation of privacy, which is Key Number 61 within Searches and Seizures. The text of headnote 24 states:

> The mere fact that a driver in lawful possession or control of a rental car is not listed as an authorized driver on the rental agreement will not defeat his or her otherwise reasonable expectation of privacy under the Fourth Amendment; abrogating *U.S. v. Kennedy*, 638 F.3d 159, *U.S. v. Seeley*, 331 F.3d 471, *U.S. v. Wellons*, 32 F.3d 117, *U.S. v. Roper*, 918 F.2d 885. U.S.C.A. Const.Amend. 4.

That same language would be reprinted in the *Federal Digest* under Key Number 61 of the Searches and Seizures topic. If the reader wished to read the paragraph that was the basis of this headnote, the reader would find [**24**] at the beginning of the next-to-the-last full paragraph of Justice Kennedy's majority opinion.

Briefing a Case

"Briefing a case" means taking notes of the most important parts of a case so that you can later refer to your "case brief" to quickly refresh your memory rather than have to read the case over again. When you write out a case brief, you have engaged in active learning as you write a summary in your own words. This leads to better understanding of the case than underlining or rereading. Professors may require you to brief cases, with class time spent discussing the cases and "synthesizing" them. Synthesizing involves analyzing how cases deal with a particular subject matter and extracting a "rule of law" from them.

A second reason to brief cases is as a research and writing tool. When researching a problem, you should brief the cases found, synthesize them to determine the rule of law, and apply the rule of law to the problem.

> **LEGAL ANALYSIS TIP**
>
> ***A Brief***
>
> When attorneys refer to a "brief," they may be referring to a case brief, but more likely than not, they are referring to an "appellate brief." An appellate brief is the document containing the arguments of a party to a case that is usually prepared by the party's attorney and is submitted to the appellate court when a case is appealed.

The format description that follows is a fairly standard one, but there is no one right way to brief a case. If a professor asks you to brief cases, it may be a good idea to ask the professor if a particular format is preferred. The desired format may vary from professor to professor, with some requiring a longer brief of three to four pages.

As the name suggests, a case brief should be fairly concise. If your case brief is as long as or longer than the case, you might as well just reread the entire case rather than refer to the case brief. For most cases, a good length is a page or less. Some portions of the case brief, such as the issue(s), holding(s), and reasoning, may be quoted directly from the case, while the case brief may summarize the facts. To avoid being accused of plagiarism, you should make a practice of placing any borrowed language in quotation marks.The case brief format is explained in the following section.

Case Brief Format

A standard format for briefing a case is the following:

Correct case citation—The correct case citation is determined by applying *Bluebook* rules.

Facts—This section should only contain the significant facts in light of the legal question asked, but it may state what facts are not known if the absence of facts is significant.

History—State briefly what happened at trial and at each level before the case reached the court whose opinion you are briefing.

Issue(s)—State the issue or issues considered by the court. Each issue should be one sentence in length, and the issues should be numbered if there is more than one. An issue is easier to understand if it is stated in the form of a question, rather than beginning with the word "whether," and it should end with a question mark.

Holding(s)—Generally, you will have the same number of holdings as you do issues, with each holding containing the answer to the corresponding issue. Sometimes you may have one issue and more than one holding if the issue is a broad one and there is more than one answer to it. Each holding should be one sentence. Even if the court does not explicitly state the holding or gives a simple "yes" or "no" answer to an issue, reread the case until you can write a one-sentence holding.

Reasoning—State the court's reasoning for reaching the holding from the issue considered.

Disposition—State what the court did with the lower court's decision: affirmed, reversed, vacated, etc.

Correct Case Citation When a citation to a case is given, the citation format must conform to the *Bluebook*.

Facts The occurrences on which a case is based.

History What happened at trial and at each level before the case reached the court whose opinion you are briefing.

Issue A question that a judge or a jury must decide in a case.

Holding The holding of a case is the court's decision and the significant or material facts upon which the court relied in arriving at its determination. This is the binding portion of the case.

Reasoning The main portion of the case, which discusses the law involved in deciding the case and the court's reasons for reaching a particular holding.

Disposition The final result in the case in relation to the lower court decision, such as affirmed or reversed.

Case Brief for Byrd

The following is a suggested case brief for *Byrd*. It would be good practice for you to try to brief *Byrd* yourself and compare your case brief with the following case brief.

Byrd v. United States, 138 S. Ct. 1518 (2018).

Facts—Terrence Byrd was driving a rental car even though the rental agreement did not authorize him to do so when he was pulled over by Officer Long for an alleged traffic violation. After ascertaining that Byrd was not the authorized driver and Byrd had prior convictions, Long and another officer who had arrived at the scene requested consent to search Byrd's vehicle. They proceeded to search the vehicle without Byrd's consent, finding body armor and heroin in the trunk.

History—After Byrd was arrested, he moved to suppress the evidence. After his motion was denied by the federal trial court, Byrd entered a conditional guilty plea but reserved his right to appeal the denial of his motion. The federal intermediate appellate court affirmed.

Issue—"Does a driver of a rental car have a reasonable expectation of privacy in the car when he or she is not listed as an authorized driver on the rental agreement?"

Holding—"The Court now holds that, as a general rule, someone in otherwise lawful possession and control of a rental car has a reasonable expectation of privacy in it even if the rental agreement does not list him or her as an authorized driver."

Reasoning—The two keys to Byrd having a reasonable expectation of privacy in the vehicle were that his possession of it was legal, and he had the right to exclude others from the vehicle. "The Court sees no reason why the expectation of privacy that comes from lawful possession and control and the attendant right to exclude would differ depending on whether the car in question is rented or privately owned by someone other than the person in current possession of it...."

Disposition—The Court vacated the lower court decision.

Summary

- A court's jurisdiction is the power of the court to decide cases. To decide a case, a court must have geographical jurisdiction, subject matter jurisdiction, and hierarchical jurisdiction.
- The Supreme Court of the United States is the highest federal court. The thirteen United States courts of appeals are federal intermediate appellate courts. The United States district courts are federal trial-level courts.
- The state court system varies from state to state. Some states have a simplified court structure (also called a unified court structure) with three or four tiers; the court structure of other states is more complex.
- Cases are easier to read and understand once you are familiar with typical case style and format.
- The syllabus (case summary) and the headnotes (summaries of important legal principles contained in the case) that precede the opinion were prepared by the publisher and have no official authority.
- The main parts of a typical opinion are the facts, the procedural history of the case before it reached the court writing the opinion, the issue(s) (legal questions considered by the court), the holding(s) (the rules of the case), and the court's explanation of why it reached the particular holding(s).

- "Briefing a case" means taking notes of the most important parts of a case so that you can later refer to your "case brief" to quickly refresh your memory.
- A standard format for briefing a case contains:
  - correct case citation
  - facts
  - history
  - issue(s)
  - holding(s)
  - reasoning
  - disposition

Key Terms

admissible
appellate briefs
appellate court
appellate jurisdiction
bench trial
charge
Chief Justice
correct case citation
court of last resort
defendant
discretionary jurisdiction
disposition
dissenting opinion
diversity jurisdiction
facts
federal question jurisdiction
general jurisdiction
geographical jurisdiction
hierarchical jurisdiction
history
holding
in personam jurisdiction
in rem jurisdiction
intermediate appellate court
issue
jurisdiction
Justices
limited jurisdiction
majority

motion
motion for a directed verdict
motion for a summary judgment
oral argument
original jurisdiction
panel
petition for writ of certiorari
plaintiff
questions of fact
questions of law
reasoning
remand
reporter
subject matter jurisdiction
Supreme Court of the United States
testimony
trial courts
unified court structure
United States court of appeals
United States district courts

Cyberlaw Exercises

1. Go to the website https://www.usa.gov and read about the judicial branch.
2. Go to the website https://www.usa.gov and read about the various federal courts.
3. Go to the website https://www.usa.gov and read about how the United States Supreme Court works.
4. The website www.uscourts.gov contains a map showing the geographical arrangement of the federal circuits. Access the map and determine which circuit covers your geographical location.
5. Each state contains one or more districts of the United States district courts. Access the map at www.uscourts.gov and determine the outlines of the federal district courts making up your state. Determine which district covers your geographical location.
6. Locate the official website or websites providing information on the judicial branch of your state. Determine the number and the names of the state courts comprising your state judicial branch. Formulate a chart showing the structure of the state courts of your state similar to the chart above for the Florida State courts.

QUESTIONS FOR CASE LAW ASSIGNMENT

1. What are the names of the three reporters containing current decisions of the United States Supreme Court?

2. What is the name of the loose-leaf service containing current decisions of the United States Supreme Court?

3. What are the names of the two reporters containing current decisions of the United States circuit courts of appeals?

4. What are the names of the reporter containing current decisions of the United States district courts?

5. What is the name of the highest court in your state, and what is the name of the reporter containing current decisions of that court?

6. What is the name of your state's intermediate appellate court, and what is the name of the reporter containing current decisions of that court?

7. What is the name of the loose-leaf service containing decisions of your state's courts?

8. What is the name of your state's trial-level courts? (Name all trial level courts, if more than one.) What is the name of the reporter containing current decisions of those courts?

9. Answer the following questions regarding the case found at 139 S.Ct. 1514:

   a. What is the correct citation for this case?

   b. What was Apple's argument in the case?

   c. What was the holding of the case?

   d. What were the plaintiffs' allegations?

   e. Who wrote the majority opinion and which Justices joined the majority opinion?

f. Who wrote the dissenting opinion and which Justices joined the dissenting opinion?

10. Answer the following questions regarding the case found at 139 S.Ct. 706:

a. What is the correct citation for this case?

b. What was the issue?

c. What were the underlying facts in this case that made the date of the judge's death important?

d. What was the holding?

e. What was the reasoning?

11. Answer the following questions regarding the case found at 139 S.Ct. 2525:

a. What is the correct citation for this case?

b. How many Justices joined Justice Alito's opinion?

c. How many Justices dissented?

d. Did Justice Thomas concur in Justice Alito's opinion or in the judgment?

e. Was Justice Alito's opinion a majority or what other type of opinion was it?

f. What was the issue?

g. What was the holding?

h. What was the reasoning?

i. What does Justice Thomas add to Justice Alito's opinion?

j. What was the main point of each of the dissenting opinions?

12. Answer the following questions regarding the case found at 138 S.Ct. 1518:

    a. What is the correct citation for this case?

    b. What was the issue?

    c. What was the holding?

    d. What was the reasoning?

    e. What was the main point of each of the concurring opinions?

13. Answer the following questions regarding the case found at 138 S.Ct. 1663:

    a. What is the correct citation for this case?

    b. What was the issue in this case?

    c. What were the relevant facts?

    d. What are the two components of the Fourth Amendment that the United States Supreme Court considered in this case?

    e. What did the Court hold?

    f. Why did Justice Thomas write a concurring opinion?

    g. Why did Justice Alito dissent?

14. Answer the following questions regarding the case found at 135 S.Ct. 2218:

    a. What is the correct citation for this case?

    b. What was the issue in this case?

    c. What were the relevant facts?

d. What are the three categories of signage covered by the town code?

e. What did the Court hold?

f. How does the First Amendment support the Court's decision?

g. Why did Justice Alito write a concurring opinion?

h. Why did Justice Breyer write a concurring opinion?

i. Why did Justice Kagan write a concurring opinion?

15. Answer the following questions regarding the case found at 137 S.Ct. 1178:

a. What is the correct citation for this case?

b. What was the issue in the case?

c. What was the holding of the case?

d. What were the relevant facts concerning the original lawsuit?

e. What did the respondents' attorney learn from a newspaper article?

f. In the trial court's view, what could the sanctions of attorney fees and costs include?

g. What standard did the Court apply in calculating attorney fees?

16. Answer the following questions regarding the case found at 913 F.3d 1371:

a. What is the correct citation for this case?

b. What were the two issues in the case?

c. What action did the court take with respect to *Haas v. Peake*?

d. What was the holding of the case?

e. Why do you think that the decision was an en banc rather than a panel decision?

f. How many judges joined the majority opinion and how many joined the dissenting opinion?

g. How many judges joined the concurring opinion who did not also join the majority opinion?

17. Answer the following questions regarding the case found at 848 F.3d 803:

a. What is the correct citation for this case?

b. What was the issue in the case?

c. What were the relevant facts?

d. What was the holding of the case?

e. What two basic points emerge from cases in which courts have faced a similar question?

18. Answer the following questions regarding the case found at 911 F.3d 260:

a. What is the correct citation for this case?

b. What was the issue in the case?

c. What were the relevant facts?

d. What were the claims of the representatives of the victims?

e. What was the holding of the case?

f. What role does the smartphone play in contributing to the user's tortious acts?

19. Answer the following questions regarding the case found at 893 F.3d 1276:

a. What is the correct citation for this case?

b. What was the issue in the case?

c. What were the relevant facts?

d. What was the holding of the case?

e. What was the purpose of the liquidated damages provision?

f. Does the provision provide a reasonable pre-breach estimate of damages?

20. Answer the following questions regarding the case found at 891 F.3d 929:

a. What is the correct citation for this case?

b. What was the issue in the case?

c. What were the relevant facts?

d. What was the holding of the case?

e. What was the reasoning that a painted flag does not comply with the requirement?

21. Answer the following questions regarding the case found at 887 F.3d 716:

a. What is the correct citation for this case?

b. What was the issue in the case?

c. What were the relevant facts?

d. What was the holding of the case?

e. What was the reasoning?

Chapter 5

Primary Sources: Constitutions, Statutes, Court Rules, and Administrative Law

Introduction

As identified by the chapter title, this chapter introduces:

- constitutions
- statutes
- court rules
- administrative law

The chapter provides information on each of the four primary sources and explains their correct citation form. The second portion of the chapter, on statutes, is the longest and most complex. In addition to discussing citation form, the statutes portion provides information concerning:

- the legislative branch
- Congress
- state legislatures
- publication of statutes
- the process of statutory research
- local law

Constitutions

Because there is a United States Constitution and each state has its own **constitution**, constitutional law research may be done at the federal and the state level.

Constitution 1. A document that sets out the basic principles and most general laws of a country, state, or organization. 2. The U.S. Constitution is the basic law of the country on which most other laws are based and to which all other laws must yield.

As explained in Chapter 1, Article VI of the United States Constitution contains the **supremacy clause.** The supremacy clause makes the Constitution prevail over any federal statute or state constitutional provision or statute in conflict with the Constitution.

Supremacy Clause The provision in Article VI of the U.S. Constitution that the U.S. Constitution, laws, and treaties take precedence over conflicting state constitutions or laws.

Congress is given certain **enumerated powers** in Article I, section 8 of the Constitution. Sections 9 and 10 of Article I prohibit the federal and state governments from taking certain actions (e.g., passing any **ex post facto law**). The Tenth Amendment to the Constitution reserves all other powers to the states.

Enumerated Powers The powers specifically granted to a branch of government in a constitution.

Ex Post Facto Law (Latin) "After the fact." An ex post facto law is one that retroactively attempts to make an action a crime that was not a crime at the time it was done, or a law that attempts to reduce a person's rights based on a past act that was not subject to the law when it was done.

A written constitution is the document setting forth the fundamental principles of governance. For example, Article I of the United States Constitution deals with the legislative branch, Article II deals with the executive branch, and Article III deals with the judicial branch of the federal government. A state constitution sets forth the basic framework of state government in a similar fashion.

Some people differentiate between the written and the **living constitution.** The written United States Constitution, including all amendments to it, is less than twenty pages in length. The living constitution would include those pages in addition to all case law interpretations of the Constitution. If printed, the living constitution would require numerous volumes. Scholars and laypersons alike have hotly debated constitutional interpretation. Some believe that any interpretation should be based on the plain language of the Constitution and should not stray far from it. Others believe that the broad language of the Constitution should be interpreted as needed to deal with legal questions never dreamed of when the Constitution was first enacted.

Living Constitution The written United States Constitution, including all amendments to it, is less than twenty pages in length. The living constitution would include those pages and all case law interpretations of the Constitution.

The language of the United States Constitution is very broad, setting up a framework of government, often without much detail. For example, Article III of the Constitution establishes the United States Supreme Court, with the establishment of other federal courts left to Congress. State constitutions may be much longer than the United States Constitution and may deal with many subjects that are dealt with on the federal level by statute. The only limit on state constitutions is that they may not conflict with the United States Constitution or any federal statute concerning a matter given exclusively to the federal government.

Constitutions generally have the same basic format. A constitution usually begins with a preamble. A preamble is a paragraph or clause explaining the reason for the enactment of the constitution and the object or objects it seeks to accomplish. The body of the document is divided into various parts (called "articles" in the United States Constitution and many state constitutions) corresponding to the various subjects dealt with in the constitution and the parts into subparts (called "sections" and "clauses" in the United States Constitution). Near the end of the constitution is a provision describing the procedure for amending it. Any amendments to a constitution are either printed at the end of the constitution (the procedure followed for the United States Constitution) or the new language is simply incorporated into the body of the document (the procedure followed for the Florida Constitution and the constitutions of many other states).

The United States Constitution is unique in that it was adopted in 1787 and has been the fundamental document of American government ever since. There are twenty-six amendments to it, with the first ten amendments known as the Bill of Rights. The Fourteenth Amendment, adopted in 1868, has been interpreted to make most of the provisions of the Bill of Rights applicable to the states. In contrast, many states have been governed under more than one constitution. For example, Illinois has had four constitutions since it became a state in 1818; the present Constitution of the State of Illinois is dated 1970 and is a revision of the constitution of 1870. The Illinois Constitution has been amended a number of times since 1970.

Initiation of Constitutional Amendments

Article V of the Constitution states, in part:

> The Congress, whenever two thirds of both Houses shall deem it necessary, shall propose Amendments to this Constitution, or on the Application of the Legisla-

> tures of two thirds of the several States, shall call a Convention for proposing Amendments, which, in either Case, shall be valid to all Intents and Purposes, as Part of this Constitution, when ratified by the Legislatures of three fourths of the several States, or by Conventions in three fourths thereof, as the one or the other Mode of Ratification may be proposed by the Congress....

Accordingly, there are two methods of initiating a constitutional amendment. Congressional resolution is the first, in which two-thirds majorities in both houses of Congress are required. The president does not play a role in this process. Second, with two-thirds of the state legislatures or more, a convention can be convened to propose amendments. To date, initiation by Congress is the only method that has been successfully used to initiate amendments.

Regardless of which method of proposal is employed, Congress is empowered to decide the method of ratification. There are two methods: by concurrence of three-fourths of the state legislatures or by conventions in three-fourths of the states.

Congress holds considerable authority in the amendment process. It may establish a time limit for ratification of a proposal, regardless of the method of proposal, and it is empowered to decide whether an amendment has been ratified.

Locating Constitutions

The text of constitutions may be found in many reference books in the law library. If you just want to read the United States Constitution, you could read it from a constitutional law textbook or other source. (Even many dictionaries contain a copy of the United States Constitution.) The text of your state's constitution may be printed in the set of books containing the official version of your state's statutory code.

An annotated version of the United States Constitution is found in the sets of books containing the annotated *United States Code*. If you want to know how the first amendment to the United States Constitution has been interpreted concerning restrictions on prayers in public schools, you would look at the case summaries of cases interpreting the First Amendment. The case summaries are found in *United States Code Service* or *United States Code Annotated* following the text of the First Amendment. You would follow a similar procedure to research your state's constitution. Often, codes and annotated codes contain a separate index located at the end of a constitution. The index is designed to help you locate a particular provision within the constitution.

Don't forget to update your research. Hardbound volumes of the annotated codes are updated by pocket parts. The pocket parts are updated by quarterly supplements. Because of the lag time between the announcement of an important United States Supreme Court decision interpreting the Constitution and the printing of the annual pocket part to the annotated code, the annotated code may be as much as two years behind current case law. Update your research by using **citators** and **computer-assisted**

legal research. When researching, you may find it helpful to consult one or more of the various treatises dealing with constitutional law in addition to reading the annotations in the annotated codes.

> **Computer-Assisted Legal Research** Legal research performed on a computer.
>
> **Citators** A set of books or a database that lists relevant legal events subsequent to a given case, statute, or other authority.

Citations for Constitutions

The clause prohibiting ex post facto laws and section 1 of the Fourteenth Amendment to the Constitution may be cited as follows (with an explanation of the citation in parentheses):

U.S. Const. art. I, § 9, cl. 3.

(abbreviation for United States Constitution, Article I, section 9, clause 3)

U.S. Const. amend. XIV, § 1.

(abbreviation for United States Constitution, Fourteenth Amendment, section 1)

Give the section number when the Constitution specifically identifies a portion of an article as a section. When a section, such as section nine of article I, is long and contains a number of paragraphs, you can reference a particular paragraph as a "clause." Some copies of the United States Constitution identify the amendments as "articles" instead of "amendments." This is because the amendments are technically articles in amendment of the Constitution. To avoid confusion, cite the amendments to the Constitution as "amendments" rather than as "articles." State constitutions can be cited using the same citation form given or using your state's citation rules.

> **CITATION TIP**
>
> ***Check for Correct Citation***
>
> Do not assume that the legal citations found when researching are in correct citation form. Citations, even those included in cases, may or may not comply with the citation rules your professor has asked you to use. Always check your citations against the appropriate citation rule for correct form.

State Constitutionalism and the New Federalism

Every state has its own constitution. Like the federal Constitution, state constitutions contain declarations or bills of individual rights. In fact, many clauses in state bills of rights are worded identically, or nearly so, to the federal Constitution.

State constitutional law may not decrease or limit federally secured rights, but a state may extend civil rights beyond what the federal Constitution secures. In some cases, this may occur expressly. For example, both the Florida and Alaska constitutions expressly protect privacy, whereas the federal constitution does not. Rather, a national right to privacy was declared by the United States Supreme Court (as a penumbra or implied protection), and it is somewhat controversial because of the absence of express language in the Constitution establishing the right. The Florida State constitution protects one's privacy through two constitutional provisions.

Statutes

The Legislative Branch

The United States Constitution gives Congress the power to pass legislation. Article I, section 1 of the United States Constitution provides:

> All legislative Powers herein granted shall be vested in a Congress of the United States, which shall consist of a Senate and House of Representatives.

Article I, section 7, clause 2 of the United States Constitution provides:

> Every Bill which shall have passed the House of Representatives and the Senate, shall, before it become a Law, be presented to the President of the United States; If he approve he shall sign it, but if not he shall return it, with his Objections to that House in which it shall have originated, who shall enter the Objections at large on their Journal, and proceed to reconsider it. If after such Reconsideration two thirds of that House shall agree to pass the Bill, it shall be sent, together with the Objections, to the other House, by which it shall likewise be reconsidered, and if approved by two thirds of that House, it shall become a Law. But in all such Cases the Votes of both Houses shall be determined by yeas and Nays, and the Names of the Persons voting for and against the Bill shall be entered on the Journal of each House respectively. If any Bill shall not be returned by the President within ten Days (Sundays excepted) after it shall have been presented to him, the Same shall be a Law, in like Manner as if he had signed it, unless the Congress by their Adjournment prevent its Return, in which Case it shall not be a Law.

Similarly, state constitutions give state legislatures power to pass legislation. Nebraska's legislature is unique among all state legislatures in the United States because it has a **unicameral** (single-house) system. All other states and the federal government have **bicameral** legislatures. A two-part legislature, such as the U.S. Congress is bicameral, composed of the Senate (the "upper house" or "upper chamber") and the House of Representatives (the "lower house" or "lower chamber").

Unicameral A legislature with a single-house system.

Bicameral Having two chambers.

The process of **legislation** and its effect differs significantly from **adjudication** (judges deciding cases). Adjudication resolves a dispute between particular parties based on the facts presented to the court and the law applied by the judge. The judge's opinion is directly binding only on the parties before the court. In the future, other courts may look to the judge's opinion as authority in deciding future cases.

Legislation 1. The process of thinking about and passing or refusing to pass bills into law (statutes, ordinances, etc.). 2. Statutes, ordinances, etc.

Adjudication The formal giving, pronouncing, or recording of a judgment for one side or another in a lawsuit.

In contrast, legislation is expected to have universal application. Universal application means that the legislation applies to all individuals subject to the legislation. The legislation applies as of its effective date and into the future unless amended, repealed, or held to be unconstitutional. Ex post facto laws are forbidden under the United States Constitution. Ex post facto laws are criminal statutes with retroactive effect. Civil statutes are usually interpreted to be **prospective** rather than **retrospective** in effect. A prospective law is one that applies to situations that arise after it is enacted. Most laws are prospective only.

Retrospective A retrospective or retroactive law is one that changes the legal status of things already done or that applies to past actions.

Prospective Looking forward; concerning the future; likely or possible.

Congress

The Constitution creates the Senate and the House of Representatives as the two houses of Congress. The Senate comprises 100 senators, two from each state, and the House of Representatives comprises 435 representatives, with at least one from each state and otherwise apportioned among the states according to population.

A term in Congress lasts for two years, beginning in January of the year following the biennial election of members. Each Congress is divided into two one-year sessions. For example, the first session of the 116th Congress began on January 3, 2019, and the second session of the 116th Congress began on January 1, 2020. The 117th Congress will begin on January 3, 2021, and will last through calendar year 2022.

Bills are either public bills or private bills. A public bill applies to the general public. Sometimes, Congress authorizes relief to a named individual or an organization pursuant to a private bill. Common subjects of private bills are claims against the United States and immigration and naturalization matters. For example, a private bill may authorize the federal government to pay an individual's claim against the United States; a private bill is needed where the individual's claim would ordinarily be barred under sovereign immunity.

Bills in each house are identified by "H.R." (House of Representatives) or "S." (Senate), followed by sequential numbers identifying the order in which they are introduced in the house. Any member of either house may introduce a bill. The member introducing the bill is the "sponsor"; the bill may have an unlimited number of co-sponsors. A member of the House of Representatives introduces a bill by signing and placing it in the "hopper," a wooden box located at the side of the House rostrum. A senator introduces a bill by signing it and delivering it to one of the clerks at the presiding officer's desk; in the alternative, a senator may orally introduce the bill from the Senate floor.

After being introduced, a bill is referred to the appropriate committee and copies of the bill are made available to the committee members and to the public. The House has 20 standing committees, the Senate has 16 standing committees, and four standing joint committees have oversight responsibilities. In addition, a house may form select committees and task forces as needed. Each committee has jurisdiction over certain matters; the committee may have a number of subcommittees to deal with particular issues within the jurisdiction of the committee. Committee members are assisted in their committee work by a professional staff.

A committee or a subcommittee may hold meetings or public hearings on a bill. After hearings have been held, a committee or subcommittee considers the bill in a "markup" session. A markup session is the committee or subcommittee members' opportunity to comment and then vote on a bill. A subcommittee may vote to report the bill favorably, with or without recommendation, unfavorably, or without recommendation to the committee. A bill would not leave the subcommittee if the vote were to table or postpone action on the bill. Similarly, a committee may vote to report a bill to the floor of the chamber, or may table or postpone action on the bill.

A committee staff member prepares the committee report once a committee has voted favorably to report the bill to the chamber floor. The committee report usually outlines the purpose and scope of the bill and provides a detailed explanation of each section of the bill.

After leaving a committee, a bill may be debated on the chamber floor; during the debate, the bill may be amended numerous times. Once a chamber passes a bill, the bill technically is transformed from a bill to an "act," signifying that it is the **act** of one chamber of Congress. Although it is technically an act, it is still commonly called a bill. The enrolling clerk prepares a copy of the bill, including all amendments adopted. The final copy of the bill is often referred to as the "**engrossed**" copy because it contains the definitive text approved by the chamber. If passed by the House of Representatives, the engrossed bill is printed on blue paper and the Clerk of the House signs it. If passed by the Senate, the engrossed bill is printed on white paper and is attested to by the Secretary of the Senate. A bill approved by one chamber is delivered to the other chamber. There it is referred to the appropriate committee for study and public hearings. The second chamber may pass the bill, with or without amendments. If there were no amendments, the bill is enrolled for presentation to the president.

Engrossed The final copy of the bill is often referred to as the "engrossed" copy because it contains the definitive text approved by the chamber.

Act A law passed by one or both houses of a legislature.

If the second chamber passes the bill with amendments, it is returned to the chamber in which it originated. The first chamber may approve the amendments. If the amendments are substantial, differing provisions may be resolved in a conference committee comprised of members from both chambers. The conference committee prepares a report containing the recommendations of the committee. A bill is considered approved by Congress if both chambers agree to the conference report.

An **enrolled** bill approved by both chambers in identical form is prepared for the president. The term enroll means to prepare the final perfect copy of the bill approved by both chambers in perfect final form. The enrolled bill is printed on parchment paper and is signed by the authorized member of each chamber.

The president may approve the bill by signing it, may veto the bill, or may take no action on the bill. If the president takes no action while Congress is in session, the bill becomes law ten days (Sundays excepted) after it was presented to him. If the president takes no action but Congress is not in session, the bill does not become law. This is commonly referred to as the "pocket veto." The president's veto can be overridden by the vote of two-thirds of each chamber.

Enrolled Registered or recorded a formal document in the proper office or file.

State Legislatures

Except for Nebraska, which has a unicameral legislature, all states have bicameral legislatures. The upper house in the state legislatures is called the Senate; the lower house is called the House of Representatives, the General Assembly, or the House of Delegates.

A primary role of state legislatures is enacting statutes. The legislative procedure followed to enact statutes differs from state to state, but many states follow a procedure similar to that followed in Congress and described previously.

As in Congress, the idea for a new statute may come from a variety of sources, including a constituent, a legislator, or an organization. A legislator introduces the bill, and it is referred to a committee. After committee hearings and discussion, the bill is considered on the floor of the chamber. There it is debated and amended. If the bill passes in that chamber, it is transmitted to the other chamber for consideration. A similar procedure is followed in the second chamber. Once both chambers pass a bill, it may go to a conference committee to clear up any differences in wording. If both chambers passed the bill in identical form, it is transmitted to the governor. The governor may sign or veto the act. A veto may be overridden by the vote of two-thirds of each house.

Publication of Statutes

Although federal and state statutes are published in a number of different formats, there is a general pattern to the order in which the formats are used. The general names for the formats of statutory publication, in chronological order, are as follows:

slip law
advance session law service
session laws
code
annotated code

The chart in Chapter 1 lists the types of reference materials and the names of the reference materials containing the law made by Congress. Another section below uses Florida as an example to provide information on a state constitution, state statutes, and state administrative law. The state constitution, state statutes, and state administrative law may be similar for your state.

Slip Law

A new statute is first published as a **slip law**. In this form, a single statute is printed in an unbound pamphlet, with each pamphlet individually paginated. Although the slip law is the first official form of publication, distribution of the slip law form of statutes is generally limited to law school libraries and libraries designated as official government depositories. A researcher would find researching slip laws cumbersome; they are unindexed and individual slip law pamphlets may easily be misshelved or misplaced.

Slip Law A printed copy of a bill passed by Congress that is distributed immediately once signed by the president.

Federal statutes are first published in slip law form. Each federal statute is numbered with a public law or a private law number that contains the session number of Congress and is separated by a hyphen from the number corresponding to the statute's sequence.

For example, the first public law in the 116th session of Congress would be "Public Law 116-1" and the first private law in that session would be "Private Law 116-1." Each slip law pamphlet is identified by a public or private law number, the approval date (or an explanatory notation if it became law without presidential approval), and the bill number.

Session Laws

The next publishing format is called **session laws.** Session law format involves the publication of slip laws produced in a legislative session, with the laws published in chronological order. Each state and the federal government publish session laws, generally in hardbound volumes. As typical of a government publication, the session laws published by a state or the federal government appear some time after the end of the legislative session. In most states, commercial publishers produce **advance session law services** to fill the gap between the passage of the statutes and the appearance of the government-published session laws. The format for advance session law services for one legislative session may be a number of paperbound volumes, each volume with a numerical and subject index. The numerical index typically indexes the existing statute numbers, as codified, and indicates if the statutes have been amended or repealed.

Session Laws Statutes printed in the order that they were passed in each session of legislature.

Advance Session Law Services Publications that contain the text of recently passed statutes and statutory amendments produced by commercial publishers to fill the gap between the passage of the statutes and the appearance of the government-published session laws.

The *United States Code Congressional and Administrative News* is an advance session law service for federal statutes. This publication contains the text of new statutes as well as selected legislative history information, such as House and Senate reports.

Paperbound pamphlets (often referred to as advance pamphlets) produced to supplement *United States Code Service* and *United States Code Annotated* also contain the text of newly passed federal legislation.

> **United States Code Congressional and Administrative News** An advance session law service for federal statutes.

The ***United States Statutes at Large*** is the session law publication for federal statutes. The *United States Statutes at Large* contains the statutes, as enacted, arranged in chronological order. The *United States Statutes at Large* is the legal evidence of the laws contained in the publication; however, the legal researcher might find it difficult to determine the text of a statute currently in effect. The material in them is not arranged by subject matter, and statutes are not consolidated with later amendments. Typically, publication lags two to three years behind passage of the statutes.

> **United States Statutes at Large** A collection of all statutes passed by the United States Congress, printed in full and in the order of their passage.

Statutory Code

A **code** is the compilation of the existing statutes of a jurisdiction, with the statutes arranged by subject. The code is generally recompiled at regular intervals into a multi-volume hardbound set; the recompilation incorporates statutes still in effect, statutory amendments, and newly passed statutes, while omitting statutes that have been repealed and portions of statutes amended by deletion. Codes generally contain the text of the statutes, brief historical notes, and subject index volumes at the end of the set.

> **Code** 1. A collection of laws. 2. A complete, interrelated, and exclusive set of laws.

The official code containing federal statutes is the ***United States Code***. The *United States Code* presents the laws in effect in a much more concise and usable form than the *United States Statutes at Large*. The *United States Code* presents the federal laws currently in effect organized according to subject matter under "titles." A title is one of the major organizational divisions of the *United States Code*. The title headings are largely arranged in alphabetical order. Each **title** is divided into chapters and the chapters into sections. A new edition of the *United States Code* is published every six years. The edition contains the current text of the statutes, including all amendments and omitting all text previously amended. Cumulative supplements to the *United States Code* are published following each regular session of Congress. A cumulative supplement contains any statutory amendments and any new statutes passed since the last edition of the *United States Code*. As typical of a government publication, production of the volumes can lag eight months to two years behind the passage of legislation.

> ***United States Code*** The official law books containing federal laws organized by subject. They are recompiled every six years, and supplements are published when needed.
>
> **Title** The *United States Code* presents the federal laws currently in effect organized according to subject matter into 54 "titles."

Statutes Passed as an "Act"

The legislature may either pass statutes singly or as part of an **act**. Single statutes are passed when the legislative provision is short. When the new statute is codified, it will be inserted into the statutory code with statutes concerning the same or related subject matter. Where the new statutory language is longer and, often, where it concerns matters not previously dealt with by statute, the legislature may pass an "act" comprised of several consecutively numbered statutes.

An act often is identified by a name given by the legislature and for easy reference is often referred to by that name. This **short title** or **popular name** is usually found in one of the first sections of an act, at the beginning of a table of contents preceding the act, or, in annotated codes, in the historical references following each provision of the act.

> **Short Title** A legislative act often is identified by a name given it by the legislature and for easy reference is often referred to by that name. This is the "short title" or "popular name" of the act.
>
> **Popular Name** *See* short title.

For example, 42 U.S.C. § 1983, which prohibits a state from depriving persons of their constitutional rights, was passed as part of the Civil Rights Act of 1871. Other common provisions of an act are a **preamble**, which identifies the objective or the objectives of the act, and a **definitional section**, which defines terms used in the act.

> **Preamble** An introduction (usually saying why a document, such as a statute, was written).
>
> **Definitional Section** A common provision of a legislative act that defines terms used in the act.

Annotated Code The annotated code contains the text of existing statutes, in language identical to that contained in the code for the jurisdiction, together with annotated material after each statutory section.

Annotated Code

The publication often used for statutory research is the **annotated code.** The annotated code is a commercial publication and often appears on a more timely basis than a code published by the federal or a state government; the annotated code is generally supplemented frequently by pocket parts and supplementary pamphlets. The annotated code contains the text of existing statutes, in language identical to that contained in the code for the jurisdiction. It is referred to as an annotated code because it contains annotated material after each statutory section. An **annotation** is a paragraph summary of a relevant court opinion, attorney general opinion, or an administrative decision interpreting the preceding statutory section.

Annotation An annotation is a paragraph summary of a relevant court opinion, attorney general opinion, or an administrative decision interpreting the preceding statutory section. The paragraph ends with a citation to the opinion or decision.

A newly passed statutory section may have no annotated material following it because the statute has not yet been interpreted in a published decision. Other research references following a statutory section may include citations to relevant administrative code sections, legal encyclopedia sections, law reviews, and treatises and references to digest sections and online services. There may be references to the legislative history of the statutory section and the text of the section prior to an amendment or the text of amendments.

United States Code Annotated *(U.S.C.A.)* (published by West) and ***United States Code Service*** *(U.S.C.S.)* (published by LexisNexis) are the two annotated codes for federal statutes. Volumes of *U.S.C.A.* and *U.S.C.S.* contain the text of the United States Constitution, the Federal Rules of Civil, Criminal, Bankruptcy, and Appellate Procedure, and the Federal Rules of Evidence.

A volume in each set contains a popular name table, allowing the researcher to use the name under which a statute is popularly known to locate the statute's session law and code citations. The researcher may access the two sets by searching for key terms in the multivolume general index (located at the end of the set) or volume-specific indexes located at the end of the volumes.

United States Code Annotated A multivolume commercial publication containing annotated codes for federal statutes, the United States Constitution, court rules, and other materials to aid the legal researcher.

United States Code Service *See United States Code Annotated.*

Each volume of an annotated code is annually updated with a cumulative pamphlet, generally referred to as a "pocket part." The pocket part is inserted inside the back cover of the volume for easy reference and the pamphlet from the prior year is discarded; the pocket part contains textual material and citations, new since the copyright date of the hardbound volume. Over time, the information for the annual pocket part supplement becomes too voluminous to be easily stored inside the volume's back cover; the information is printed in a separate paperbound volume, shelved next to the hardbound volume. The researcher should consult both the hardbound volume and the supplement.

The copyright date of the hardbound volumes varies greatly. Volumes are recompiled and reprinted from time to time when the supplementary material becomes unwieldy. A recompiled volume incorporates new material and eliminates out-of-date information; volumes relating to more rapidly changing areas of the law are reprinted more frequently than other volumes.

Commercial publishers publish annotated versions of statutory codes. To research case law interpretations of the *United States Code*, consult *United States Code Service* or *United States Code Annotated.*

Wiretapping and Eavesdropping Statutes

This section provides in-depth information on federal wiretapping and eavesdropping statutes as an example of federal statutes. You can use the information in this section to better understand other statutes you might be researching. These are the statutes you would find if you are researching the Joshua Smeek fact pattern included in Chapter 2.

As described previously, the *United States Code* is divided into fifty-four broad subject categories called titles. For example, the federal wiretapping and eavesdropping statutes, 18 U.S.C. §§ 2510–2523, portions of which are quoted in this chapter, are part of title 18. Title 18 deals with crimes.

The federal wiretapping and eavesdropping statutes are in title 18 because the purposes of the statutes are to prohibit law enforcement officers and private individuals from intercepting certain types of conversations and to prohibit the use of devices capable of interception. The protected conversations include private face-to-face conversations and telephone conversations, whether made on landline, cellular, or cordless telephones. A law enforcement officer may intercept communications if the officer is a party to the conversation or obtains a **court order** authorizing the taping of a conversation of private individuals.

Court Order	An order issued by the court requiring a party to do or not do a specific act.

Conversations intercepted in violation of the statutes may not be used as evidence in court. An individual who illegally intercepts a conversation may be subject to a fine and up to five years imprisonment.

Federal statutes are further grouped by subject matter into chapters within a title of the *United States Code*. For example, the federal eavesdropping and wiretapping statutes are found in chapter 119 of title 18. Chapter 119 is entitled "Wire and Electronic Communications Interception and Interception of Oral Communications." Although the federal statutes are grouped into chapters within a title, the citation to the statutes references the title and section numbers; the citation does not reference the chapter. Notice in the *United States Code* that several statutes will appear numbered consecutively and then there may be a break in numbering before the next group of statutes; there is also a break in numbering between chapter numbers. The break in numbering allows new statutes to be inserted in the middle of a title without having to renumber existing statutes or chapters. For example, the federal wiretapping and eavesdropping statutes, comprising chapter 119, are numbered consecutively 2510 through 2523; they are preceded by chapter 118, "War Crimes," which contains sections 2441 and 2442 and are followed by chapter 121, "Stored Wire and Electronic Communications and Transactional Records Access," which contains sections 2701 through 2713. When researching, a table of contents for a group of consecutively numbered statutes is accessible. The table of contents for the federal wiretapping and eavesdropping statutes contains the section numbers of the statutes and the title of each section. A table of contents is helpful because it allows you to overview a series of statutes and to ascertain at a glance the general scope of those statutes. When examining the table of contents for the federal wiretapping and eavesdropping statutes, you see that section 2510 contains definitions; section 2511 prohibits the interception and disclosure of certain types of conversations; and section 2515 prohibits the use of intercepted conversations as evidence. The complete text of sections 2510, 2511, and 2515 are located in Appendix F of this book, should you need to consult those sections.

Section 2510 (1) defines "wire communication." Although the definition is complex, a wire communication is a telephone conversation. Section 2510(2) contains the definition of an "oral communication":

> "oral communication" means any oral communication uttered by a person exhibiting an expectation that such communication is not subject to interception under circumstances justifying such expectation....

This definition means that a face-to-face conversation is an "oral communication," so long as the conversants expect that the conversation is private and the expectation is reasonable.

Section 2511(1) prohibits the intentional interception (tape recording) of telephone and face-to-face conversations:

> Except as otherwise specifically provided... any person who... intentionally intercepts... any wire [or] oral... communication... shall be punished as provided in subsection (4)....

Section 2511 (4) provides that "whoever violates subsection (1) of this section shall be fined under this title or imprisoned not more than five years, or both."

There are certain exceptions to the prohibition against tape recording conversations. Those exceptions are found in section 2511(2). Section 2511(2)(c) allows a law enforcement officer ("a **person acting under color of law**") to intercept a conversation if the law enforcement officer is a party to the conversation. Section 2511(2)(d) allows a private individual to intercept a conversation if the individual is a party to the conversation.

Person Acting Under Color of Law One taking an action that looks official or appears to be backed by law.

Researching Wiretapping and Eavesdropping Statutes in an Annotated Code

Many legal researchers like to use an annotated code to research statutes because an annotated code contains the text of the statutes, legislative history, and various research tools, including annotated material.

The legislative history of a statute may aid in its interpretation. Various textual versions of the statute prior to passage, transcripts of committee hearings, committee reports, debates, and other legislative documents may shed light on the meaning of a statute. An annotated code gives you information you can begin with in researching the legislative history of a statute. For example, following the statutory text of 18 U.S.C.A. § 2510, you see:

> (Added Pub.L. 90-351, Title III, § 802, June 19, 1968, 82 Stat. 212; amended Pub.L. 99-508, Title I, § 101(a), (c)(1)(A), (4), Oct. 21, 1986, 100 Stat. 1848, 1851; Pub.L. 103-414, Title II, §§ 202(a), 203, Oct. 25, 1994, 108 Stat. 4290, 4291; Pub.L. 104-132, Title VII, § 731, Apr. 24, 1996, 110 Stat. 1303; Pub.L. 107-56, Title II, §§ 203(b)(2), 209(1), 217(1), Oct. 26, 2001, 115 Stat. 280, 283, 290; Pub.L. 107-108, Title III, § 314(b), Dec. 28, 2001, 115 Stat. 1402; Pub.L. 107-273, Div. B, Title IV, § 4002(e)(10), Nov. 2, 2002, 116 Stat. 1810.)

The first portion of the information provided states that section 2510 was passed as public law 90-351 on June 19, 1968, and its text is available in volume 82 of *United States Statutes at Large* beginning on page 212. The public law information means that section 2510 was the 351st bill passed in the 90th Congress. This information also shows that the statute was amended in 1986, 1994, 1996, 2001, and 2002.

An annotated code typically cross-references you to related secondary sources, including law review articles, *American Law Reports* annotations, sections in legal encyclopedias, and sections in treatises. For many statutes, this section cross-references you to primary sources, such as administrative law and other federal statutes.

> **CITATION TIP**
>
> ***Check for Correct Citation Form***
>
> Do not assume that the legal citations found when researching are in correct citation form. Citations, even those included in cases, may or may not comply with the citation rules your professor has asked you to use. Always check your citations against the appropriate citation rule for correct form.

An annotated code typically contains a section entitled "Notes of Decisions." Attorneys commonly refer to "Notes of Decisions" as annotated material. Similar to digest annotated material, each paragraph of annotated material in the Notes of Decisions section gives a summary of a legal principle contained in a case interpreting § 2510 and the citation to the case. If you would like to know how § 2510 has been interpreted, you can read through the annotations and use the citation to pull and read the case. Although the citations are usually to cases, sometimes they can be to other legal authority. When you are researching statutes in hardbound volumes, make sure to check the pocket part for later annotations. Also, do not assume that an annotated code contains the most recent cases interpreting a statute. Use the cases you find from the annotated materials to find more recent cases through the digests or citators.

Citations for Statutes

A citation to the *United States Code* is the preferred citation because the *United States Code* is the official code. Title 18 U.S.C. § 2510 can be cited as follows:

18 U.S.C. § 2510 (2018).

In the above citation, 2018 is the date of the latest version of the Code containing the statute. However, publication of the *United States Code* (every six years) and its annual supplements lag behind recent amendments to federal statutes. If the *United States Code* is unavailable or does not contain the cited statute, you can use the following citation templates to cite to either *United States Code Annotated* (published by West) or *United States Code Service* (published by LexisNexis):

18 U.S.C.A. § 2510 (West ____ & Supp. ______).
18 U.S.C.S. § 2510 (LexisNexis ____ & Supp. ______).

The parenthesis at the end of the citation gives the name or an abbreviation of the commercial publisher's name and the location of the statute. In the two citation templates, "LexisNexis" indicates that it publishes *United States Code Service* and "West" indicates that it publishes *United States Code Annotated.* Select the applicable citation template above and fill in the blanks in the parentheses with the year of the hardbound volume and the year of the pocket part. Omit the reference to the supplement if the hardbound volume was published sufficiently recently that there is no pocket part. If the statutory language cited is found entirely in the hardbound volume, you need only include information on the hardbound volume in the parenthesis. Conversely, if the statutory language is found entirely in the pocket part supplement, you need only include information on the pocket part supplement in the parenthesis.

If the above citation information is unavailable, you may cite to a commercial electronic database:

18 U.S.C.A. § 2510 (West, Westlaw through P.L. 116-130).

West publishes *United States Code Annotated*, which is also available on Westlaw®. The currency of a statute on Westlaw is gauged by the Public Law (P.L.) through which the statute has been updated. The public law number is stated at the bottom of the screen containing the text of the statute.

If you are referring to a portion of the statute rather than to the entire statute, pinpoint the portion by subsection. If you do give the subsection in your citation, be sure the subsection is designated just as it is in the statute, including whether letters are lower- or uppercase, whether numbers are Arabic or roman, and whether numbers and letters are enclosed in parentheses or not. For example, "18 U.S.C. § 2511(2)(c) (2018)" refers to sub-subsection (c) of subsection (2) of section 2511 of title 18 of the *United States Code.*

CITATION TIP

Symbols for Sections

The symbol § means "section." Use two section symbols (§§) when citing to two or more sections.

Statutory Research

The first step in statutory research is to read the statute carefully and read any other statute or material cross-referenced in the first statute. Generally, statutes are drafted in broad language to set forth a legal principle rather than to deal with a specific problem. Great care must be taken in drafting statutory language so that the language is neither underinclusive nor overinclusive. A statute that is underinclusive may leave loopholes allowing practices that the statute was intended to preclude. A statute that sweeps too broadly may be held to be unconstitutionally vague.

As described more fully in Chapter 2, a court faced with statutory interpretation will look first to the language of the statute itself and its context. A statute that is part of an act should be interpreted by the way it fits into the scheme of the act. Another tool for statutory interpretation is legislative history. Committee reports and other legislative documents may shed light on the meaning of a statute. A source of congressional legislative history available in many law libraries is *United States Code Congressional and Administrative News*. This publication contains the text of federal acts and selected committee reports. *United States Code Congressional and Administrative News* was described more fully earlier in this chapter. A court will also look to prior case law interpretation of the statute. An interpretation by the same or a higher court would be mandatory authority, while an interpretation by a lower court or the courts of another jurisdiction would be persuasive.

Remember to update your research. Once passed, a statute may be amended, repealed, or held to be unconstitutional. Pocket parts update hardbound volumes of the annotated codes. The pocket parts of *United States Code Service* and *United States Code Annotated* are updated by quarterly supplements. You can further update your research by Shepardizing, KeyCiting, or BCiting and using computer assisted legal research. (Shepardizing, KeyCiting, and BCiting are discussed in Chapter 6.) If you are researching state statutes, update the annotated code by researching session laws.

RESEARCH TIP

Use of Hardbound Volume and Pocket Part

When researching in-print sources, the researcher must make it a practice to check both the hardbound volume and the pocket part to obtain complete information.

State Constitution, State Statutes, and State Administrative Law

This section provides an overview of Florida legal research as an example of legal research for a state. It might be interesting for you to compare the information below with similar information for your state.

The Constitution of the State of Florida, ratified in 1968, is the basic governing document that sets forth the structure and function of the state government and the powers and duties of Florida State officials and entities. As is typical of a state government, the Florida State government is divided into judicial, legislative, and executive branches.

The researcher tasked with researching Florida State law must be familiar with the publications containing the primary sources for Florida. The following chart contains information on publications used in researching primary sources of Florida law, with additional information provided below in the following section.

Judicial Branch	**Legislative Branch**	**Executive Branch**
Florida Supreme Court and District Courts of Appeal	Florida Legislature	Governor
Southern Reporter	*Florida Statutes*	
Florida Law Weekly	*Florida Statutes Annotated*	Administrative Agencies
		Florida Administrative Code
	West's Florida Session Law Service	
Circuit and County Courts	*Laws of Florida*	
Florida Law Weekly Supplement		

The publication *Florida Statutes* contains all statutes of general applicability and is published annually after the conclusion of the regular legislative session. The *Florida Statutes* are codified, meaning that each chapter covers a particular topic. In a statute citation, the numbers to the left of the decimal point correspond to the chapter and the numbers to the right of the decimal point correspond to the section.

The publication *Florida Statutes Annotated* contains the statutory text found in *Florida Statutes*, with the addition, following each statute, of summaries of court decisions, regulations, attorney general opinions, and secondary sources relevant to the statute.

Session laws contain all the general and special laws enacted by the Florida Legislature in a calendar year. The two session law publications for Florida are *West's Florida Session Law Service* and *Laws of Florida*. *West's Florida Session Law Service* is a paper-bound publication produced by a private publisher. *Laws of Florida* is a hardbound publication produced by the State of Florida.

Numerous Florida Statutes give Florida State administrative agencies the power to adopt rules and regulations. The *Florida Administrative Code* is the publication compiling the rules and regulations adopted by Florida administrative agencies.

To be current when researching in print volumes, you must consult the hardbound volume and the pocket part. You may still have to check session laws if the pocket part does not contain statutes from the most current legislative session. The first few pages of the pocket part will tell the latest legislation covered in the pocket part.

Local Law

The many smaller units of government include counties, cities, and villages. Local laws passed by these units govern many areas of day-to-day concern. Matters regulated by local law include zoning, traffic, education, health, occupational licensing, and housing. Courts interpret these local laws, sometimes called **ordinances**, in a manner similar to statutes.

> **Ordinances** A local or city law, rule, or regulation.

Court Rules

Court rules govern the procedure of beginning a lawsuit and handling a case before a court. The rules cover such mundane matters as the size paper on which documents are to be submitted to the courts and the format for appellate briefs. They also set forth important time limitations such as the time period within which the defendant has to answer a complaint and the time period within which a party may appeal a decision.

> **Court Rules** Govern the procedure of beginning a lawsuit and handling a case before a court.

Generally, each jurisdiction has a number of sets of court rules. **Rules of civil procedure** govern the conduct of civil cases at the trial level. **Rules of evidence** govern the gathering of information for use at trial and admission of information as evidence at trial. **Rules of criminal procedure** govern the conduct of criminal cases at the trial level. **Rules of appellate procedure** govern the conduct of cases before an appellate court. Courts of limited jurisdiction and specialized courts may have their own sets of court rules. In addition, a court may have promulgated **local court rules** that govern procedure in that court and supplement other court rules.

> **Rules of Civil Procedure** Court rules that govern the conduct of civil cases at the trial level.
>
> **Rules of Evidence** Court rules that govern whether information may be considered by the fact finder.
>
> **Rules of Criminal Procedure** Court rules that govern the conduct of criminal cases at the trial level.
>
> **Local Court Rules** Court rules that govern procedure in a particular local court and supplement other court rules.
>
> **Rules of Appellate Procedure** Court rules that govern the conduct of cases before an appellate court.

Each jurisdiction has its own procedures for promulgating court rules. In some jurisdictions, the legislature creates the court rules; in other jurisdictions, such as the federal courts, the highest court is responsible for creating court rules; and in other jurisdictions, the creation of court rules requires legislative and judicial action. In many jurisdictions, the judicial branch promulgates court rules under the statutory authority given to it by the legislative branch.

Congress has delegated the power to make court rules to the federal courts. The United States Supreme Court promulgates the rules for the Court and the rules for the lower federal courts. The United States Supreme Court is required to submit any proposed court rule to Congress by May 1 of the year in which the court rule is to take effect. Congress has until December 1 to review any proposed court rule. Congress must take action before a rule concerning an evidentiary privilege is effective. For any other proposed court rule, the proposed court rule becomes effective if Congress fails to act by December 1.

For federal courts, the basic court rules used at the trial level are the Federal Rules of Civil Procedure, the Federal Rules of Criminal Procedure, and the Federal Rules of Evidence. At the appellate level, the Federal Rules of Appellate Procedure are used in the United States Courts of Appeals, and the Revised Rules of the Supreme Court of the United States are used in the United States Supreme Court. In addition, each federal court may promulgate its own supplementary local rules so long as the local rules do not conflict with the rules promulgated by the United States Supreme Court.

Researching Court Rules

Your state probably has similar sets of rules and may have sets of rules for courts of limited jurisdiction such as traffic court and small claims court. You will become familiar with some of your state's court rules by completing the legal research assignment on court rules.

Locating Court Rules

All the federal rules identified, except for the local rules of the United States district courts, may be found in *United States Code Service* or in *United States Code Annotated.* West also publishes paperbound volumes of certain of the federal court rules, including certain of the United States district court local rules and the court rules for certain states. The paperbound volumes have the virtue of being fairly inexpensive and easily transportable and contain an index following each set of rules. The paperbound volumes are not annotated, however. The paperbound volumes are printed annually. Be sure you are researching in the most current version available.

Besides being printed in a publication containing just court rules, you may find your state's court rules in volumes of the publication containing your state's annotated code. Court rules may be in separate volumes, or, if enacted by the legislature, they may be part of the statutory code. For example, the Florida Rules of Evidence comprise Chapter 90 of the *Florida Statutes*, while the balance of the state's court rules are printed in volumes at the end of *Florida Statutes Annotated*.

Local Court Rules

Most courts have local rules that must be followed in addition to or in lieu of federal or state rules. Some local court rules may be found in *United States Code Service* or in *United States Code Annotated*. Many are available on the Internet or for purchase from the clerk of the court. The attorney has a duty to research and be familiar with local rules.

Citations for Court Rules

The following are sample citations to the most important types of court rules identified previously (with the explanation of the citation in parentheses following the citation):

Fed. R. Civ. P. 23.	*(Rule 23 of the Federal Rules of Civil Procedure)*
Fed. R. Crim. P. 1.	*(Rule 1 of the Federal Rules of Criminal Procedure)*
Fed. R. App. P. 5.	*(Rule 5 of the Federal Rules of Appellate Procedure)*
Fed. R. Evid. 610.	*(Rule 610 of the Federal Rules of Evidence)*
Sup. Ct. R. 1.	*(Rule 1 of the Rules of the United States Supreme Court)*

Administrative Law

As discussed in Chapter 1, administrative agencies play a vital role in government.

Publication of Administrative Regulations

Administrative regulations are published chronologically as they are adopted and they are later codified. Federal administrative regulations are published chronologically in the ***Federal Register***, and they are codified in the ***Code of Federal Regulations***. The *Federal Register* is published each business day. The *Code of Federal Regulations* is divided into titles, with the regulations contained within most of the titles roughly related to the same subject matter as contained in the same number title within the *United States Code*. For example, title 26 of both the *United States Code* and the *Code of Federal Regulations* concern the Internal Revenue Service. The regulations within a particular title are arranged by the agencies responsible for them rather than by subject matter. Regulations governing a particular topic are grouped in the same "part," with the parts divided into sections. As in the *United States Code*, where each section is considered a separate statute, one section of the *Code of Federal Regulations* contains one administrative regulation.

Federal Register A federal government source published each business day that contains federal administrative regulations arranged chronologically.

> ***Code of Federal Regulations*** A multivolume set of books containing federal administrative regulations arranged by federal agencies and by topic.

Citations for Administrative Law

The following are sample citations to the *Federal Register* and the *Code of Federal Regulations*:

81 Fed. Reg. 59131 (Aug. 29, 2016).
21 C.F.R. § 101.2 (2010).

In the citation for the *Federal Register*, "81" is the volume, "59131" is the page number, and August 29, 2016, is the date of publication. In the citation for the *Code of Federal Regulations*, "21" is the title, "101" is the part, "2" is the section, and the year 2010 is the year of publication.

Summary

- Constitutions, statutes, court rules, and administrative law, like cases, are primary authority.
- The United States Constitution sets forth the fundamental principles of governance for the country; state constitutions set forth the fundamental principles of governance for the states.
- To find how a provision of a constitution has been interpreted by the courts, you would consult an "annotated" version of the constitution.
- Federal and state statutes first appear as slip law, then as "session laws" (arranged chronologically), and later are "codified" (grouped by subject matter).
- To understand a statute, you must read the text of the statute and any annotations summarizing how the statute has been interpreted by the courts.
- The Federal Rules of Civil Procedure, the Federal Rules of Criminal Procedure, and the Federal Rules of Evidence govern litigation procedure in federal trial courts.
- Similar sets of rules govern litigation procedure in state trial courts.
- Separate sets of rules govern litigation procedure in federal and state appellate courts.
- Administrative agencies promulgate administrative regulations that have the force of law.
- Federal administrative regulations are published chronologically in the *Federal Register* and are later codified in the *Code of Federal Regulations*.
- State administrative regulations are generally published in similar fashion.

Key Terms

act
adjudication
administrative regulations
advance session law services
annotated code
annotation
bicameral
citators
civil damages
code
Code of Federal Regulations
computer-assisted legal research
constitution
court order
court rules
definitional section
engrossed
enrolled
enumerated powers
ex post facto law
Federal Register
legislation
living constitution
local court rules
ordinances
person acting under color of law
popular name
preamble
prospective
retrospective
rules of appellate procedure
rules of civil procedure
rules of criminal procedure
rules of evidence
session laws
short title
slip law
supremacy clause
title
unicameral

United States Code
United States Code Annotated
United States Code Congressional and Administrative News
United States Code Service
United States Statutes at Large

Cyberlaw Exercises

1. Go to the website https://www.usa.gov and read about the federal legislative branch.
2. Go to the website https://www.usa.gov and read about the federal executive branch administrative agencies.
3. Go to the website https://www.house.gov/, investigate the materials available at the website, and read about the United States House of Representatives.
4. Go to the website https://www.senate.gov, investigate the materials available at the website, and read about the United States Senate.
5. Find a website providing information on your state's government. Read about its organization and locate individual websites, if any, providing information on the three branches of states government.

QUESTIONS FOR CONSTITUTIONS ASSIGNMENT

1.
   a. In what sets of books would you be able to research how case law has interpreted the United States Constitution?

   b. In what set of books would you be able to research how case law has interpreted your state's constitution?

2. What do the following articles of the United States Constitution deal with?

   a. Article I

   b. Article II

   c. Article III

3. What is the citation to that portion of your state's constitution dealing with the following matters?

a. The executive branch

b. The legislative branch

c. The judicial branch

4. Which provision of the United States Constitution contains the "enumerated powers" of Congress?

5. Which provision of the United States Constitution is commonly known as the "supremacy clause"?

6.

   a. Which provision of the United States Constitution is frequently cited as giving people the right to own handguns?

   b. If your state constitution guarantees the same right, give the citation to that provision.

7.

   a. Which provision of the United States Constitution guarantees the right to a speedy and public trial?

   b. If your state constitution guarantees the same right, give the citation to that provision.

8.

   a. Which provision of the United States Constitution deals with freedom of the press?

   b. Which provision of your state constitution deals with freedom of the press?

9. What 1868 change to the United States Constitution made much of the Bill of Rights applicable to state governments as well as the federal government?

10.

   a. Which provision of the United States Constitution specifically guarantees a "right to privacy"?

b. If your state constitution guarantees the right to privacy, give the citation to that provision.

11.

a. Which provision of the United States Constitution guarantees "the right of the people to be secure in their persons, houses, papers and effects"?

b. If your state constitution guarantees the same right, give the citation to that provision.

12.

a. Which provision of the United States Constitution guarantees free speech?

b. If your state constitution guarantees the same right, give the citation to that provision.

13.

a. Which provision of the United States Constitution prohibits laws "establishing" religion?

b. If your state constitution guarantees the same right, give the citation to that provision.

14.

a. Which provision of the United States Constitution prohibits cruel and unusual punishment?

b. If your state constitution contains a similar prohibition, give the citation to that provision.

QUESTIONS FOR STATUTES ASSIGNMENT

1. Name the advance session law service containing federal statutes.

2. Name the set of books containing federal statutes arranged in chronological order.

3. Name the set of books containing the official codified version of federal statutes.

4. Name two sets of books containing the codified version of federal statutes and annotations to those statutes.

5. Name the advance session law service for your state.

6. Name the set of books for your state containing state statutes arranged in chronological order.

7. Name the set of books for your state containing the official codified version of state statutes.

8. Name the set of books for your state containing the codified version of state statutes and annotations to those statutes.

Find the answers to the following questions in the federal statutes.

9. What are three circumstances pursuant to which a passport may be revoked or denied? What is the correct citation for the statutes?

10. What is the penalty for making a false statement on a passport application? What is the correct citation for the statute?

11. What is perjury and what is the penalty for perjury? What is the correct citation for the statute?

12. How are national monuments created? What is the limitation on creating national monuments in Wyoming? What is the correct citation for the statute?

13. What is the permanent seat of the United States government? State the correct citation for your answer.

14. Name the fifteen departments within the executive branch of the United States government. State the correct citation for your answer.

15. Name the three military departments of the United States government. State the correct citation for your answer.

16. What is the effective date of the next United States census of population? State the correct citation for your answer.

17. Over what type of controversy does the United States Supreme Court have original and exclusive jurisdiction? State the correct citation for your answer.

18. Over what type of controversy does the United States Supreme Court have original but not exclusive jurisdiction? State the correct citation for your answer.

19. What statute gives the United States district courts jurisdiction over civil lawsuits concerning United States statutes and the United States Constitution? What is this type of jurisdiction commonly called?

20. What is the minimum amount in controversy required to file a diversity of citizenship case in United States district court? State the correct citation for your answer.

21. What is the federal minimum hourly wage? State the correct citation for your answer.

22. Under what conditions does one lose his or her nationality as a United States citizen? State the correct citation for your answer.

23. What is the method of choosing the designs for quarters in commemoration of each of the fifty states? State the correct citation for your answer.

24. Which federal agency has the power to prevent use of unfair methods of competition in or affecting commerce and unfair or deceptive acts or practices in or affecting commerce? State the correct citation for your answer.

25. What is the method for the United States Supreme Court to review final judgments of the highest court of a state? State the correct citation for your answer.

26. What are the prohibitions related to a biological weapon and what is the penalty for violating the prohibitions? State the correct citation for your answer.

27. What are the circumstances under which it is illegal to bribe a public official or accept a bribe if one is a public official? State the correct citation for your answer.

28. What are the provisions making it a crime to use a weapon of mass destruction? State the correct citation for your answer.

29. What is the penalty for distributing a switchblade knife? State the correct citation for your answer.

30. What is the composition of the Joint Chiefs of Staff, and what is the function of the Chairman of the Joint Chiefs of Staff? State the correct citation for your answer.

31. What is the president's annual compensation, and what is his expense allowance? State the correct citation for your answer.

32. What is the duration of a copyright created after January 1, 1978? State the correct citation for your answer.

33. What is the term of a patent? State the correct citation for your answer.

34. What are the categories of persons considered United States citizens at birth? What is the correct citation for the statute?

35. What are the two methods by which the United States Supreme Court reviews decisions of the federal courts of appeals? What is the correct citation for the statute?

36. What is the mission of the Food and Drug Administration? What is the correct citation for the statute?

Find the answers to the following questions in the statutes for your state.

State statutes 1. Does your state permit marijuana for medical purposes? If so, what is the correct citation to the state statute permitting medical marijuana?

State statutes 2. Does your state have a "red flag law" that permits law enforcement to petition a judge to remove guns from individuals posing a threat? What is the correct citation to the state statute?

State statutes 3. Does your state have a statute requiring public school education on the dangers of sex trafficking? What is the correct citation to the state statute?

State statutes 4. Does your state have a statute banning styrofoam? What is the correct citation to the state statute?

State statutes 5. Does your state have a statute banning drinking straws? What is the correct citation to the state statute?

State statutes 6. Does your state have a statute permitting college athletes to get paid for their name or likeness? What is the correct citation to the state statute?

State statutes 7. Does your state have a statute regulating driverless vehicles? What is the correct citation to the state statute?

State statutes 8. Does your state have a statute preventing businesses from passing tax-free profits out of a state? What is the correct citation to the state statute?

State statutes 9. Does your state have a statute enforcing privacy rights? What is the correct citation to the state statute?

State statutes 10. Does your state have a statute preventing texting while driving? What is the correct citation to the state statute?

State statutes 11. Does your state have a minimum hourly wage? What is the correct citation to the state statute?

State statutes 12. Does your state have restrictions on abortion? What is the correct citation to the state statute?

State statutes 13. Does your state have restrictions on gun sales? What is the correct citation to the state statute?

State statutes 14. Does your state have a statute permitting sports gambling? What is the correct citation to the state statute?

State statutes 15. Does your state have restrictions on a law enforcement agency gathering evidence on privately owned real property through the use of a drone? What is the correct citation to the state statute?

State statutes 16. Does your state have a minimum age to obtain a marriage license? Are there exceptions to the minimum age? What is the correct citation to the state statute?

State statutes 17. Does your state have a statute pursuant to which a vehicle driver is deemed to have consented to breath or blood tests if an officer has reason to believe that the motorist as committed a drug- or alcohol-related driving offense? What is the correct citation to the state statute?

QUESTIONS FOR COURT RULES ASSIGNMENT

1. Using the Federal Rules of Civil Procedure, answer questions a through c:

   a. Which courts are governed by the Federal Rules of Civil Procedure?

   b. What is the purpose of the rules?

   c. What is the correct citation?

   d. Using your state's rules of civil procedure, what are the answers to a through c?

2. Using the Federal Rules of Civil Procedure, answer questions a and b:

   a. How does one begin a civil lawsuit?

   b. What is the correct citation?

   c. Using your state's rules of civil procedure, what are the answers to a and b?

3. Using the Federal Rules of Civil Procedure, answer questions a through c:

a. Who must sign a pleading and what additional information must be included below the signature?

b. What is being certified to?

c. What is the correct citation?

d. Using your state's rules of civil procedure, what are the answers to a through c?

4. Using the Federal Rules of Civil Procedure, answer questions a and b:

a. Who may serve the summons?

b. What is the correct citation?

c. Using your state's rules of civil procedure, what are the answers to a and b?

5. Using the Federal Rules of Civil Procedure, answer questions a and b:

a. What pleadings are allowed?

b. What is the correct citation?

c. Using your state's rules of civil procedure, what are the answers to a and b?

6. Using the Federal Rules of Civil Procedure, answer questions a through c:

a. What request may a party serve on another party?

b. What are the contents of the request?

c. What is the correct citation?

d. Using your state's rules of civil procedure, what are the answers to a through c?

7. Using the Federal Rules of Civil Procedure, answer questions a and b:

    a. When must the court grant a motion for summary judgment?

    b. What is the correct citation to the rule?

    c. Using your state's rules of civil procedure, what are the answers to a and b?

8. Using the Federal Rules of Civil Procedure, what are the answers to a and b?

    a. What is the maximum number of interrogatories a party must answer and how long does a party have to answer the interrogatories?

    b. What is the correct citation?

    c. Using your state's rules of civil procedure, what are the answers to a and b?

9. Using the Federal Rules of Civil Procedure, answer questions a and b:

    a. What is the effect of a party's failure to respond to a written request to admit?

    b. What is the correct citation?

    c. Using your state's rules of civil procedure, what are the answers to a and b?

10. Using the Federal Rules of Civil Procedure, answer questions a and b:

    a. What is the number of jurors in a civil lawsuit?

    b. What is your correct citation?

    c. Using your state's rules of civil procedure, what are the answers to a and b?

11. Using the Federal Rules of Civil Procedure, answer questions a and b:

a. What are the grounds for entering a default judgment?

b. What is the correct citation?

c. Using your state's rules of civil procedure, what are the answers to a and b?

12. Using the Federal Rules of Civil Procedure, answer questions a and b:

    a. What are the grounds for entering a temporary restraining order?

    b. What is the correct citation?

    c. Using your state's rules of civil procedure, what are the answers to a and b?

13. Using the Federal Rules of Civil Procedure, answer questions a and b:

    a. What are the prerequisites to a class action?

    b. What is the correct citation?

    c. Using your state's rules of civil procedure, what are the answers to a and b?

14. Using the Federal Rules of Evidence, answer questions a and b:

    a. What is the purpose of the rules?

    b. What is the correct citation?

    c. Using your state's rules of evidence, what are the answers to a and b?

15. Using the Federal Rules of Evidence, answer questions a and b:

    a. What type of fact may be judicially noticed?

    b. What is the correct citation?

    c. Using your state's rules of evidence, what are the answers to a and b?

16. Using the Federal Rules of Evidence, what are the answers to a and b?

    a. When may the court exclude relevant evidence?

    b. What is the correct citation to the rule?

    c. Using your state's rules of evidence, what are the answers to a and b?

17. Using the Federal Rules of Evidence, answer questions a through c:

    a. When waiving the attorney–client or work product privilege, does the waiver extend to undisclosed communication or information?

    b. Does an inadvertent disclosure operate as a waiver?

    c. What is the correct citation?

    d. Using your state's rules of evidence, what are the answers to a through c?

18. Using the Federal Rules of Evidence, answer questions a through c:

    a. When may witnesses be excluded from the courtroom?

    b. What are the exceptions to excluding witnesses?

    c. What is the correct citation?

    d. Using your state's rules of evidence, what are the answers to a through c?

19. Using the Federal Rules of Evidence, answer questions a through c:

    a. What is hearsay?

    b. What statements are not hearsay?

    c. What is the correct citation to the rule?

d. Using your state's rules of evidence, what are the answers to a through c?

20. Using the Federal Rules of Criminal Procedure, answer questions a and b:

 a. What is the scope of the rules?

 b. What is the correct citation?

 c. Using your state's rules of criminal procedure, what are the answers to a and b?

21. Using the Federal Rules of Criminal Procedure, answer questions a and b:

 a. What is the purpose of the rules, and how are they to be construed?

 b. What is the correct citation?

 c. Using your state's rules of criminal procedure, what are the answers to a and b?

22. Using the Federal Rules of Criminal Procedure, answer questions a through c:

 a. How many members does a grand jury have?

 b. Who may be present when the grand jury is in session?

 c. What is the correct citation?

 d. Using your state's rules of criminal procedure, what are the answers to a through c?

23. Using the Federal Rules of Criminal Procedure, answer questions a and b:

 a. What happens during an arraignment?

 b. What is the correct citation?

c. Using your state's rules of criminal procedure, what are the answers to a and b?

24. Using the Federal Rules of Criminal Procedure, answer questions a and b:

    a. What are the reasons that allow trial in a district other than the one in which the offense was committed?

    b. What is your correct citation?

    c. Using your state's rules of criminal procedure, what are the answers to a and b?

25. Using the Federal Rules of Criminal Procedure, answer questions a and b:

    a. When may a court order separate trials?

    b. What is the correct citation to the rule?

    c. Using your state's rules of criminal procedure, what are the answers to a and b?

26. Using the Federal Rules of Criminal Procedure, answer questions a through c:

    a. Under what circumstance must a defendant notify an attorney for the government of an intended alibi defense?

    b. When must the defendant provide the intended alibi defense and what information must the defendant provide?

    c. What is the correct citation?

    d. Using your state's rules of criminal procedure, what are the answers to a through c?

27. Using the Federal Rules of Criminal Procedure, answer questions a through c:

a. What is the required content of a subpoena?

b. What documents and objects are subject to being produced and what are the conditions of producing them?

c. What is the correct citation?

d. Using your state's rules of criminal procedure, what are the answers to a through c?

28. Using the Federal Rules of Criminal Procedure, answer questions a through c:

a. How many members does a trial jury have?

b. What is the minimum number of jurors to return a valid verdict?

c. What is the correct citation?

d. Using your state's rules of criminal procedure, what are the answers to a through c?

29. Using the Federal Rules of Criminal Procedure, answer questions a and b:

a. What happens during closing argument?

b. What is the correct citation?

c. Using your state's rules of criminal procedure, what are the answers to a and b?

30. Using the Federal Rules of Appellate Procedure, answer questions a and b:

a. What courts are governed by these rules?

b. What is the correct citation?

c. Using your state's rules of appellate procedure, what are the answers to a and b?

31. Using the Federal Rules of Appellate Procedure, answer questions a and b:

a. What items constitute the record on appeal?

b. What is the correct citation?

c. Using your state's rules of appellate procedure, what are the answers to a and b?

32. Using the Federal Rules of Appellate Procedure, answer questions a and b:

a. How may service of papers be made?

b. What is the correct citation?

c. Using your state's rules of appellate procedure, what are the answers to a and b?

33. Using the Federal Rules of Appellate Procedure, answer questions a and b:

a. When must the appellant's brief be filed?

b. What is the correct citation?

c. Using your state's rules of appellate procedure, what are the answers to a and b?

34. Using the Federal Rules of Appellate Procedure, answer questions a through c:

a. How is service accomplished?

b. How is proof of service accomplished?

c. What is the correct citation to the rules?

d. Using your state's rules of appellate procedure, what are the answers to a through c?

35. Using the Federal Rules of Appellate Procedure, answer questions a through c:

a. What are the requirements for hearing or rehearing a case en banc?

b. What are the standards for a court to hear or rehear a case en banc?

c. What is the correct citation to the rule?

d. Using your state's rules of appellate procedure, what are the answers to a through c?

36. Using the Federal Rules of Appellate Procedure, answer questions a through c:

a. What is the procedure for making local rules?

b. What are the limits on local rules?

c. What is the correct citation?

d. Using your state's rules of appellate procedure, what are the answers to a through c?

37. Using the Rules of the Supreme Court of the United States, answer questions a through c:

a. What is the term of the Court?

b. What happens to the cases pending on the docket at the end of the term?

c. What is the correct citation to the rule?

38. Using the Rules of the Supreme Court of the United States, answer questions a and b:

a. How many members of the Court constitute a quorum?

b. What is the correct citation?

39. Using the Rules of the Supreme Court of the United States, answer questions a and b:

a. Is review on writ of certiorari discretionary or mandatory?

b. What is the correct citation?

40. Using the Rules of the Supreme Court of the United States, answer questions a and b:

    a. When must a petition for writ of certiorari be filed with the Court?

    b. What is the correct citation?

41. Using the Rules of the Supreme Court of the United States, answer questions a and b:

    a. What is the filing fee for a petition for writ of certiorari?

    b. What is the correct citation?

42. Using the Rules of the Supreme Court of the United States, answer questions a through c:

    a. What is the purpose of oral argument?

    b. Normally, how much time is each party permitted for oral argument?

    c. What is the correct citation to the rule?

43. Using the Rules of the Supreme Court of the United States, answer questions a and b:

    a. What are the restrictions on an employee of the Court practicing law?

    b. What is the correct citation?

44. Using the Rules of the Supreme Court of the United States, answer questions a and b:

    a. What are the requirements concerning a part of the record in a language other than English?

b. What is the correct citation?

QUESTIONS FOR ADMINISTRATIVE LAW ASSIGNMENT

1.

a. What is the name of the set of books containing the codified version of federal administrative rules?

b. What is the name of the publication containing new administrative rules not found in the code?

2.

a. What is the name of the set of books containing the codified version of your state's administrative rules?

b. What is the name of the publication containing new administrative rules not found in the code?

3.

a. What two federal government agencies are the subject of title 11 of the *Code of Federal Regulations*?

b. What two federal government agencies are the subject of title 17 of the *Code of Federal Regulations*?

c. What federal government agency is the subject of title 26 of the *Code of Federal Regulations*?

4.

a. What is the purpose of the Note at 16 C.F.R. Part 17?

b. What is the purpose of 16 C.F.R. §§ 1615.1–1616.65?

c. What is the purpose of 16 C.F.R. §§ 1501.1–1501.5?

d. What is the purpose of 16 C.F.R. §§ 238.0–238.4?

e. What is the purpose of 16 C.F.R. §§ 233.1–233.5?

5.

   a. What is the citation to the rules promulgated under the Magnuson-Moss Warranty Act?

   b. What is the citation to the rules requiring care labels (stating whether the item is recommended to be machine washed or dry cleaned) in clothing?

   c. What is the citation to the rules requiring clothing labels to state the fabric content and the country of origin?

6. What is the definition in the *Code of Federal Regulations* for the following terms, and what is the correct citation for your answer?

   a. Beer

   b. Wine

   c. Milk

   d. Cream

7. Locate the federal regulations concerning the *Code of Federal Regulations* and the *Federal Register* and answer the following questions:

   a. How often is each volume of the *Code of Federal Regulations* updated?

   b. What is the correct citation for a?

   c. What are the categories of documents published in the *Federal Register*?

   d. How often is the *Federal Register* published?

   e. What is the correct citation for c and d?

8. Locate the federal regulations in the *Code of Federal Regulations* concerning labeling of alcoholic beverages, and answer the following questions:

   a. What is the wording for the warning required to be placed on alcoholic beverages?

b. What is the effective date of the labeling regulation?

c. What is the correct citation for a and b?

9. Answer the following questions, and state the correct citation for your answers:

   a. When may a petition for pardon be filed by someone seeking executive clemency?

   b. Is a federal prisoner eligible for parole?

   c. In whose name must a patent application be made?

   d. Why has the Consumer Product Safety Commission banned lawn darts?

10. Answer the following questions, and state the correct citation for your answer:

   a. What must a seller of mail-order merchandise do when unable to ship merchandise within the applicable time period?

   b. How long does a consumer who purchased a consumer item in a "door-to-door" sale have to cancel the purchase, and how long after receiving buyer's cancellation notice does the seller have to refund any money paid?

   c. May someone operate a brewery in his or her home?

Chapter 6

Citators

Introduction

Although **citators** are one of the last sources to be studied in a legal research class, they are one of the most important tools in legal research. Citators are important because they allow the legal researcher to ascertain the history of a case and which cases and other legal sources have cited to the case. Citators allow similar research on other legal sources as well. **KeyCite**®, found on Westlaw®, ***Shepard's Citations***, available on LexisNexis®, and **BCite**, found on Bloomberg Law®, are the three leading citators. In addition, *Shepard's Citations* is available in a number of different print sets.

> **Citators** A set of books or database that lists relevant legal events subsequent to a given case, statute, or other authority.
>
> | ***Shepard's Citations*** | **KeyCite** | **BCite** |
> |---|---|---|
> | A leading citator. | A leading citator. | A leading citator. |

This chapter discusses:

- citators
- online use of citators
- citation of a lower court case with subsequent history

Using a citator is essential to legal research, and an attorney's failure to use citators will be quickly criticized by the court. As more fully explained in Chapter 14, an attorney has an ethical duty as an officer of the court to bring directly adverse authority to the court's attention. An attorney should be able to identify such adverse authority by using a citator. An attorney's credibility is at risk if a court discovers an attorney's failure to fulfill this ethical obligation. A court may point out an attorney's failure to use a citator in open court, much to the embarrassment of the attorney. This court admonishment is sometimes referred to as a "benchslap." A similar admonishment in an opinion ramps up the embarrassment several more degrees, as the court benchslap is available in print for years to come. Such a benchslap is illustrated in the following case.

The Supreme Court of Idaho noted that the attorney for the City had omitted citing to an adverse authority in *Galvin v. City of Middleton*, 434 P.3d 817, 823 n.3 (Idaho 2018). The court noted in its opinion that the attorney's omission was due to the attorney's failure to use citators. "The failure to acknowledge the existence of adverse controlling precedent from this Court was not willful. At oral argument, counsel for the City candidly admitted that he had failed to Shepardize or Key-Cite our decision...." *Id.*

YOU BE THE JUDGE

What action could have caused the court to make the following comment?

Upon signing a pleading, motion or other paper, an attorney certifies that he or she has conducted a reasonable inquiry into the law.... A signer's inquiry is not reasonable if the law is discoverable by using basic legal research tools, such as citators, digests, annotated codes, or computerized searches, if available.
Gutierrez v. City of Hialeah, 729 F. Supp. 1329, 1332 (S.D. Fla. 1990).

Note on Online Citators

Thirty to forty years ago, the standard was for law libraries to have print volumes of *Shepard's Citations* on their shelves, KeyCite did not exist, and legal researchers were beginning to use *Shepard's Citations* in digital form. There has certainly been a sea change in citators since those days. Nowadays, many libraries do not include print volumes of *Shepard's Citations* in their collections, and the standard is for individuals performing legal research to use online citators. Using one of these online services to cite check is much faster than manually checking all applicable issues of *Shepard's*, and there is probably less chance of error. Cite checking online using *Shepard's*, KeyCite, or BCite will yield the most up-to-date information.

Citators

As explained in Chapter 2, the doctrine of stare decisis requires judges to rely on past cases to decide controversies in front of them. Attorneys research case law to advise clients and to predict the outcome of a lawsuit. Judges and attorneys look for authoritative case law; however, a reporter fails to indicate the subsequent history of a promising-looking case. Thus, the researcher cannot determine whether the case is still good law (is still authoritative) without consulting a citator.

A case, once authoritative, may no longer be good law for a number of reasons. It may have been reversed or overruled. A case may no longer be authoritative because subsequent decisions have created so many exceptions or so limited its effect that the legal principle announced in the case is no longer viable. There is a difference between a court reversing a decision and a court overruling a decision. You might think of reversal as vertical in effect. A higher court reverses a case decided by a lower court; the result is that a higher court nullifies the decision of a lower court. Overruling a case is horizontal in effect. A case is overruled by the same court that originally decided the case. The result is that a court nullifies one of its past decisions. The court may decide, because of the passage of time or changes in society, that case law should be changed. The court accomplishes this, by stating in a case presently before it, that it is overruling a prior case.

Although a court usually states that it is "overruling" a prior case, a court may use a term such as "abrogate" to indicate that it is discrediting the precedential effect of the prior case, at least in part. A 1957 United States Supreme Court case, *Conley v. Gibson*, 355 U.S. 41 (1957), is marked with a KeyCite red flag that indicates that *Conley* is no longer good law. In 2010, a court expressed its displeasure with an attorney relying on *Conley*. "The rule in *Conley*... has been abrogated by *Ashcroft v. Iqbal*, 556 U.S. 662 (2009), and *Bell Atlantic Corporation v. Twombly*, 550 U.S. 544 (2007). Counsel is reminded that 'diligent research, which includes Shepardizing cases, is a professional responsibility.'" *Baumgardner v. Bimbo Food Bakeries Distribution, Inc.*, 697 F.Supp.2d 801, 807 n.4 (N.D. Ohio 2010) (citations omitted).

A case may have been appealed, with the case subsequently decided by a higher court. Even if the higher court affirmed the lower court, it is important to know that a higher court reached a decision in the case. If the lower court decided an issue and the higher court subsequently decided the same issue, the holding and reasoning of the higher court, rather than the lower court, is authoritative. One might want to cite to the lower court opinion for an issue not considered by the higher court or for facts or procedural history of the case not described in the higher court opinion. Even so, citation rules require the citation to the lower court opinion to include information informing the reader that the case was later decided by a higher court.

Without correctly using a citator, one may fail to ascertain that a case upon which one is relying has been reversed or overruled. This may result in an attorney giving a client incorrect legal advice, being admonished by a judge, or even losing a case. An attorney might be benchslapped in a written and reported opinion, where the admonishment will be accessible for all to read. For a judge, it may mean being reversed on appeal and being chastised by the higher court. At the very worst, it may be the ground for a legal malpractice lawsuit against the attorney or disciplinary proceedings against the attorney or the judge. If this happened because the paralegal forgot to use the citator and the attorney relied on the paralegal's research, the paralegal can lose his or her job. In short, do not forget to use citators!

YOU BE THE JUDGE

What action could have caused the court to make the following comment in connection with the attorney's failure to Shepardize?

"Defendant's sloppy effort to curry favor with the court is of a piece with its general sloppiness in connection with Mrs. Shepherd's matter."

Shepherd v. Law Offices of Cohen & Slamowitz, LLP, 668 F.Supp.2d 579, 582 n.2 (S.D.N.Y. 2009).

The researcher uses the citator to verify the status of a case and update it. Frank Shepard founded Shepard's Company in 1873 in Illinois, and the company published citators for many years. Shepard's is now a part of LexisNexis, which continues to publish a separate set of citators for each jurisdiction. *Shepard's Citators* are sets of indexes that enable you to look up cases, statutes, administrative regulations, and some secondary sources to discover if they have been cited. Although in a different format, the online citator provides the same substantive information. Thus, the citator allows the researcher to verify the status of primary sources and ascertain whether and where sources were cited. A statute or administrative regulation may no longer be good law for a number of reasons; it may have been amended, repealed, or held to be unconstitutional.

Shepard's Citators have been such an indispensable tool to the researcher for so long that the process of case verification and updating is commonly referred to as "Shepardizing."® Some thirty years ago, attorneys began to talk of "KeyCiting" to verify and update primary sources. KeyCite is the online citator introduced into Westlaw a number of years ago and KeyCite became the exclusive citator on Westlaw in June 1999. Some ten years ago, BCite made its appearance with the appearance of Bloomberg Law. The explanation of citators in this chapter will be limited to the procedure used for cases. Once you understand the procedure for those sources, the same procedure can be used for other materials. *Shepard's* is available online on LexisNexis, as is KeyCite on Westlaw and BCite on Bloomberg Law.

For inclusiveness and ease, this chapter will talk of verifying a case through the use of a citator rather than Shepardizing, KeyCiting, or BCiting it to reference the process of verifying and updating a case.

The scheme of the citator is quite simple. The citator lists each instance in which the case being verified has been cited, with the information given as citations to the pages on which the case being verified is cited. For example, imagine a case was later decided by a higher court in a published opinion and, in addition, the case was cited twice, once in another published opinion and once in a law review article. Verifying would yield three citations; one citation is to the higher court opinion, one is to the other case, and the third is to the law review article. The citations found by verifying yield the page on which the verified case was cited, which may not necessarily be the first page of the source.

Using Online Citators for Cases

The citator has two primary uses. It is used to determine the current status of a case, that is, whether the case is still authoritative. This is the history of the case, in other words, whether there are lower court opinions and higher court opinions in the case.

The citator is also used as a tool to find cases and other authorities citing to the case being verified. The researcher is looking for citing references to the case being verified. For example, the researcher may have found an older case that is of interest because it contains facts and issues similar to those in the problem being researched. If newer cases with similar facts and issues cited the case being verified, verifying will enable the researcher to locate those cases. Consulting citing references can result in locating other authorities, such as law review articles and other secondary sources citing to the case being verified. These secondary sources can clarify the importance of the case and how it fits with primary and secondary sources.

Two primary uses for citators are:

1. To determine the history of the case; and
2. To find cases and other authorities citing to the case being verified.

Shepard's, KeyCite, and BCite are similar in a number of respects. When the researcher finds a case, the first thing to do is to check for a visual indicator symbol to the left of the case name. If there is an indicator, the researcher immediately knows something about the status of the case.

To illustrate some of the points made in this section, online use of a citator will be discussed using *Byrd v. United States*, 138 S. Ct. 1518 (2018), the case discussed in some detail in Chapter 4.

The visual indicator symbols in *Shepard's* are called **signals**. The red stop sign is an indication of strong negative treatment such as the case having been overruled or reversed. The yellow triangle is an indication of the case having received negative treatment. The researcher can click on a signal other than a red stop sign or a yellow triangle to determine the meaning of the signal.

The author reviewed *Byrd* in LexisNexis, finding the following information at the time this book was being written. *Byrd* has a yellow triangle at the beginning of the case to the left of the case name. Rolling the mouse over the indicator brings up the message: "Caution: Possible negative treatment is indicated." Clicking on that yellow triangle brings up excerpts of all 170 cases that cited to *Byrd* and indicating the reason for the citing. The cases are arranged in hierarchical order, with the United States Supreme Court cases first, followed by federal cases grouped by federal circuit number, and followed by state cases grouped alphabetically by state. The first United States Supreme Court case listed, *Carpenter*, indicates that *Byrd* was cited in *Carpenter* in a dissenting opinion. The vertical reviewing pane visible to the right indicated that there were twenty-two cases that cited to *Byrd* and were marked with a yellow triangle. Clicking on the yellow triangle in the reviewing pane brings up the twenty-two cases. An excerpt from each of those cases indicates that the cases cited to *Byrd* but distinguished those cases from *Byrd*. In other words, in each of those cases there was a factor that made *Byrd* inapplicable to the case.

The visual indicator symbols in KeyCite are called **status flags**. The red status flag is an indication that the case is no longer good for at least one point of law. The yellow status flag is an indication of the case having received negative treatment but not having been overruled or reversed. The researcher can click on a status flag other than a red or yellow status flag to determine the meaning of the indicator.

The author reviewed *Byrd* in Westlaw, finding the following information at the time this book was being written. *Byrd* has a yellow status flag at the beginning of the case to the left of the case name. Rolling the mouse over the indicator brings up the message: "KeyCite Yellow Flag—Negative Treatment." Clicking on that yellow flag brings up information on the eleven cases that gave *Byrd* negative treatment, indicating the reason for the citing was either "Declined to Extend" or "Distinguished." In other words, in each of those cases there was a factor that made *Byrd* inapplicable to the case.

In BCite, the **composite analysis** is the visual representation of the direct history and the case analysis of the case. The red square with a minus sign is a visual indication that the case was reversed, vacated, de-published, or overruled in full or in part. The yellow square with a white triangle inside is a visual indication symbol that the researcher should exercise caution because of the case having been modified, clarified, or amended in its direct history or having been criticized in another case but not having been overruled. The researcher can click on a visual indicator symbol other than a red or yellow square to determine the meaning of the indicator.

Signals The visual indicator symbols in *Shepard's* are called signals. The red stop sign is an indication of strong negative treatment such as the case having been overruled or reversed. The yellow triangle is an indication of the case having received negative treatment.

Status Flags In KeyCite, a red or yellow status flag located in the upper left-hand corner of a primary source warns the researcher of any negative history. A red flag appearing on a case means that the case is no longer good law for at least one of the points it contains. A yellow flag appearing on a case means that the case has some negative history, but it has not been reversed or overruled.

Composite Analysis In BCite, the composite analysis is the visual representation of the direct history and the case analysis of the case. The red square with a minus sign is a visual indication that the case was reversed, vacated, de-published, or overruled in full or in part. The yellow square with a white triangle inside is an indication that the researcher should exercise caution because of the case having been modified, clarified, or amended in its direct history or having been criticized in another case but not having been overruled.

The tabs at the top of the screen of a case in Westlaw are an important feature of KeyCite. The tabs are labeled "Filings," "Negative Treatment," "History," "Citing References," and "Table of Authorities." Probably the ones most useful to you at this point are the "Negative Treatment," "History," and "Citing References" tabs. The "Filings" are the court documents filed in the case being verified and the "Table of Authorities" are the authorities cited in the case being verified. Some of the information found by clicking on the "Negative Treatment" and "History" tabs can also be accessed by clicking on a case status flag.

Clicking on the "Citing References" tab automatically brings up the documents that have cited to the case you are KeyCiting. Thus, with KeyCite, citations concerning the history of the case are separated from citations to cases that have cited the case being KeyCited. "Citation References" materials are separated into several sections. Typical sections might include "Cases," "Trial Court Orders," "Secondary Sources," and "Appellate Court Documents."

Both *Shepard's* and BCite provide information similar to the information grouped by tabs in KeyCite. In the LexisNexis version of a case, the researcher would click on a link in the right-hand vertical reviewing pane that invites the researcher to Shepardize the case. Clicking to Shepardize would bring up four subtabs labeled "Appellate History," containing direct and indirect history of the case being verified, "Citing Decisions," containing cases citing to the case being verified, "Other Citing Sources," containing primary sources and secondary sources citing to the case being verified, and "Table of Authorities," containing cases cited to within the case being verified. In the Bloomberg Law version of the case, click on the BCite Analysis icon, which brings up tabs for "Direct History," containing prior and subsequent cases that affect or are affected by the outcome of the main opinion, "Case Analysis," containing cases citing to the case being verified with excerpts from those cases, "Table of Authorities," containing cases citing to the case being verified with an analysis of the treatment of those cases, and "Citing Documents," containing primary and secondary authorities citing to the case being verified.

Another similarity among *Shepard's*, KeyCite, and BCite is inclusion of segmented visual bars next to a case citing to the case being verified. The number of the colored segments indicates the strength of discussion provided by the citing case about the case being verified, with the maximum colored segments indicating the most discussion down to a single colored segment indicating the least discussion. *Shepard's* refers to the visual as a **depth of discussion indicator**, KeyCite refers to the visual as **depth of treatment bars**, and BCite refers to the visual as **citation frequency**.

Depth of Discussion Indicator In *Shepard's*, a visual bar segmented into four portions next to a case citing to the case being verified and indicating the strength of the discussion provided by the citing case about the case being verified.

Depth of Treatment Bars In KeyCite, a visual bar segmented into four portions next to a case citing to the case being verified and indicating the strength of the discussion provided by the citing case about the case being verified.

Citation Frequency In BCite, a visual bar segmented into five portions next to a case citing to the case being verified and indicating the strength of the discussion provided by the citing case about the case being verified.

For *Shepard's*, a citing case marked with four colored segments indicates "Analyzed," meaning that the citing case fully considered the case being verified. A citing case marked with three colored segments indicates "Discussed," meaning that the citing case discussed the case being verified with some measure of analysis. A citing case marked with two colored segments indicates "Mentioned," meaning that the citing case briefly mentioned the case being verified. A citing case marked with one colored segment indicates "Cited," meaning that the citing case cited the case being verified with minimal if any discussion.

For KeyCite, the cases with the fullest discussion of the case being KeyCited are marked with four colored depth of treatment bar segments, meaning "Examined." A case in this category would include an in-depth discussion of the KeyCited case, usually more than a page. The cases in which the KeyCited case is discussed are marked with three colored depth of treatment bar segments, meaning "Discussed." A case in this category includes a substantial discussion of the KeyCited case, usually more than a paragraph but less than a page. The cases in which the KeyCited case is cited and discussed briefly are marked with two colored depth of treatment bar segments, meaning "Cited." A case in this category includes a brief discussion of the KeyCited case, usually less than a paragraph. The cases that simply cite the KeyCited case are marked with one colored depth of treatment bar segment, meaning "Mentioned." A green double quotation mark indicates that the KeyCited case is quoted in the listed case.

Within each depth of treatment grouping in KeyCite, the cases are listed hierarchically, with United States Supreme Court cases preceding federal court of appeals cases, which precede federal district court cases, which precede state court cases. The federal court of appeals cases are listed in numerical order by circuit. State court cases are listed alphabetically by state. Other information retrieved by clicking the "Citing References" link in KeyCite includes headnote numbers of the case the researcher is KeyCiting, the substance of which headnote is referenced in the citing document.

Similarly for BCite, the cases with the fullest discussion of the case being verified are marked with five colored citation frequency segments. The number of colored citation frequency segments declines as the depth of discussion lessens, with the least treatment of the case being verified marked with one colored citation frequency segment.

Using Online Citators for Statutes

Shepard's, KeyCite, and BCite can also be used with statutes. When viewing a statute online, the researcher should take note of the presence of indicators and other information discussed above.

Citation of a Lower Court Case with Subsequent History

When citing to a case, you must give your reader all subsequent history except for a withdrawn opinion, history on remand, and denial of certiorari or denial of review by a court with discretionary review unless the case for which certiorari or review is sought is less than two years old. Where an intermediate appellate court issued an opinion and the intermediate appellate court en banc issued an opinion subsequent history would include both opinions; the italics preceding the en banc decision should identify the decision as an en banc decision, for example "*aff'd en banc*" or "*rev'd en banc*."

The reason you would not give the citation for the denial of a rehearing is that many parties routinely petition for a rehearing and the rehearing is routinely denied. A denial of a rehearing is different from a court denying review or the United States Supreme Court denying a petition for certiorari. A rehearing is denied by the same court that has already rendered a decision.

In contrast, only a higher court can deny review or deny a petition for certiorari. Therefore, a denial of review or a denial of a petition for certiorari is important enough to be given as subsequent history for two years after the case has been decided, whereas denial of rehearing is not. The two-year period was selected because the appeal of a case to a higher court is generally concluded within two years of the lower court decision. Subsequent history indicating denial of certiorari or denial of review within the two-year period tells the reader the lower court decision is final.

When citing to a case, you would not give subsequent history for the United States Supreme Court granting certiorari unless the Court has granted certiorari, but has not yet reached a decision in the case. The reason that you would not include the grant of certiorari is because it is obvious that the Court granted certiorari if the Court issued a decision in the case. By the same token, when citing to a case, you would not give subsequent history for an appellate court granting review or a rehearing unless the court has granted review or a rehearing, but has not yet reached a decision in the case. The reason that you would not include the grant of review or rehearing is because it is obvious that the court granted review or rehearing if the court issued a decision in the case.

When an appellate court remands a case, it sends it back to the lower court to redo something the lower court did incorrectly before. The appellate decision in which the appellate court lays down the rule of law to be followed by the lower court on remand, and not the lower court decision in which the rule of law is carried out, is more important for its precedential value. For that reason, history on remand is not usually cited in subsequent history.

An Example of a Lower Court Case with Subsequent History

CITATION TIP

Subsequent History

Connect subsequent history to the end of the citation of the lower court decision by explaining what the higher court did, underlining the explanation, and setting it off by commas. "Certiorari denied" should be abbreviated to "*cert. denied*," "affirmed" should be abbreviated to "*aff'd*," and "reversed" should be abbreviated to "*rev'd*." Otherwise the explanation should be written out, for example, "*vacated*." *The Bluebook* instructs you to omit information on denial of certiorari unless the case is less than two years old or there is a particular reason to include the information.

Imagine that you are researching a products liability case in which the plaintiffs asked the court to require the defendant to pay the plaintiffs' attorney fees as a sanction for the defendant's failure to disclose highly relevant information during discovery. Your research might very well lead you to a 2017 United States Supreme Court case, *Goodyear Tire & Rubber Co. v. Haeger*, 137 S. Ct. 1178 (2017).

By clicking on the "History" tab of the case in Westlaw, you find that there was a reported decision at the trial court level. *Haeger v. Goodyear Tire and Rubber Co.*, 906 F. Supp. 2d 938 (D. Ariz. 2012). That decision was affirmed by the federal intermediate appellate court. *Haeger v. Goodyear Tire & Rubber Co.*, 813 F.3d 1233 (9th Cir. 2016). When the case reached the United States Supreme Court, the Court reversed.

The United States Supreme Court decision is the most important as far as the law is concerned; however, you might want to cite to the trial court's extensive findings of fact on pages 941 through 954. In including pages 941 through 954 you are providing a pinpoint citation, often called a "pincite." In providing a pinpoint citation, you are pinpointing for your reader the page or pages of the opinion that are particularly significant to your discussion.

If you cite to a lower court decision, you are required to inform the reader of the subsequent history of the case in the federal intermediate appellate court and in the United States Supreme Court. The preceding section explained that subsequent history would not include any denial of a rehearing, the grant of a petition of certiorari by the United States Supreme Court, or a decision on remand.

Therefore, to cite to the 2012 federal trial court decision requires you to combine the citations for that decision, the federal intermediate appellate court decision, and the United States Supreme Court decision. You also need to include the information that the intermediate appellate court affirmed the lower court decision and the United States Supreme Court reversed.

Haeger v. Goodyear Tire and Rubber Co., 906 F. Supp. 2d 938, 941-54 (D. Ariz. 2012), *aff'd*, 813 F.3d 1233 (9th Cir. 2016), *rev'd*, 137 S. Ct. 1178 (2017).

Summary

- Citators allow the legal researcher to determine whether and where the authority found has been cited in any source.
- The two reasons for consulting citators are to discover whether your authority is still good law and to locate more recent authority dealing with the same legal principle found in your authority.
- Using a citator is a necessary part of legal research and must be done systematically.
- KeyCite, found on Westlaw, is one citator.
- *Shepard's Citations*, another citator, is available online on LexisNexis and in a number of different print sets.
- BCite, found on Bloomberg Law, is a third citator.

Key Terms

BCite
citators
depth of treatment bars
direct history
KeyCite
negative indirect history

Shepard's Citations
status flags

Cyberlaw Exercises

1. For an overview of online citators, see the library guide for using online citators accessible at https://libguides.law.gonzaga.edu.
2. A number of law libraries provide online guides explaining how to Shepardize. Find one of these library guides and compare the information available in the guide to the information included in this chapter.
3. A number of online sources explain how to KeyCite. Find one of these online sources and compare the information available in the guide to the information included in this chapter.
4. A number of online sources explain how to BCite. Find one of these online sources and compare the information available in the guide to the information included in this chapter.

QUESTIONS FOR CITATOR ASSIGNMENT

Citator 1. The United States district court case found at 832 F.Supp.2d 1070 was appealed to the federal intermediate appellate court and was later decided by the United States Supreme Court.

a. Give the proper citation to the case in the United States district court.

b. Give the proper citation to the case in the federal intermediate appellate court.

c. Give the proper citation to the case in the United States Supreme Court.

d. Give the proper citation to the case in the United States district court, including subsequent history in the federal intermediate appellate court and the United States Supreme Court.

Citator 2. The United States district court case found at 172 F.Supp.3d 104 was appealed to the federal intermediate appellate court and was later decided by the United States Supreme Court.

a. Give the proper citation to the case in the United States district court.

b. Give the proper citation to the case in the federal intermediate appellate court.

c. Give the proper citation to the case in the United States Supreme Court.

d. Give the proper citation to the case in the United States district court, including subsequent history in the federal intermediate appellate court and the United States Supreme Court.

Citator 3. The United States district court case found at 906 F.Supp.2d 938 was appealed to the federal intermediate appellate court, and was later decided by the United States Supreme Court. Note: There were two decisions by the federal intermediate appellate court, the second decision amending and superseding the first on denial of rehearing en banc. Cite only to the second of the two decisions.

a. Give the proper citation to the case in the United States district court.

b. Give the proper citation to the case in the federal intermediate appellate court.

c. Give the proper citation to the case in the United States Supreme Court.

d. Give the proper citation to the case in the United States district court, including subsequent history in the federal intermediate appellate court and the United States Supreme Court.

Citator 4. The United States district court case found at 40 F. Supp.3d 744 was appealed to the federal intermediate appellate court and was later decided by the United States Supreme Court.

a. Give the proper citation to the case in the United States district court.

b. Give the proper citation to the case in the federal intermediate appellate court.

c. Give the proper citation to the case in the United States Supreme Court.

d. Give the proper citation to the case in the United States district court, including subsequent history in the federal intermediate appellate court and the United States Supreme Court.

Citator 5. A United States Supreme Court case decided on June 21, 2018, overruled two prior cases.

a. Give the proper citation to the case.

b. Give the proper citation to the two cases overruled.

Citator 6. Locate the case found at 525 F.3d 1168.

a. Give the proper citation to the case.

b. Is the case still good law? (In your answer state why or why not and give any applicable citation.)

Citator 7. Give the proper citation to the December 2019 case that quoted from and examined (four depth of treatment bars) *Procopio v. Wilkie*, 913 F.3d 1371 (Fed. Cir. 2019) and dealt with the legal concept of headnotes 3 and 4 of *Procopio*.

Citator 8. Give the proper citation to a 2020 updated section from *Corpus Juris Secundum* discussing an expectation of privacy as basis of protectable interest that discussed *United States v. Paxton*, 848 F.3d 803 (7th Cir. 2017) and dealt with the legal concept of headnotes 5, 6, and 7 of *Paxton*.

Citator 9. Give the proper citation to a 2018 *American Law Reports* annotation discussing federal regulation of drones that dealt with the legal concept of headnotes 3 and 9 of *Taylor v. Federal Aviation Administration*, 895 F.3d 56 (D.C. Cir. 2018).

Citator 10. Give the proper citation to the December 2019 case that quoted from and discussed (three depth of treatment bars) *Meador v. Apple, Incorporated*, 911 F.3d 260 (5th Cir. 2018) and dealt with the legal concept of headnotes 5, 9, and 10 of *Meador*.

Citator 11. Give the proper citation to the September 2019 case that quoted from and mentioned (one depth of treatment bar) *United States v. Obando*, 891 F.3d 929 (11th Cir. 2018) and dealt with the legal concept of headnotes 2, 4, and 9 of *Obando*.

Citator 12. Give the proper citation to a 2020 updated section from *American Jurisprudence 2d* discussing how an offense level is calculated generally that cited to *United States v. Maturino*, 887 F.3d 716 (5th Cir. 2018) and dealt with the legal concept of headnote 8 of *Maturino*.

Chapter 7

Overview of the Research Process and Ethical Considerations

Introduction

This chapter is designed to provide you with an overview of the research process. Now that you have learned about the basic types of law books a legal researcher would use, it is time to discuss how to use them together and to explore basic research strategies. The chapter discusses considerations preliminary to beginning legal research, basic approaches to legal research, and the steps in the research process.

The Eight Steps of Legal Research

Generally, legal research encompasses a series of steps, beginning with a research problem and ending with an answer to the problem. Following are the eight steps of legal research:

- step one requires you to gather all relevant factual information
- step two requires you to identify relevant key words that you will use as search terms in indexes to secondary and primary sources
- step three requires you to use secondary sources
- steps four and five require you to find relevant primary sources
- step six requires you to update your primary sources
- step seven requires you to determine whether you have completed your research
- step eight requires you to formulate an answer to your research problem

As you become more experienced in performing legal research, you may choose to vary the steps you pursue in answering your research problem.

Remember that your goal is to find all relevant authority, not just the authority favorable to you. You need to uncover adverse authority so you can formulate a defense to the adverse authority.

Preliminary Considerations

Getting Organized

Legal research can be time-consuming, and details are important. To be successful, you must be organized, methodical, and thorough. One way to organize your research is to keep a research journal in which you record any relevant information you have found. A research journal may seem time-consuming at the beginning of your research. However, the time you spend writing in your research journal should help you focus your research.

Jurisdiction

A preliminary question to tackle is **jurisdiction**, that is whether federal, state, or local law will likely govern your research problem. A research problem may be governed by the law of more than one jurisdiction.

The researcher is hoping to find mandatory authority, but may have to rely on persuasive authority if there is no mandatory authority on point.

> **Jurisdiction** 1. The geographical area within which a court (or a public official) has the right and power to operate. 2. The persons about whom and the subject matters about which a court has the right and power to make decisions that are legally binding.

Currency

Currency is critical in legal research. Each source should be updated as you use it, and any sources you intend to use as authority should be updated at the end of your research. Updating includes checking both the hardbound volume and the pocket part, if performing your research in print sources, and using a citator to determine if your source is good law. Research should be updated again if there is a time lag between the completion of your research and the time you use the results of your research. If you have updated your sources as you have gone along, you only need to update your authority from the date of your last update.

> **Currency** The principle that a legal source is authoritative as of the date of the research.

Three Basic Approaches to Legal Research

There are at least three approaches to the research process, depending on the amount of knowledge you possess concerning the areas of law involved in your research problem and depending on whether you are starting with a known primary source. The three approaches to the research process are the overview approach, the topic approach, and the known primary source approach.

Overview Approach: Learning about the General Topic

If you have little or no knowledge about the areas of law you are researching, you may want to begin the research process with secondary sources to gain a basic understanding of the areas of law. The secondary sources should give you an overview of the areas of law related to your legal question. Your background reading may help you focus your later research and help you generate more key terms to use.

Topic Approach: Learning about the General Topic

The topic approach differs from the overview approach in that someone pursuing the topic approach narrows the scope of research at the outset to a single topic. As described in the following paragraphs, the topic approach can be pursued beginning either with primary sources or secondary sources. The danger with focusing your research early on is that you may miss something in another area of law.

If you have knowledge about the areas of law you are researching, you may decide to begin the research process with primary sources to quickly locate relevant primary sources. If searching for case law, you might begin your research by examining the outline of a particular topic in a digest. If searching for statutes or administrative regulations, you might begin your research in the index to those statutes or regulations.

A researcher pursuing the topic approach in primary sources skips from step two to step four, omitting background research in secondary sources.

Another option for the knowledgeable researcher is to perform focused research in secondary sources. Even a knowledgeable researcher would be glad to quickly locate a law review or legal periodical article on point. The article usually saves the researcher time by summarizing the law in the area and citing relevant authority. The researcher can pull the cited authority, read it, update it, and pursue another avenue of research.

A researcher pursuing the topic approach in secondary sources follows all eight steps in the research process, but may not explore the secondary sources as thoroughly as someone pursuing the overview approach.

Known Primary Source Approach: Starting from a Primary Source You Have

The third approach is the known primary source approach. Sometimes you are starting with a known primary source. Read the primary source carefully and then explore links to other research tools.

A researcher pursuing the topic approach in primary sources skips from step two to step four, omitting background research in secondary sources.

Step One: Gathering Information

The length of time you spend researching in the law library will probably be shortened by the time you spend organizing and gathering information beforehand. If you start researching without gathering all relevant information, you may spend hours researching a question that could have been answered by reviewing pertinent documents or gathering more facts.

Thus, the first step in the legal research process is to gather and study all relevant factual information pertaining to your research problem. In all likelihood, someone gave you some information concerning the research problem. If you brainstorm, you might determine other sources of relevant information.

A warning is in order here. Unless you are licensed to practice law, you are performing tasks, like gathering information, under the supervision of an attorney. You may not offer legal advice and must not give the impression that you are licensed to practice law. Hold this in mind when gathering facts from the client and from others.

Once you have gathered all the relevant information, it is time to move on to step two and identify key terms.

Step Two: Identifying Key Terms

The next step is to review all the information you have gathered and use it to identify **key terms** and issues that you might find in conducting legal research. The key terms can be used to start your research in the indexes to secondary or primary sources or to input into a query box in an online database. Because the indexes and online sources you consult may use words other than the ones you have identified, brainstorm to identify related words. A legal thesaurus might be helpful at this point. From brainstorming and consulting a legal thesaurus, you might think of a number of potentially relevant terms. As you progress in your research, add any other key words you find to your list.

Key Terms Words central to a legal research problem that can be used by the legal researcher to begin researching in print indexes or to formulate a query in computer-assisted legal research.

Identification of key terms is a very important step in your research, whether you are proceeding with the overview approach, the topic approach, or the known primary source approach. Due to its importance, this section discusses these three approaches to conduct legal research, which can also be used to identify key terms. Your professor may favor one method of identifying key terms over the other two, in which case that is the approach you should employ. As you develop expertise in performing legal research, you may decide which of the three methods would be the most productive.

Step Three: Learn More about the Area of Law You Are Researching through Secondary Authority

If you know little or nothing about the area of law involved in the problem you are researching, a good beginning point in your research is to read a textual explanation of that area of the law. Legal encyclopedias and *American Law Reports* are the two most widely available sources giving you this type of information. Check to see whether your library has any loose-leaf services that cover the area you are researching. Use the key words you have identified to locate relevant topics in the legal encyclopedias, relevant annotations in *American Law Reports*, and relevant materials in loose-leaf services.

Step Four: Locating Primary Authority

Often, the hardest part of the research process is locating the first piece of relevant information. Once you locate the first piece of relevant information, use some of the techniques that follow to move from that information to more relevant information.

There is no one right place to start to locate primary sources. You may first want to locate primary sources by using the citations noted in your learning journal. Most legal sources have an index. Part of the research process involves researching the key terms you have developed in the appropriate index. If you think the problem involves a statute, constitution, administrative regulation, or court rule, consult the appropriate index. While reporters are not accompanied by indexes, digests function as indexes for reporters.

Consult a digest to find relevant cases. Locate cases in the digest either by consulting the Descriptive-Word Indexes (located at the end of the digest set) or reviewing a topic outline (printed at the beginning of each topic). When you locate a primary source, use that source to locate other primary sources. For example, you could look in the Descriptive-Word Index of the most current series of a digest to locate an appropriate topic. Once you have found a relevant topic, you could look at the outline at the beginning of the topic to gain information on the topic coverage and to identify relevant Key Numbers.

Once you have found some primary authority that might answer your legal problem, it is now time to proceed to step five.

Step Five: Locating Other Primary Authority

If the legal problem is simple, perhaps answered by a statute or court rule, then a single source may be sufficient. However, a more complex legal problem usually calls for additional legal research to flesh out the answer to the problem.

To locate other primary authority, it is helpful to understand the relationship among primary sources, secondary sources, and finding tools. In the preceding chapters, legal research tools (primary sources, secondary sources, and finding tools) have been discussed individually. When researching a legal problem, you must combine their use.

Research tools are linked to each other in a variety of different ways. Information in one research tool can lead to more information in the same or another research tool. Note links to other research tools and follow up the links as you move through the research process.

What do you do after you find a relevant statutory or constitutional provision? Once you find a relevant statutory or constitutional provision, there are three ways to use the provision to locate other primary authority. First, read the provision carefully and note any cross-references to other statutory or constitutional authority. Then, pull the authority referenced. Also examine how the provision fits with other statutory or constitutional provisions. You may find definitions of terms or related statutory provisions.

The second way is to consult an annotated code or constitution. Locate the applicable statute or constitutional provision and begin reading the references following the provision. The references may refer you to related constitutional provisions, statutes, and administrative regulations as well as digest topics, legal encyclopedia topics, and law review articles. Then, read the case summaries. If a reference or case summary involves the same question you are researching, note the citation, pull the authority, and read it. A third way to locate other authority is to consult a citator to find additional information on your constitutional or statutory provision.

What do you do after you find a relevant case? Once you find a relevant case, there are three ways to use the case to locate other cases. The first way is to read the case and note the citations to earlier cases cited in it. Then, pull and read any of those earlier cases that seem helpful. A second way is to make note of relevant headnotes from the case, locate the same digest topic in the digest, and read the digest abstracts to locate more cases. A third way of locating cases is to use a citator. Using a citator will give you citations to later cases citing the case. The case also may cite other primary sources such as statutes, constitutional provisions, court rules, or administrative regulations.

Use citations in the footnotes and pocket parts of legal encyclopedias, *American Law Reports* annotations, and other secondary sources to lead you to relevant cases and statutes.

Once you find a relevant case, read it, noting internal citations to other primary sources, including other cases, statutes, court rules, and administrative regulations. Note the digest topic and number from relevant headnotes and use that information to locate summaries of relevant cases under the same topic and number of the appropriate digest. Use a citator to ascertain whether the case is still good authority and to find more recent relevant cases.

Once you find a relevant statute, read it, noting internal citations to other statutes. Carefully read the research references following the statute for citations to related constitutional provisions, statutes, administrative regulations, secondary sources, and digest topics. Read the case summaries to find relevant cases. Do not forget to check the pocket part to the volume and any interim pamphlets. Use a citator to double-check the status of the statute and to find relevant cases.

Once you find a relevant constitutional provision, locate it in an annotated code. Carefully read the research references, following the provision for citations to related constitutional provisions, statutes, administrative regulations, secondary sources, and digest topics. Read the case summaries to find relevant cases. Do not forget to check the pocket part to the volume and any interim pamphlets. You probably do not need to use a citator to check the status of a provision from the United States Constitution, but do so for a state constitutional provision. Using a citator will allow you to find relevant cases.

Now, continue to step six.

Step Six: Reviewing Found Sources and Updating

Legal research involves discovering what the law is and how it will affect the client's case. Your goal in legal research is to find all applicable constitutional provisions, statutes, court rules, and administrative regulations. As far as case law is concerned, your goal is to find cases that constitute mandatory authority; if there is no mandatory authority, you are searching for cases that constitute persuasive authority. When primary authority is unavailable, you can look to secondary sources. Certain types of secondary sources, such as restatements, law review articles, and well-respected treatises, generally carry more weight than other secondary sources and may be highly persuasive.

Step six requires you to evaluate what you have found thus far and determine which sources need to be updated by checking any applicable pocket parts and using a citator to ascertain that your primary sources are still good law. Once you have finished this, you may continue to step seven.

Step Seven: Deciding Whether You Are Finished with Your Research

Your research process must be as efficient as possible to save you unnecessary wasted time and to limit the client's fees; at the same time, the research must be as thorough as possible. You may have a limited amount of time to research a particular issue because you must meet a filing deadline. Your office may have quoted the client a certain amount in attorneys' fees.

When are you finished with your research? You are probably finished when you have checked each of the main primary and secondary sources and you keep finding the same authorities. Before you stop, double-check to make sure you have updated any authorities you intend to use by using a citator and follow any other avenues of research suggested by the information you obtain from the citator.

Once you have decided that you have finished your research, it is time to proceed to step eight.

Step Eight: Evaluate What You Have Found and Determine the Answer to Your Research Question

Recall that what started you on the process of legal research was the legal problem that had been presented to you. Once you have completed finding your sources, you must critically evaluate them and formulate an answer to your research problem

Do not be surprised if your research does not turn up a clear-cut answer to your research problem. You will likely be disappointed if you were expecting to find a case with facts identical to your legal problem. (This is referred to as a case on all fours.) The most you may be able to find is a case with similar facts or a statute that appears to apply to your legal problem. Your research might discover a conflict in authorities, in which case you might have to predict which line of reasoning a judge may follow. You might not find primary sources that are mandatory in the jurisdiction if the problem is of first impression. (Something is of first impression if it presents a novel fact pattern.) You may have found primary sources from sister jurisdictions that you can use as persuasive authority.

Inadequate Legal Research as an Ethics Violation

Besides causing the client problems, the lawyer can be disciplined or disbarred under state lawyer ethics rules that require adequate legal research. In addition, the lawyer must supervise non-lawyer assistants and may be held responsible for the actions of the non-lawyer assistants. Thus, a lawyer may be held responsible if a paralegal was given the responsibility of performing legal research and failed to adequately research the law.

Each state has its own lawyer ethics rules that are required to be followed by lawyers admitted to practice law in the state. Many states, such as Maryland, have lawyer ethics rules patterned on the American Bar Association's *Model Rules of Professional Conduct*. Rule 1.1 of the Maryland Rules of Professional Conduct generally describes the type of representation the lawyer must provide the client. Rule 1.1 of the Maryland Rules of Professional Conduct states:

Rule 1.1 Competence

A lawyer shall provide competent representation to a client. Competent representation requires the legal knowledge, skill, thoroughness, and preparation reasonably necessary for the representation.

Incompetence may mean inadequate legal research or poor writing skills. Often, an attorney who violated Rule 1.1 because of inadequate research may have problems complying with Rule 1.3, which requires the attorney to perform in a timely manner. Rule 1.3 of the Maryland Rules of Professional Conduct states:

Rule 1.3 Diligence

A lawyer shall act with reasonable diligence and promptness in representing a client.

In 2019, the Court of Appeals of Maryland (the Maryland state court of last resort) decided a case involving Scott A. Conwell, who had been accused of violating a number of Maryland attorney ethics rules, including Rules 1.1 and 1.3. The court concluded that Conwell had violated Rule 1.1. "[T]he pleadings filed by Conwell on Mr. DeSerio's behalf demonstrated Conwell's failure to apply the requisite thoroughness and preparation to properly represent the DeSerios, were unnecessary, lacked merit and prejudiced Mr. DeSerio's case by not furthering his cause of action, thereby violating Rule 1.1." *Attorney Grievance Commission of Maryland v. Conwell*, 200 A.3d 820, 835 (Md. 2019).

The cumulative effect of Conwell's ethics rules violations was the basis of the court ordering that Conwell be disbarred:

> In the present case, the severity of the sanction is dependent on, among other things, the Rule 8.4(d) violations with regard to Conwell's representations of Ms. Brewington, the DeSerios, and Mr. Olsen, as well as the finding that Conwell acted with "dishonest or selfish motive." Rule 8.4(d), which requires a finding that an attorney engaged in conduct prejudicial to the administration of justice, is based upon, here, Conwell acting dishonestly, with selfish motive and without regard to the impact of his actions on the profession. In similar circumstances, we have imposed the sanction of disbarment.

Id. at 843.

YOU BE THE JUDGE

What would you do if an attorney failed to articulate a legal theory, perhaps because the attorney's legal research was inadequate?

In reaching your decision, consider the following alternatives:

- You could dismiss the case.
- You could perform the necessary legal research and, in your opinion, roundly chastise the attorney for failing to adequately research the law.

To see how one state court and two federal courts dealt with inadequate legal research, see *Attorney Grievance Com'n of Maryland v. James*, 870 A.2d 229 (Md. 2005); *Bradshaw v. Unity Marine Corporation, Inc.*, 147 F. Supp. 2d 668 (S.D. Tex. 2001); *Ernst Haas Studio, Inc. v. Palm Press, Inc.*, 164 F.3d 110 (2d Cir. 1999). Try locating any of these cases using one of the online research sites referenced in the Internet exercises below.

Summary

- Before you start researching in the law library, gather and organize information and read all pertinent documents.
- Throughout the research process, take notes of what you have found, citations to relevant authority, and ideas for other avenues of research.
- Review all the information you have gathered and use it to identify key terms and issues.
- You may want to learn more about the area of law you are researching by consulting secondary sources such as legal encyclopedias, *American Law Reports* annotations, loose-leaf services, and law review articles.
- Locate primary authority by using citations found in secondary authority, indexes, and digests.
- Use primary authority to locate other primary authority through reading cited primary authority, case summaries in annotated codes and constitutions, and Shepardizing or KeyCiting.
- You are probably finished with your research when you have checked each of the main primary and secondary sources and keep finding the same authorities.
- Consult the Eight Steps of Legal Research discussed in this chapter to develop a research strategy or explore other avenues of research.

Key Terms

currency
jurisdiction
key terms

Cyberlaw Exercises

1. Westlaw's home page is located at https://www.westlaw.com. The home page offers training options to those new to Westlaw. Explore some of those options.
2. The Legal Information Institute at Cornell Law School maintains a home page with a wealth of legal information. The homepage is located at https://www.law.cornell.edu/. Explore some of the material accessible via this home page.
3. LexisNexis' home page is located at https://www.lexis.com/. The home page offers a tour of the site. Take the tour.
4. A fee-based legal research site offering an alternative to Westlaw and LexisNexis is VersusLaw (https://www.versuslaw.com). Compare the types of sources available there to the sources available at Westlaw and LexisNexis.
5. FindLaw (https://www.findlaw.com) is a well-known legal research starting point. Research a legal question using this site.
6. The American Bar Association's home page (https://www.americanbar.org) contains links to federal government sites, selected law libraries, and other online research sites. Try accessing a few of the links.
7. Also try https://www.law.com. The site has current legal news plus links to multiple legal resources. Access and read a few of the current news items.

Discussion Points

1. Think of a legal problem that you have encountered lately. What specific steps would you take to research the problem?
2. Which of the three approaches seems to be more beneficial and why?
3. Which of the three approaches to identifying key terms would you attempt first and why?

Chapter 8

Legal Research in the Information Age

Introduction

This chapter is designed to build on the information from Chapters 1 through 7 to help you navigate online legal research. The chapter provides you with an understanding of:

- the types of online information available,
- the value of questioning pieces of online information for reliability,
- the need to recognize nature of the authority, and
- the importance of weighing the significance of the authority.

Computer-Based Legal Research

Computer-based legal research is a method for conducting legal research using computers, smart phones, and other electronic devices to access **databases** of information using research software or the Internet.

> **Databases** A collection of information organized in such a way that a computer program can quickly select desired pieces of data; a type of electronic filing system.

Traditional databases are organized by fields, records, and files. A field is a single piece of information, a record is one set of fields, and a file is a collection of records. Technology offers legal researchers an alternative to the traditional print law library to locate statutes, case law, administrative regulations, secondary sources, and legal reference materials. Access to a wide variety of content, including business and economic journals, newspapers, and tax and financial data is also easily accessible. The increasing availability and comprehensiveness of online sources through free websites lower the access barriers to such information. Computer databases greatly improve the speed, currency, and cost-efficiency of conducting legal research.

When computer-assisted legal research was first developed in the 1970s, it borrowed Boolean searching techniques from the field of computer programming. A **Boolean search** looks for a particular term or group of terms in a specific relationship to one another. Boolean searches can include limits with respect to time; for example, court opinions are always dated, so the legal researcher can use a Boolean search to locate cases decided in a given year or in a range of years.

Boolean search Most database searching is based on the principles of Boolean logic. A Boolean search looks for a particular term or group of terms in a specific relationship to one another.

Many legal subscription database service providers, such as Westlaw® and LexisNexis®, discussed later in this chapter, also have a natural (plain) language search option as an alternative to Boolean searching. With the natural language approach, the search query is typed in common English in the form of a question or as a string of words without the use of Boolean connectors such as the words "and," "or," "near," or "not."

The Internet and Law Practice

The Internet has made a significant impact on the practice of law and the way in which the legal professional performs legal research. As more fully explained below, attorney competence includes knowledge of relevant technology.

Each state has its own lawyer ethics rules that are required to be followed by lawyers admitted to practice law in the state. Many states have lawyer ethics rules patterned on the American Bar Association's *Model Rules of Professional Conduct*. Rule 4-1.1 of The Florida Bar Rules of Professional Conduct (the Florida version of ABA Rule 1.1) states:

Rule 4-1.1 Competence

A lawyer must provide competent representation to a client. Competent representation requires the legal knowledge, skill, thoroughness, and preparation reasonably necessary for the representation.

The American Bar Association provides comments on each of the ethics rules; in 2012, the ABA adopted an amendment to Comment 8 to Rule 1.1. This comment obligates attorneys to be competent in relevant technology. States have the option of adopting ABA Comments. The Florida Bar adopted Comment 8 effective January 1, 2017. The Florida version of Comment 8 states:

Maintaining Competence

To maintain the requisite knowledge and skill, a lawyer should keep abreast of changes in the law and its practice, engage in continuing study and education, including an understanding of the benefits and risks associated with the use of technology, and comply with all continuing legal education requirements to which the lawyer is subject.

Lack of relevant technology came into play in *Emerald Coast Utilities Authority v. Bear Marcus Pointe, LLC*, 227 So. 3d 752 (Fla. Dist. Ct. App. 2017). In the case, the trial court ordered Emerald Coast Utilities Authority to pay attorneys' fees and sent the order to the attorney for Emerald Coast via email. According to the local newspaper, the amount ordered in attorneys fees was approximately $600,000. The attorney missed the arrival of the emailed order and failed to file an appeal within the requisite time period because of the configuration of the attorney's email system. The intermediate appellate court affirmed the trial court, refusing to find excusable neglect on the part of the appellant's attorney. *Id.* at 753. The appellate court reasoned: "the trial court could conclude that [the attorney for the appellant] made a conscious decision to use a defective email system without any safeguards or oversight in order to save money. Such a decision cannot constitute excusable neglect." *Id.* at 757. The appellate court added: "Counsel has a duty to have sufficient procedures and protocols in place to ensure timely notice of appealable orders. This includes use of an email spam filter with adequate safeguards and independent monitoring of the court's electronic docket." *Id.*

Online The condition of being connected to a network of computers or other devices. The term is frequently used to describe someone who is currently connected to the Internet.

The proliferation and ease of electronic research is accelerating the transition from print to **online**. The *American Bar Association Profile of the Legal Profession 2019* provides a snapshot of the attorney's use of technology. The typical attorney reports telecommuting forty times a year, with 72% telecommuting. Of attorneys working away from the office, 95% use smartphones, 81% use laptops, and 49% use tablets.

The *Profile* provides information on online legal research. An attorney spends a significant portion of time on legal research. The typical attorney spends up to 18% of the attorney's time conducting legal research. Much like the non-attorney researcher, the starting point for attorneys performing legal research includes 37% beginning with a general search engine such as Google. Other choices for the starting point for legal research include 31% using a fee-based database and 11% using a database accessed free through state bar membership. In completing legal research, 90% of the attorneys report using free online databases and 72% use fee-based databases. Of fee-based databases, the one used by 64% of attorneys is Westlaw, with 46% preferring it over other fee-based databases. When using free online databases, 19% of the attorneys report they use Cornell's Legal Information Institute as the one used most often, while 17% used each of Findlaw, Fastcase, and government websites most often. For many attorneys, legal research in print sources has not gone out of fashion, with 44% reporting that they regularly use print sources. A small percentage perform all legal research online, with 5% reporting that they never use print sources when performing legal research.

The shift from books to electronic legal research has been especially beneficial to small firms and solo practitioners with neither the budget nor space to house an extensive print library. In private law firms and corporate law departments, space to shelve rapidly expanding and expensive print collections is being converted to offices for attorneys and paralegals who generate revenue. For law firms with multiple locations and attorneys and staff who access information remotely, the law library is a laptop computer or mobile device with Internet access.

Online Availability of Legislative and Judicial Materials

No vocation is better suited to using the Internet as a research tool than the legal profession. Legal researchers are in the business of locating, retrieving, analyzing, organizing, and disseminating information, and the Internet is the single most comprehensive collection of data ever compiled. Information that once took hours, days, and even weeks to obtain can now be viewed, downloaded, and printed without ever leaving the office. The "virtual" aspect of the Internet provides access to a much broader collection of legal information than would be possible with traditional print resources.

RESEARCH TIP

No vocation is better suited to using the Internet as a research tool than the legal profession.

There are two kinds of Internet legal research sites:

1. free electronic databases; and
2. proprietary **fee-based** legal sites.

There are many examples of Internet resources that are virtually free, although some sites require online registration and a user password, and may offer a combination of free and fee-based services. Websites often provide the most current information available and may offer resources that cannot be found in any other format. A good example is the trend toward web-only electronic publishing of many law journals, legal newsletters, and law reviews. LexisNexis and Westlaw are the two most widely used subscription services used by legal researchers.

> **Fee-Based** Used to describe online database services that require users to pay a fee before being able to access the information; users are generally charged fees to search the database based on annual or monthly contracts, or on a pay-as-you-go "per transaction" basis.

Many online subscription services, such as LexisNexis and Westlaw, include extensive coverage of federal and state legislative information (e.g., bills, laws, statutes, legislative histories). Alternatively, most recent federal and state legislation is easily accessible free on the Internet. Archived coverage of older bills and laws varies depending on the jurisdiction and web resource. Refer to Chapter 5 for a discussion of legislative sources of the law.

Today, federal court case dockets, court rules, and the full-text of every United States Supreme Court decision from 1893 to the present is available free on the Internet. The same is true for the federal appellate courts. Additional information, such as court rules, trial calendars, and biographical data on federal judges and magistrates, is generally available from a court's website.

Internet coverage of court opinions, court rules of procedure, and court forms is fairly comprehensive at the state supreme and appellate court levels. Availability of case law on the Internet at the state court level varies by jurisdiction. Generally, expect to find the most comprehensive coverage at the highest state court levels (supreme and appellate courts), with scope and coverage decreasing as you move down the state judicial court structure (e.g., trial courts). At the trial court level, most courts have a web presence, but the scope and content of information provided varies by jurisdiction. Generally, court forms, administrative procedures, and local rules are available online. Access to official court case dockets and pleadings filed in a case, especially scanned document images, is not always available free on state court websites and must be obtained by contacting the respective court clerk's office. Refer to Chapter 4 for information on the judicial branch, court structure, and case law.

Computer-Based Legal Research: Pros and Cons

While legal instruction programs continue to teach an effective use of traditional print resources to locate primary and secondary law, the use of computers and the Internet for legal research has become an integral part of today's law practice and legal education. Refer to Chapter 1 of this text for a discussion of primary and secondary sources of the law. Computer-assisted legal research is not intended to replace manual research and is often best used in conjunction with print resources. As a result, attorneys and others performing legal research need to be proficient in both print and computerized legal research tools.

RESEARCH TIP

Use Online Legal Research

When cite checking a case, statute, or administrative law decision using a citator.

Online research is recommended when:

- currency is very critical.
- a comparable print source is unavailable.
- information is not published in paper format.
- researching a new and emerging area of law or current event.
- an online version is easier to use than its print counterpart.
- researching facts, persons, or entities that can be described with specificity.
- there is a narrow time limit to retrieve information.
- cite checking a case, statute, or administrative decision using a citator.

RESEARCH TIP

Use Manual Legal Research

When you know little or nothing about the area of law or subject you are researching.

Manual research is recommended when:

- researching older materials or historical data.
- dealing with a procedural or evidentiary question of law.
- you know little or nothing about the area of law or the subject you are researching.
- a print source is preferable to the online version.
- information is not available from a reliable online source.
- you found too much (or irrelevant) information using online resources.
- establishing general knowledge of an area of law.
- exploring complex concepts and legal theories.
- dealing with a concept that can be phrased in many different ways using multiple synonyms.
- search terms are too common, ambiguous, have alternate meanings, or have too many synonyms to effectively narrow your online search.

When deciding whether to use computer or manual research tools, consider what sources are readily available, what are the cost considerations, and your online searching skills. Computer-based legal research can be very effective when conducted by a legal professional skilled in database searching and when one is familiar with the area of law or subject being researched.

Evaluative Guidelines of Internet Resources for Accuracy and Timeliness

The term "fake news" has been widely used recently. Typically, the concept is based on the person or entity who authors the piece providing inaccurate information because sources were not checked thoroughly enough, the author misinterprets sources, the sources are not reliable, or the author relies on outdated sources. A similar problem can happen to the legal researcher who fails to double check the accuracy and timeliness of a source before relying on it. One can imagine the problem when a reader, perhaps a judge or a law firm partner, finds that the author of a legal document relied on a faulty Internet source. This mistake can have serious negative consequences for the legal researcher who failed to ascertain the currency of the source. A paramount goal for the legal researcher when evaluating any resource is to determine whether the information presented is accurate and timely. This is especially true with legal and government information, both print and online. One would think that information found at a government website would be trustworthy; however, the information may not have been updated recently.

Unlike print resources or fee-based databases, such as LexisNexis, Westlaw, and Bloomberg Law®, which go through a lengthy editorial and filtering process, information posted on the Internet is mostly unfiltered. This places the burden of evaluating the authority and reliability of web-based resources on the legal researcher. The legal researcher would do well to critically evaluate online databases using the eight criteria in the left-hand column of the chart below by asking the questions in the right-hand column of the chart.

Evaluative Criteria for Internet Resources

Criteria	Key Components
Authority of Source (Sponsorship)	• Who is the author? Is the author clearly identified? • What are the author's credentials? • Are the author and publisher the same entity? • Is there an organizational sponsor for the site? • Can you easily determine the author/publisher's reputation? • Can you easily contact the author with questions or comments? • Is the content author also the site webmaster? • Is the author and/or webmaster responsive to your questions?
Currency (Timeliness)	• Is the date of the last update or revision to the page content readily available? • Is the site current? • Is the information updated on a regular basis? • If the content is time sensitive, is it out of date? • Is the site archived?

Purpose and Usefulness	• Is the purpose (intent or focus) of the site clearly stated? • Is the intended audience easily determined from the main (home) page? • Does the site contain advertising (i.e., a marketing focus)? If so, does it distract from the resource content? • Is the information too old (or too new) for your needs? • Is the information copyrighted?
Scope and Content	• Is the scope (time span, coverage) of the information easily determined? • Is the content easy to understand (i.e., layman vs. expert level)? • Does the site include a variety of well-organized links? • Does the site include advertisements or promotional material? Is it excessive? • If so, does it distract from the information content? • Is there a political, cultural, or religious bias? • Are the sources for the content cited? • Does the author/sponsor's affiliation influence views presented on the site?
Objectivity and Balance	• Do you know the purpose of the site (news, personal, entertainment, informational, marketing, etc.)? • Is the author/publisher/sponsor's reason for publishing the information posted? • Is the information presented with a minimum of bias?
Accuracy and Reliability	• Is the information content accurate? • Does the site contain spelling or grammar errors? • Does the site contain technical errors? How do you know? • If the site contains links, are they reliable? • Does the site include any reviews or a rating system? • If so, are the reviewers' qualifications and/or rating criteria provided?
Technical Design	• Is the page well organized and easy to use? • Is the site design (colors, background, fonts, layout) appealing? • Does the page load reasonably fast? • If a highly graphic site, is there a text-only option? • Is the site searchable? • Is there an index, table of contents, and/or site map to help with navigation? • How well does the page print out? • Are any required plug-ins or "helper" applications clearly identified (with links to any necessary software downloads)?

Uniqueness	• Is the information available elsewhere in print, in digital form, or from another website? • If so, would using another resource be preferable?

Legal Analysis of Online Information

The legal researcher can be overwhelmed by the vast quantities of information available online. The legal researcher should keep in mind information presented in Chapters 1 through 7. This information should provide a framework for analyzing potentially relevant pieces of information obtained online as to its usefulness. Online legal research at first blush is deceptively similar to general online research that perhaps one has done frequently in the past. However, online legal research is much more complicated and sophisticated. Being an expert on general electronic research does not guarantee expertise in legal research. The online legal researcher who treats all relevant information found without considering the weight and significance of the information does so at the legal researcher's peril.

When performing print research, the legal researcher easily distinguishes among secondary authorities, cases from the jurisdiction, cases from outside the jurisdiction, statutes and other codified laws from the jurisdiction, and codified laws outside the jurisdiction. The legal researcher finds these different types of legal authorities in separate sets of law books and can ascertain the relationship, context, and hierarchy of the various legal authorities based on the organization of the print sources. Secondary authorities provide background information. Cases from the jurisdiction that are substantially related to the problem being researched are binding authority, while similar cases from outside the jurisdiction are persuasive authority. Relevant codified laws from the jurisdiction are binding authority, while similar codified laws from outside the jurisdiction are persuasive authority.

The legal researcher should perform the same analysis of the nature of legal information found online. The legal researcher must identify the type and importance of the legal information found online. Thus, the legal researcher can separate online information into the following categories:

Background authorities;
Binding case law;
Binding codified law; and
Persuasive authorities.

The legal researcher must keep in mind the category into which a particular piece of information falls when formulating an answer to a legal research question.

Copyright in a Digital Environment

Rapid changes in information technologies pose new issues for **copyright** law. Many primary sources are considered to be in the **public domain**; primary sources falling within the public domain are unprotected by copyright. However, commentary accompanying primary sources is typically protected by copyright. Thus, case syllabi and headnotes are copyright protected. Today, a digital file can be copied and instantaneously distributed worldwide through the Internet, potentially depriving the copyright holder of revenue from licensed sales. Existing United States copyright law is governed by the Copyright Law of the United States, contained in Title 17 of the *United States Code*. Since its enactment, there have been several key pieces of federal legislation passed by Congress in an attempt to address the omission of provisions covering copyright protection of electronic information, and Congress continues to address this oversight in an effort to provide adequate protections for both electronic publishers and consumers.

For now, publishers of original information on the Internet are provided the same copyright protections as those who publish in other mediums. You should not reproduce or reprint in any manner the complete, or a substantial portion of, text or graphics from a website without permission. More information on copyright is available on the United States Copyright Office website at https://www.copyright.gov.

Copyright A form of government protection provided by the laws of the United States (Title 17, *United States Code*) to the authors of "original works of authorship" including literary, dramatic, musical, artistic, and certain other intellectual works. This protection is available for both published and unpublished works. Copyrighted works are identified by the © symbol.

Public Domain The public domain comprises the body of all creative works and other knowledge (writings, artwork, music, inventions) in which no person or organization has any proprietary interest (usually represented by a copyright or patent).

Legal Research Starting Points and Web Search Tools

It is very important when researching legal and government information on the Internet that resources be reliable. The legal researcher can gauge that a website is reliable if it meets a majority of the evaluative criteria set forth in the chart above entitled "Evaluative Criteria for Internet Resources." This section highlights some of the most reliable websites and search tools designed to make locating free legal and government information on the Internet faster and more cost-effective. Refer to Chapters 1, 4, and 5 of the text for a discussion of primary sources of the law.

Cornell Law School Legal Information Institute
https://www.law.cornell.edu/

The Legal Information Institute (LII) is a free research and electronic publishing activity of the Cornell University Law School, providing electronic versions of core legal materials in numerous areas of the law.

Government Publishing Office
https://www.gpo.gov

The United States Government Publishing Office (GPO) provides free online access to official federal government publications and documents.

FindLaw for Legal Professionals
https://lp.findlaw.com/

A popular legal search engine and web directory is FindLaw for Legal Professionals, devoted exclusively to information for legal professionals, including links to primary law sources.

Google Scholar
https://scholar.google.com/

Google Scholar offers researchers the ability to search scholarly and professional information across many disciplines and sources, including law.

HG Legal Resources
https://www.hg.org/

A commercial web directory providing access to United States federal and state government websites and primary law sources, international law, and law-related organizations and bar associations.

Justia
https://www.justia.com/

Justia provides Internet users with free case law, codes, regulations, legal articles, and legal blog and twitter databases, as well as additional community resources.

Open Jurist
https://openjurist.org

Open Jurist is a resource providing free access to an extensive collection of federal case law.

Oyez
https://www.oyez.org/

Oyez provides information on the United States Supreme Court, including audio of oral arguments.

USAGov
https://www.usa.gov/

USAGov is the official gateway connecting all of the federal government's online resources with links to federal and state government webpages.

Federal Law Web Resources

This section highlights several websites used to locate free United States federal government information on the Internet, including federal agencies, federal legislative materials, federal courts, and judicial opinions.

Most United States federal district courts (civil and criminal) and bankruptcy courts provide access to case dockets and images of filed documents for a nominal cost through the subscription service PACER (discussed in detail later in this section). Selected opinions (usually high-profile cases), court rules, administrative forms, filing fees, and other information are generally available from a court's official website.

Congress.gov
https://www.congress.gov/

This website provides extensive coverage of federal legislative information, with free access to full-text documents.

Emory Law School Electronic Resources
https://www.law.emory.edu

From the main page, select "Library: Electronic Resources" to access a list of links to free Internet-based legal resources, arranged by subject areas.

Federal Agency Index
https://www.lib.lsu.edu

Hosted by the Louisiana State University (LSU) libraries and located under "Government Information: Federal" on the main library page, this is an extensive directory listing of federal government agencies on the Internet.

Federal Government Legal Resources
https://law.sc.edu

Maintained by the Law Library at the University of South Carolina School of Law, this is one of the most comprehensive web directories used to locate primary sources of the law from all branches of the federal government at Law Library ➡ Research ➡ Law Electronic Resources.

Regulations.gov
https://www.regulations.gov

One of the most user-friendly websites for locating federal administrative law materials is Regulations.gov at https://www.regulations.gov, the government site devoted to free public access to federal rulemaking.

United States Courts
https://www.uscourts.gov/

This website provides links to the home pages for the United States Supreme Court, the federal courts of appeal, and the federal district and bankruptcy courts.

RESEARCH TIP

Using PACER to Retrieve Court Case Dockets

PACER is a subscription service for the United States courts where subscribers can obtain case information and federal court dockets.

Court case dockets provide a complete index, entered by a court clerk, of all pleadings and papers filed in a case. Case dockets generally include the style of the case, case number, parties and their counsel, nature of the controversy or cause of action, and the judge assigned to the case. Public Access to Court Electronic Records, referred to by the acronym PACER (https://www.pacer.gov), is a subscription service of the United States courts, allowing registered users to obtain case information and court dockets from federal appellate, district, and bankruptcy courts. There is no fee to register for access to PACER, although a valid login and password issued by the PACER Service Center are required to access the system. Once logged in, users are billed a nominal per-page charge (currently 10¢) for retrieving and printing court dockets and other reports and for viewing and printing imaged documents. The $0.10 per-page charge is based on the number of pages that result from each search and each requested report or document.

State and Municipal Government Law Web Resources

State constitutions, statutes (also called codes or compiled laws), legislation (bills, amendments, resolutions), session laws (bills that have become law in a given year), and related materials promulgated by the legislative branch of all fifty states are readily available free on the Internet. Access to state and local administrative codes, registers, rules, and regulations published by state agencies is becoming more readily available on the web, but scope and coverage varies by jurisdiction.

A good place to begin any state law research is the State and Local Government Internet Directory at http://www.statelocalgov.net/, a convenient one-stop access to the official websites for state agencies and city and county government. The following portion of this section summarizes several websites providing free access to state and local government law and related legal resources on the Internet.

Law Library of Congress
http://www.loc.gov/law/

A product of the Law Library of Congress, this comprehensive web directory includes links to hundreds of state and local government resources, arranged alphabetically by state.

Municode
https://www.municode.com

Municode is a commercial subscription-based host for official city and county codes and ordinances and offers a free trial period.

National Center for State Courts
https://www.ncsc.org/

The National Center for State Courts (NCSC) is an independent, nonprofit organization and the website includes a comprehensive listing of state courts and law-related Internet sites.

National Conference of State Legislatures
https://www.ncsl.org/

The National Center for State Legislatures website provides access to current state and federal legislation and a comprehensive list of state documents including state statutes, constitutions, pending and passed legislation, and bill and statute summaries.

Commercial Online Legal Databases

LexisNexis, Westlaw, and Bloomberg Law are the leading online legal information providers, with comprehensive coverage of United States (federal and state) and international legal materials, news, and business information. LexisNexis, Westlaw, and Bloomberg Law have had a profound impact on the way law-related materials are distributed, offering timely, convenient access to federal and state primary and secondary law materials. Their non-legal databases provide access to national and regional newspapers, scholarly journals, company and financial data, and **public records**. Although Bloomberg Law is gaining in popularity, at the present time legal research using commercial online databases focuses more on LexisNexis and Westlaw.

> **Public Records** Documents or other written records required by law to be maintained by a governmental agency, filed with a court clerk, or recorded with a county comptroller's office; generally open to view by the public.

There are other web-based subscription services providing access to case law, federal and state statutes, legal forms, research guides, and other legal information. While the scope and content of these databases is substantially less than LexisNexis, Westlaw, or Bloomberg Law, they are generally less expensive, making them attractive alternatives for solo practitioners and small law firms. Examples include Casemaker at https://public.casemakerlegal.net/, FastCase at https://www.fastcase.com, LOISLaw at http://www.loislaw.com, the National Law Library at http://www.itislaw.com, and VersusLaw at http://www.versuslaw.com. Casemaker has a partnership with several state and local bar associations to provide its members with free access to primary legal research, such as court opinions and statutes.

LexisNexis went online nationally in 1973 and holds the distinction of being the oldest computer-assisted legal research information service provider. That same year, West Publishing Company began work on its own computer-assisted legal database—Westlaw. The earliest version of Westlaw was launched in 1975. Over the years, both products have undergone major redesigns and enhancements in an effort to keep pace with technology, competitors, and the demands of their users. Some ten years ago, Bloomberg Law made its appearance.

LexisNexis and Westlaw are similar in overall organization. Both LexisNexis and Westlaw divide database content into the following general content folders: all content, federal materials, state materials, and practice-specific materials. The federal materials content folder is divided into sub-folders for cases, statutes, and regulations. The state materials content folder is divided into sub-folders for cases, statutes, regulations, secondary sources, forms, and court documents. The first step a legal researcher should take in beginning a research session is to identify the applicable jurisdiction and select the corresponding folder and sub-folder.

One should have a thorough understanding of the applicable plan and pricing prior to beginning an online legal research session. The applicable subscription may be limited to certain databases, with additional charges for accessing documents outside the applicable subscription. If web access to a subscription database, such as Westlaw or LexisNexis, is based on transactional pricing, users are not charged per minute for reading retrieved data online—only for each new transaction (e.g., running a search, executing a new search, editing a search query, changing databases or files, linking to a new document, or printing a document). With hourly pricing database contracts, users pay set charges based on the time spent searching or browsing in a specific database. Pricing varies by vendor and database. If the database contract allows users to select from hourly or transactional pricing, rely on the "10-Minute Rule"—if online for ten minutes or less, use the hourly option; otherwise, select transactional. Transactional pricing should be avoided when running a search in multiple databases or editing your initial search query, but is recommended when reading results online before sending selected documents to print or download.

Summary

- Attorneys must embrace technology to keep abreast of the ever-expanding amount of legal information disseminated electronically worldwide.
- Familiarity with the operation and applications of computers in legal research and litigation support are necessary skills for persons pursuing a legal career.

- The Internet is fundamentally changing the way law firms are organized, how they relate to clients, the courts, information suppliers, and employees, and how attorneys and other legal professionals conduct legal research.
- Technology and the Internet are integral parts of today's law practice.
- There are two kinds of Internet legal research sites: proprietary legal sites, or pay sites, and free electronic databases. LexisNexis and Westlaw are the two most popular proprietary electronic subscription services used in law firms and corporate legal departments.
- The legal researcher needs to be proficient in both print and computerized legal research tools.
- Computer-assisted legal research is not intended to replace manual research and is often best used in conjunction with print resources.
- Online research is recommended when currency is critical, the online version is easier to use than its print counterpart, or when a comparable print source is unavailable.
- Unlike print products that go through a lengthy editorial and filtering process, information posted on the Internet is mostly unfiltered. This places the burden of evaluating the reliability of web-based resources on the legal researcher.
- An important goal when evaluating any information resource is to determine whether the information presented is accurate and timely. This is especially true with legal and government information, regardless of the format. The chart entitled "Evaluative Criteria for Internet Resources" contains a list of recommended criteria for evaluating web resources.
- Online information must undergo a legal analysis to determine its weight and significance.
- Publishers of original information on the Internet are provided the same copyright protection as those who publish in other mediums—print and electronic.
- Most federal trial courts—United States district courts (civil and criminal) and bankruptcy courts—provide access to case dockets and scanned images of filed documents for a nominal cost through the subscription service PACER.
- Availability of case law at the state court level varies by jurisdiction, with the most comprehensive coverage at the highest state court levels. Scope and coverage decreases as you move down the state judicial court structure.

Key Terms

Boolean search
copyright
database

fee-based
headnote
online
PACER
public domain
public records

Exercises

1. When conducting legal research on the Internet, what criteria are most important for evaluating an online website? Explain your answer.
2. When conducting legal research on the Internet, what criteria are most important for evaluating online information? Explain your answer.

Cyberlaw Exercises

1. The United States Supreme Court case, *Byrd v. United States*, was discussed in Chapter 4 of this text. Locate a copy of this 2018 published opinion using only free Internet resources. Which website did you use, and why?
2. Use the rulemaking information available on the official United States Courts site at https://www.uscourts.gov to locate the current version of the *Federal Rules of Civil Procedure*.
   a. What does Rule 11 cover?
   b. Which rule (and subsection) sets forth the prerequisites for filing a class-action lawsuit?
   c. Which United States constitutional amendment governs the right of a defendant to a jury trial?
   d. What rule did you use to answer question (c)?
3. Find and watch an online Westlaw tutorial at https://legal.thomsonreuters.com/en/support/westlaw. What did you find helpful about the tutorial?
4. Find and watch an online LexisNexis tutorial at http://www.lexisnexis.com/pdf/lexis-advance/quick-reference-guide.pdf. What did you find helpful about the tutorial?
5. Using the "Evaluative Criteria for Internet Resources" chart included in this chapter, evaluate the reliability of one of the websites listed in this chapter as a legal research starting point.
6. Using the "Evaluative Criteria for Internet Resources" chart included in this chapter, evaluate the reliability of one of the websites listed in this chapter as a federal law web resource.

7. Using the "Evaluative Criteria for Internet Resources" chart included in this chapter, evaluate the reliability of one of the websites listed in this chapter as a state and municipal government law web resource.

Discussion Points

1. How has technology changed the way legal research is conducted?
2. How would you respond to a supervising attorney who wants to cancel the firm's online subscriptions to LexisNexis and Westlaw now that "everything is free on the Internet"?
3. When is online computer-assisted legal research recommended overusing print materials? Discuss specific examples of legal information that can be located more cost-efficiently using free Internet resources.
4. What are the advantages of using Westlaw KeyCite or *Shepard's* online over a print citator?

Chapter 9

Introduction to Legal Writing

Introduction

The material in Chapters 9 and 10 introduces you to legal writing and fundamental writing skills. Chapter 9 briefly discusses many different types of legal documents and later chapters discuss some of the most important ones in detail — transmittal and client opinion letters and e-mail correspondence (Chapter 11), pleadings (Chapter 12), law office memos (Chapter 13), memoranda of law (Chapter 14), and appellate briefs (Chapter 15). Chapter 10 discusses fundamentals of writing that apply to all types of legal documents.

This chapter is designed to provide you with an understanding of:

- basic concepts to consider when writing legal documents
- elimination of mechanical errors
- types of legal writing
- ethical obligations relevant to legal writing

WRITING TIP

Keep Copies of Your Documents

You should keep copies of the documents you completed in your legal writing class. At some point you may be applying for a job and your potential employer may request a writing sample. You can use a document written for class as a writing sample; however, you need to make your potential employer aware that the document is based on a hypothetical situation, and there is no confidential client information being disclosed when you share the document. Another reason to retain copies of documents produced for class is that they can serve as samples should you be asked to write a similar document in the future. Prior to using a previously written document, revise the document to incorporate any feedback your professor provided.

The first portion of the chapter introduces you to concepts fundamental to legal writing such as the importance of legal writing to the law, writing as communication, a warning against communicating too much, and elimination of mechanical errors. The second portion of the chapter discusses relevant attorney ethics rules, with examples from recent cases in which attorneys were disciplined for violating ethics rules related to legal writing. The third portion of the chapter discusses legal documents designed to inform, persuade, and record information.

YOU BE THE JUDGE

Is it appropriate for a judge to "benchslap" an attorney in a written opinion?

Some see a written admonishment as presenting a teachable moment and others see it as bullying. What should a court do if an attorney, in a brief filed with the intermediate appellate court, refers to the trial judge as "attractive"?

To read how one court handled the incident, see *Briganti v. Chow*, 254 Cal. Rptr. 3d 909, 914-15 (Cal. Ct. App. 2019).

Importance of Good Legal Writing to the Law

Good legal writing is vitally important to those professionally involved with the law. Attorneys, judges, and paralegals are in the business of communicating, and their success depends in good measure on how well they write. As explained in this chapter, the goal of a legal document is to inform, to persuade, or to record information, depending on the document. Serious problems with meeting any of these goals may have negative consequences. For the judge, a poorly written opinion or order may result in reversal on appeal. For the attorney, errors in legal writing may result in the loss of a case, loss of a client, litigation of ambiguously written legal documents, legal malpractice lawsuits, or professional sanctions. An attorney's failure to abide by ethics rules or court rules may result in a mention in a court opinion. A paralegal may lose a job over a poorly written document.

Even if the client should win on the merits, a poorly written document can obscure the legal analysis needed for the judge to rule in the client's favor. On the other hand, in a close case a well-written document may persuade the decision-maker that the law is on your side and may lead to a decision in your favor.

Do not be intimidated by legal writing. Although certain things, such as citation form and the format for some legal documents, are peculiar to legal writing, legal writing in many ways is not that different from writing you have done in the past. You can think of learning legal writing as fine-tuning the writing skills you already have. In addition, just because you are doing legal writing does not mean that you leave your common sense behind. You will often have to pull on your own experiences in analyzing problems and in brainstorming to arrive at solutions.

YOU BE THE JUDGE

What caused a judge to include an 870-word catalogue of prior court decisions in a written opinion?

The plaintiff made a spoliation claim because the store failed to preserve evidence that a swing on display at the store allegedly contributed to a shopper's death. The judge wrote: "The Court believes that Wal-Mart's conduct and arguments are not sound, bordering on disingenuous, and sanctions are accordingly warranted." The judge introduced the lengthy catalogue of prior court decisions in stating: "The Court is also concerned by Wal-Mart's apparent track record of having spoliation sanctions imposed on it with alarming frequency and under strikingly similar circumstances."

To read the court's opinion, see *Rivera v. Sam's Club Humacao*, 386 F. Supp. 3d 188, 207, 208-09 (D.P.R. 2018).

Writing is not easy — not for good writers, nor even for professional writers. Your writing will improve with practice and a good grasp of the fundamentals. The following chapters are designed to give you practice in legal writing and to explain those fundamentals.

Writing as Communication

The purpose of all writing, including legal writing, is to communicate. For centuries, legal writing has been criticized for being wordy and hard to understand because of the use of Latin phrases and legal terms. Although not universally accepted, the trend today is to write legal documents in plain English. (Statutes in some states require consumer contracts to be written in plain English; the Plain Writing Act of 2010 requires documents of federal agencies to be in "plain writing.") Writing in plain English means writing so the document can easily be understood. It requires good organization and format combined with elimination of excess words, Latin phrases, and unnecessary legal terms. Practice plain English whenever possible.

One commonsense thing you have probably done in your past writing is to think of your audience. You need to do the same in legal writing. Before you start writing, determine who your audience will be. For a client letter, it will be the client. For a memorandum of law, it will be the judge and opposing counsel. For a contract, it will be the parties to the contract. These are the obvious answers. Then think who else you need to make sure understands what you have written. For example, documents designed to record information, such as deeds, contracts, and wills, may end up being litigated. A cautious writer of those types of documents will keep in mind the attorneys who might litigate and the judge who might interpret the meaning of those documents.

YOU BE THE JUDGE

How did the court sanction an attorney whose "comments made by respondent which are the subject matter of this disciplinary proceeding went beyond the bounds of zealous advocacy and were derogatory, undignified and inexcusable"?

The court suspended the attorney for three months.

To read the court's opinion, see *Matter of Giorgini*, 166 A.D.3d 43, 46, 48 (N.Y. App. Div. 2018).

While writing, ask yourself whether your intended (and perhaps your unintended) audience will understand what you have written. If you are writing to the client, will the client understand what you have written? If not, explain your message in simpler terms. Are the words you use too abstract or inexact? If so, use more specific words or explain yourself in more detail. Are any words too ambiguous? If so, try defining any ambiguous word.

WRITING TIP

Warning on Metadata

In the electronic age, you need to be wary of inadvertently communicating too much through metadata. Metadata is information invisible to the reader of a print document but visible or accessible in an electronic document. The information can include the client's name, the author's name, the name of the author's employer, history of the document, hidden text, comments, revisions to the document, and prior versions of the document. Depending on the circumstances, this information can be the type you do not want to disclose because it is confidential or sensitive. You may need to use a "scrubbing" program to remove metadata prior to transmission, and the hard drive of a computer that is being discarded should be scrubbed to remove confidential or sensitive information.

Your ultimate goal is to have your reader understand what you have written. If you think your reader will have trouble understanding what you have written, revise your document. Even if your reader will understand what you have written, can you add more transitional language or signposts to make the document easier to understand? (The terms transitional language and signposts are explained in Chapter 10.) One way to determine whether your writing is easy to understand is to read the document out loud. Revise the parts of the document that do not read well when being read out loud. Another way is to have someone unfamiliar with the subject matter read your document. Ask that person which passages were hard to understand and revise them.

A Warning against Communicating Too Much

You must be careful not to communicate too much. If you were playing poker, you would not let the other players see your hand. Just as you would guard your poker hand, an attorney representing the client's best interest will guard against certain information being disclosed and will be careful in the way information is presented. Care in word choice is extremely important because anything in writing may be used against the writer later. An attorney dealing with a confidential matter may refrain from putting the matter in writing for this reason. If the information is adverse to the client, it may be better to communicate the information orally rather than to put it in writing.

In contrast, a paper or digital trail is often useful as proof of exactly what was communicated. Certain information needs to be written so it can have legal effect now and be referred to later (contracts, wills, deeds, court documents). An attorney may put advice or information in writing in case there is any question later as to what the attorney communicated. A client opinion is often put in writing so the client can study it in detail and refer to it later; putting the advice in writing protects the attorney if the client tries to apply the advice to some future situation beyond the scope of the opinion letter. Certain information may be given to the opposing attorney in writing to furnish proof that the opposing attorney was aware of the information.

> **WRITING TIP**
>
> ***Warning on E-mail Correspondence***
>
> Much law practice these days is conducted via e-mail because of the ease of transmission. However, because of this ease of transmission, the attorney must be especially cautious prior to hitting the send button to double- and triple-check to whom the e-mail is being sent. Other tips on successfully navigating potential e-mail pitfalls are introduced in Chapter 10.

Elimination of Mechanical Errors

Communicating is the fun part of legal writing. The other necessary, though tedious, part is eliminating mechanical errors. You need to do your best to eliminate mechanical errors for two reasons. First, you want your reader to concentrate on your message and not be distracted by mechanical errors. Second, a reader who spots a number of mechanical errors will begin to wonder if the writer was sloppy. If the writer did not take the time to proof for typographical and spelling errors, perhaps the writer's sloppiness extended to legal research, too. You do not want to lose your credibility over a few easily eliminated mechanical errors.

In this author's experience, students typically have trouble with three categories of mechanical errors. You are already familiar with the first category of mechanical errors from your previous writing experience. These errors include problems with apostrophes, antecedents, spelling, run-on sentences, sentence fragments, parallel construction, and sequence of tenses. These are discussed below.

The second category of mechanical errors will be new to you if you have not had previous legal writing experience. This category includes problems with quotations and citations. The rules for quotations and citations are covered in the *Bluebook* and in Appendix C.

Third-category mechanical errors include errors other than second-category errors. This category includes errors such as quoting from a headnote or case syllabus, not using plain English, not giving a page reference to material from a primary or secondary source, not quoting exactly, plagiarizing, using contractions in more formal legal documents, using the word "I" in more formal legal documents, and elegant variation (using more than one word to refer to the same thing). These errors are discussed in Chapter 10.

Mechanical Errors

You know your own writing, and you probably know from past experience what types of mechanical errors give you problems. Keep in mind those types of mechanical errors that have given you problems in the past so you can eliminate them when editing and proofing your legal writing. If you have trouble spotting them yourself, ask a fellow student to help you proof your writing. Do the same for that student in return.

This section covers nine different mechanical errors. You have certainly been warned about a number of mechanical errors discussed in this section. They include incorrect use of apostrophes, sentence fragments, and run-on sentences. Problems with passive voice, parallel construction, and antecedents may be less familiar to you. Two other errors covered in this section are using excess words and changing tenses without reason.

Use of Apostrophes

Apostrophes have two uses. They tell your reader that something belongs to someone (possessive use) and that letters have been omitted (use in contractions). This section will deal primarily with the use of apostrophes in possessives because contractions are generally too informal to be used in legal writing. The following box contains rules for the use of apostrophes.

Rules for Use of Apostrophes in Possessives

1. To make a singular noun possessive, add an apostrophe and an "s." (If your noun already ends in an "s," refer to rule 2.)

Example: the car of the officer = the officer's car

2. To make a plural noun (or a singular noun ending in "s") possessive, add an apostrophe.

Example: the car of the officers = the officers' car

3. Do not, under pain of mortal embarrassment, use an apostrophe with a pronoun like "its" to make it possessive. "It's" means "it is."

Examples: the speed of it (when it refers to a car) = its speed
it is a speedy car = it's a speedy car

Sentence Fragments

A sentence fragment occurs when the writer attempts to write a sentence, but the thought is expressed incompletely. There are three common causes of sentence fragments. The first is omission of the verb; obviously, this can be easily corrected by supplying the verb. A second cause is beginning a sentence with a subordinating conjunction, such as "while" or "although," and not following the dependent clause with an independent clause. "While" and "although" tell the reader: "I'm going to tell you something less important before I tell you the really important information." The reader reads what he or she was cued to think was the less important information and is left hanging when the sentence does not supply the "important information" promised. This error can be corrected either by deleting the subordinating conjunction or adding the "important information." The third cause of sentence fragments is incorrect punctuation. This happens when the writer puts a period where a comma should be and capitalizes the next word in the sentence. Correct this error by putting the comma back in and changing the capital to lower case.

Run-On Sentences

Run-on sentences are usually caused by trying to pack too much information into a sentence. The solution is to break up the run-on sentence into several sentences. Another cause of run-on sentences is wording. The wording of a sentence may make the reader think the reader is reading a run-on sentence. The solution is to reword and reorganize the sentence so the reader can handle the information as a single sentence.

Another solution might be to place a semicolon between two sentences closely related in subject matter. You would replace the period at the end of the first sentence with a semicolon. The initial word in the second sentence should not be capitalized unless it is a proper noun or a word otherwise requiring capitalization.

Parallel Construction

When you write about a series of items or activities, you must use parallel construction. This means that the wording of each item or activity must be similar in grammatical structure. For example, the following sentence discusses three different activities:

> The officers stopped the car, were questioning the occupants, and searched the car trunk.

The sentence is an example of poor parallel construction because the verb tense in the middle of the sentence does not match the verb tense at the beginning and at the end of the sentence. "Stopped" and "searched" are simple past tense while "were questioning" is past progressive tense. "Stopped" and "searched" describe two completed actions and "were questioning" describes an action in progress. The parallel construction problem can be corrected by changing the second verb to match the tense of the other two verbs in the sentence:

> The officers stopped the car, questioned the occupants, and searched the car trunk.

Antecedents

To understand the problems that can arise with antecedents, look at the following example:

> The DEA agents made an investigative stop of the suspect and his companion because they fit the drug courier profile as well as other information they had obtained.

There are three pronouns in the sentence: "his," "they," and "they." Out of context the reader would not know what these pronouns refer to. The reader will determine to whom the pronoun refers by assuming that it refers to the last person or persons identified (the "antecedent"). In the example provided, "his" refers back to "suspect," "they" refers back to "the suspect and his companion," and "they" refers back to "the suspect and his companion." Do you see any problems? The problem is that the second "they" in the sentence should refer back to "the DEA agents" rather than to "the suspect and his companion." The way to correct this is to replace the second "they" with "the agents." Then the sentence would read:

> The DEA agents made an investigative stop of the suspect and his companion because they fit the drug courier profile as well as other information the agents had obtained.

The pronoun must agree in number with its antecedent. Many students have problems with antecedents and the word "court." Even though there are a number of judges making up the court, court is a singular noun. The proper pronoun to use with "court" would be "it" rather than "they."

Active versus Passive Voice

To understand active and passive voice, look at the following sentences:

> The officer returned the money to the driver.
> The money was returned to the driver by the officer.

The first sentence is written in active voice. "Officer" is the subject, "returned" is the verb, "money" is the object, and "driver" is the indirect object. The "officer" is also the person taking the action of "returning" the money. Sentences written in active voice have the "performer" as the subject of the sentence, with the subject preceding the verb. The second sentence is written in passive voice. In passive voice sentences, the object of the action (the thing or person performed on) comes first, then the verb, and then the "performer."

Active voice is preferable in legal writing because it makes the sentence more powerful and easier to understand. See whether this is true by reading the two sentences above. Which do you prefer? Passive voice is fine for those instances when you do not know or do not want to identify the performer. In the example provided, if you did not know who returned the money you could write:

The money was returned to the driver.

When you edit your writing and you find a sentence in passive voice, rewrite it in active voice. Even if the "performer" is not specifically identified in the sentence, you may be able to identify the performer by the context of the sentence.

WRITING TIP

Locating the Direct and Indirect Objects

- To find the direct object in a sentence, ask "what" or "who."
- To find the indirect object in a sentence, ask "to whom" or "for whom."

So, to find the direct object in the first sentence, "what" or "who" did the officer return? The officer returned the money; thus "money" is the direct object.

To find the indirect object, "to whom" or "for whom" did the officer return the money? The officer returned the money to the driver; thus "driver" is the indirect object.

Change in Tenses

Usually sentences and paragraphs are written in a single tense unless there is a reason for changing tenses. Your reader will be distracted from what you are trying to communicate if you change tenses in midstream without a reason. The following sentence contains a distracting change in tenses:

> DEA agents arrested Smith and Swindell and charged them with conspiracy to possess cocaine with intent to distribute. Defendants file motions to suppress. The motions were denied.

Why did the writer change from past tense ("arrested" and "charged"), to present tense ("file"), and back to past tense ("were denied")? Your reader may be wondering about that more than the writer's message. Keep your tenses consistent unless you have a reason for changing tenses.

Excess Words

Do not tire your reader by making the reader wade through excess words to understand your point. Your message will be easier to understand if you delete unnecessary wording. At the editing stage, look at each sentence again. Identify the meaning of the sentence and then attempt to eliminate any excess words.

The following sentences contain excess words. Review each sentence, identifying any excess words. Then compare your results with the suggested answers. The suggested answers are only suggestions. Your results may be better.

1. The United States Constitution provides for protection against unreasonable search and seizure.
2. The similarities among *Smith*, *Forfeiture*, and *Nelson* are almost identical.
3. The Court found that the factors taken together, as they were, amounted to reasonable suspicion.
4. In deciding the *Nelson* case, the court will have the difficult job of balancing Nelson's constitutional right against unreasonable search and seizure and society's interest in controlling drug trafficking on the nation's highways.
5. In regards to investigatory stops, there must be a balance between an individual's right to privacy and society's interest in being safe.

Suggested Answers

1. The United States Constitution prohibits unreasonable search and seizure.
2. *Smith*, *Forfeiture*, and *Nelson* are almost identical.
3. The Court found that the factors taken together amounted to reasonable suspicion.
4. In deciding *Nelson*, the court will have the difficult job of balancing Nelson's constitutional right against unreasonable search and seizure and society's interest in controlling drug trafficking on the nation's highways.
5. Investigatory stops must balance an individual's right to privacy and society's interest in enforcing the law.

Ethical Obligations

Ethics rules from various states have an impact on the information included in written documents. The attorney ethics rules of your state may be similar in wording or intent to those of other states or the American Bar Association *Model Rules of Professional Conduct*. With the prevalence of online communications and social media, much of the communication attorneys previously completed in print may now be completed online. Attorney ethics rules, discussed more thoroughly below, cover attorney online communications.

For example, on February 27, 2019, the Florida Supreme Court granted The Florida Bar petition to suspend Ashley Ann Krapacs from the practice of law. In its petition,

The Florida Bar alleged that attorney Krapacs had violated various ethics rules, including the Florida version of ethics rules 4.4 and 8.4, which are discussed below. According to The Florida Bar petition, Krapacs allegedly targeted two Florida attorneys "with a variety of vicious social media online continuous attacks," characterized as "terrorist legal tactics," because the two attorneys represented clients in litigation with certain of Krapacs' clients. Apparently, the attacks were so vicious that one of the two was forced to obtain a Temporary Injunction for Protection Against Stalking and the second filed a lawsuit against Krapacs for Libel, Slander, and Malicious Prosecution.

The writer should be mindful of the attorney ethics rules; a number of them concern the contents of written documents and the consequences for violating them can be very serious, as shown in the excerpts from disciplinary cases accompanying the rules. The following is a brief explanation of these ethics rules.

Competence in Writing

An attorney must have the legal knowledge and engage in necessary preparation to competently represent the client. Incompetence may mean inadequate legal research, poor writing skills, or both. A comment to Rule 1.1 of the American Bar Association *Model Rules of Professional Conduct* states in part, "To maintain the requisite knowledge and skill, a lawyer should keep abreast of changes in the law and its practice, including the benefits and risks associated with relevant technology."

In 2005, the Supreme Court of Kansas disbarred a fledgling attorney, Bret Landrith, for violating a number of Kansas ethics rules, including Rule 1.1. Rule 1.1 of the Kansas Rules of Professional Conduct generally describes the type of representation the lawyer must provide the client. Rule 1.1 of the Kansas Rules of Professional Conduct, patterned on Rule 1.1 of the American Bar Association's *Model Rules of Professional Conduct*, states:

Rule 1.1 Competence

A lawyer shall provide competent representation to a client. Competent representation requires the legal knowledge, skill, thoroughness, and preparation reasonably necessary for the representation.

Landrith's disciplinary case before the Supreme Court of Kansas was based on ethics complaints arising from two of the first four cases he handled in practice. In the first of the two cases, Landrith represented Price, the biological father whose parental rights had been terminated. The judge deciding the case stated:

> [W]e are compelled to express consternation over most of the issues framed and argued by the appellant in this appeal. We generally conclude that, with the exception of a legitimate appeal from the termination of parental rights, [Price] and his counsel [Landrith] have asserted claims that have no factual or legal ba-

> sis, often citing only conclusory and unsupported allegations of fact or without providing any supportive legal authority. We are inclined to admonish that vigorous advocacy certainly does not require or tolerate such conduct. We have diligently reviewed and addressed all claims asserted, but our objective discussion and determinations should not be viewed as condoning the assertion of such unsupported claims in our court.

In re Landrith, 124 P.3d 467, 472 (Kan. 2005).

In the second case, the federal magistrate stated:

> the undersigned wishes to express some words of caution to both plaintiff and Mr. Landrith. This case has been handled in an extremely haphazard manner. The court is mindful of and sympathetic to plaintiff's statement during the recent pretrial conference ... that no attorney other than Mr. Landrith was willing to take plaintiff's case and that plaintiff is therefore thankful for Mr. Landrith's loyalty. But plaintiff would be prudent to bear in mind that loyalty and competence are different qualities. Stated more directly, the court is deeply troubled by Mr. Landrith's apparent incompetence. The pleadings he has filed [citations omitted], and his non-responsive, rambling, ill-formed legal arguments during the pretrial conference, suggest that he is not conversant with even the most basic aspects of the Federal Rules of Civil Procedure. The court doubts that Mr. Landrith has any better grasp of the substantive law that applies to this case.
>
> Based on what transpired at the pretrial conference, plaintiff appears more articulate that Mr. Landrith. Plaintiff may be better served by representing himself without any attorney if indeed Mr. Landrith is the only attorney willing to take the case.

Id. at 475.

The time Landrith spent practicing before being disbarred was roughly equivalent to the three years a full-time student spends in law school. Landrith graduated from Washburn Law School in 2001 and passed the bar in 2002. Normally, one would imagine that a court would give an inexperienced attorney some leeway with ethical violations and perhaps impose suspension rather than disbarment; however, Landrith's actions in his three years of practice were examples of how not to practice law, causing havoc with his clients, the courts, and other attorneys. The following statement by the Supreme Court of Kansas indicates why the court meted out the ultimate sanction to an attorney so early in his career:

> [Landrith] violated his duty to his clients to provide competent representation. He violated his duty to refrain from interfering with the administration of justice. He violated his duty to the legal profession to maintain personal integrity. He violated these duties intentionally. As a result of his misconduct, [Landrith] caused actual injury to the adoptive parents of Baby C; to Vincent, their counsel;

> and to the legal system and the legal profession. [Landrith]'s behavior cost Baby C's adoptive parents more than $20,000. Vincent forgave the parents an additional $10,000 in attorney fees. In addition, the personal anxiety and stress experienced by the adoptive parents in their experience with the legal system was dramatically increased due to [Landrith]'s conduct.
>
> Furthermore, the legal system itself suffered injury as a result of [Landrith]'s misconduct. The Kansas Court of Appeals and the United States District Court for the District of Kansas wasted valuable resources because of [Landrith]'s absolute incompetence and interference with the administration of justice. Finally, the legal profession has been damaged by [Landrith]'s false accusations against members of the judiciary; attorneys; court personnel; and other state, county, and municipal employees.

Id. at 485.

Confidential Information

Rule 1.6 generally requires an attorney to safeguard confidential client information. However, an attorney may be required or permitted to disclose otherwise confidential client information as described in subsections (b), (c), and (d). Online communications present a potential pitfall for attorneys that may result in a violation of Rule 1.6. Many attorneys are not as technologically savvy as they should be and may inadvertently transmit electronic documents containing sensitive metadata or may send unencrypted e-mails containing confidential client information. Rule 1.6 provides:

Rule 1.6 Confidentiality of Information

(a) A lawyer shall not reveal information relating to representation of a client unless the client gives informed consent, the disclosure is impliedly authorized in order to carry out the representation, or the disclosure is permitted by subsection (b), (c), or (d).

(b) A lawyer shall reveal such information to the extent the lawyer reasonably believes necessary to prevent the client from committing a criminal or fraudulent act that the lawyer believes is likely to result in death or substantial bodily harm.

(c) A lawyer may reveal such information to the extent the lawyer reasonably believes necessary to:

  (1) Prevent the client from committing a criminal or fraudulent act that the lawyer believes is likely to result in substantial injury to the financial interest or property of another;

  (2) Prevent, mitigate or rectify the consequence of a client's criminal or fraudulent act in the commission of which the lawyer's services had been used;

  (3) Secure legal advice about the lawyer's compliance with these Rules;

  (4) Comply with other law or a court order.

(d) A lawyer may reveal such information to establish a claim or defense on behalf of the lawyer in a controversy between the lawyer and the client, to establish a defense to a criminal charge or civil claim against the lawyer based upon conduct in which the client was involved, or to respond to allegations in any proceeding concerning the lawyer's representation of the client.

In 2018, the Supreme Court of Ohio suspended attorneys Thomas Charles Holmes and Ashleigh Brie Kerr from the practice of law for six months for violating Rule 1.6, with the suspension stayed on the condition that the attorneys commit no further misconduct. As to the facts, the attorneys stipulated that they engaged in a two-year personal relationship while they had separate law practices and represented different public school districts. During the relationship, they sent each other e-mails in which they disclosed confidential client information and shared legal documents prepared for clients. In exchanging e-mail documents, Holmes prepared legal documents for Kerr. *Disciplinary Counsel v. Holmes*, 120 N.E.3d 820, 821 (Ohio 2018).

In *Holmes*, the court recognized that the attorneys' intentional pattern of misconduct extended over a two-year period, even after their law firms discovered their misconduct. The mitigating factors were that the attorneys had clean disciplinary records and the conduct caused their clients no harm. The court stayed the suspension because of the mitigating factors. *Id.* at 822.

Meritorious Claim

The attorney's argument for the client must have a legal basis and an attorney filing a frivolous claim is committing an ethics violation. For example, Rule 3.1 of the Louisiana Rules of Professional Conduct provides:

Rule 3.1. Meritorious Claims and Contentions

A lawyer shall not bring or defend a proceeding, or assert or controvert an issue therein, unless there is a basis in law and fact for doing so that is not frivolous, which includes a good faith argument for an extension, modification or reversal of existing law....

In 2019, the Supreme Court of Louisiana decided that Carol E. Parker should be suspended from the practice of law for six months, with all but thirty days deferred, for violating Rule 3.1 and other ethics rules. Parker had filed two motions to recuse judges in a pending case as a delaying tactic to give her additional time to prepare her case and knowing that a motion to recuse would stay the case progress until the motion could be heard. Parker filed the first motion to recuse against the judge assigned to decide the case and the second motion to recuse against the judge assigned to hear the first motion to recuse. One Justice dissented in part, joined by a second Justice, and stated:

> [T]he sanction imposed is too lenient. Respondent's egregious conduct, including filing baseless recusal motions engineered to unfairly and illegally delay the proceedings, cluttering the public record, and undoubtedly costing the opposing counsel time and expense, violated duties owed to her client, opposing counsel, the court, and the administration of justice.

In re Parker, 280 So.3d 569, 570–71, 575 (La. 2019).

Candor toward the Tribunal

The judge often relies on statements of the attorneys appearing in court, at least initially, and is understandably dismayed if an attorney intentionally misstates the law. In this role, the attorney functions as an officer of the court, charged with the duties of making true statements and disclosing to the judge adverse authority not disclosed by the opposing attorney. The bar association has the power to discipline an attorney for violating ethics rules, as does the judge.

For example, Rule 3.3 of the *Model Rules of Professional Conduct* provides:

Rule 3.3 Candor Toward the Tribunal

(a) A lawyer shall not knowingly:

(1) make a false statement of fact or law to a tribunal or fail to correct a false statement of material fact or law previously made to the tribunal by the lawyer;

(2) fail to disclose to the tribunal legal authority in the controlling jurisdiction known to the lawyer to be directly adverse to the position of the client and not disclosed by opposing counsel; or

(3) offer evidence that the lawyer knows to be false. If a lawyer, the lawyer's client, or a witness called by the lawyer, has offered material evidence and the lawyer comes to know of its falsity, the lawyer shall take reasonable remedial measures, including, if necessary, disclosure to the tribunal. A lawyer may refuse to offer evidence, other than the testimony of a defendant in a criminal matter, that the lawyer reasonably believes is false....

In 2019, the United States Court of Appeals for the Ninth Circuit indicated that the attorney representing the appellant might have included passages from documents, cases, or characterizations of legal arguments that appeared to differ from what the court had found. Therefore, the court ordered the attorney to address:

> Substitution of words in the language of an easement;
>
> Substitution of words in four cases;
>
> Characterization of the opposing party's argument on two separate pages of the attorney's opening brief; and

Characterizations of prior negotiations on two separate pages of the attorney's opening brief.

Swinomish Indian Tribal Community v. BNSF Railway Company, No. 18-35704, 2019 WL 3074050, at *1-3 (9th Cir. May 22, 2019). The court gave the attorney 28 days to respond to the court's order by letter brief and limited the response to 25 pages. The court permitted, but did not require, the appellee's attorney to respond to whatever the appellant's attorney filed. *Id.* at *3.

In December of 2019, the United States District Court for the District of Massachusetts cited to *Swinomish* in footnote 1 of its decision, stating:

> The Court is disturbed by the apparent lack of candor shown by counsel for Wellington and Argyle in citing *Taylor* for the unqualified proposition that "there is a presumption against the application of Massachusetts statutes outside the United States," Defs.' Mem. 4, while omitting without comment the preceding words of the *Taylor* Court that it was "[a]ssuming without deciding" the issue. Counsel for Wellington and Argyle repeats this misleading characterization (albeit in less egregious fashion) in its reply brief, stating that the *Taylor* Court "assumed that there is a presumption against extraterritorial application outside the United States." Defs.' Reply 2 (emphasis in original). Counsel's attempt to explain these misrepresentations, id. at 2 n.2, is wholly inadequate. The Court harbors serious concerns that these misleading descriptions of *Taylor*, which would be controlling authority had it said what counsel told the Court it said, amount to "a false statement of ... law to a tribunal." Model Rules of Prof'l Conduct r. 3.3(a)(1) (Am. Bar Ass'n 2019); *cf. Swinomish Indian Tribal Cmty.* v. *BNSF Ry. Co.*, ... (ordering counsel to show cause why misleading citations of law were candid representations). Counsel is therefore admonished to maintain scrupulous candor with this Court and all other tribunals.

Gigi Kai Zi Chan v. Wellington Management Company LLP, 2019 WL 6496930, at *1 n.1 (D. Mass. Dec. 3, 2019).

Fairness to Opposing Party and Counsel

The attorney must be fair to opponents by refraining from certain activities specified in the ethics rules.

Rule 3.4 of the Kansas Rules of Professional Responsibility, illustrated in the short discussion of *Landrith* below, contains this ethical requirement. Rule 3.4 provides:

Rule 3.4 Fairness to Opposing Party and Counsel

A lawyer shall not:

(a) unlawfully obstruct another party's access to evidence or unlawfully alter, destroy or conceal a document or other material having potential evidentiary value.

A lawyer shall not counsel or assist another person to do any such act;

(b) falsify evidence, counsel or assist a witness to testify falsely, or offer an inducement to a witness that is prohibited by law;

(c) knowingly disobey an obligation under the rules of a tribunal except for an open refusal based on an assertion that no valid obligation exists;

(d) in pretrial procedure, make a frivolous discovery request or fail to make reasonably diligent effort to comply with a legally proper discovery request by an opposing party;

(e) in trial, allude to any matter that the lawyer does not reasonably believe is relevant or that will not be supported by admissible evidence, assert personal knowledge of facts in issue except when testifying as a witness, or state a personal opinion as to the justness of a cause, the credibility of a witness, the culpability of a civil litigant or the guilt or innocence of an accused; or

(f) request a person other than a client to refrain from voluntarily giving relevant information to another party unless:

   (1) the person is a relative or an employee or other agent of a client; and

   (2) the lawyer reasonably believes that the person's interests will not be adversely affected by refraining from giving such information.

In *Landrith*, the 2005 Kansas case discussed above, the court found that Landrith violated Rule 3.4(c) by knowingly and intentionally failing to follow court rules. Landrith's almost complete failure to follow court rules prolonged the litigation, at considerable extra cost to the other party.

Impartiality and Decorum of the Tribunal

The attorney must not improperly influence the judge or others involved in a court case and must not disrupt the courtroom.

For example, Rule 3-503.5 of the Nebraska Rules of Professional Conduct, patterned on Rule 3.5 of the American Bar Association's *Model Rules of Professional Conduct*, spells out the requirement that the attorney preserve the impartiality and decorum of the courtroom. Rule 3-503.5 provides:

---

§ 3-503.5. Impartiality and Decorum of the Tribunal

(a) A lawyer shall not:

   (1) seek to influence a judge, juror, prospective juror or other official by means prohibited by law;

   (2) communicate ex parte with such a person during the proceeding unless authorized to do so by law or court order;

   (3) communicate with a juror or prospective juror after discharge of the jury if:

      (i) the communication is prohibited by law or court order;

      (ii) the juror has made known to the lawyer a desire not to communicate; or

(iii) the communication involves misrepresentation, coercion, duress or harassment; or

(4) engage in conduct intended to disrupt a tribunal.

(b) A lawyer shall reveal promptly to the court improper conduct by a venireperson or a juror, or by another toward a venireperson or a juror or a member of his or her family, of which the lawyer has knowledge.

In a 2017 case from the Nebraska Supreme Court, the court suspended William E. Gast from the practice of law for one year, followed by two years' probation for violating §§ 3-503.5, 3-508.2, and 3-508.4 of the Nebraska Rules of Professional Conduct. The disciplinary charges were based on communications that Gast sent to Douglas County District Court Judge Peter C. Bataillon and attorney Robert Craig. Craig was the opposing counsel in a long-running case, *State of Florida v. Countrywide Truck Insurance Agency*, originally filed in 1998, and Judge Bataillon was the judge when the case was finally decided. Gast had filed a motion to recuse Judge Bataillon alleging that there was a close personal relationship between Craig and Judge Bataillon that Judge Bataillon had failed to disclose; this allegation was also the subject matter of the communications that were the basis of the disciplinary charges against Gast. *State ex rel. Counsel for Discipline of Nebraska Supreme Court v. Gast*, 896 N.W.2d 583, 586–90 (Neb. 2017).

Mitigating factors were that Gast had no prior disciplinary record and his actions did not harm his client or the public. One of the chief aggravating factors was Gast's lack of remorse. The court stated:

> Gast seems to lack any appreciation of how serious his violations were and how baseless and inappropriate his attacks on the integrity of Judge Bataillon were. What is troubling is Gast's inability to see anything wrong with his conduct. His lack of remorse is a significant aggravating factor, as is the serious nature of his infractions.
>
> We also agree with the referee that during the hearing in this case, Gast engaged in unnecessary and inappropriate verbal attacks on the Counsel for Discipline. The Counsel for Discipline has an important job to do in our profession and has performed that job ably in this case.

Id. at 599.

Truthfulness in Statements to Others

In addition to making true statements to the judge, the attorney must make true statements to others and must disclose certain information.

The Court of Appeals of Maryland, the Maryland state court of last resort, disbarred attorney Andrew Steinberg for violating fourteen Maryland ethics rules, one of which was Rule 4.1 of the Maryland Lawyers' Rules of Professional Conduct. Rule 4.1 prohibits the attorney from making false statements and requires the attorney to disclose certain information.

Rule 4.1 provides:

Rule 4.1. Truthfulness in Statements to Others

(a) In the course of representing a client a lawyer shall not knowingly:
 (1) make a false statement of material fact or law to a third person; or
 (2) fail to disclose a material fact when disclosure is necessary to avoid assisting a criminal or fraudulent act by a client.

(b) The duties stated in this Rule apply even if compliance requires disclosure of information otherwise protected by Rule 1.6.

This violation occurred in connection with Steinberg's representation of Christine Serabian based on the following facts:

> [Rule] 4.1 prohibits a lawyer from making false statements of material fact to third persons. This includes misrepresentations made to clients, opposing counsel, or any other third person. Throughout his representation of Ms. Serabian, the record reveals several instances where [Steinberg] made misrepresentations. The most glaring is the misrepresentation made to Mr. Meng, [opposing counsel] regarding the 13 November deposition, when [Steinberg] told opposing counsel that his client refused to be deposed. Ms. Serabian testified at the *ex parte* hearing that she did not make such a statement. A second major misrepresentation followed Steinberg's discharge, when he informed both Ms. Serabian and Mr. Meng that he had filed a motion to withdraw. He had not filed and did not file the motion until months later.

Attorney Grievance Com'n of Maryland v. Steinberg, 910 A.2d 429, 446 (Md. 2006).

Respect for Rights of Third Persons

The attorney must respect others' rights by refraining from taking actions only to harass others.

In *Landrith*, the 2005 Kansas case discussed above, the court found that Landrith violated Rule 4.4 of the Kansas Rules of Professional Responsibility by falsely accusing public officials and others connected with his cases of improprieties. Rule 4.4 provides:

Rule 4.4 Respect for Rights of Third Persons

(a) In representing a client, a lawyer shall not use means that have no substantial purpose other than to embarrass, delay, or burden a third person, or use methods of obtaining evidence that violate the legal rights of such a person.

(b) A lawyer who receives a document relating to the representation of the lawyer's client and knows or reasonably should know that the document was inadvertently sent shall promptly notify the sender.

Landrith made some of these accusations after the disciplinary proceeding was filed against him:

> [Landrith] filed an 85-page document in this disciplinary proceeding, repeating accusations he had made in previous filings and adding new accusations. He accused now Justice Luckert and Judge Anderson of mismanaging funds; Justice Luckert of backdating an entry of appearance; the Shawnee County District Court staff of telling deliberate falsehoods; Chief Justice Kay McFarland and appellate clerk Green of obstructing justice and denying Price his constitutional rights; two other district judges of obstructing justice; Judge Pierron of deliberate and knowing falsehoods; and Vincent of altering records and other crimes, including operating "a baby export business." Additional accusations continued in this vein.
>
> [Landrith] also stated that, having "since researched and investigated the matter further," he was "now certain" that Vincent, Wichita attorney Martin Bauer, attorney Alan Hazlett, and Stanton Hazlett, were engaged "in a common enterprise to kidnap Kansas babies through deception and coercion and sell the infants in an illicit commerce that is entirely dependent upon the participation of some officials in the Kansas Judicial Branch."
>
> [Landrith] also made numerous accusations against specific named Topeka city officials and generally against the Topeka Police Department for harassing and stalking his clients and his witnesses. Both Price and Bolden, as well as several of [Landrith]'s witnesses, presented affidavits attesting to the conspiracy involved in these cases and to the fact that Topeka police began harassing and stalking them once [Landrith] instituted the appeals for Price and Bolden.

In re Landrith, 124 P.3d 467, 476 (Kan. 2005).

The Attorney's Responsibility Regarding Non-Attorney Assistants

The attorney must supervise non-attorney assistants, and the attorney is responsible for their actions. For example, Rule 5.3 of the Georgia Rules of Professional Conduct provides:

Rule 5.3. Responsibilities Regarding Nonlawyer Assistants

With respect to a nonlawyer employed or retained by or associated with a lawyer:

(a) a partner, and a lawyer who individually or together with other lawyers possesses managerial authority in a law firm, shall make reasonable efforts to ensure that the firm has in effect measures giving reasonable assurance that the person's conduct is compatible with the professional obligations of the lawyer;

(b) a lawyer having direct supervisory authority over the nonlawyer shall make reasonable efforts to ensure that the person's conduct is compatible with the professional obligations of the lawyer;

(c) a lawyer shall be responsible for conduct of such a person that would be a violation of the Georgia Rules of Professional Conduct if engaged in by a lawyer if:

  (1) the lawyer orders or, with the knowledge of the specific conduct, ratifies the conduct involved; or

  (2) the lawyer is a partner in the law firm in which the person is employed, or has direct supervisory authority over the person, and knows of the conduct at a time when its consequences can be avoided or mitigated but fails to take reasonable remedial action; and

(d) a lawyer shall not allow any person who has been suspended or disbarred and who maintains a presence in an office where the practice of law is conducted by the lawyer to:

  (1) represent himself or herself as a lawyer or person with similar status; or

  (2) provide any legal advice to the clients of the lawyer either in person, by telephone or in writing.

The maximum penalty for a violation of this Rule is disbarment.

In 2019, the Supreme Court of Georgia ordered a public reprimand in open court for Cheryl Joyce Braziel for her violation of Rule 5.3(a), (b), (c)(2) of the Georgia Rules of Professional Conduct. Attorney Braziel was looking for a document to support a client's Medicaid lien that would have allowed the client to recover certain hospital expenses under the uninsured motorist provision of the client's insurance policy. While traveling, Braziel called her assistant and asked the assistant to pull a Medicaid lien letter from another client's file. The assistant misunderstood Braziel's request because of a faulty telephone connection and the assistant prepared a new Medicaid lien letter patterned on the letter from the other client but incorporating the current client's information. Braziel admonished the assistant but failed to destroy the falsified letter, which made its way to the attorney for the hospital. *Matter of Braziel*, 830 S.E.2d 730, 731–32 (Ga. 2019).

Statements Concerning Judges

The attorney must treat the judge with respect and must refrain from making any statement impugning the judge's integrity. An attorney who disagrees with a judge's decision can take certain steps to question the wisdom of the decision, all the while staying within the bounds of the jurisdiction's ethics rules. The disappointed attorney might file a motion for the judge to vacate the decision and, if that fails, might appeal the decision.

The Supreme Court of Pennsylvania disbarred Eugene Wrona in 2006 for violating three ethics rules, one of which was Rule 8.2, while handling his first court case on his own. Rule 8.2 of the Pennsylvania Rules of Professional Conduct prohibits the attorney from making a false statement concerning a judge's integrity. Rule 8.2 provides:

Rule 8.2. Statements Concerning Judges and Other Adjudicatory Officers

(a) A lawyer shall not make a statement that the lawyer knows to be false or with reckless disregard as to its truth or falsity concerning the qualifications or integrity of a judge, adjudicatory officer or public legal officer, or of a candidate for election or appointment to judicial or legal office.

(b) A lawyer who is a candidate for judicial office shall comply with the applicable provisions of the Code of Judicial Conduct.

The court found that Wrona violated Rule 8.2 based on the following facts:

> [Wrona] represented [Farouk Z. Hamoui] in a child support matter in the Court of Common Pleas of Lehigh County. [Wrona] came to believe that original audiotapes of court proceedings in the case had been altered to omit statements or testimony and that the transcripts of those proceedings, prepared from the audiotapes, therefore did not accurately reflect all that had been said in the course of those proceedings. After filing unsuccessful motions to "correct the record" to have the allegedly omitted statements added to the record, [Wrona] began in late 2000 to accuse the presiding judge in the support case, Alan M. Black, and other court personnel in the Court of Common Pleas of Lehigh County of involvement or complicity in the criminal alteration of audiotapes of court proceedings. These accusations were made in a succession of letters, pleadings, court filings, affidavits and internet postings. These accusations continued to the time of [Wrona]'s filings and testimony in this disciplinary proceeding.

Office of Disciplinary Counsel v. Wrona, 908 A.2d 1281, 1288 (Pa. 2006).

The Pennsylvania Disciplinary Board investigated the case and recommended that Wrona be disbarred even though this was the first case that Wrona had handled on his own. The Supreme Court of Pennsylvania adopted the Board's recommendation, perhaps in part because it did not appear that Wrona could be rehabilitated.

> More than in any other case of this nature, [Wrona] is truly unfit to practice law. He exhibited no awareness of his responsibilities and obligations to the court. He was prepared to fight his case in any way possible, including making false and injurious accusations against a judge in a persistent manner through a number of years and to a variety of audiences. This "zealous" representation goes far beyond that contemplated by the ethical rules governing this profession. [Wrona] has not demonstrated that he possesses the qualities and character necessary to practice law in this Commonwealth. Despite his own opinion of his actions, the record is clear that [Wrona] did not serve his client well. It is the Board's opinion that the general public is well-served to have [Wrona] removed from the roll of active attorneys.

Id. at 1290.

Attorney Misconduct

Most sets of ethics rules contain something of a catchall rule that broadly prohibits the attorney from violating any of the ethics rules, doing anything dishonest, fraudulent, deceitful, or criminal, or doing anything prejudicial to the administration of justice. For example, Rule 8.4, the Kansas version of the above-described catchall rule, provides:

Rule 8.4 Misconduct

It is professional misconduct for a lawyer to:

(a) Violate or attempt to violate the rules of professional conduct, knowingly assist or induce another to do so, or do so through the acts of another;

(b) commit a criminal act that reflects adversely on the lawyer's honesty, trustworthiness or fitness as a lawyer in other respects;

(c) engage in conduct involving dishonesty, fraud, deceit or misrepresentation;

(d) engage in conduct that is prejudicial to the administration of justice;

(e) state or imply an ability to influence improperly a government agency or official;

(f) knowingly assist a judge or judicial officer in conduct that is a violation of applicable rules of judicial conduct or other law; or

(g) engage in any other conduct that adversely reflects on the lawyer's fitness to practice law.

In 2014, the Supreme Court of Kansas suspended attorney Eric Michael Gamble from the practice of law for six months, instead of the sixty-day suspension recommended by the hearing panel, for Gamble violating subsections (d) and (g) of Rule 8.4 of the Kansas Rules of Professional Conduct. At the time of the incident, Gamble was representing the biological father in parental-rights termination and adoption proceedings in which the father opposed the adoption. The unwed mother, who was unrepresented, had consented to the adoption and strongly expressed her desire not to revoke her consent. Gamble sent the mother a social media message that the hearing panel found to be unethical in that the message "contain[ed] false statements of fact regarding the adoptive parents" and "us[ed] emotionally manipulative language" in an attempt to have the mother revoke her consent to the adoption. *In re Gamble*, 338 P.3d 576, 577–80 (Kan. 2014).

The Supreme Court of Kansas imposed a lengthier suspension than that recommended by the hearing panel because:

> [Gamble's] conduct "amounted to emotional blackmail" of an unrepresented 18–year–old who was dealing with a process that was already "'emotionally exhausting.'" His "electronic message was designed to embarrass, burden, and create guilt in the mind of the biological mother." These "bullying tactics directly reflect on [Gamble's] fitness to practice law as an attorney."

Id. at 586.

Types of Legal Writing

The purposes of legal documents are to inform, to persuade, to record information, and to set forth the law to be followed. The balance of this chapter will discuss the different types of legal documents falling within the first three categories — documents designed to inform, persuade, or record information. Cases, statutes, court rules, and administrative rules and regulations are specialized types of legal writing that set forth the law. You are already somewhat familiar with the substance and format of these documents from your legal research course, although further discussion of them is beyond the scope of this book.

Legal Writing Designed to Inform

The purpose of a transmittal letter, a client letter, a letter to a third party, an opinion letter, and an office memo is to inform. (The client letter and the letter to a third party are also dealt with in the following section because another purpose of those documents is to persuade.) As the name suggests, a client letter is written to the client. The subject matter of a client letter may be anything from a simple cover letter explaining a document attached to the letter, to a letter containing basic facts, such as the time and date of a closing, to a letter answering a legal question the client has asked. The first two types of client letters are often referred to as *transmittal letters*. The purpose of a transmittal letter is to communicate basic information. The letter answering a legal question the client has asked is often referred to as a *client opinion letter*. It is the most complicated and takes care to write.

A client letter and a letter to a third party may be similar in subject matter but usually differ in treatment of that subject matter. The two letters will likely differ in substance and wording because there are certain things that would be discussed in confidence with the client that would not be revealed to a third party. Care in word choice is essential, because anything contained in a letter may be later used against the writer should the matter be litigated.

Be careful not to confuse a client opinion letter with an opinion letter. When attorneys refer to an *opinion letter*, they are usually referring to a formal letter written by an attorney in which the attorney gives the opinion that the transaction is legal. The attorney writing the opinion letter is the attorney for one of the parties to the transaction. For example, an opinion letter may be required in a loan closing, a securities offering, or a real estate closing. The opinion letter is usually addressed to one of the other parties to the transaction. Its status is that of a professional work product, and the party may sue the attorney who wrote the letter if the transaction does not result as the attorney has stated in the letter. This type of opinion letter is beyond the scope of this book, but the client opinion letter is discussed extensively in Chapter 11.

The *law office memo* is used to inform the reader of the results of legal research. The information in the law office memo is used by the client or the attorney to solve the problem researched. The office memo is discussed extensively in Chapter 13.

Legal Documents Designed to Persuade

As discussed below, a second purpose of the client letter and the letter to the third party is to persuade. This is also the purpose of a pleading, a memorandum of law, and an appellate brief. The job of the attorney is to represent the client's best interests by persuading others that the client's argument is the one that should be adopted.

Think for a moment how the client's argument is formulated. Imagine that two parties have a contract dispute. The attorneys have in front of them the same contract and, if they have competently performed their legal research, the same primary and secondary authority. Each attorney reviews the contract and any authority in the light most favorable to the client. Just as there are two sides to every story, there are at least two arguments that can be made on the same set of facts. Each attorney will argue that the contract interpretation most favorable to the client applies and distinguish away any interpretation not supporting the client's position. If the law seems to be contrary to the client's position, the attorney can argue for a change in the law or can argue that the law should not be enforced because it is unconscionable or unconstitutional.

The client letter, the letter to the third party, the pleading, the memorandum of law, and the appellate brief may all contain the same legal argument. The differences among them are the time frame in which each is used and the format. Take a closer look at each of these documents.

Although the client letter and the letter to the third party may be used at any time, they are often used as persuasive documents prior to or in anticipation of litigation. Both types of letters analyze a problem and argue persuasively that the problem should be resolved in a certain way. The letter to the third party may conclude by saying that the client will be forced to file a lawsuit if the third party does not resolve the problem as suggested in the letter. After the lawsuit has been filed, the letter to a third party may also be used as a persuasive document in pre-trial settlement negotiations.

Pleadings are formal statements by the parties to a lawsuit setting forth their claims or defenses. Examples of pleadings include a complaint, an answer, and a counterclaim. The format and basic substance of civil law pleadings are governed by the Federal Rules of Civil Procedure for federal courts and are governed by the state rules of civil procedure for state courts.

> **Pleadings** Formal statements by the parties to a lawsuit setting forth their claims or defenses. Sometimes, written motions and other court papers are called pleadings, but this is not strictly correct.

A **memorandum of law** is a written document containing the attorney's argument substantiated by relevant authority. At the trial level, an attorney may prepare, or may be required to prepare, a memorandum of law, the purpose of which is to persuade the judge to reach a particular decision. The format for the memorandum of law is discussed extensively in Chapter 14.

> **Memorandum of Law** A brief of law. It is often submitted to a judge in a case. The purpose of the memorandum of law is to support and argue the client's position in the lawsuit.

An **appellate brief** is a formal statement by a party submitted to the appellate court. When a case is appealed, each attorney submits a written statement to the appellate court to persuade the court of the correctness of the client's position. An appellate brief argues the facts of the case and the applicable law, supported by citations to authority. The format for the appellate brief is discussed extensively in Chapter 15.

> **Appellate Brief** Written statement submitted to an appellate court to persuade the court of the correctness of one's position. An appellate brief argues the facts of the case, supported by specific page references to the record, and the applicable law, supported by citations of authority.

Anyone writing persuasive documents must be mindful of ethics rules. The prior section of this chapter discusses ethical obligations associated with legal writing.

Legal Documents Designed to Record Information

The primary purpose of a deed, a contract, a will, a case brief, or a corporate document is to record information so the information can be reread later. These documents are sometimes referred to as planning documents because they set forth a plan of what will happen in the future so the parties can avoid litigation. Well-written planning documents should prevent rather than encourage litigation. Look at these planning documents.

A **deed** is a document by which real property or an interest in real property is transferred from one person to another. A deed contains the names of the parties, the date, the operative words transferring the property, and the property description. A warranty deed contains title covenants (promises made by the person transferring the property that certain things are true concerning the title to the property), whereas the quitclaim deed does not. Although there are similarities in the format for deeds from state to state, real property transactions are largely creatures of state law, so the law of the state in which the property is located should be consulted as to any particular format required.

Deed A document by which one person transfers the legal ownership of land to another person.

A **contract** is an agreement entered into to do or refrain from doing a particular thing. The contract must be supported by adequate consideration (that which is given in exchange for performance or the promise to perform), must involve an undertaking that is legal to perform, and must be based on mutuality of agreement and obligation between at least two competent parties.

Contract An agreement that affects or creates legal relationships between two or more persons. To be a contract, an agreement must involve: at least one promise, consideration (something of value promised or given), persons legally capable of making binding agreements, and a reasonable certainty about the meaning of the terms.

A **will** is an instrument by which a person makes a disposition of his or her property, to take effect after death. A will contains the name of the person making the will, the date, the operative words willing that person's property, and the property description. In contrast to a deed, a will is revocable during a person's lifetime. While there are similarities in the format for wills from state to state, wills are also largely creatures of state laws, so the law of the state in which the property is located should be consulted as to any particular format required.

Will A document in which a person tells how his or her property is to be handed out after death. If all the necessary formalities have been taken care of, the law will help carry out the wishes of the person making the will.

A **case brief** is an outline or summary of a published court opinion. One reason to brief a case is to understand the case better by identifying its important parts. The other reason to brief a case is to be able to refer to the case brief to refresh one's memory without having to read the whole case again. Although the format for a case brief varies from person to person, some standard parts of a case brief are the case citation, the facts, the history of the case, the issue(s), the holding(s), the reasoning, and the disposition.

Case Brief An outline or summary of a published court opinion.

Corporate documents are those documents necessary, usual, or permitted for the establishment and operation of a corporation. Because the corporation is a creature of statute, it comes into existence only upon complying with requirements of state statute. Generally, state statutes require articles of incorporation or a corporate charter to be filed with the secretary of state and an incorporation fee be paid. Other corporate documents include bylaws, rules, and minutes. The format for corporate documents is beyond the scope of this book.

Summary

- Good legal writing is vitally important to attorneys, judges, and paralegals.
- The trend is to write legal documents in plain English (writing so the document can be easily understood).
- Your ultimate goal is to have your reader understand what you have written.
- Legal writing also involves eliminating mechanical errors; this book tells you how to eliminate mechanical errors common to writing in general and how to avoid errors with quotations and citations, as well as to avoid mechanical errors peculiar to legal writing.
- When writing, one must be cognizant of ethics rules.
- Poor writing may violate attorney ethics rules and lead to disciplinary action.
- The purposes of legal documents are to inform, to persuade, to record information, and to set forth the law to be followed.
- This book devotes a chapter to the office memo (designed to inform) and a chapter to the memorandum of law (designed to persuade).
- The purpose of a transmittal letter is to communicate information, and the client opinion letter answers a client's legal questions.

- Pleadings are formal statements by the parties to a lawsuit setting forth their claims or defenses.
- The office memo is used to inform the reader of the results of legal research.
- A memorandum of law is a written document usually filed with the court that contains the attorney's argument substantiated by relevant authority.
- An appellate brief is a formal statement by a party submitted to the appellate court.

Key Terms

appellate brief
case brief
contract
deed
memorandum of law
pleadings
will

Exercises

1. Why is good legal writing important to the legal profession?
2. How does legal writing resemble or differ from writing you have done in the past?
3. Who are the audiences for the different types of legal writing referred to in the chapter?
4. Is it always a good idea for legal writing to communicate as much as possible?
5. Where could you look in this book to find out how to eliminate mechanical errors from legal writing?
6. Name types of legal writing not covered in depth in this book.
7. What is the purpose of these types of legal writing?

Discussion Points

1. Is it fair to suspend an attorney for poor writing skills?
2. What types of legal documents have you read? What are the purposes of those documents?
3. Which documents will you be writing as class assignments? Why do you think your professor has assigned those documents?

Cyberlaw Exercises

1. Bryan Garner is an authority on legal writing and his company's website is located at http://www.lawprose.org/. He has interviewed a number of judges concerning the importance of legal writing and linked the video interviews to the website. Go to the website and watch one or more videos that relate to elimination of mechanical errors, a topic covered in this chapter.
2. A number of interesting videos are posted on https://www.youtube.com/, some of which are related to legal writing. Go to the website and find a video providing legal writing tips. How do the legal writing tips add to your understanding of writing well? How do the tips differ from the legal writing advice provided in this chapter?
3. Information on grammar, style, and editing are accessible at https://www.law.cuny.edu/legal-writing/students/writing-sample/. Access that information from the website and compare it to the information included in this chapter.
4. Monthly plain language columns are accessible at https://www.michbar.org/generalinfo/plainenglish/home. Review several of the columns that are of interest to you.
5. The website https://abovethelaw.com features law-related news, including benchslaps that have been issued. Locate news on some of the benchslaps and analyze how they are related to information included in this chapter.
6. Several **You Be the Judge** boxes providing information on selected cases are included in this chapter. At the end of each box, there is a citation to the referenced case. Use a portion of the case citation, such as the case name or the volume number, abbreviation for the reporter, and the first page of the case to find the case online. Read the case to determine why it was included in this chapter.

Chapter 10

Fundamentals of Writing

Introduction

This chapter introduces you to certain writing fundamentals that apply to all types of legal writing. The writing process comprises three steps, from the prewriting stage, to writing, to editing and proofing. After covering the prewriting stage, the chapter discusses matters to keep in mind while writing, editing, and proofing. These include organization, topic sentences, transitional language, signposts, paragraphing, format, and avoiding errors peculiar to legal writing other than errors in quotations and short-form citations. These errors include quoting from a headnote or case syllabus, not using plain English, not giving a page reference to material from a primary or secondary source, not quoting exactly, plagiarizing, using contractions in more formal legal documents, using the word "I" in more formal legal documents, and elegant variation (using more than one word to refer to the same thing).

Writing Process

The writing process should have three steps:

1. prewriting;
2. writing; and
3. editing and proofing.

The novice writer plunges into writing without going through the prewriting step and may not spend enough time on the third step. Some of you will be slow to be convinced, and some of you will never be convinced that all three steps are necessary. If your professor does not force you to proceed through all three steps by requiring you to turn in an outline, a written document, and a revision of the written document, try completing the three steps on your own. You will be pleased with the results.

Prewriting

Prewriting involves performing any necessary research, formulating a writing "plan," and outlining. Do not skimp on any of these activities. Your "research strategy" should include good note-taking and case briefing as you go along. You may spend a little more time doing research, but a little extra time on research should shorten the time you spend formulating your writing plan and outlining.

From time to time you may need to pause and collect your thoughts. Mentally review what you have accomplished, and think about the direction you are heading. You need to pay attention to detail yet not lose sight of the big picture.

The research required to write letters, deeds, contracts, and wills may be limited to gathering facts and identifying the information to be included. In writing an office memo, a memorandum of law, or an appellate brief, your research usually will be more extensive than for other types of documents. Performing research may mean various things, from gathering facts by reviewing documents and interviewing people to doing legal research in the law library. Research needs to have been completed as fully as possible before you start writing, or you may find yourself backtracking later.

As you do your research, you should start to decide what your writing plan will be. In other words, how will you organize your facts and the results of your research to make sense to your reader? As you look at the information in front of you, you will probably identify a number of ideas you want to communicate to your reader. In formulating your plan, you must decide on a scheme for arranging these ideas and developing them for the reader.

Your plan is somewhat dictated by the type of document you are writing. Research the standard format for the type of document you are writing. For certain documents, such as deeds and wills, you must follow governing statutes, and you will probably want to follow the organizational format customarily used in your area, but do not depend entirely on the recognized format. Make any organizational changes necessary to make sure your reader understands what you have written. The format for court documents may be dictated by court rule. Even though you must follow the overall organizational framework set out in the rule, make sure you have good internal organization.

If you are writing an office memo, a memorandum of law, or an appellate brief, prewriting should involve developing a thesis. Think about your facts in relation to the results of your research. Then try to step back and look at the "whole picture." If you think about it long enough, you will find a central idea that runs through your facts and research material. This is your thesis. Think of your thesis as the border to a puzzle. Once you have established your thesis, use it as a framework and fit your facts and research material within it.

Try to develop a "flowchart" or "road map" as part of your writing plan for your office memo, memorandum of law, or appellate brief. A flowchart should help you understand the legal analysis applicable to the legal problem you are researching. If you can complete a flowchart, you are probably on the right track with your legal analysis. Frequent reference to your flowchart will help you write your outline. If you cannot construct a flowchart because you cannot make sense of your research, you either need to spend more time to "fit the pieces" together or you need to do more research.

Once you have completed your flowchart, start writing an outline. The outline can be as brief or as detailed as you like. An outline that does not contain very much detail will not take as long to write but will be less helpful in the writing process. An outline that is too skeletal is not very useful. You need to include enough information in your outline to organize yourself before you start writing and determine whether your legal analysis flows. A more detailed outline will take more time to write but should speed up the writing process and cut down on revision time.

If your writing plan is not clear, your writing will be unclear. If your writing is unclear, your reader will end up doing the organization that should have been your job. A reader saddled with this task will not enjoy reading what you have written and may become very frustrated in the attempt.

Writing

After you have completed the prewriting step, you can progress to writing your document. This section explains how you can help your reader understand your document by organizing it well.

Overall Organization and Organization within Sections

Good organization is essential for readability. Depending on the complexity of your document, you may have various levels of organization. Your document must be well organized at each level. The first impression is important because this impression, whether good or bad, may color the reader's impression of the balance of the document. Follow any formatting rules for the document, including appropriate margins, typeface, color of printing, binding, and page numbering. Section headings provide overall organization. Then, you must organize your writing within each section, and you must organize what you say within each paragraph and within each sentence.

Keep the reader in mind when formulating a plan for overall organization. Development of and exposition of a thesis, theme, or theory ties the document together, helps you with organization, and provides a framework to help the reader understand the document proposed. Provide basic or background information, such as the standard of review, at the outset and then organize issues with the most important, such as a dispositive issue, preceding less important ones. It is your job, not the reader's, to organize the document to make it the most reader-friendly possible. Main points or conclusions should be included early in the document, so as not to be overlooked.

The section containing the facts must be carefully crafted to include the essential ones, stated accurately, and omit the others. Do not hide material unfavorable facts, but there is no need to highlight them; the writer can state them simply and move on. The writer should tell the story from the client's perspective, such that the story comes alive for the reader.

WRITING TIP

Keep Your Intended Reader in Mind in Organizing Your Document

It is important to keep your intended reader in mind when organizing your document. Spend some time determining what is important for your intended reader to know and provide that information as early as possible in the document. A well-organized document is more professional and may produce a better result than one in which the reader is tasked with combing the document to locate relevant information. For example, when an appellate court reviews the trial court grant of a motion for summary judgment to the defendants on a number of counts de novo, the appellate court must determine whether there is a genuine issue of material fact for each count. The plaintiff/appellant can help the appellate court by separately discussing the law and the evidence showing disputed material facts for each count toward the beginning of the appellate brief.

A discussion or reasoning portion of a legal document should contain an introduction, explain the relevant law, and apply the law to the facts. Be careful to accurately state the law and provide a logical application of the law to the facts. Use quotations where appropriate. but do not let long block quotes consume the document. Accurately cite to authority, including a pinpoint page reference, and explain the relevance of cited material. The conclusion may be part of the body of the document or may be in a separate section.

In explaining the relevant law and applying it to the facts, the body of the discussion should develop the idea introduced in the introduction and lead up to the conclusion. Develop the idea step by step so you do not lose your reader along the way, explaining even the most obvious steps. Just because you can see the connection between steps two and three does not necessarily mean that your reader will be able to unless the connection is spelled out. The development can be logical or chronological depending on the nature of the discussion.

Organization of an Office Memo

To understand what was explained in the preceding section, look at the various levels of organization of an office memo. The office memo is used to record the law found as a result of the research, to explain how the researcher analyzed the law and applied it to the facts, and to propose a solution to the problem. The overall organizational framework is set by the typical office memo format: facts, issue(s), answer(s), reasoning, and conclusion. This is the first level of organization.

The key to the second level of organization is your formulation of the issue(s). An issue must be well organized to contain as much information as possible while still being readable. If you have more than one issue, you need to carefully consider the order in which you will present the issues. The way you formulate your issue(s) dictates everything else in the office memo. Look at your issue(s) and decide what facts are relevant or significant to the issue(s). These are the only ones that should be included in the facts section. Your answer(s), as the terms imply, are simply answer(s) to your issue(s) and should mirror your issues. The reasoning section flows from the issue(s) because it tells the reader how you got from your issue to your answer. The conclusion is a more detailed statement of your answer(s).

The reasoning section should contain a thesis paragraph that serves as an introduction, an explanation of relevant law, and an application of the law to the facts. If you have more than one issue, you may want to follow the thesis paragraph with an explanation of the law that is applicable to all the issues first and then discuss each issue separately. For example, a section entitled "reasoning" may begin with a thesis paragraph that serves as an overall introduction and may continue with a statement of the law relevant to all issues. The balance of the reasoning portion of the office memo is broken up into the same number of sections as there are issues. You may visually break up the reasoning portion of the office memo for your reader by using headings for each issue such as "reasoning for issue one" and so on. More levels of organization may be needed if you have sub-issues within issues.

Organization at the Paragraph Level

The final levels of organization are at the paragraph and sentence levels. You will lose your reader if your overall organization and the organization within the various sections is good but your paragraphs and sentences are not well organized. This section discusses organization at the paragraph level. The following section discusses organization at the sentence level.

Do you remember your English teacher talking to you about topic sentences? Most paragraphs need topic sentences. (A paragraph reciting a string of chronological events might get along without a topic sentence.) A topic sentence summarizes the topic being discussed in the paragraph. The rest of the paragraph should develop and expand on the idea introduced in the topic sentence. Because the reader will best remember the first and last sentences of the paragraph, the topic sentence is usually, but not always, in one of those two positions.

Look at the preceding paragraph. The first sentence in the paragraph caught the reader's attention. The second sentence is the "topic sentence" and contains the main idea of the paragraph: paragraphs usually need topic sentences. The rest of the paragraph expands on the idea contained in the topic sentence. The rest of the paragraph gives an exception to the use of topic sentences, explains what a topic sentence does, explains how the rest of the paragraph relates to the topic sentence, and gives the typical location of the topic sentence.

If your discussion sounds disjointed, check your paragraph structure. Do you deal with a single idea in each paragraph? If you have more than one idea in a paragraph, split up the paragraph so you give each idea its own paragraph. Do you have a topic sentence? If not, write a sentence that contains the essence of the rest of your paragraph. Did you develop the idea introduced in the topic sentence? If not, decide what else you can say about the idea and add it to the paragraph. If you cannot develop a topic sentence, perhaps the idea needs to be part of another paragraph or you need to eliminate it.

Word Order within Sentences

Although readers may enjoy a challenge, do not challenge your reader too often with unconventional word order. Most sentences should follow the conventional structure for English sentences: subject, verb, and object (if any). Your reader should easily understand your sentences without having to hunt for the subject and the verb. Help your reader by keeping the subject, verb, and object close together and near the beginning of the sentence. Every now and then you may want to vary the conventional subject/verb/object structure to emphasize certain words. Because your reader will remember the beginning and end of your sentence better than the middle of the sentence, put the information you want to emphasize either at the beginning or at the end of the sentence.

The following are "mixed-up" sentences from student writing. Read them, determine which word order rules have been broken, and decide how the sentences can be corrected.

1. The United States Supreme Court in two cases had to determine whether an investigatory stop was based on reasonable suspicion.
2. Trooper Vogel testified that the appellants, based on a reasonable suspicion created by a drug courier profile, were hauling drugs.
3. In *Smith*, relying on a drug courier profile, Trooper Vogel stopped a car.

Here are suggested corrections to these sentences. They are only suggestions. You may have come up with better answers.

1. In two cases, the United States Supreme Court had to determine whether an investigatory stop was based on reasonable suspicion.
2. Trooper Vogel testified he had a reasonable suspicion that the appellants were hauling drugs and that his suspicion was based on the drug courier profile.
3. In *Smith*, Trooper Vogel stopped the car in reliance on the drug courier profile.

Transitional Language and Signposts

Be kind to your reader by using transitional language and signposts as frequently as possible. Think of the textbooks you have been assigned to read this semester. You probably dread trying to read one or two of them, and you may actually enjoy reading some of them. Even the most impenetrable subject matter can be made less so through the use of transitional language and signposts. On the other hand, easier subject matter can seem just as impenetrable without transitional language and signposts. After reading this section, it would be interesting for you to take a look at your textbooks and analyze the authors' writing style for use of transitional language and signposts.

Transitional language provides a "transition" or link between what you have just written and what you are going to write about.

> **Transitional Language** Provides a "transition" or link between what you have just written and what you are going to write about.

For example, the first sentence in this chapter provides a subject matter transition from Chapter 9 to Chapter 10 by explaining that Chapter 10 introduces the reader to the fundamentals of legal writing. Although transitional language introducing a new topic can be used anyplace in the paragraph, it is usually used at the beginning of the paragraph (as it was in the example) or at the end of the paragraph. Use of transitional language at the end of a paragraph allows the writer to introduce the topic of the next paragraph. The writer can then emphasize the new topic by discussing it again immediately in the first sentence of the new paragraph. You can also use transitional words like "although," "even if," "after," "before," and "because" to show the reader the relationship between sentences in a paragraph.

Signposts are words or phrases that point the reader in the right direction and provide a framework for understanding the document.

The signposts in the first paragraph of this chapter are the words "the first part of the chapter," "the second part of the chapter," and "the third part of the chapter." They make it easier for the reader to understand the chapter by preparing the reader to expect the chapter to discuss three main topics: the writing process, writing structure, and certain kinds of mechanical errors. Signposts can also highlight main points in a discussion. For example, the words "the main issue before the court" tells the reader that that will be the central focus of the discussion and provides a context for the rest of the discussion.

> **Signposts** Words or phrases in a document that point the reader in the right direction and provide a framework for understanding the document.

Paragraphing and Tabulation

To paragraph or not to paragraph: that is the question. There is no one right paragraph length. Some paragraphs may be one sentence long while other paragraphs may contain a number of sentences. One gauge of correct paragraph length is the subject matter of the paragraph. Each paragraph should discuss one main idea. If a paragraph is long and sounds disjointed, it may be because you are trying to discuss more than one idea in a single paragraph. Break up the paragraph into shorter paragraphs.

Another gauge of correct paragraph length is readability. Each page of print should contain a minimum of two or three paragraphs. A reader faced with a long, solid block of print will retain less of what you said than if the same material were broken up into a number of shorter paragraphs. A page containing a series of one- and two-sentence paragraphs is just as bad. If you find yourself with a series of one- and two-sentence paragraphs, see whether your text is easier to read if you combine several of the paragraphs.

Tabulation can be used very effectively in legal writing where you have a list of items or activities. When you tabulate, you place each item or activity on a separate line.

> **Tabulation** A format that enhances readability when the writer wants to convey information concerning a number of items or activities, with the writer listing each item or activity on a separate line.

Each line, except for the last and next to the last lines, ends with a semicolon. The next to the last line ends with a semicolon and the word "and" or "or." The last line ends with a period.

The first page of this chapter contains the following example of tabulation:

The writing process should have three steps:

1. prewriting;
2. writing; and
3. editing and proofing.

Compare the tabulated material with the following:

The writing process should have three steps: prewriting, writing, and editing and proofing.

The only difference between the two sentences is tabulation. Tabulation makes the sentence much easier to read and understand.

Graphics

Usually, the writer thinks of conveying ideas to the reader through words alone; however, a complicated sequence of events or a complex argument might be easier for the reader to understand through the use of graphics. Graphics might include timelines, flowcharts, diagrams, and tables. The reader may understand the convoluted procedural history of a case better through the inclusion of a timeline.

An explanation of the consequences of pursuing each of several alternatives may be better explained through the use of a flowchart. The differences and similarities between two cases may be more easily grasped by including them in a table or spreadsheet.

Mechanical Errors

Legal writing students typically have trouble with three categories of mechanical errors. The first and second categories of mechanical errors are discussed in Chapter 9. This section discusses a third category of mechanical errors—errors that are peculiar to legal writing other than errors in quotations and short-form citations. This section will discuss the following errors:

1. quoting from a headnote or case syllabus;
2. not italicizing a case name;
3. not using plain English;
4. not giving a page reference to material from a primary or secondary source;
5. not quoting exactly;
6. plagiarizing;
7. using contractions in more formal legal documents;
8. using the word "I" in more formal legal documents; and
9. using elegant variation.

Quoting from a Headnote or Case Syllabus

The error that will most quickly identify you as a novice legal writer is quoting from a headnote or case syllabus. The reason that you should not use any material other than the opinion itself, such as the headnotes and case syllabus, is that the material other than the opinion is not the law. It is appropriate to refer to or quote from the opinion because it is the law. The publisher or the official reporter for the court prepared the material in the reporter other than the opinion itself. The non-opinion material is usually, but not always, accurate. It may on occasion contain outright errors. Because the non-opinion material is a summary of material from the case, you may have a different impression of what the law is from reading the non-opinion material than from reading the opinion itself. In addition, the summary may not refer to a part of the case important for your research. The only way to find that material is to read the entire case.

Not Italicizing a Case Name

A person's last name

1) may be part of a case name; or
2) may be used when referring to a person as an individual.

In legal writing, a case name is italicized in the text of a document. In contrast, when the writer is referencing the individual, the person's last name is not italicized. The distinction is important because not italicizing a case name or italicizing a reference to the individual will give the reader the impression that the writer is not knowledgeable about the law.

Not Using Plain English

Writing in plain English means writing so the reader can understand the document easily. An easily understood document requires good organization and format combined with the elimination of excess words, Latin phrases, and unnecessary legal terms and jargon. Organization and format were discussed in an earlier section of this chapter.

Some attorneys seem to think that the more Latin phrases and legal terms they include, the better their writing will be, but the contrary is usually true. Although there are some Latin terms (like "*res ipsa loquitur*") whose meanings are clear to attorneys but are hard to translate into English, use of most Latin terms is unnecessary and may alienate your reader. *Res ipsa loquitur* is a Latin term meaning "the thing speaks for itself"; it is a rebuttable presumption (a conclusion that can be changed if contrary evidence is introduced) that a person is negligent if the thing causing an accident was in his or her control only, and if that type of accident does not usually happen without negligence. Eliminate all Latin terms if possible. Where you have to use a Latin term like *res ipsa loquitur*, do so with caution. If there is any question whether your reader will understand the term, define it. You can often slip in a definition in a parenthetical phrase within the sentence without insulting your reader's intelligence.

The same thing holds true with legal terms. Eliminate any legal terms or words you think your reader will have trouble understanding and replace them with words your reader will understand. For example, attorneys often speak of "drafting" a document and the client "executing" it. The client may be confused if the attorney's cover letter refers to the document the attorney has "drafted" and asks the client to "execute" the document. For the legally unsophisticated client, it would be preferable to refer to the document the attorney has "written" and ask the client to "sign" it.

Omitting a Page Reference to Material from a Primary or Secondary Source

Most students know they need to give a page reference when they quote from a case so the reader can quickly find and read the passage in the case. In legal writing, you must also give a page reference when you are referring to specific material from a case even if you are not quoting the material. For example, you may give the facts from the case in your own words. As a courtesy to your reader, you need to tell your reader the page or pages on which the facts are located so the reader can refer to that part of the case without reading the entire opinion. A reference to a specific page is sometimes referred to as a **pinpoint citation** because the citation pinpoints or specifically locates the information for the reader.

> **Pinpoint Citation** A citation including the page number(s) on which a quotation or referenced material appears. You do not have to give a page reference if you are referring to the case in general, rather than referring to specific material from the case, and you have previously given the full citation to the case.

A pinpoint citation may precede or follow the information to which it is referring. The location of the pinpoint citation (before or after the applicable information) is unimportant. You must provide the pinpoint citation and locate it so the reader is clear what information is being referenced. In the next paragraph, the first pinpoint citation precedes the information being referenced and the second pinpoint citation follows the information being referenced. "*Terry*" appears by itself in the middle of the paragraph where the case is being referred to in general terms.

> *Terry v. Ohio*, 392 U.S. 1, 27 (1968) was the landmark case that lowered the burden of proof necessary for a stop from probable cause to "reasonable suspicion." In *Terry*, the United States Supreme Court held that police officers could stop someone on the street to investigate possible drug activity so long as the stop is based on something more than "inarticulate hunches." *Id.* at 22.

Not Quoting Exactly

A writer's stock in trade is his or her credibility. You will lose your credibility quickly if you do not quote accurately. It is important that anything you quote, but especially primary sources, be accurate. If your quotes are not accurate, your reader will think, at best, that you are sloppy and, at worst, that you are intentionally misleading the reader. You must disclose to your reader any intentional alteration of quoted material. *The Bluebook* explains how to show alterations. If you quote a passage that was printed with a typographical error or other mistake, do not correct the passage. Instead, quote the passage as originally printed and insert "[sic]" after the mistake. "[Sic]" tells the reader that the mistake was that of the original author.

Plagiarizing

Plagiarism is adopting another writer's work as your own without giving proper credit to the other writer. Plagiarism exists when you quote from a primary or secondary source without putting the language in quotation marks. It also exists when you have generally followed another writer's style and word choice even though not every word is the other writer's. Instead of plagiarizing, you should either quote the other writer directly or put the material entirely in your own words. To put the material in your own words, you need to know the substance of it well enough that you can "retell" it without referring back to the text.

> **Plagiarism** Taking all or part of the writing or idea of another person and passing it off as your own.

Using Contractions in More Formal Legal Documents

Most legal documents, except for letters and memos to business associates who are also friends, have at least a slightly formal tone of voice. Certain words, such as contractions, that are common in oral communication do not fit in formal legal documents because the tone of these words is too informal. When you are writing a legal document, think twice before you use a contraction or informal word. Chances are it does not belong in your document.

Use of the Word "I" in More Formal Legal Documents

When giving an opinion in a document, such as a client letter, an office memo, a memorandum of law, or an appellate brief, keep the words "I," "you," and "we" out of your writing. Although you have a personal opinion and the legal opinion you give very likely coincides with your own opinion, your analysis must be backed up with the law rather than your personal opinion. Rephrase your sentences in the third person (e.g., "The virtual identity of the facts in the two cases means that . . .") instead of in the first person singular (e.g., "I think that . . ."). You can include your personal opinion in more formal legal documents so long as you state it in impersonal language.

Elegant Variation

One English teacher or another in the past has probably suggested to you that you make your writing interesting by using as many different words as possible to refer to the same thing. This is called **elegant variation**. Elegant variation is terrific for most writing other than legal writing. In legal writing, pick a word to refer to something and use it whenever you refer to the same thing.

> **Elegant Variation** Use of a number of different words to refer to the same thing. For example, this book uses "attorney" to refer to a person licensed to practice law. It would be elegant variation to also refer to that person as a "lawyer," "counselor," or "practitioner." A legal thesaurus can profitably be used when you are trying to choose the right term. Once you chose your term, stick with it throughout your document.

Elegant variation is not appropriate in legal writing because attorneys focus so intently on word choice. If in writing a contract, you first referred to the document as a "contract," you have defined the document as a "contract." If you later referred to it as an "agreement," an attorney will wonder why you have changed the wording from "contract" to "agreement." The attorney will wonder whether the writer might have made a mistake or whether the writer was referring to two different documents, one of which was a "contract" and the other was an "agreement." Although it may seem uncomfortable at first to keep using the same word over and over again, you will soon get used to it.

WRITING TIP

Start Writing the Document Early Enough that You Have Time for Revisions

If possible, complete the first draft of your document with plenty of time prior to your deadline. Put your document away for a while and bring it out when you have sufficient time to edit and proofread. Because of the lapse of time, you can take a fresh look at the document and approach it more objectively, finding errors that you might not otherwise have noticed. If time constraints do not allow you to let your document lie fallow for a while, try one of the other editing and proofreading techniques recommended below.

Editing and Proofing

The final step, editing and proofing, is perhaps the most important step in the writing process, yet often the one overlooked by the novice writer. Good writing is a product of careful planning and writing, followed by revising multiple times. Editing and proofing are difficult because the writer has been so absorbed in the writing process that the writer has lost the objectivity necessary to proofread, which leads to an inability to spot errors easily noted by others. This difficulty is compounded by the fact that the typical legal document is quite complex. The writer must base the legal document on applicable law, the writer must communicate the substance of the document clearly to the reader, the writer must avoid mechanical errors, and the writer must cite correctly.

WRITING TIP

Spell Check Does Not Replace the Need for Careful Proofreading

Relying on the computer to highlight typographical errors is no substitute for careful proofreading. For examples of embarrassing errors this might cause, go to http://www.youtube.com and view the video the "impotence of proofreading."

To revise effectively, the writer should tackle one thing at a time, revising first for substance and meaning, then to eliminate mechanical errors, and then to correct citation form. Often you can find someone to help you check your document for meaning and readability by reading it. It is a good sign if the person understands what you are trying to explain; you can provide a fuller explanation of whatever the person finds unclear. Another technique is to read the document out loud, perhaps into a tape recorder. This technique provides sufficient distance between the writer and the document that the writer notices missing words and other problems that the writer may miss when reading silently.

Your word processing program can help you catch obvious typographical and grammatical errors; however, do not place all of your faith in spell and grammar checks. Your computer program will not catch the use of a correctly spelled word that is the wrong word in context.

Summary

- The three steps of the writing process are:
  - prewriting;
  - writing; and
  - editing and proofing.
- Before you start writing, you should perform any necessary research and formulate a writing plan.
- It is a good idea to develop a flowchart and/or outline before you start writing.
- Good organization is essential for readability.
- Carefully organize words within sentences, sentences into paragraphs, and paragraphs into an entire document.
- Overall organization may be dictated by the traditional format of the type of document you are writing.
- Most paragraphs need topic sentences.
- Do not challenge your reader too often with unconventional word order.
- Use transitional language to provide a link between what you have just written and what you are going to write about.
- Use signposts to point the reader in the right direction and provide a framework for understanding the document.
- Paragraph and tabulate to enhance readability.
- Make sure you know how to eliminate the eight mechanical errors discussed at the end of the chapter.

Key Terms

elegant variation
pinpoint citation
plagiarism
signposts
tabulation
transitional language

Exercises

1. What do you do before you write?
2. How can you improve your prewriting step?
3. Take a document you have written and analyze it:
   a. How is the overall organization?
   b. Do you use topic sentences?
   c. Is the word order within sentences logical?
   d. Can you use more transitional language and signposts?
   e. Do you paragraph about the right amount, too often, or too infrequently?
   f. Can you make more use of tabulation?
   g. Are you prone to any of the eight mechanical errors discussed in the chapter?

Discussion Points

1. How can organization help your reader understand what you have written?
2. What are some examples of transitional language?
3. What are some examples of signposts?
4. What is tabulation, and how can it be incorporated into a document?
5. What is the reason for giving a page reference to authority used in your document?
6. What is plagiarism, and how can you avoid it?

Cyberlaw Exercises

1. Bryan Garner, a legal writing authority, has interviewed many judges and other writers, many of whom give tips on legal writing. Go to http://www.lawprose.org/ and watch videos of one or more of the judges or writers. How does the advice they provide support or differ from the legal writing advice provided in this chapter?
2. A number of interesting videos are posted on https://www.youtube.com/, some of which are related to legal writing. Go to the website and find a video providing legal writing tips. How do the legal writing tips add to your understanding of writing well? How do the tips differ from the legal writing advice provided in this chapter?
3. Information on revision is accessible at https://www.law.cuny.edu/legal-writing/students/writing-sample/. Access the information on revision

from the website and compare it to the information included in this chapter.

4. Monthly plain language columns are accessible at https://www.michbar.org/generalinfo/plainenglish/home. Review several of the columns that are of interest to you.

Chapter 11

Transmittal Letter, Client Opinion Letter, and Email Correspondence

Introduction

This chapter discusses the transmittal letter, the client opinion letter, and email correspondence.

Two types of letters an attorney often writes to clients are the transmittal letter and the client opinion letter. This chapter explains the purpose and use of the letters and their proper format. It also includes a sample transmittal letter and two sample client opinion letters. The first sample client opinion letter has been footnoted to provide you with writing tips. It would be helpful to refer to the footnotes when writing client opinion letters.

Email correspondence is increasingly prevalent and has replaced letters in many instances. In addition, information formerly communicated in a law office memo (Chapter 13) may increasingly be communicated via email. Thus, the reader needs to know about appropriate email usage and format.

Purpose of the Transmittal Letter

One of the most common types of letters written in the law office is the transmittal letter, the cover letter used when forwarding a document or other information to the client or to a third party. The purposes of the transmittal letter are to explain the information being transmitted, to instruct the recipient in any further action to be taken, and to cover any related matters. For example, the sample transmittal letter below is the cover letter for an attorney-client retainer agreement (the contract between the attorney and client memorializing the employment relationship between client and attorney). The transmittal letter explains to the client what the attached document is, asks the client to sign the two copies of the agreement and return one copy to the attorney, and suggests that the client schedule an appointment with the attorney.

Another purpose of the transmittal letter is to document that the information attached to the letter was sent to the client and to document the instructions given. Usually the attorney places a copy of the transmittal letter and attachment in the client file. Later, the attorney can refer to the file copy to learn what was sent to the client. If the client loses the transmittal letter or the attachment, the material can be resent.

Style of Letters

Clients judge the competency of the attorney by the way the attorney presents himself or herself. Clients may lose confidence in the attorney if they spot errors in letters received from the attorney. In contrast, a clear but knowledgeable letter will strengthen the attorney-client relationship and may cause the client to recommend the attorney to others.

SAMPLE TRANSMITTAL LETTER

Florida Attorney
101 Main Street
Anytown, Anystate
May 4, 2020

Esteemed Client
201 Oak Street
Anytown, Anystate

Re: Attorney-Client Retainer Agreement

Dear Ms. Client:

It was a pleasure to meet with you in my office yesterday to discuss your potential lawsuit against Rack & Ruin, Inc. Enclosed are two copies of the Attorney-Client Retainer Agreement we had discussed. The Agreement states the terms of our attorney-client relationship.

Please sign both copies of the Agreement on page 2 in the space provided for your signature and keep one copy of the Agreement for your files. Please return the second signed copy to me in the enclosed stamped, self-addressed envelope.

I would like to meet with you again to discuss any paperwork you are able to find on Rack & Ruin, Inc. Once you have gathered any applicable information, please call my office and schedule an appointment with me.

Very truly yours,

Florida Attorney

The ten style tips listed on this page are applicable to the transmittal letter and the client opinion letter. The list probably contains nothing new. Most of the suggestions listed are a matter of common sense. They are things that you would wish someone writing a letter to you would do.

Glance over the style tips and try to keep them in mind as you write your transmittal or client opinion letter. As you revise the letter, use the list as a checklist and make sure you have complied with it.

WRITING TIPS

What to Do in a Letter

Keep the following writing tips in mind:
Do

1. Use plain English.
2. Be precise and specific.
3. Write at a level of formality appropriate for the recipient.
4. Be consistent in maintaining the same level of formality throughout the letter.
5. Keep your sentences fairly short.
6. Break up each page of the text with paragraphs.
7. State the purpose of the letter early in the letter (preferably in the "Re:" or in the opening line of the body of the letter).
8. Proofread the letter.
9. Double-check that any enclosures are included.
10. Note any special transmittal method other than regular mail (facsimile, certified mail, etc.).

Purpose of the Client Opinion Letter

From time to time, a client will ask an attorney a question that requires the attorney to do some research before giving the client an answer. After the attorney researches the question, the attorney may give the client the answer orally or in writing. The letter the attorney writes to the client explaining the answer is usually referred to as a client opinion letter because it gives the client the attorney's legal opinion. Another alternative is to tell the client the answer and follow up the conversation with a client opinion letter. The client opinion letter repeats what the client was told in the conversation and would add any additional information suggested by the conversation.

Generally, it is wise for the attorney to give the answer to the client's question in a client opinion letter. The client can reread the opinion letter as many times as necessary and refer to it later. Putting the opinion in writing means that the client will more likely understand the opinion as it was stated by the attorney. The client opinion letter usually states that the opinion it contains is limited by the facts stated in the letter and by the law as of the date of the letter. This language, and the fact that the opinion is in writing, protect the attorney to the extent possible from having the attorney's advice misconstrued or applied in the future to a different set of facts. An attorney might decide not to put the attorney's opinion in writing if the subject matter of the attorney's opinion is confidential. Another reason not to put the opinion in writing is that a written opinion may be discoverable in litigation.

The main purpose of the client opinion letter is to answer the client's question, but the opinion letter does not just contain the answer. A good client opinion letter also contains a statement of the facts on which the opinion was based, an explanation of applicable law, and an explanation of how the law applies to the facts. The tone of the client opinion letter is usually objective, rather than persuasive, because it explains the law, whether favorable or unfavorable to the client. There is no need to be persuasive and argue the client's position because the letter is directed to the client.

Chapter 13, which discusses the law office memo, may sound very similar to what you read in this chapter. The reason is that both a client opinion letter and the office memo require the same type of research and analysis to answer a legal question or problem. The client opinion letter and the office memo differ in content because the audience is different. Unless the client is sophisticated, the client opinion letter should be stated in lay terms and include few quotations or citations. (If the client is sophisticated, he or she may be sent the office memo itself rather than a separate client opinion letter.) Another difference is format. A client opinion letter more closely resembles a business letter, although it may have internal headings similar to those of a law office memo.

Format of the Client Opinion Letter

Although there is no one format for client opinion letters, the format given in this chapter is fairly standard. As you read the explanation in this chapter, compare it with the sample client opinion letters below.

Heading

The heading contains the name and address of the attorney, the date, the name and address of the client, and the subject matter (the "re"). The date is important because, unless otherwise stated in the letter, it is assumed that the opinion is based on the law current through the date of the letter. For ease of reading and reference, the "re" will identify the subject matter of the letter with a reasonable amount of detail.

Opening

The opening paragraph sets the stage. It typically reminds the client of the context of the client's question and reiterates the client's question. This is a good place to state any limitations on the opinion contained in the letter. The attorney typically states that the opinion is limited to the facts contained in the letter and the law of the state (or federal law, if federal law applies) as of the date of the letter. It is advisable to state that the opinion may be different given different facts or a different date.

Facts

The facts significant to the opinion are stated objectively in this section. If important facts are not known, this should be stated. It is wise to ask the client to review the facts and advise the attorney of any necessary additions or changes.

Answer

The answer section explains the answer to the client's question, with any necessary detail and clarification.

Explanation

In the explanation section, the attorney explains the law in lay terms and then explains how the law applies to the facts. The challenge is to support the answer with the law, yet explain it in a way the client can understand. Generally, the attorney would not use quotations or citations in this section, but they may be included if the client is knowledgeable concerning the law. Even if the client is not knowledgeable, the opinion may quote the relevant portion of an important statute or case. If a source is quoted or a case is referred to specifically, the citation should be given. The subject matter content and the way it is presented must be geared to the particular client.

Closing

The closing is no different from the closing in any other business letter. The attorney may want to tell the client what action needs to be taken and may direct the client to contact the attorney with any further questions concerning the opinion.

Sample Client Opinion Letters

Introduction

This section contains two sample client opinion letters. The first sample letter has been footnoted to provide you with writing tips. Normally, the client opinion letter includes no footnotes; the footnotes in the first sample client opinion letter should not be considered part of the letter.

The sample client opinion letter below was written to a mother whose son had been arrested for possession of cocaine. The cocaine was found in the car trunk when the son's car was stopped on Interstate 95 in Florida. The son is originally from Florida but had been attending an out-of-state university. Prior to the arrest, the son had returned to Florida with a friend to visit his mother and to enjoy spring break. The mother hired the attorney to represent the son and has asked the attorney whether the cocaine found can be suppressed.

FIRST SAMPLE CLIENT OPINION LETTER

Florida Attorney
Main Street
Anytown, Florida
April 6, 2020

Ms. Mom Campbell
Oak Street
Anytown, Florida

Re: Whether cocaine found in the Campbell car when it was stopped on I-95 may be suppressed.

Dear Ms. Mom Campbell:

You hired me to represent your son who had been arrested for possession of cocaine on April 1, 2020. On April 3, 2020, I met with you and with your son and you asked me whether the cocaine could be suppressed. This opinion is limited to the facts contained in the facts section of this letter and to federal law as of the date of this letter and is solely for your benefit and for the benefit of your son.[1]

Facts

The following facts were gathered from the April 3, 2020, interview with you and Mike Campbell, your son, and a review of the police report. Please contact me or have your son contact me if there are any inaccuracies to be corrected or any additions to be made.[2]

Your son and his best friend, John Wright, were driving north on I-95 returning from spring break in Florida, when they were stopped by members of a drug task force made up of Volusia County sheriff officers and federal drug enforcement agents. The agents requested permission to search the car. When your son refused consent, the agents brought in a drug dog that alerted to the trunk of the car. The agents then claimed that the dog's actions gave them probable cause to search the trunk and gave your son the choice of either opening the trunk or waiting until the agents obtained a search warrant. After your son opened the trunk, the agents found two kilograms of cocaine in a brown paper bag. Your son and Wright were arrested and charged with possession with intent to distribute cocaine.

1. This sentence protects the attorney by naming the persons who can rely on the opinion. Perhaps the attorney was trying to avoid having the other defendant (the son's best friend) rely on the letter, by stating that the letter's benefit is limited to the mother and son. This language is usually used when third parties not represented by the attorney may try to rely on the opinion.

2. This language protects the attorney by requesting that both mother and son verify that the facts are accurate. The prior sentence identifies the source of the attorney's information.

The agents claimed they stopped your son's car because your son was following the car in front of him too closely and because the following facts fit a drug courier profile used by the Volusia County Sheriff officers:

1. The car was a large late model;
2. The car had out-of-state tags;
3. The car was being driven cautiously at the speed limit;
4. The car was being driven on a known drug corridor, I-95;
5. There were two passengers in the car;
6. The passengers were in their twenties;
7. The car was being driven in the early evening; and
8. The passengers were dressed casually.[3]

Although not listed by the agents, your son and Wright believe the real reason they were stopped is because they are African Americans.

Answer

The court should suppress the cocaine if it decides that your son did not commit a traffic violation. In opposition to the motion to suppress, the government will likely make two arguments.

One argument is that the agents had reasonable suspicion that your son's car contained illegal drugs. They may claim that their reasonable suspicion was based on a drug courier profile. The government should lose this argument because of the similarity between the facts in your son's case and another case. In the other case involving a car stop based on a drug courier profile, the court granted the defendant's motion to suppress the illegal drugs found because the stop violated the defendant's constitutional rights to be free from unreasonable search and seizure.

The second argument is that the agents had probable cause to stop your son's car for following too closely. In a 1996 case, the United States Supreme Court decided that a police officer may stop a car for any type of traffic violation, no matter how minor. This means that the traffic stop is valid so long as there is a technical violation; it does not matter if the reason the agents gave was a pretext for a stop based on race. The Court stated that a challenge to a stop allegedly based on race should be brought under the equal protection clause and not under the Fourth Amendment. The Court did not explain that an equal protection clause challenge is difficult to prove because it requires evidence of intentional discrimination.

---

3. When you have a list of items, make it easier for your reader to skim down the list by tabulating. Number each item, follow each item except for the last one by a semicolon, and place the word "and" after the semicolon following the next-to-last item. Make sure that you follow parallel construction for all items. If you are unsure what parallel construction means, refer to Appendix D.

The applicable Florida motor vehicle statute prohibits a vehicle from following another vehicle "more closely than is reasonable and prudent, having due regard for the speed of such vehicles and the traffic upon, and the condition of, the highway." Unfortunately, there is no simple test to determine if your son violated the statute. The court will have to determine from any evidence presented whether the distance at which your son was following the car in front of him was reasonable and prudent.

The court should grant the motion to suppress if we can convince the judge that your son was following the car at an appropriate distance; the cocaine would not have been found had the car not been stopped.

Explanation of the Government's First Argument

The Fourth Amendment to the United States Constitution protects your son "against unreasonable searches and seizures." The Fourth Amendment does not prohibit all searches and seizures—just unreasonable searches and seizures. The courts have allowed officers to stop cars on the highway to investigate a "reasonable suspicion" of illegal drug activity. In a case involving facts almost identical to those in your son's case, the court found that a highway stop was not reasonable under the Fourth Amendment even though the stop was made based on a drug courier profile. *United States v. Smith*, 799 F.2d 704, 712 (11th Cir. 1986).[4] (This was the drug courier profile case referred to in the answer section.)

You will probably be interested to know more about *Smith* because the facts in that case are nearly identical to the facts in your son's case. This letter will first give you the facts from *Smith* and then compare them to the facts from your son's case.

Smith

One night in June of 1985, Trooper Robert Vogel, a Florida Highway Patrol trooper, and a DEA agent were observing cars traveling in the northbound lanes of I-95. They hoped to intercept drug couriers. When Smith's car passed through the arc of the patrol car headlights, Vogel noticed the following factors that matched his drug courier profile:

1. The car was traveling at 3:00 a.m.;

---

4. The number "704" is the first page of *Smith* and "712" is the page on which the finding of the court referred to in the preceding sentence is located. As a courtesy to the reader, a page reference should be given when specific material from a case is referred to even if the material is not directly quoted.

The two types of sentences in legal writing are textual sentences and citation sentences. A *textual sentence* is the type of sentence you have been writing all your life. It is a complete grammatical sentence with a subject and a verb. A *citation sentence* contains only citations. A *string citation* is a citation sentence with more than one citation. In a string citation, the citations should be separated by semicolons.

A sentence is more difficult to read when it contains a full case citation, especially if the citation is long. To avoid including a full citation in a textual sentence, you can refer to a case in very general terms or refer to a legal principle from a case and give the full citation to the case in a citation sentence following the textual sentence.

2. The car was a 1985 Mercury, a large late model car;
3. The car had out-of-state tags;
4. There were two occupants of the car who were around 30; and
5. The driver was driving cautiously and did not look at the patrol car as the Mercury passed through the arc of the patrol car headlights.

Id. at 705–06.[5]

The above drug courier profile is almost identical to the profile used by the officers in your son's case.[6] In both *Smith* and your son's case, the cars were traveling after dark, the cars were large late models with out-of-state tags, the cars were being driven "cautiously," and each car contained two passengers in their twenties or thirties. The differences between the two profiles are very minor. Your son and Wright were dressed casually while it is not known how Smith and Swindell were dressed. Smith and Swindell did not look at Vogel as they passed. It is not known whether your son and Wright looked in the agents' direction as your son drove past. Your son and Wright claim that race was a factor in their stop even though it was not listed as such by the agents. Smith and Swindell's race is unknown.[7]

In *Smith*, Vogel followed the Mercury for a mile and a half and noticed that the Mercury "wove" several times, once as much as six inches into the emergency lane. Vogel pulled Smith over. When a drug dog alerted on the car, a DEA agent searched the trunk and discovered one kilogram of cocaine. Smith and his passenger, Swindell, were arrested and were charged with conspiracy to possess cocaine with the intent to distribute it. *Id.* at 706. On appeal, the *Smith* court held that the stop of Smith's car violated Smith's constitutional rights and found that Smith's motion to suppress should have been granted. *Id.* at 712.

---

5. When you need to cite a block quote or other material set off from the rest of the text, as is the tabulation here, bring the citation back to the left margin. "*Id.*" is used here because "*id.*" refers back to the immediately preceding citation, *Smith*. When citing inclusive pages with three or more digits, drop all but the last two digits of the second number and place a hyphen between the numbers.

6. This is an example of a topic sentence. A topic sentence contains one main idea summarizing the rest of the paragraph, with the rest of the paragraph developing the idea presented in the topic sentence. Most paragraphs should have topic sentences. The typical location of a topic sentence is the first sentence in the paragraph. Sometimes the topic sentence is the last sentence in the paragraph and pulls together the rest of the paragraph. Some paragraphs, typically narrative paragraphs, do not have a topic sentence.

If a paragraph sounds disjointed or unorganized, try pulling it together using a topic sentence. If a topic sentence does not help, think about breaking the paragraph up into more than one paragraph.

7. This paragraph applies the facts in *Smith* to the facts in *Campbell*. Applying facts from one case to another case involves explaining the similarities and differences between the two sets of facts. Instead of simply stating that the facts from the two cases are very similar, the paragraph specifically states which facts are the same. Sometimes, in the application, you need to explain in what way the facts are similar if they are not identical.

You can either apply the *Smith* facts to *Campbell* as done here or you can wait until you have thoroughly discussed *Smith*. When you prepare your outline prior to starting to write the client opinion letter, spend some time moving parts of your reasoning around to determine the best flow for your reasoning.

Just as there was nothing in your son's drug courier profile to differentiate your son and Wright from other innocent college students returning from spring break in Florida, there was nothing in Vogel's drug courier profile to differentiate Smith and Swindell from other law-abiding motorists on I-95. It is usual to drive after dark to avoid heavy traffic or to complete an interstate trip. Although many motorists speed on the highways, motorists driving "cautiously" at or near the speed limit are simply obeying traffic laws. Many people other than drug couriers drive large late model cars with out-of-state tags. A motorist between the ages of twenty and forty is not unusual.

Explanation for the Government's Second Argument

In 1996, the United States Supreme Court decided that a stop for a traffic violation does not violate the driver's constitutional right against unreasonable search and seizure. *Whren v. United States*, 517 U.S. 806, 818 (1996). In *Whren*, Brown was driving a Pathfinder in which Whren was a passenger. While Brown was stopped at a stop sign, he looked down into Whren's lap. Plain clothes police officers were patrolling this "high drug area" of the District of Columbia in an unmarked patrol car. The Pathfinder caught the attention of the officers because Brown remained stopped at the stop sign for approximately twenty seconds. When the patrol car made a U-turn to follow the Pathfinder, Brown turned right without signaling and started off at an "unreasonable speed." The patrol car stopped the Pathfinder. When one of the officers approached Brown's window and peered in, the officer saw that Whren had two plastic bags of crack cocaine on his lap. The officers arrested Whren and Brown. *Id.* at 808, 809.

Prior to *Whren*, some courts, including the court deciding *Smith*, had decided that a car stop for a traffic violation was unconstitutional unless a reasonable officer would have made the stop. The *Smith* court found that the cocaine should have been excluded from evidence because a reasonable officer would not have stopped Smith's car for the alleged traffic violation. 799 F. 2d at 711. However in *Whren*, the United States Supreme Court rejected the argument that the reasonable officer standard should apply. 517 U.S. at 813. The Court decided that the stop was constitutional because the officers observed Brown violate the traffic code. *Id.* at 819.

Whren and your son's case are very similar in that in both cases, the government claimed that the stop of a suspect's car did not violate the driver's right against unreasonable search and seizure because there was some irregularity in the way the car was being driven that gave the officer reason to stop the car. The driving "irregularities" are similar in that failure to use a turn signal in changing lanes, speeding, and following too closely are moving violations that can pose a severe safety hazard; under the circumstances, none appeared to adversely impact any other vehicle's safety.

After *Whren*, it would be very difficult to convince a court that a stop for an alleged traffic violation is unconstitutional. However, if the court finds that the driver did not violate any traffic regulation, then the stop would be unconstitutional.

The Florida motor vehicle statute identified by the officer in your son's case states: "The driver of a motor vehicle shall not follow another vehicle more closely than is reasonable and prudent, having due regard for the speed of such vehicles and the traffic upon, and the condition of, the highway." Fla. Stat. Ch. 316.0895 (1) (2019). No simple test determines if your son violated the statute. The court must determine from any evidence presented whether the distance at which your son was following the car in front of him was reasonable and prudent.

The alleged driving irregularities in *Whren* and your son's case are dissimilar in certain respects. While it was clear that Brown committed a traffic violation, the Florida statute cited in this case does not apply to your son if he was following at a safe distance. Determining whether one vehicle is following another vehicle too closely involved much more of a judgment call than determining whether the Pathfinder failed to signal when turning right and exceeded the speed limit. The position of the vehicles on the highway and the weather and road conditions must all be considered to determine if your son violated the statute.

I will be meeting with your son within the next few days to discuss the facts in more detail, and I anticipate filing a motion to suppress after that meeting. Should you or your son have any questions concerning this matter do not hesitate to call me.

Very truly yours,
Florida Attorney

The second sample client opinion letter below was written to a client who had been arrested for possession of methamphetamines. The client was a passenger in a car stopped on the interstate. The drugs were found in the client's purse. The client's conversation with the car's driver was tape-recorded while they sat in the patrol car as the officer searched their car. The passenger hired the attorney to represent her and has asked whether the methamphetamines and the tape-recorded conversation can be suppressed.

SECOND SAMPLE CLIENT OPINION LETTER

Florida Attorney
Main Street
Anytown, Florida
March 23, 2020

Ms. Cruz Estrada
Main Street
Mytown, Florida

Re: Whether drugs found in your purse may be suppressed

Dear Ms. Estrada:

You hired me to represent you after you were arrested for possession of methamphetamines on March 14, 2020. On March 17, 2020, I met with you and you asked me whether the drugs could be suppressed. This opinion is limited to the facts contained in the facts section of this letter and to federal law as of the date of this letter and is solely for your benefit.

Facts

The following facts were gathered from the March 17, 2020, interview with you and a review of the police report. Please contact me if there are any inaccuracies to be corrected or any additions to be made.

You were riding with your friend, Luis Briones, when Luis's car was pulled over. You and Luis were traveling south on I-95 toward Miami to visit friends. The officer said he had stopped the car because Luis was speeding.

After he stopped you, the officer stood at the window on the driver's side and asked for Luis's license and car registration. While Luis searched his wallet for the documents, the officer noticed a glass vial containing small kernels of an off-white substance in Luis's lap. Believing the vial to contain crack cocaine, the officer announced that he was seizing it. He asked you and Luis to exit the car and asked Luis for his wallet.

You got out of the car with your purse strap slung over your shoulder. The officer approached you and said, "You don't mind if I search this, do you?" Without giving you time to respond, the officer grabbed your purse and began to search it. Inside your purse, he found a brown paper envelope. You told the officer that someone had given it to you to give to a friend in Miami.

Still holding your purse, the officer asked you and Luis to wait in the patrol car while the officer searched Luis's car. You and Luis nervously waited in the back seat of the patrol car. You admitted to Luis that the envelope was yours and that it contained illegal drugs.

After you were arrested, you discovered that the police officer had tape-recorded your conversation in the back of the patrol car. Luis believed that the reason the officer gave for stopping Luis's car must have been a pretext because, at the most, he was driving five miles over the speed limit. He said he suspected that he had been stopped for what is jokingly referred to as the offense of DWH or Driving While Hispanic.

You were charged under the federal drug statutes.

Answer Concerning the Motion to Suppress the Drugs Found in Your Purse

The court should suppress the drugs if you file a motion to suppress. In opposition to the motion to suppress the drugs, the government will likely make two arguments.

One argument is that you consented to the search of your purse. If you had consented to the search, then the drugs would be admissible. Whether you consented is determined by what a reasonable person would believe. The government should lose this argument because a reasonable person would probably not believe that you had consented. The officer gave you no time to respond after he stated, "You don't mind if I search, do you?" You would not likely give the officer consent because your purse held personal items.

The second argument is that the officer had probable cause to search Luis's car after he discovered that Luis had drugs. Where an officer has probable cause to search the car, the officer can search containers found in the car that might hold the object of the search. Even though the officer can search containers found in the car, the officer would not be able to search your person, at least without more evidence than he had.

Once the court rules against the government on the government's two arguments, the court should grant the motion to suppress the drugs found in your purse.

Answer Concerning the Motion to Suppress the Tape Recording

The court should deny the motion to suppress the tape-recorded conversation if judged solely under the federal eavesdropping statutes; however, the court may suppress your conversation with Luis if the court finds that the tape-recorded conversation was tainted by the unconstitutional search of your purse.

The federal eavesdropping statutes prohibit the taping of private conversations unless the officer was a party to the conversation and consented to the taping. The taped private conversation may not be used as evidence. To gauge whether a conversation is private, the federal statutes require the court to consider whether you expected the conversation to be private and whether society perceived the expectation to be reasonable.

In a case with similar facts, the court held that there is no reasonable expectation of privacy where the conversation took place in the rear seat of a patrol car. If a conversation in the rear seat of a patrol car is not considered private, then the tape-recorded conversation may not be suppressed under the federal eavesdropping statutes.

Even though the tape-recorded conversation may not be suppressed under the federal eavesdropping statutes, we can use the argument that the unconstitutional search of your purse tainted the taped conversation. The court might find that you would not have told Luis about the contents of your purse while you were in the patrol car, had your purse not been searched a few minutes earlier.

Explanation of the Government's First Argument

The Fourth Amendment to the United States Constitution protects you "against unreasonable searches and seizures." The Fourth Amendment does not prohibit all searches and seizures—just unreasonable searches and seizures. Although obtaining a search warrant before conducting a search is preferable, the courts have allowed a number of exceptions to the search warrant requirement over the years. The search of your purse is constitutional if you consented to the search.

The United States Supreme Court has stated the standard for determining when an individual has consented to the search of a car. *Florida v. Jimeno*, 500 U.S. 248, 251 (1991). "The standard for measuring the scope of a suspect's consent under the Fourth Amendment is that of 'objective reasonableness'—what would the typical person have understood by the exchange between the officer and the suspect?" *Id.*

Applying the objective reasonableness standard, it would not be objectively reasonable to believe that you consented to the search of your purse. You did not verbally consent nor did your actions demonstrate consent. A woman's purse often contains objects of a personal nature that the individual wants to guard from prying eyes. A purse is often considered an extension of the individual's outer clothing. Because of the private nature of your purse, it probably would take some overt action or response on your part before it would be reasonable to believe that you consented.

Explanation for the Government's Second Argument

An exception to the search warrant requirement is stopping a vehicle to investigate a traffic violation. Once a vehicle is stopped, the officer can search the car if there is probable cause of criminal activity. Even without consent, the officer can search containers found in the car and suspected of holding the object of the officer's search, no matter who owns the container. An officer may not search someone's person without probable cause.

As far as the container exception is concerned, the United States Supreme Court held that "police officers with probable cause to search a car may inspect passengers' belongings found in the car that are capable of concealing the object of the search." *Wyoming v. Houghton*, 526 U.S. 295, 307 (1999). The facts of *Houghton* and your case will be compared to determine if the search of your purse was constitutional.

In *Houghton*, David Young was stopped for speeding and a faulty brake light. After the officer saw a hypodermic syringe in Young's pocket, Young admitted that he used it to take drugs. The officer asked the two female passengers seated in the front seat to exit the car and the officer searched the car. The officer found Sandra Houghton's purse on the back seat of the car. Searching the purse, the officer found a brown pouch that contained drug paraphernalia and a syringe containing methamphetamine in a large enough quantity for a felony conviction. Houghton claimed that the brown pouch was not hers. The officer also found a black container that contained drug paraphernalia and a syringe containing a smaller amount of methamphetamine, insufficient for a felony conviction. Houghton's arms showed fresh needle-marks. The officer arrested her. 526 U.S. at 297–98.

In *Houghton*, the Court held "that police officers with probable cause to search a car may inspect passengers' belongings found in the car that are capable of concealing the object of the search." *Id.* at 307. The Court noted that an individual carrying a package in a vehicle travelling on the public roads has a reduced expectation of privacy; however the Court did note the "unique, significantly heightened protection afforded against searches of one's person." *Id.* at 303. The Court found no reason to afford more protection to a container owned by a passenger than a container owned by the driver. *Id.* at 305.

The facts of *Houghton* and your case are similar in that the two cars were stopped for alleged traffic violations and the officers searched a passenger's purse. The facts of the two cases differ in that Houghton's purse was on the back seat of the car, Houghton had exited the car without taking the purse with her, and Houghton at first disclaimed ownership of the purse. In contrast, you took your purse with you when you exited the car and it was attached to you when the officer snatched it from your shoulder.

In *Houghton*, the Court drew a distinction between the permissible search of containers and the search of an individual. The officer would not have been permitted to search Houghton without probable cause that she was carrying drugs or a weapon on her person.

Explanation Concerning the Motion to Suppress the Tape Recording

The federal eavesdropping statutes protect certain types of face-to-face conversations against interception. A conversation is not an oral communication unless the conversants expect that the conversation is private and an objective third party would consider that expectation reasonable. It is illegal to intercept an oral communication. If an oral communication is taped in violation of the eavesdropping statutes, the conversation cannot be used as evidence in court.

Thus, if your and Luis's conversation was an oral communication, it should be suppressed. Whether the conversation is an oral communication turns on whether you had a reasonable expectation of privacy while seated in the rear seat of the patrol car. One prong of the two-prong test is satisfied; you had an expectation of privacy or you would not have discussed the contents of your purse. The other prong of the test is whether your expectation was reasonable. On one hand, the conversation was not audible outside the patrol car. The only way the officer could have heard the conversation was by taping it. On the other hand, you were not sitting in Luis's car. You were sitting in the officer's car. While an expectation of privacy in Luis's car would have been reasonable, it is unclear from the statutes whether an expectation of privacy in the officer's car was reasonable. Some might equate the officer's car to the officer's office. If you were conversing in an office of a police station, it might not be reasonable to expect privacy.

In a case with similar facts, the issue before the United States Court of Appeals for the Eleventh Circuit was "whether the district erred in denying the motion to suppress the tapes resulting from the secret recording of McKinnon's pre-arrest conversations while he sat in the back seat of the police car." *United States v. McKinnon*, 985 F.2d 525, 526 (11th Cir. 1993).

In *McKinnon*, police officers stopped a pick-up truck for failure to travel in a single lane on the Florida Turnpike. Theodore Pressley was driving and Steve McKinnon was the passenger. Pressley consented to the search of his vehicle. While the officers were searching, McKinnon and Pressley waited in the rear seat of the patrol car. There they made incriminating statements that were secretly recorded by the officers. The officers arrested McKinnon and Pressley after finding cocaine in the truck, and they were again placed in the rear seat of the patrol car. The officers again recorded McKinnon's and Pressley's incriminating statements. *Id.*

The *McKinnon* court considered the meaning of the term "oral communication" under the federal statutes. An oral communication is protected against taping. If a conversation is taped in violation of the statutes, the tape may be suppressed. A conversation is an oral communication only if the conversants exhibited a subjective expectation of privacy and the expectation of privacy was objectively reasonable. The court seemed to agree with the government's argument that a patrol car functions as the officer's office and the rear seat of the patrol car functions as a jail cell. *Id.* at 527. The court held "that McKinnon did not have a reasonable or justifiable expectation of privacy for conversations he held while seated in the back seat area of a police car." *Id.* at 528.

In examining the facts of *McKinnon* and your case, the facts concerning the taping seem virtually identical. In each case, an officer asked two individuals to wait in the patrol car prior to their arrest. The officer taped their conversation in the rear seat of the patrol car; the conversation contained incriminating statements. One difference between the two cases is that the officer in *McKinnon* also taped McKinnon's conversation following his arrest. This difference is not significant because an arrestee held in the back of a patrol car would have a lesser expectation of privacy than a person not under arrest.

Where a police officer obtained evidence in an unconstitutional manner, that evidence is excluded from use at trial. If that evidence leads the officer to other evidence, the other evidence is derivative of the first evidence. The derivative evidence is known as fruit of the poisonous tree and is also inadmissible. Generally, evidence that is tainted by the prior unconstitutional conduct is inadmissible; however, in some instances the second evidence is admissible because the connection between the unconstitutionally seized evidence and the subsequently obtained evidence is marginal.

We will argue that the taped conversation is derivative of the evidence the officer discovered searching your purse. If the court finds that the taped conversation is tainted from the unconstitutional search of your purse, the conversation will also be inadmissible.

I will be meeting with you within the next few days, and I anticipate filing a motion to suppress the drugs and the taped conversation after that meeting. Should you have any questions concerning this matter do not hesitate to call me.

Very truly yours,
Florida Attorney

Email Correspondence

With a computer on almost each person's desk and a cell phone in hand, it is tempting to send an email or text message rather than telephone someone, visit someone, or send a letter. Attorneys provide much of their legal advice through emails, perhaps via "e-memos"; emails have become central to the practice of law. This central role of emails to legal practice may put pressure on attorneys to provide legal advice within a short time-frame in emails that are shorter than the legal documents that attorneys were accustomed to writing in the past. Obviously, these short bursts of email advice should have been researched as thoroughly as longer documents.

Although you write countless emails each day, you need to think of emails composed and sent in the professional setting as distinct from personal emails you might send. Most of you have grown up using emails to communicate rather than sending letters, and many of you may have had little practice in letter writing. In certain circumstances, an email is preferable if one wants a quick answer to a specific question or wants to set up an appointment. Email correspondence can provide answers to simple questions and allow busy professionals to coordinate schedules without speaking on the telephone at the same time.

Your familiarity with email correspondence in an informal setting may not have adequately prepared you for using it appropriately in the professional setting. The purpose of this portion of the chapter is to offer guidelines on when email correspondence is appropriate and style tips to keep in mind in composing the email.

In deciding whether to send an email, it might be helpful to consider the differences between an email message and other types of communication. An email is similar to a letter in that it is written and can be referenced later. This semi-permanence is an advantage for recordkeeping and can be an advantage when dealing with a complex matter; however, the semi-permanency of emails and letters means that one must carefully scrutinize their contents to determine if there is anything in them that could come back to haunt the writer later. Although a letter can be copied and forwarded to a recipient unintended by the letter writer, copying and mailing a letter takes a great deal more effort than forwarding an email. In some circumstances, an email recipient may give in to the temptation of forwarding an email demeaning or insulting someone behind the person's back. In addition, the recipient of the forwarded email receives the entire exchange of correspondence contained in the email and a computer archive may contain a wealth of email correspondence potentially discoverable later in a request for production or in an investigation.

One should also consider whether the information is confidential in nature and whether the sender has the recipient's correct and current email address. Because an email message sometimes goes to someone other than the intended recipient, it is customary in law practice to include a confidentiality warning at the bottom of the email message stating that the message is only for the intended recipient and should not be considered a communication with others. Another way to protect confidential information is to encrypt it. Even though including a confidentiality warning or encrypting information may protect the sender in some circumstances, there is a risk of sending confidential information via email. A misdirected email message became the subject matter of a lawsuit when a law firm sent an individual's confidential and sensitive information to the individual's former email address rather than to the individual's current email address; the information was accessed by the individual's former employer.

One advantage of a telephone conversation over a letter or email message is that the conversation is not in writing and is not semi-permanent unless tape recorded; thus, if you have something sensitive to discuss, you might want to discuss the matter in a telephone conversation or in person. However, be aware that there is a chance that the conversation might be tape recorded, either legally or illegally. Of course, even if the conversation is not taped, a person who is a party to a conversation may be able to testify about the conversation, but the testimony does not capture the tone and inflection of the speaker and is subject to being disputed as being inaccurate. Other advantages of a "live" conversation are that a participant hears the other person's tone of voice, there is more of a context for the conversation, the participants can immediately clarify any misunderstandings, and the participants can discuss a matter in great length. Without being able to hear the sender's voice as one would during a telephone or in-person conversation, the reaction to the sender's email might be very different than intended. The sender should consider how the email message could be interpreted. For example, what the sender perceives as light and joking in tone could be perceived by the recipient as sarcastic and wounding.

The advantages of sending an email message are that it is much quicker than composing and sending a letter through the mail, and the typical email correspondent is very familiar with corresponding in that fashion. A recommended practice is to reread an email, including recipients, the email subject matter, and email text, prior to sending it to make sure the sender has no revisions. If in doubt if revisions are needed or that the email should be sent at all, an email can be saved in draft form, to be revised, sent, or not sent later; sometimes one can be more objective given a little time between initially composing the email and sending it.

A writer's familiarity with informal email correspondence is a disadvantage if the writer does not recognize that one should maintain a certain level of formality with business correspondence. A young legal professional from Generation X, Generation Y, or Generation Z may be corresponding with someone from the Mature Generation (born prior to 1946) or a baby boomer who grew up with print correspondence and expects email messages to mirror print correspondence. This may mean that the sender should include a greeting typical of a letter such as "Dear — —:" and a closing such as "Very truly yours" followed by a signature, especially if the sender's name is not obvious from the email address. The sender can anticipate what the recipient expects by reviewing prior correspondence. It is usually advisable for the sender to set up the sender's email program to generate an automatic signature line with contact information.

If sending a law office memo via email, the sender can use the law office memo format in the body of the email or attach a document containing the law office memo. Because email message formatting can be different when viewed by the recipient, it may be preferable to attach the law office memo as a document to the email. However, great care should be taken that the correct document is attached to an email. A suggestion is to preview the substance of each attachment prior to sending the email. That precautionary step lessens the likelihood that an incorrect attachment, perhaps containing sensitive or confidential information, is not disclosed inadvertently.

The speed with which one can reply to an email message can be a disadvantage; if the email recipient had an emotional reaction to an email message, the natural response might be to reply in kind. A heated email response has the advantage over a telephone conversation or personal visit in that there is no direct simultaneous confrontation. Even though the temptation to respond immediately is great, the better advice usually is not to respond immediately because one often regrets sending a hasty response composed in the heat of the moment. It might be better for the recipient of an angry email not to respond at all or send a response later when one has had the opportunity to craft a more appropriate response. Although satisfying at the time, one should avoid sarcasm, insults, accusations, derogatory language, and otherwise uncivil language in emails. After cooling down, the sender may regret having sent the email, and the email may be used against the sender in the future.

Just as with print correspondence, the recipient may very well judge the writer based on the substance and style of the email correspondence. The recipient may not have the best impression of the writer of an email that contains spelling or grammar errors. One should avoid abbreviations or symbols common to informal email correspondence, spelling mistakes, grammar mistakes, and punctuation mistakes. One should use wording appropriate to the recipient and carefully consider the substance of the message. Some part of the message that is other than the main focus of the message and that the sender wrote in haste may become crucial later, especially if the subject matter of a lawsuit. Make sure you state facts accurately.

Many of the writing tips for letters discussed in this chapter also apply to email messages. Use plain English, be precise and specific, keep your sentences fairly short, and break up the message into paragraphs, double-spacing between paragraphs. Consider that the recipient may be reading the email on a small screen; formatting using bold, italics, headings, numbered lists, and bullet points may be advisable to ensure that the main points of the writer's message are communicated well. The visual appeal of email text can enhance or impede the reader's comprehension. The ease with which the reader understands the email substance can be a benefit or an impediment to the writer achieving the desired result from the email.

The organization of the email message is as important as the organization of other legal writing. Your recipient is busy and may not read your entire email unless the recipient knows that it is in his or her best interest to do so. Put the most important information at the beginning of the email so that the recipient will not have to scroll down to read it. If your email is a little long or the substance is complex, you can make your organization obvious by using headings and numbering paragraphs.

One should also consider matters seemingly extrinsic to the email message itself. These include the email address of the sender, the sender's screen name, the subject matter of the email, the email recipients, and attachments referenced in the email. The sender's email address or screen name should not be used if objectionable to the intended receiver or possible recipients. For example, in a 2008 Virginia appellate court case, the screen name on a document that an attorney sought to introduce into evidence before Judge West was "westisanazi."

Because many recipients of email correspondence decide whether to read an email message based on the subject matter, the subject line of an email should accurately reflect the subject of the email and should be changed if the correspondence has shifted from one topic to another. The subject line is an opportunity to communicate specific and meaningful information.

Before sending, one should check the recipients; all of us have been on a listserv where an obviously personal message was sent out to the entire listserv. The consequence of doing this on a listserv is embarrassment, but the consequence of doing this in the legal profession can be considerably more serious. The sender should double-check to ascertain that all attachments referenced in the email were actually attached to the email.

Perhaps the most important advice is to reread and proofread an email message before sending it. If possible, the sender should imagine what the recipient knows and then determine whether the recipient will understand the message. It is common when composing an email to omit words when one is typing quickly. Rereading the message from the viewpoint of the recipient and adding additional wording or an additional explanation may help keep the sender from being embarrassed or receiving questions from the recipient when the meaning of the message is unclear. Rereading and proofing may also help avoid technical errors (spelling, grammar, punctuation) and errors with the subject line, recipients, and attachments.

Summary

- The transmittal letter is the cover letter used when forwarding a document or other information to the client or to a third party.
- The client judges the competency of the attorney by the way the attorney presents himself or herself. A client letter may either cause the client to lose confidence in the attorney or may strengthen the attorney-client relationship.
- The client opinion letter answers the client's question and contains a statement of the facts, an explanation of applicable law, and an explanation of how the law applies to the facts.
- The format of the client opinion letter generally contains a heading, an opening, the facts, an answer, an explanation, and a closing.
- The client opinion letter should state that it is limited to the facts in the letter, to federal and/or state law of a certain date, and to the benefit of the client.
- Gear the language in the client opinion letter to the knowledge of the client.
- You may or may not want to include citations or quotations in the client opinion letter.

Exercises

1. What are important style tips to remember when writing a transmittal letter?
2. What does the heading of a client opinion letter contain?
3. What does the opening of a client opinion letter contain?
4. What facts should a client opinion letter contain?
5. What does the answer section of a client opinion letter contain?
6. What does the explanation section of a client opinion letter contain?
7. What does the closing of a client opinion letter contain?

Cyberlaw Exercises

1. Bryan Garner, a legal writing authority, has interviewed many judges and other writers, many of whom give tips on legal writing. Go to http://www.

lawprose.org/, watch videos of one or more of the judges or writers, and identify three writing tips that you could use when you are asked to write a transmittal letter or a client opinion letter.

2. A number of interesting videos are posted on https://www.youtube.com/, some of which are related to writing a transmittal letter. Go to the website and find a video providing legal writing tips on writing effective transmittal letters. How do the legal writing tips add to your understanding of writing well? How do the tips differ from the legal writing advice provided in this chapter?
3. A number of interesting videos are posted on https://www.youtube.com/, some of which are related to writing a client opinion letter. Go to the website and find a video providing legal writing tips on client opinion letters. How do the legal writing tips add to your understanding of writing well? How do the tips differ from the legal writing advice provided in this chapter?
4. A sample client letter is accessible at https://www.law.cuny.edu/legal-writing/students/writing-sample/. Access the sample client letter from the website and compare it to the two sample client opinion letters included in this chapter.

Discussion Points

1. Locate a transmittal letter you have received. Does it follow the style tips in this chapter?
2. What are your reactions to the first client opinion letter?
3. What are your reactions to the second client opinion letter?

Chapter 12

Pleadings

Introduction

Pleadings are the formal statements by the parties to an action setting forth their claims or defenses. This chapter explains the purpose, use, and format of the "complaint" and the "answer" and includes two sample complaints and answers.

The sample pleadings have been extensively footnoted to provide you with writing tips. The footnotes in the sample pleadings are not part of the pleadings themselves. If the footnotes do not make sense to you right now, read them again when you are writing your own complaint and answer.

Purpose and Use

A civil lawsuit begins with the plaintiff filing the **complaint** with the court. The complaint is the initial **pleading** in a **civil action**, in which the plaintiff alleges a **cause of action** and asks the court to remedy the wrong done to the plaintiff. The purposes of the complaint are for the plaintiff to state what happened and to state the relief that the plaintiff is requesting from the court.

Complaint The first main paper filed in a civil lawsuit. It includes, among other things, a statement of the wrong or harm done to the plaintiff by the defendant, a request for specific help from the court, and an explanation why the court has the power to do what the plaintiff wants.

Pleading The process of making formal, written statements of each side of a civil case. First the plaintiff submits a paper with "facts" and claims; then the defendant submits a paper with "facts" (and sometimes counterclaims); then the plaintiff responds; until all issues and questions are clearly posed for a trial.

Civil action A lawsuit that is brought to enforce a right or to redress a wrong, rather than a court action involving the government trying to prosecute a criminal.

Cause of action Facts sufficient to support a valid lawsuit; the legal theory upon which a lawsuit ("action") is based.

The **answer** is a pleading in response to the complaint. The answer may deny the allegations of the complaint, agree with them, state that the plaintiff is without knowledge of them, or introduce **affirmative defenses** intended to defeat the plaintiff's lawsuit or delay it. The purposes of the answer are for the defendant to reply to the claims plaintiff raised in the complaint, to state the defendant's affirmative defenses, and to state related claims (called **counterclaims**) that the defendant has against the plaintiff.

Answer The first pleading by the defendant in a lawsuit. It responds to the charges and demands of the plaintiff's complaint.

Affirmative Defense That part of a defendant's answer to a complaint that goes beyond denying the facts and arguments of the complaint. The burden of proof for an affirmative defense is on the defendant.

Counterclaim A claim made by a defendant in a civil lawsuit that, in effect, "sues" the plaintiff. It can be based on entirely different things from the plaintiff's complaint (a permissive counterclaim) and may even be for more money than the plaintiff is asking.

Look for a moment at the first sample complaint and answer included in this chapter. The plaintiff is Jake Carson and the defendant is Tom Harris. Jake and Tom ran against each other for the position of student body president at Collegiate University. The basis of Jake's suit was the statement Tom made about Jake in Tom's political skit, presented on the eve of the election. In the skit, Tom stated to a student playing the part of Jake that "Jake" was HIV-positive. Jake claims that the skit also depicted him as a homosexual. Jake was so outraged by the skit that he hired an attorney to sue Tom for slander and for depicting him in a "false light" as being a homosexual. The pleadings were filed in Florida State court.

A second sample complaint and answer follows the first set of pleadings. The plaintiff, Phone Addicted, alleges that the defendant, Nosy Neighbor, has used a scanner to listen to Phone Addicted's cordless telephone conversations. The second set of pleadings were filed in federal court because a federal statute gives the federal court jurisdiction over lawsuits alleging interception of telephone conversations.

Format

Court Rules

Once you determine the court in which the complaint will be filed, you must carefully review any applicable court rules and statutes. The first sample set of pleadings should comply with the Florida Rules of Civil Procedure because they were filed in Florida State court; the second sample set of pleadings should comply with the Federal Rules of Civil Procedure. It might also be helpful to review court files to learn the format customarily used in the particular court.

Court rules may specify the contents of the complaint and the answer. For example, Rule 8 of the Federal Rules of Civil Procedure requires the complaint to state "a claim for relief." The same rule requires the answer to "state in short and plain terms its defenses to each claim asserted against it; and... [to] admit or deny the allegations asserted against it by an opposing party."

Commonly, the court rules and official forms accompanying the court rules specify the content and format of the caption (the heading of the court paper) and the body of the pleading. For example, Rules 7 through 13 of the Federal Rules of Civil Procedure govern the content of the complaint, answer, affirmative defenses, and counterclaim.

Forms

Although pleadings can be written entirely from scratch, someone writing a pleading will usually try to find one or more pleadings that are similar to the one the person is writing and use those pleadings as a guide. An attorney may recall a similar lawsuit the attorney has dealt with in the past and use a pleading from that matter as a guide.

Another option is to consult forms and formbooks. Court rules may have appended to them official forms. A number of commercial publishers publish formbooks. As the term implies, formbooks are volumes containing forms that may be referred to as a guide. There is a wide variety of formbooks. The forms contained in a particular publication may be much simpler than those contained in another formbook. Some formbooks are written in plain English while others contain a lot of "legalese." Many forms are now available on the Internet.

If you use a form, you must tailor it to the particular situation you are dealing with. Just because material is contained in a form does not mean that the material is correct for your jurisdiction. Be sure to research the cause of action and defenses for your jurisdiction to ascertain you have all the elements of the cause of action and have correctly stated the relief available and any affirmative defenses.

Besides including forms, a formbook often contains checklists of typical provisions included in a particular pleading. When writing a pleading, it is helpful to glance over the checklist to make sure you have included all necessary provisions.

Format of the Complaint

This section gives a brief explanation of the various parts of the complaint and then the various parts of the answer. It might be helpful for you to read the rest of this section and the "format of the answer section" while comparing the explanation to the two sets of sample pleadings in this chapter.

Complaint: Caption, Title, and Introductory Clause

This section (called the "caption") contains the name of the court, the names of the parties, and the case number. The title indicates the type of pleading. Rule 10 of the Federal Rules of Civil Procedure specifies the content of the caption and the pleading title. Rule 10(a) of the Federal Rules of Civil Procedure states:

> Every pleading must have a caption with the court's name, a title, a file number, and a Rule 7(a) designation. The title of the complaint must name all the parties; the title of other pleadings, after naming the first party on each side, may refer generally to other parties.

Rule 7(a) limits the types of documents that can be filed to motions and the following pleadings:

> (1) a complaint;
> (2) an answer to a complaint;
> (3) an answer to a counterclaim designated as a counterclaim;
> (4) an answer to a crossclaim;
> (5) a third-party complaint;
> (6) an answer to a third-party complaint; and
> (7) if the court orders one, a reply to an answer.

After the caption and title and before the first numbered paragraph, an unnumbered sentence (called the "introductory clause" or "commencement") states who is filing the complaint and against whom it is being filed.

Complaint: Body

This section (called the "body" or "charging portion" of the complaint) contains a series of numbered paragraphs telling the court why it has jurisdiction of the case and what has happened. For example, Rule 8(a) of the Federal Rules of Civil Procedure requires the complaint to contain:

> (1) a short and plain statement of the grounds for the court's jurisdiction, unless the court already has jurisdiction and the claim needs no new jurisdictional support; [and]
> (2) a short and plain statement of the claim showing that the pleader is entitled to relief....

Rule 8(d) encourages claims to be stated simply: "Each allegation must be simple, concise, and direct. No technical form is required"; but the rule allows alternative statements of a claim and inconsistent but separate claims.

Rule 10(b) of the Federal Rules of Civil Procedure specifies the format for the body of the pleading:

> A party must state its claims or defenses in numbered paragraphs, each limited as far as practicable to a single set of circumstances. A later pleading may refer by number to a paragraph in an earlier pleading. If doing so would promote clarity, each claim founded on a separate transaction or occurrence—and each defense other than a denial—must be stated in a separate count or defense.

YOU BE THE JUDGE

Does a complaint by a company against an employee for breach of a confidentiality agreement warrant sanctions under Rule 11 of the Federal Rules of Civil Procedure?

In reaching your decision, consider the following information:

- The term of the confidentiality agreement was five years and the disclosure took place outside the five-year term.
- The information disclosed was not confidential in nature.

To see how a court answered the question, see *Superior Consulting Services, Inc. v. Steeves-Kiss*, 786 F. App'x 648, 651 (9th Cir. 2019).

Complaint: Prayer for Relief

This section of the complaint (called the "prayer for relief") states what the plaintiff wants the court to do. For example, Rule 8(a)(3) of the Federal Rules of Civil Procedure requires the complaint to contain "a demand for the relief sought, which may include relief in the alternative or different types of relief." A plaintiff may ask the court for various types of damages, for an injunction, for specific performance, or for some other type of relief.

Complaint: Signature Block

The signature block usually contains the name of the attorney, the name and designation of the person the attorney is representing, the attorney's address, and the attorney's telephone number. Many state courts require the attorney's bar membership number. Rule 11(a) of the Federal Rules of Civil Procedure provides:

> Every pleading, written motion, and other paper must be signed by at least one attorney of record in the attorney's name—or by a party personally if the party is unrepresented. The paper must state the signer's address, e-mail address, and

telephone number.... The court must strike an unsigned paper unless the omission is promptly corrected after being called to the attorney's or party's attention.

Complaint: Verification

The verification is a notarized statement of the party, rather than of the attorney, "verifying" the statements contained in the complaint. Some states dispense with verification of court documents unless specifically required by an applicable rule or statute. You should check to determine whether the court in which your complaint is being filed requires verification. Rule 11(a) of the Federal Rules of Civil Procedure states that court documents need not be verified: "Unless a rule or statute specifically states otherwise, a pleading need not be verified or accompanied by an affidavit."

Although Rule 11 does not require verification, the effect of the rule is to certify that certain matters are true.

> (b) **Representations to the Court**. By presenting to the court a pleading, written motion, or other paper—whether by signing, filing, submitting, or later advocating it—an attorney or unrepresented party certifies that to the best of the person's knowledge, information, and belief, formed after an inquiry reasonable under the circumstances:
>
> (1) it is not being presented for any improper purpose, such as to harass, cause unnecessary delay, or needlessly increase the cost of litigation;
>
> (2) the claims, defenses, and other legal contentions are warranted by existing law or by a nonfrivolous argument for extending, modifying, or reversing existing law or for establishing new law;
>
> (3) the factual contentions have evidentiary support or, if specifically so identified, will likely have evidentiary support after a reasonable opportunity for further investigation or discovery; and
>
> (4) the denials of factual contentions are warranted on the evidence or, if specifically so identified, are reasonably based on belief or a lack of information.

If the matters are not true, the judge may sanction any person seeking to rely on the matters. Rule 11 sanctions have become a powerful tool of the judge, allowing monetary or nonmonetary sanctions.

YOU BE THE JUDGE

What should a court do where the plaintiff's attorney challenges the summary judgment granted in favor of the defendants?

In reaching your decision, consider the following information:

- There was no evidence to support the plaintiff's claims.
- The district court found that "responses to defendants' statements of material facts were laden with disingenuous and misleading statements."

To see how a court answered the question, see *McGreal v. Village of Orland Park*, 928 F.3d 556, 559–60 (7th Cir. 2019).

Format of the Answer

Answer: Caption, Title, and Introductory Clause

The caption for the answer is the same as the caption for the complaint. The title reflects that this is an answer. The introductory clause identifies the defendant and introduces the body of the answer.

Answer: Defenses

As stated previously, the answer states the defendant's defense, admitting or denying plaintiff's claims. Rule 8(b) of the Federal Rules of Civil Procedure requires the defendant to "state in short and plain terms its defenses to each claim asserted against it," "admit or deny the allegations asserted against it by an opposing party," and quite specifically state how any denial is to be made:

(2) *Denials–Responding to the Substance.* A denial must fairly respond to the substance of the allegation.

(3) *General and Specific Denials.* A party that intends in good faith to deny all the allegations of a pleading—including the jurisdictional grounds—may do so by a general denial. A party that does not intend to deny all the allegations must either specifically deny designated allegations or generally deny all except those specifically admitted.

(4) *Denying Part of an Allegation.* A party that intends in good faith to deny only part of an allegation must admit the part that is true and deny the rest.

(5) *Lacking Knowledge or Information.* A party that lacks knowledge or information sufficient to form a belief about the truth of an allegation must so state, and the statement has the effect of a denial.

(6) *Effect of Failing to Deny*. An allegation—other than one relating to the amount of damages—is admitted if a responsive pleading is required and the allegation is not denied. If a responsive pleading is not required, an allegation is considered denied or avoided.

Affirmative Defenses and Counterclaims

Rule 8 of the Federal Rules of Civil Procedure requires any affirmative defense to be stated in the same format as the body of the complaint. A counterclaim, like the body of the complaint, would be followed by a prayer for relief.

Certificate of Service

If the attorney for the defendant serves the answer on the plaintiff's attorney, a certificate of service must be included. There was no certificate of service included in the first sample complaint because the complaint was served on the defendant by the court, not by the plaintiff's attorney.

Evidentiary Facts, Ultimate Facts, and Legal Conclusions

An understanding of the terms *evidentiary facts*, *ultimate facts*, and *legal conclusion* is vital in drafting allegations of a complaint. This section will first explain what these terms mean. Then, the section will explain the relationship among the terms and drafting allegations.

Evidentiary facts are facts admissible in evidence. **Ultimate facts** are the facts in a case upon which liability is determined or based. Ultimate facts establish the elements of the cause of action. A **legal conclusion** is a statement of the result in a situation that involves applying the law to a set of facts. A legal conclusion states an element of the cause of action.

Evidentiary Facts Facts that are learned directly from testimony or other evidence. Important factual conclusions inferred from evidentiary facts are called ultimate facts.

Ultimate Facts Facts essential to a plaintiff's or a defendant's case. Often facts that must be inferred from other facts and evidence.

Legal Conclusion A statement about legal rights, duties, or results that is drawn from specific facts.

As shown below, there is an overlap between evidentiary facts and ultimate facts, and there is an overlap between ultimate facts and conclusions of law. To understand these terms, examine how they relate to the first sample complaint.

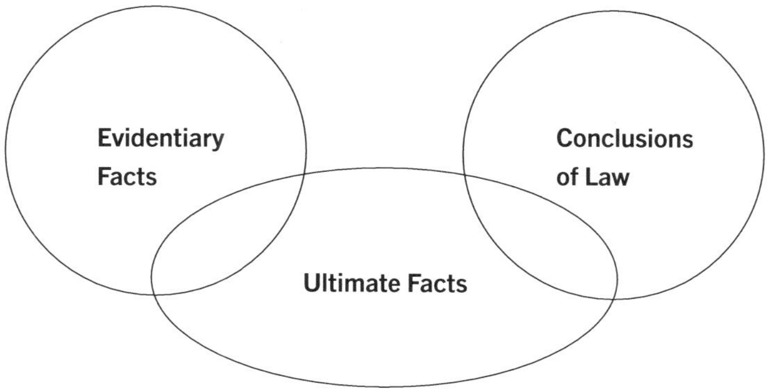

Evidentiary Facts

Paragraphs 2 through 6 and 8 contain evidentiary facts. For example:

In October 2010, plaintiff was a student at Collegiate University, a member of the Collegiate Beta Fraternity, and a candidate for student body president of Collegiate University.

In October 2010, defendant was a student at Collegiate University, a member of the Collegiate Alpha Fraternity, and a candidate for student body president of Collegiate University.

In defendant's skit, defendant portrayed "plaintiff's doctor" and another student portrayed plaintiff.

Paragraph 7 contains a mixture of evidentiary and ultimate facts. The "kernel" of the ultimate facts has been bracketed:

In defendant's skit, defendant, [in the presence and hearing of] plaintiff, and the students and faculty watching the skit, [maliciously and falsely announced] that plaintiff had tested HIV-positive, saying "you tested HIV-positive."

Ultimate Facts

Paragraphs 9 and 10 contain ultimate facts (establishing elements of defamation):

Plaintiff at the time of defendant's statement was in good health and free from any disease, and the statements of defendant were wholly untrue.
As a result of defendant's slanderous statement, plaintiff suffered, and continues to suffer, great nervousness and mental anguish.

Conclusions of Law

Paragraph 11 contains conclusions of law:

Plaintiff, as the direct result of defendant's statement, in addition to the nervousness and bodily injury, has been injured in plaintiff's good reputation in the Collegiate University community. Defendant published such false and slanderous statements about plaintiff to numerous students and faculty of Collegiate University, who have changed their attitude toward plaintiff, and who have begun to question whether plaintiff tested HIV-positive, which the slanderous remark of defendant wrongly, maliciously, and untruthfully imputed to plaintiff.

The essence of paragraph 11 is that:

Tom Harris made a defamatory statement about Jake Carson;
Tom Harris published the statement to numerous students and faculty of Collegiate University; and
The statement damaged Jake Carson's reputation.

Drafting Allegations

Now that you have an idea of the difference among evidentiary facts, ultimate facts, and conclusions of law, notice how these terms relate to drafting allegations. The body of the complaint will contain evidentiary facts, ultimate facts, and conclusions of law. The complaint should be drafted so that defendant admits as much as possible and denies as little as possible. Defendant is more likely to admit evidentiary facts than to admit ultimate facts and will routinely deny the conclusions of law. Therefore, the body of the complaint should, as much as possible, separate evidentiary facts from ultimate facts from conclusions of law. In the answer, defendant admitted paragraphs 2 through 6 and part of paragraph 7. The paragraphs defendant admitted contained evidentiary facts. The following box contains tips for drafting a complaint.

In drafting the complaint, follow this list of things to do:

Do

1. Separate evidentiary facts, ultimate facts, and conclusions of law. (Defendant will be more likely to admit allegations if evidentiary facts are separated from ultimate facts.)
2. Write in plain English. (Make your allegations clear to the judge.)
3. Place only one or two sentences in each numbered paragraph. (If a number of facts are included in a paragraph and one of the facts is wrong, defendant may deny the whole paragraph.)
4. Do not include more evidentiary facts than necessary. (Plaintiff will be faced with proving facts not admitted.)
5. Use descriptive words for allegations favorable to plaintiff; use abstract words for allegations adverse to plaintiff. (The judge will more likely remember a description that brings a picture to mind than an abstract statement of adverse facts.)
6. Use objective rather than subjective language. (It is harder for the defendant to deny objectively state facts.)
7. State facts precisely. (Defendant can easily deny inaccurate facts.)

FIRST SAMPLE SET OF PLEADINGS

First Sample Complaint

IN THE CIRCUIT COURT
OF THE NINTH JUDICIAL CIRCUIT
IN AND FOR ORANGE COUNTY, FLORIDA

JAKE CARSON,	)	
Plaintiff,	)	
	)	CIVIL ACTION
- vs -	)	No. 19-000-00
	)	
TOM HARRIS,	)	
Defendant.	)[1]	

COMPLAINT[2]

Plaintiff, JAKE CARSON, sues defendant, TOM HARRIS, and alleges:[3]

---

1. The caption contains the name of the court, the names of the parties, and the case number. There is one plaintiff and one defendant in this lawsuit. If there were more parties, all of them would be named in the caption of the initial complaint. In all other documents, only the first party on each side would be named, followed by "*et al.*" replacing all other parties. "*Et al.*" is short for "*et alia*," meaning "and others." "Jake Carson, plaintiff vs. Tom Harris, Defendant" is often referred to as the style of the case. The case number is supplied by the court clerk. The number "19" indicates the year the case was filed. The next number indicates the order of filing. Cases are given consecutive numbers based on the order filed. For example, "100" would mean that the case was the one hundredth case filed in 2019. The sample complaint is unnumbered—"000"—to show that it is not an actual case.

2. Rule 1.100 of the Florida Rules of Civil Procedure requires that court documents "indicate clearly the subject matter of the paper and the party requesting or obtaining relief." The form complaints at the end of the Florida Rules of Civil Procedure (see, for example, Forms 1.932–1.942) are simply named "Complaint." Some jurisdictions may require the pleading name to indicate the relief requested, for example, "Complaint for Damages."

3. This introductory clause (also referred to as the "commencement") states who is suing whom. Notice that the introductory clause is not numbered.

This introductory clause is modeled on the one contained in the forms at the end of the Florida Rules of Civil Procedure: "Plaintiff, A.B., sues defendant, C.D., and alleges:" (see Forms 1.932–1.942). This plain English clause is much easier to read than the traditional introductory clause filled with legalese. For example, the introductory clause rewritten in legalese might look something like this:

> Now comes the above-named plaintiff, Jake Carson, by and through his attorney of record, Florida Attorney, and for cause of action and complaint against the defendant herein alleges unto this honorable court:

Write your pleadings in plain English, complying with the court rules of your jurisdiction. Plain English pleadings are easier for the client to understand and are less time-consuming in the long run.

For simplicity's sake, there is one plaintiff and one defendant in this sample complaint. For ease of reference, they are referred to as "Plaintiff" and "Defendant" throughout the complaint. If this were a real complaint, Jake might have also named the Alpha Fraternity and Collegiate University as defendants. Multiple defendants could be referred to by short forms established in the introductory clause. For example:

> Plaintiff, JAKE CARSON, sues Defendants, TOM HARRIS ("Defendant Harris"), ALPHA FRATERNITY ("Defendant Fraternity"), and COLLEGIATE UNIVERSITY ("Defendant University") and says:

Count I—Defamation[4]

1. This is an action for damages that exceed $15,000.[5]

2. In October 2019, plaintiff was a student at Collegiate University, a member of the Collegiate Beta Fraternity, and a candidate for student body president of Collegiate University.[6]

3. In October 2019, defendant was a student at Collegiate University, a member of the Collegiate Alpha Fraternity, and a candidate for student body president of Collegiate University.[7]

4. The October 21, 2019, issue of the Collegiate University student newspaper reported that plaintiff and defendant "were running neck and neck" in the student body president race.[8]

5. On October 21, 2019, the day before the student body president election, plaintiff and defendant presented skits to Collegiate University students and faculty at the Collegiate University football stadium.

6. In defendant's skit, defendant portrayed "plaintiff's doctor" and another student portrayed plaintiff.

7. In defendant's skit, defendant, in the presence and hearing of plaintiff and the

---

> or
>
> Plaintiff, JAKE CARSON, sues Defendants, TOM HARRIS ("Harris"), ALPHA FRATERNITY ("Fraternity"), and COLLEGIATE UNIVERSITY "University" and says:

Once you establish short forms, you should use them consistently throughout the rest of the complaint. For readability, you may want to put party names in all capital letters.

4. In a complaint with more than one count, the counts are usually numbered for ease of reference. The count heading may also state the cause of action (here "Count I—Defamation" and "Count II—False Light Invasion of Privacy") or relief sought. The relief sought in another complaint, for example, may be "Specific Performance" and "Damages." If the complaint contains a single count, the count need not be headed.

In this complaint, the background for both counts is alleged in numbered paragraphs 1 through 8. Paragraph 12 of Count II realleges paragraphs 1 through 8. Another way to organize the complaint is to provide a heading "Common Allegations" after the introductory paragraph. The "Common Allegations" section of the complaint would contain numbered paragraphs 1 through 8. Then the complaint would state:

> Count I—Defamation
>
> 9. Plaintiff realleges and incorporates paragraphs 1–8.

5. The paragraphs of the body of the complaint (sometimes referred to as the "charging portion" of the complaint) are numbered consecutively. In the body of the complaint, the plaintiff alleges plaintiff's "ultimate facts." This paragraph establishes the court's jurisdiction. In Florida, the circuit court handles cases with more than $15,000 in controversy.

6. Paragraphs 2 through 11 contain the ultimate facts on which plaintiff relies. The two purposes of the body of the complaint are to:

> 1. give the defendant notice of plaintiff's claims; and
>
> 2. include all the elements of the cause of action plaintiff alleges.

Before you write the body of the complaint, make a list of the elements of the cause of action. After you have completed the body of the complaint, double check to make sure you have included ultimate facts needed for all elements.

7. Paragraphs 2 and 3 identify the parties. Usually the parties are identified early in the complaint.

8. Plaintiff begins to narrate what happened. The narrative is written in past tense.

students and faculty watching the skit, maliciously and falsely announced that plaintiff had tested HIV-positive, saying "you tested HIV-positive."

8. In the student body president election on October 22, 2019, plaintiff received 10 percent of the vote and defendant received 90 percent of the vote.

9. Plaintiff at the time of defendant's statement was in good health and free from any disease, and the statements of defendant were wholly untrue.

10. As a result of defendant's slanderous statement, plaintiff suffered, and continues to suffer, great nervousness and mental anguish.

11. Plaintiff, as the direct result of defendant's statement, in addition to the nervousness and bodily injury, has been injured in plaintiff's good reputation in the Collegiate University community. Defendant published such false and slanderous statements about plaintiff to numerous students and faculty of Collegiate University who have changed their attitude toward plaintiff and who have begun to question whether plaintiff tested HIV-positive, which the slanderous remark of defendant wrongly, maliciously, and untruthfully imputed to plaintiff.

Count II—False Light Invasion of Privacy

12. Plaintiff realleges and incorporates paragraphs 1–8.[9]

13. Prior to October 21, 2019, a rumor had circulated on the Collegiate University campus that plaintiff was a homosexual, and the rumor was traced back to defendant's fraternity.

14. Defendant's statement during the skit and the manner of its presentation, in light of the rumor that plaintiff was a homosexual, falsely depicted plaintiff as a homosexual.

15. Plaintiff is not a homosexual, and defendant's depiction of plaintiff as a homosexual was highly offensive to plaintiff.

16. Defendant's depiction of plaintiff as a homosexual was done with knowledge of its falsity or reckless disregard whether the depiction gave a false impression or not.

17. As a result of defendant's depiction of plaintiff as a homosexual, plaintiff suffered, and continues to suffer, great nervousness and mental anguish.

18. Plaintiff, as the direct result of defendant's depiction of plaintiff as a homosexual, in addition to the nervousness and bodily injury, has been injured in plaintiff's good reputation in the Collegiate University community. Such false depiction has been circulated also among plaintiff's personal friends who have changed their attitudes toward plaintiff and who have begun to question as to whether plaintiff is a homosexual, which depiction defendant wrongly, maliciously, and untruthfully imputed to plaintiff.

9. Paragraph numbering is consecutive from one count to the next.

Plaintiff therefore requests judgment granting the following relief as to Counts I and II:[10]

A. an award of compensatory damages in an amount to be set at trial;

B. an award of punitive damages in an amount to be set at trial;

C. an award of costs and attorney's fees; and

D. such other relief as the court deems appropriate.[11]

Jury Demand

Plaintiff demands trial by jury.[12]

____

Florida Attorney
Bar No. 0000000
101 Main Street
Anytown, Florida
(407) 000-0000
Attorney for Plaintiff

---

10. This is the beginning line of plaintiff's prayer for relief. The line is not numbered but the various types of relief sought are lettered with capital letters. Traditionally, the first line of the prayer for relief would have read as follows:

> Wherefore, Plaintiff, Jake Carson, demands that this honorable court grant judgment for the following relief:

This line has been rewritten in the sample complaint to eliminate legalese. Also the word "requests" (a word sounding less strident) has been substituted for "demands."

Another way to organize the complaint would be to have two prayer for relief sections—one following paragraph 11 and the other as it is in the sample complaint following paragraph 18.

11. This "catchall phrase" typically is included in the prayer for relief. It allows the court to grant relief other than that specifically requested.

12. Typically the plaintiff will request a jury trial. If plaintiff decides later against a jury trial, the right may be waived.

First Sample Answer

IN THE CIRCUIT COURT
OF THE NINTH JUDICIAL CIRCUIT
IN AND FOR ORANGE COUNTY, FLORIDA

JAKE CARSON,	)	
Plaintiff,	)	
	)	CIVIL ACTION
- vs -	)	No. 19-000-00[13]
	)	
TOM HARRIS,	)	
Defendant.	)	

Answer[14]

Defendant TOM HARRIS answers Plaintiff's complaint and says:

1. He admits paragraph 1 for jurisdictional purposes only and otherwise denies it insofar as it is applied to him.

2. He admits paragraph 2.[15]

3. He admits paragraph 3.

4. He admits paragraph 4.

5. He admits paragraph 5.

6. With respect to paragraph 6, he denies making the quoted statement maliciously or falsely. Otherwise he admits paragraph 6.[16]

7. He is without knowledge of paragraph 7.

8. He is without knowledge of paragraph 8.

9. He is without knowledge of paragraph 9.

10 He is without knowledge of paragraph 10.

---

13. The case number is copied from the complaint.

14. Because there is a single defendant, "Answer" is a sufficient title. If there were multiple defendants and the answer was that of all defendants, title the pleading "Defendants' Answer." If the answer was that of less than all the defendants, the title should indicate the party filing the answer. For example, "Answer of Defendant Collegiate University."

15. Here the defendant's numbered paragraphs correspond to the numbering of the paragraphs in the complaint. Another way to organize the answer would be for the defendant to list in a single numbered paragraph the paragraphs of the complaint admitted, to list in a single numbered paragraph the paragraphs of the complaint denied, and to list in a single numbered paragraph the paragraphs of the complaint of which defendant has no knowledge. For example:

> 2. He admits paragraphs 2 through 6.
>
> 3. He is without knowledge of paragraphs 8 through 11, 13, 15, 17, and 18.
>
> 4. He denies paragraphs 14 and 16.

16. Rule 1.110 of the Florida Rules of Civil Procedure requires the defendant to specify which part of the allegation is admitted and which part of the allegation is denied.

11. He is without knowledge of paragraph 11.

12. With respect to paragraph 12, he repeats his response to paragraphs 1 through 8.

13. He is without knowledge of paragraph 13.

14. He denies paragraph 14.

15. He is without knowledge of paragraph 15.

16. He denies paragraph 16.

17. He is without knowledge of paragraph 17.

18. He is without knowledge of paragraph 18.

First Affirmative Defense

19. Defendant's skit was an obvious expression of humor and could not reasonably be understood as describing an actual fact about plaintiff or an actual event in which plaintiff participated.

Second Affirmative Defense

20. Plaintiff has failed to allege facts showing that defendant's skit was presented with falsity, negligence, actual malice, or reckless disregard for the truth.

Certificate of Service

I furnished a copy of this answer to Florida Attorney, attorney for plaintiff, 101 Main Street, Anytown, Florida, by U.S. mail on ________, 2019.

____

Unnamed Attorney

Bar No. 100000

100 Court Street

Anytown, Florida

(407) 880-0000

Attorney for Defendant

SECOND SAMPLE SET OF PLEADINGS

Second Sample Complaint

UNITED STATES DISTRICT COURT
MIDDLE DISTRICT OF FLORIDA
ORLANDO DIVISION

PHONE ADDICTED,

Plaintiff,

v. Case No. 6:19-CIV-000-ORL-00AAA

NOSY NEIGHBOR,

Defendants.

_______________________________________/

Complaint

Plaintiff, PHONE ADDICTED, sues defendant, NOSY NEIGHBOR, and alleges:[17]

Count I—Interception of Wire Communication

1. This court has jurisdiction of this case pursuant to 28 U.S.C.A. § 1331 (West, Westlaw through P.L. 116-91)[18] and 18 U.S.C.A. § 2520 (West, Westlaw through P.L. 116-91).[19]

2. From 1995 to the present, plaintiff has resided at 200 Magnolia Street, Oviedo, Florida.[20]

3. From 2010 to the present, defendant has resided at 202 Magnolia Street, Oviedo, Florida.

4. Plaintiff regularly uses a cordless telephone to place and receive telephone calls at her residence.

5. Defendant owns a scanner capable of intercepting cordless telephone conversations.

6. In June and July of 2019, defendant intentionally intercepted and recorded a number of plaintiff's telephone calls.

---

17. Rule 8(a) of the Federal Rules of Civil Procedure governs the content and form of the complaint, as discussed earlier in this chapter.

18. Title 28 U.S.C.A. § 1331 (West, Westlaw through P.L. 116-91) provides: "The district courts shall have original jurisdiction of all civil actions arising under the Constitution, laws, or treaties of the United States." This is commonly referred to as federal question jurisdiction.

19. This statute authorizes a civil action by a person whose conversation has been wrongfully intercepted or disclosed.

20. Rule 8(d)(1) of the Federal Rules of Civil Procedure governs the substance and form of allegations of the complaint, as discussed earlier in this chapter.

7. Defendant's intentional interception of plaintiff's telephone calls violated 18 U.S.C.A. § 2511 (1) (West, Westlaw through P.L. 116-91).

Count II — Disclosure of Wire Communication

8. Plaintiff realleges and incorporates paragraphs 1–6.

9. In June and July of 2019, defendant played tapes of several of plaintiff's conversations.

10. Defendant amplified the tapes so that plaintiff could hear them while she was on her property.

11. At least two other neighbors could hear the tapes from their properties.

12. In broadcasting the tapes, defendant intentionally disclosed to other persons the contents of plaintiff's conversations.

13. Defendant knew that he had obtained the tapes of plaintiff's conversations through the interception of plaintiff's cordless telephone calls.

14. Defendant's intentional disclosure of the tapes of plaintiff's cordless telephone conversations violated 18 U.S.C.A. § 2511 (1) (West, Westlaw through P.L. 116-91).

Plaintiff therefore requests judgment granting the following relief as to counts I and II:[21]

A. an award of compensatory damages in an amount to be set at trial;

B. an award of punitive damages in an amount to be set at trial;

C. an award of costs and attorney's fees;

D. an injunction prohibiting defendant from intercepting, tape-recording, and broadcasting plaintiff's telephone conversations; and

E. such other relief as the court deems appropriate.

Jury Demand

Plaintiff demands trial by jury.

____

Florida Attorney

Bar No. 0000000

101 Main Street

Anytown, Florida

(407) 000-0000

Attorney for Plaintiff

---

21. Title 18 U.S.C.A. § 2511 (1) (West, Westlaw through P.L. 116-91) authorizes compensatory and punitive damages, reasonable attorney's fees and costs, and injunctive relief. The authorized compensatory damages are either actual damages or "statutory damages of the greater of $100 a day for each day of violation or $10,000."

Second Sample Answer

UNITED STATES DISTRICT COURT
MIDDLE DISTRICT OF FLORIDA
ORLANDO DIVISION

PHONE ADDICTED,

Plaintiff,

v. Case No. 6:19-CIV-000-ORL-00AAA

NOSY NEIGHBOR,

Defendants.

______________________________/

Answer

Defendant NOSY NEIGHBOR answers Plaintiff's complaint and says:[22]

1. He admits paragraph 1 for jurisdictional purposes only and otherwise denies it insofar as it is applied to him.

2. He admits paragraph 2.[23]

3. He admits paragraph 3.

4. He is without knowledge of paragraph 4.

5. He denies paragraph 5.

6. He denies paragraph 6.

7. He denies paragraph 7.

8. With respect to paragraph 8, he repeats his response to paragraphs 1 through 6.

9. He admits paragraph 9.

10 He admits paragraph 10.

11. He is without knowledge of paragraph 11.

12. He admits paragraph 12.

13. He denies paragraph 13.

14. He denies paragraph 14.

First Affirmative Defense[24]

15. Defendant recorded only those portions of plaintiff's conversations audible from defendant's property.

---

22. Rule 8(b) of the Federal Rules of Civil Procedure governs the form and substance of defenses and denials, as discussed earlier in this chapter.

23. Rule 8(b) of the Federal Rules of Civil Procedure governs the effect of failure to deny, as discussed earlier in this chapter.

24. Rule 8(c) of the Federal Rules of Civil Procedure governs affirmative defenses.

Second Affirmative Defense

16. Defendant broadcast only those portions of plaintiff's conversations recorded while defendant was on defendant's property.

CERTIFICATE OF SERVICE

I furnished a copy of this answer to Florida Attorney, attorney for plaintiff, 101 Main Street, Anytown, Florida, by U.S. mail on ________, 2019.

____

Unnamed Attorney

Bar No. 100000

100 Court Street

Anytown, Florida

(407) 880-0000

Attorney for Defendant

Summary

- The *complaint* is the initial pleading in a civil action, in which the plaintiff alleges a cause of action and asks that the court remedy the wrong done to the plaintiff.
- The *answer* is a pleading in response to the complaint.
- Pleadings must conform to applicable court rules and statutes.
- Pleading forms may be used to draft a pleading but must be tailored to the particular situation that you are dealing with.
- Generally the complaint contains a caption, claims, prayer for relief, and signature block.
- Generally the answer contains a caption, defenses, affirmative defenses and counterclaims, and a certificate of service.
- *Evidentiary facts* are facts admissible in evidence.
- *Ultimate facts* are the facts in a case upon which liability is determined or based.
- A *legal conclusion* is a statement of the result in a situation that involves applying the law to a set of facts.
- When drafting the complaint, follow these writing tips:
    1. Separate evidentiary facts, ultimate facts, and conclusions of law.
    2. Write in plain English.
    3. Place only one or two sentences in each numbered paragraph.

4. Do not include more evidentiary facts than necessary.
5. Use descriptive words for allegations favorable to plaintiff; use abstract words for allegations adverse to plaintiff.
6. Use objective rather than subjective language.
7. State facts precisely.

Key Terms

affirmative defense
answer
cause of action
civil action
complaint
counterclaim
evidentiary facts
legal conclusion
pleading
ultimate facts

Cyberlaw Exercises

1. Bryan Garner has interviewed many trial court judges concerning legal writing and has posted the educational video clips linked to his company's website at https://www.lawprose.org/. Go to the website, identify the interview of a trial court judge with connections to your state or a neighboring state, watch the video of the judge, and list three legal writing tips the judge provides.
2. The Above the Law website (http://www.abovethelaw.com/) is a legal tabloid with "news and gossip about the profession's most colorful personalities and powerful institutions, as well as original commentary on breaking legal developments." The website regularly contains information on frivolous lawsuits. Access the website, note the subject matter of several of the lawsuits, and discuss the consequences of filing the lawsuit to the parties, the attorneys, and society.
3. Several **You Be the Judge** boxes providing information on selected cases are included in this chapter. At the end of each box, there is a citation to the referenced case. Use a portion of the case citation, such as the case name or the volume number, abbreviation for the reporter, and the first page of the case to find the case online. Read the case to determine why it was included in this chapter.

4. Access several pleadings from your state on an online database and compare them to the examples in this chapter.
5. A number of interesting videos are posted on https://www.youtube.com/, some of which are related to writing pleadings. Go to the website and find a video providing legal writing tips on writing effective pleadings. How do the legal writing tips add to your understanding of writing well? How do the tips differ from the legal writing advice provided in this chapter?
6. The United States courts website, located at https://www.uscourts.gov/, offers access to federal court rules. The Legal Information Institute, located at https://www.law.cornell.edu/, offers access to federal and state court rules. See if you can access the various court rules for your state. Find local federal and state court rules that apply to the area in which you are located.

Discussion Points

1. What court rules are required to be followed when submitting pleadings to federal court?
2. What court rules are required to be followed when submitting pleadings to the state courts of your state?
3. Locate some pleadings filed in a court in your area. Which paragraphs contain evidentiary facts, ultimate facts, and legal conclusions?

Chapter 13

Law Office Memo

Introduction

One of the standard legal documents written by a paralegal or attorney is what will be referred to in this book as the "law office memo." (Sometimes it may be referred to as an "office memo" or "interoffice memorandum.") This chapter includes two sample office memos and explains the purpose and use of the office memo and its format. The first time you read this chapter, glance over the sample office memos, noting their format. Then refer back to the sample office memos as they are being analyzed in the balance of the chapter.

The first sample office memo has been extensively footnoted to provide you with writing and citation tips. If the notes do not make much sense to you right now, read them again after you have reviewed the rules for citations and quotations contained in Appendixes B and C. It might also be helpful for you to refer to the notes again when you are writing your own office memo.

Purpose and Use

Legal research is required when the client or the attorney is confronted with a legal problem and the answer to the problem is unclear. A client who is planning a business deal may be wondering how the deal can be structured most advantageously to minimize taxes. Often a client is contemplating suing someone. It is important for both the client and the attorney to know what the chances are of the client obtaining a judgment and whether the client would be entitled to attorney fees. After the lawsuit has been filed, there may be a procedural question that the attorney needs researched.

The main purposes of the office memo are to record the law found as a result of the research, to explain how the researcher analyzed the law and applied it to the facts, and to ultimately propose a solution to the problem. At the moment the research on the problems has been completed, the researcher is the "expert" on the legal principles involved, but the researcher will quickly forget many of the details of the research. Depending on the complexity of the questions, one hour, several hours, or several weeks of research might have been required. For a client being billed at an hourly rate, research is expensive but necessary. Writing an office memo allows both the client and the attorney to benefit from the research. The office memo can be read several times and discussed before a decision is made. Although you will find that your first office memo seems to take days to write, edit, and rewrite, the time spent by an experienced writer on an office memo is fairly small in comparison to the time spent doing the research.

Usually, multiple copies of the office memo are made, with one copy being kept by the researcher, one copy going to the attorney in the office who had requested the research, one copy being placed in the client file, one copy going to the client (if the client is knowledgeable enough to understand it), and one copy being placed in a research file in the office. The attorney and the client use their copies to decide how to resolve the problem discussed in the memo. The copy in the client file can be used later to quickly refer to the facts or to the analysis behind the decision made. Often the researcher has spent time pulling the facts together from various sources and organizing them. The memo may be referred to quickly to refresh one's memory on the facts without having to consult various sources or to understand later why the particular decision was made. The copy placed in the research file may be used to aid in later research; there may be further research to be done later on the same or a related problem. The researcher can quickly pull prior office memos and determine whether any of the research previously done can be used. If the researcher is lucky enough to find a prior office memo involving the same problem, all the researcher may have to do is update the research from the date of the prior memo.

Style

A number of common style errors made in office memos can be easily avoided if you know what to do and what not to do. After you have written the first draft of your office memo, read this section again and make any necessary change to your memo.

First of all, the tone of the office memo should be objective rather than persuasive. Choose words that are fairly neutral. For example, referring to the illegal drug problem as a "serious menace," as one court did in its opinion, is fine for an opinion, but that language sounds too persuasive for an office memo. Instead substitute "serious problem."

Second, keep yourself out of the memo. Even if the office memo contains your opinion, keep the tone of the office memo as impersonal as possible and do not use the word "I." Instead of saying: "I think that ..." you might substitute: "Based on similar facts in *Smith* and *Campbell*, it is obvious that ..." By the same token, do not use the words "we" and "you."

A third style tip is to avoid using contractions, slang, or any other informal expressions that are normally used in spoken rather than in written communication. Although the tone of the office memo does not have to be so formal that it is uninviting to read, it should be somewhat formal. Contractions and slang lend too informal a tone to your office memo.

A fourth error is use of elegant variation. Your English composition teacher probably told you not to use the same word twice and to use synonyms to make your writing more interesting. This is fine for English composition but not for legal writing. If you use two different words that mean the same thing, like "lawyer" and "attorney" or "purchaser" and "buyer," an attorney reading your writing will immediately want to know why you changed wording. The attorney will also assume there is some reason for the change. Perhaps you were referring to something different when you used a different word. If you are referring to the same thing a second time, use the same reference term.

The final style error is to use an abstract word when a more specific one is available. For example, in *Campbell* (the case on which the first sample office memo is based), the agents discovered cocaine in Campbell's car. Rather than talking about suppression of the "evidence" or the "drugs," tell your reader that Campbell filed a motion to suppress the "cocaine." It is just as easy to use the word "cocaine," it makes it easier for your reader to picture, and the word is more descriptive than "evidence" or "drugs."

Conducting an IRAC/IGPAC/FIRAC Analysis

One of the recommended ways to perform legal analysis is to conduct an IRAC/IGPAC/FIRAC analysis.

"IRAC" stands for issue, rule of law, application, and conclusion;

"IGPAC" stands for issue, general rule, precedent, application, and conclusion; and

"FIRAC" stands for facts, issue, rule of law, analysis, and conclusion.

These three terms are acronyms for organizational schemes that are used to write legal arguments. Even if a Legal Writing class does not formally use any of the three acronyms, students in the class are, in fact, employing an IRAC/IGPAC/FIRAC analysis when writing the office memo and the memorandum of law.

It would serve you well to become familiar with the three acronyms. Should you attend law school, your Legal Writing instructor may require you to write documents using one of the three acronyms as an organizational device. Using one of the acronyms to organize the substance of your legal document ensures that important information is included in the document. Law school students may also use one of the acronyms to brief cases and write law school exam essay answers.

The variants of IRAC are not limited to IGPAC and FIRAC; in fact, there are fifteen or more variations on the IRAC acronym. Some legal writers use a particular acronym when writing an office memo, which is objective in tone, and a different acronym for a persuasive document such as a memorandum of law or an appellate brief.

Format

Although there is no one correct format for office memos, the format given in this chapter is fairly standard. Another format frequently used has the same major sections but places the facts after the issues and answers. Ask your professor what format the professor prefers. You will need to do the same thing if you are asked to write an office memo for your job. Many law offices have a format that the attorneys prefer.

The following portion of this chapter tells you in general terms what to put in each section of the office memo. You may want to read the following sections while comparing them to the sample office memos.

To and From

These two sections contain the name of the person who assigned you the office memo and your name. If the office memo will be read by persons other than the person who assigned you the memo, you may want to add their names as well.

Re

Identify the subject matter of the office memo in a phrase with sufficient detail so a reader will know whether to read further.

Date

The memo should be dated with either the date you complete your research or the date you deliver it to your reader. The date is important for future reference because it is assumed that the research reflected in the memo is current with the date of the memo or shortly before.

Facts

Clearly state the significant facts that the reader needs to know to understand the reasoning section of the memo and limit them to one or two paragraphs. The facts are the facts; do not invent facts. If you do not know the important facts, spend more time gathering them, or, if that is impossible, state what facts are not known. Where important facts are unknown, you may have to assume facts and then base your research and your office memo on the assumed facts. This is fine so long as you clearly state your assumption and explain that your discussion and conclusion are based on your assumption. You may even want to assume facts in the alternative and explain what conclusions you would reach based on the various assumptions.

Issues(s) and Answer(s)

You should spend considerable time writing your issues and answers because they are the heart of your memo. You may have an idea of what your issues will be before you begin your research, so write down your issues at this preliminary stage. As you perform your research and write your office memo, you will probably find yourself revising your issues and answers several times.

An issue and the corresponding answer should each be one sentence in length while giving the reader the most information possible. An issue is usually stated in the form of a question, and the answer is a full sentence response to the issue. Usually there are the same number of issues as answers, with each issue being paired with an answer. Number your issues and answers to make it easier for your reader. If you find, in including as much information as possible in your issue and answer, that the issue and answer become unwieldy, experiment with splitting up an issue and answer into two issues and two answers.

An issue and answer contain a blend of fact and law, as depicted in the following text box. The text box contains the first issue and answer from the first sample office memo in this chapter.

The words relating to the facts are underlined and the words relating to the law are italicized. Some words are italicized and underlined because they relate both to law and to fact.

Issue

1. Did the agents have *reasonable suspicion* to stop the car for an *illegal* drug violation?

Answer

1. Because the *factors* in the *drug courier profile*, even if taken together, did not support *reasonable suspicion* of *illegal* drug activity, the cocaine should be *suppressed* unless the agents had *probable cause* to stop the car for a *traffic violation*.

Reasoning

The substance of the reasoning portion of the office memo usually is comprised of a thesis, a short conclusion, the statement of the rule of law, and the application of the rule of law to the facts.

Format for Reasoning

The reasoning portion of the first and second sample office memos in this chapter are examples of the way in which an office memo with more than one issue and one answer can be organized. The first sample office memo contains two issues and two answers; the second sample office memo contains three issues and three answers.

Thesis Paragraph

The reasoning portion of your office memo should begin with a **thesis paragraph**. This paragraph should contain your thesis—the central idea of your memo. It should serve as a road map, giving your reader the big picture of your memo. Besides stating your thesis in your thesis paragraph, you may want to state your final conclusion in simple terms.

> **Thesis Paragraph**
>
> This paragraph should contain your thesis—the central idea of your memo.

Rule of Law

The **statement of the rule of law** is the law contained in any legal sources and that will be applied to your facts later in your memo. Usually the law is contained in primary sources, but sometimes you may have to rely on secondary sources (such as law review articles or legal periodicals) if there are no primary sources on point.

> **Statement of the Rule of Law**
>
> The law contained in legal sources.

You need to clearly explain the rule of law to the reader so the reader has a solid basis for understanding the rest of your reasoning. If your law is contained in constitutional or statutory provisions, you may want to quote the relevant portions of those provisions. Leave out any portions of the provisions that are irrelevant and indicate any omission by the use of an ellipsis. If the provisions are very simple, you may want to explain them in your own words rather than quoting them. If your law is from case law, explain enough about the precedent case so the reader can understand what the case stands for and can better comprehend your application of the precedent case to the facts of the current problem. You may need to devote one or more paragraphs to explaining the significant facts of an important case where you will later be comparing the facts of the case to the facts of the current problem. Your reader will be able to understand the rest of your reasoning better if you have first given the reader a good foundation of the rule of law.

Application of Law to Facts

Many students spend so much energy explaining the rule of law that they do not have energy for the application and may skip from the rule of law to the conclusion. This is a fatal error because the application is the most important part of the office memo. Omission of the application in the office memo results in a reduction of the student's grade, severely hampers the reader's understanding, and greatly lessens the memo's utility.

When applying the law to the facts, you must lead the reader step by step from the law to your conclusion. You must specifically explain why a constitutional or statutory provision applies or does not apply to the facts before explaining the consequences of the application. When applying case law, specifically tell your reader what facts from a case are similar to and what facts are different from the facts in the memo and explain why. It is not sufficient to simply state that facts are similar or different without telling your reader which facts you are referring to and why. You may not be conscious of some of the steps you used in concluding that a particular case is or is not controlling. Try to consciously think of the steps you went through in moving from the law to the conclusion, and then write your steps down on paper so your reader can understand your analysis.

The following two text boxes contain charts you might use to help you brainstorm your application. Use the first chart if you have a case you will be discussing in the application portion of your reasoning. Use a separate chart for each case discussed in your application. In the first column, list facts that are similar when comparing the facts of the problem you have researched. List facts that differ in the second column. In the last column, state the rule of law from the case and state a conclusion for your research problem. Remember the doctrine of stare decisis. If the case you are using is mandatory authority and the facts are substantially the same as the facts in your research problem, then the research problem should be decided the same way. If the facts are not substantially similar, then your research problem may be decided differently than the case.

Facts that Are Similar	Facts that Are Different	Rule of Law and Conclusion

Use this next chart if you have one or more statutes you are applying to your research problem. In the first column, write the citations to your statutes. In the second column, list the ways in which the statutory language applies or does not apply to your research problem. In the third column, write your conclusion as to the applicability of the statutes to your research problem.

Relevant Statutory Sections	Relevance	Conclusion

Your writing of the statement of the rule of law and the application should be so clear that someone who has never read about the area of law before can understand your memo. You probably have a friend or relative who has a difficult time understanding a detailed explanation. Picture yourself with that person, and imagine how you could explain your office memo to that person. Have someone else who has no knowledge of that area of the law read your memo and tell you if there are any passages he or she could not understand. Rewrite those passages so almost anyone can understand them. Try reading your office memo out loud either to yourself or to someone else. A passage that seems perfectly clear when you read it silently may not sound very clear when read out loud. Rewrite any passages that are unclear or awkward.

Conclusion

Your conclusion should be a final paragraph that ties everything together. Remember that in applying case law to your facts you are guided by the *doctrine of stare decisis*. If the facts in a prior case from the same or a higher court are substantially similar, then the answer to the problem should be the same as the result reached by the court in the prior case. Summarize the similarities and differences between the case law used as authority and the facts of the memo, and explain what cases you are relying on to reach your conclusion.

FIRST SAMPLE OFFICE MEMO

To: legal research and writing classes
From: author of this memo
Re: whether cocaine found in a car stopped on I-95 should be suppressed
Date: April 5, 2019

Facts

Mike Campbell[1] and his best friend, John Wright, were driving north on I-95 returning from spring break in Florida, when they were stopped by members of a drug task force made up of Volusia County officers and federal drug enforcement agents. The agents requested permission to search the car. When Campbell refused consent, the agents brought in a drug dog that alerted the agents to the trunk of the car. The agents then claimed that the dog's actions gave them probable cause to search the trunk and gave Campbell the choice of either opening the trunk or waiting until the agents obtained a search warrant. After Campbell opened the trunk, the agents found two kilograms of cocaine in a brown paper bag. Campbell and Wright were arrested and charged with possession with intent to distribute cocaine. Prior to trial they filed a motion to suppress the cocaine, claiming that it was the fruit of an unreasonable search and seizure.

The agents claimed they stopped the Campbell car because Campbell was following the car in front of him too closely and because the following facts fit a drug courier profile used by the Volusia County officers:

1. The car was a large, late model;
2. The car had out-of-state tags;
3. The car was being driven cautiously at the speed limit;
4. The car was being driven on a known drug corridor, I-95;
5. There were two passengers in the car;
6. The passengers were in their twenties;
7. The car was being driven in the early evening; and
8. The passengers were dressed casually.[2]

Although not listed by the agents, Campbell and Wright believe the real reason they were stopped is because they are African Americans.

Issues[3]

1. Did the agents have reasonable suspicion to stop the car for an illegal drug violation?

1. It is easier for your reader to understand if you refer to people by their names (a surname is sufficient) instead of as "plaintiff," "defendant," or similar terms. An alternative is to use terms such as "suspect" or "officer."

2. When you have a list of items, make it easier for your reader to skim down the list by tabulating. Number each item, follow each item except for the last one by a semicolon, and place the word "and" after the semicolon following the next to last item. Make sure that you follow parallel construction for all items. (See Appendix D for an explanation of parallel construction.)

3. Each issue should be a single-sentence question. Between the issue and the answer, you should give your reader the most information possible. Often a reader will read the issues and the answers first to determine if he or she should read the whole memo. It is very frustrating for the reader if the reader cannot make that determination without reading the rest of the memo.

2. Did the agents have probable cause to stop the Campbell car for the driver's failure to follow at a safe distance?

Answers[4]

1. Because the factors in the drug courier profile, even if taken together, did not support reasonable suspicion of illegal drug activity, the cocaine should be suppressed unless the agents had probable cause to stop the car for a traffic violation.
2. If Campbell failed to follow the vehicle in front of him at an appropriate distance, the stop did not violate the passengers' Fourth Amendment[5] right against unreasonable search and seizure, and the cocaine cannot be suppressed on that ground.

Reasoning[6]

Federal legislation makes possession of cocaine a crime, and officers have the task of enforcing this legislation. One method used to check illegal drug activity is to cut down on the transportation of illegal drugs along the nation's highways.[7] Unfortunately, there is no accurate method to determine which cars on the highway are carrying drugs unless the cars are stopped and searched. The car driver and passengers expect that activities within the car will be private and not subject to the scrutiny of law enforcement officials. They may feel that their privacy is invaded if a law enforcement officer stops the car to investigate. A trained police officer may have a hunch that a car's occupants are engaged in illegal activity; however, a law enforcement officer may not con-

---

4. Each answer should be a complete, single-sentence answer responding to an issue. Usually there are the same number of answers as there are issues. An exception would be, for example, if the issue is so broad that there are two parts to the answer. As previously stated, between the issue and the corresponding answer, give your reader the most information possible. If you find an issue and answer getting so long as to be unwieldy, try splitting them up into two issues and answers.

5. If you refer to a constitutional or statutory provision in an issue or answer by number, also give your reader a short explanation of the provision's subject matter. Otherwise your reader will be frustrated by not knowing why you cited a particular provision. It is usually better not to give case citations in issues or answers. Instead, state the rule of law from the case in your issue or answer and cite the case in the reasoning section of your memo.

6. You should begin the reasoning portion of your office memo with a thesis paragraph. A well-written thesis paragraph provides the reader with a framework into which the balance of the memo can be placed. It also tells the reader your ultimate conclusion.

A *thesis* is the central idea running through the entire memo. The time you spend before you start writing in developing your thesis is well worth it. Once you find a central idea, it will be much easier to organize the writing of your memo. To find a thesis, think in broad terms of a problem or controversy that is the basis for your memo—the problem or controversy that caused you to do the research in the first place. This memo concerns the delicate balance between society's interest in enforcing criminal drug statutes against the individual's constitutional right against unreasonable search and seizure. The courts recognize society's interest by prosecuting those believed to have violated criminal drug statutes, but the courts also recognize the individual's constitutional right by excluding any evidence obtained in violation of the Fourth Amendment.

7. Be sure to keep your tone objective rather than persuasive.

stitutionally stop a car unless there is a reasonable suspicion of illegal activity or there is a traffic violation.[8]

The stop of Campbell's car to investigate for criminal activity was not permissible because the agents did not have reasonable suspicion of illegal drug activity. If Campbell violated a Florida statute by following too closely, the stop for a traffic violation was constitutionally justifiable.[9]

The Fourth Amendment[10] to the United States Constitution guarantees "[t]he[11] right of the people to be secure in their persons, houses, papers, and effects against unreasonable searches and seizures" and allows a search warrant to be issued only upon "probable cause."[12] The Fourth Amendment does not prohibit all searches and seizures—just *unreasonable* searches and seizures. Although obtaining a search warrant before conducting a search is preferable, the courts have allowed a number of exceptions to the search warrant requirement over the years. One exception[13] is for illegal drug activity and another exception is to investigate a traffic violation. These two exceptions are the ones involved in *Campbell* and are discussed in detail in this memo.

Terry v. Ohio, 392 U.S. 1 (1968),[14] was the landmark case that lowered the burden of proof necessary for a stop from probable cause to "reasonable suspicion." In *Terry*[15] the United States Supreme Court held that police officers could stop someone on the street to investigate possible drug activity so long as the stop was based on something more than an "unparticularized suspicion or 'hunch.'"[16] To reach the level of reasonable suspicion, the officer may rely on "reasonable inferences" from "unusual conduct." *Id.* at

---

8. This paragraph is the thesis paragraph.

9. This paragraph contains a short conclusion.

10. When quoting a constitutional or statutory provision, quote only the relevant portion. Set quotations of fifty words or more off from the rest of the text in a quotation block indented left and right but not enclosed in quotation marks. If the quoted passage contains a quotation, the internal quotation should be enclosed in quotation marks.

11. The brackets indicate a change in the quotation from the original. Originally, the "t" was upper case.

12. Periods and commas go inside quotation marks. Other punctuation is placed outside quotation marks unless it is part of the quotation.

13. Signposts are words used to guide the reader in a particular direction. "One exception" and "another" are signposts clearly identifying the two exceptions that are discussed in much more detail later in the memo.

14. The first time you are referring to a case by name you must give the full citation. After that you should use a short-form citation. Citations in the sample office memo are given in *Bluebook* form. Your professor may require you to cite according to some other citation rule (perhaps your state's citation rule). If so, always check the appropriate citation rule to make sure you are citing correctly.

15. Once you have given the full citation for a case and are referring to the case in general terms, you can refer to it by using one or two of the words from the name of the case and underlining or italicizing it. Be sure the words you select are not so common as to cause confusion. Here, for example, use *Terry* rather than *Ohio.*

16. To indicate quotes within quotes, alternate double and single quotation marks, with double quotations outermost.

27.[17] Such stops made on reasonable suspicion are often referred to as "*Terry* stops" after *Terry* and the definition of *Terry* stops has been broadened to apply to car stops. Once a *Terry* stop is made, the officers would still need probable cause or consent to search a car.

In recent years, federal courts[18] have decided a number of cases in which the defendants filed motions to suppress, claiming that the evidence seized from cars should be suppressed because of a violation of their right against unreasonable search and seizure. In a case involving almost identical facts to those in *Campbell*,[19] the United States Court of Appeals for the Eleventh Circuit found that a highway stop was not reasonable under the Fourth Amendment even though the stop was made based on a drug courier profile and the driver had allegedly committed a traffic violation. *United States v. Smith*, 799 F.2d 704, 712 (11th Cir. 1986).[20] Although the *Smith* court found that the *Smith* drug courier profile did not support reasonable suspicion, the use of drug courier profiles is not per se unconstitutional. *Id.* at 708 n.5.[21] The United States Supreme Court has allowed the use of drug courier profiles when all the factors of the drug courier profile taken together do support reasonable suspicion. *United States v. Sokolow*, 490 U.S. 1, 9 (1989).

In 1996, the United States Supreme Court decided that a stop for a traffic violation does not violate the driver's constitutional right against unreasonable search and seizure. *Whren v. United States*, 517 U.S. 806, 818 (1996). Under the Fourth Amendment, a police officer may stop a car for any type of traffic violation, no matter how minor. A traffic stop is constitutional so long as there is a technical violation of a traffic regulation; it does not matter if the reason the agents gave was a pretext for the stop based on race. If Campbell violated the Florida statute by following too closely, then the stop was constitutional. If Campbell did not violate the statute, then the stop was unconstitutional.

---

17. The word "*Id.*" means that you are referring to the immediately preceding authority cited and the number "27" tells you the page number on which your reader will find the material.

18. Capitalize the word "court" only when referring to the United States Supreme Court or to the full name of any other court.

19. Refer to "*Campbell*" showing it is a case because Campbell and Wright have had charges filed against them.

20. Page "704" is the first page of *Smith* and "712" is the page on which the finding of the court referred to in the preceding sentence is located. As a courtesy to the reader, a page reference should be given when specific material from a case is referred to even if the material is not quoted. The two types of sentences in legal writing are textual sentences and citation sentences. A textual sentence is the type of sentence you have been writing all your life. It is a complete grammatical sentence with a subject and a verb. A citation sentence contains only citations. A "string citation" is a citation sentence with more than one citation. In a string citation, the citations should be separated by semicolons. A sentence is more difficult to read when it contains a full-case citation, especially if the citation is long. To avoid including a full citation in a textual sentence, refer to a case in very general terms or refer to a legal principle from a case and give the full citation to the case in a citation sentence following the textual sentence.

21. This reference is to footnote 5 of *Smith* located on page 708.

This memo will discuss *Smith*,[22] *Sokolow*, and *Whren* and apply them to the above facts to answer the two issues being considered.[23]

Reasoning for Issue One[24]

One night in June of 1985, Trooper Robert Vogel, a Florida Highway Patrol trooper, and a DEA agent were observing cars traveling in the northbound lanes of I-95, in hopes of intercepting drug couriers. When Smith's car passed through the arc of the patrol car headlights, Vogel noticed the following factors that matched his drug courier profile:

1. The car was traveling at 3:00 a.m.;
2. The car was a 1985 Mercury, a large, late model car;
3. The car had out-of state tags;
4. There were two occupants of the car who were around 30; and
5. The driver was driving cautiously and did not look at the patrol car as the Mercury passed through the arc of the patrol car headlights.

799 F.2d at 705–06.[25]

This drug courier profile is almost identical to the *Campbell* profile.[26] In both *Smith* and *Campbell*, the cars were traveling after dark, the cars were large, late models with

---

22. Delete excess words by writing "*Smith*" instead of "the *Smith* case" or "the case of *Smith*."

23. This sentence contains transitional language helping the reader make the transition from the introductory material contained in the first part of the reasoning section to the reasoning for issue one. Your reader will understand your memo better if you make transitions from one paragraph to the next as smooth as possible by using transitional language.

24. The material that applies to both issues was placed in the preceding section. The material in this section of the memo applies to issue one. Some of the material in this section, such as some of the facts from *Smith*, also apply to issue two. Rather than state the *Smith* facts all over again in the next section, you can refer the reader back to this section, if necessary.

25. When providing a citation for a block quote or other material set off from the rest of the text, as is the tabulation here, bring the citation back to the left margin. "*Id.*" cannot be used here because "*id.*" would refer back to the immediately preceding citation, *Sokolow*, instead of to *Smith*. When "*id.*" cannot be used, give the volume number of the reporter, the abbreviation for the reporter, "at," and the page number. You could precede this short-form citation by "*Smith*," if *Smith* had not been cited for a page or more or the reader might confuse the citation with another case, especially one from the same volume of the same reporter. This is not necessary here because *Smith* has been cited fairly recently. When citing inclusive pages with three or more digits, drop all but the last two digits of the second number and place a hyphen between the numbers.

26. This is an example of a topic sentence. A topic sentence contains one main idea summarizing the rest of the paragraph, with the rest of the paragraph developing the idea presented in the topic sentence. Most paragraphs should have topic sentences. The typical location of a topic sentence is the first sentence in the paragraph. Sometimes the topic sentence is the last sentence in the paragraph and pulls together the rest of the paragraph. Some paragraphs, typically narrative paragraphs like the preceding paragraph, do not have a topic sentence. If a paragraph sounds disjointed or unorganized, try pulling it together using a topic sentence. If a topic sentence does not help, think about breaking the paragraph up into more than one paragraph.

out-of-state tags, the cars were being driven "cautiously," and each car contained two passengers in their twenties or thirties. The differences between the two profiles are very minor. Campbell and Wright were dressed casually while it is not known how Smith and Swindell were dressed. Smith and Swindell did not look at Vogel as they passed. It is not known whether Campbell and Wright looked in the agents' direction as Campbell drove past. Campbell and Wright claim that race was a factor in their stop even though it was not listed as such by the agents. Smith and Swindell's race is unknown.[27]

In *Smith*, Vogel followed the Mercury for a mile and a half and noticed that the Mercury "wove" several times, once as much as six inches into the emergency lane. Vogel pulled Smith over. When a drug dog alerted on the car, a DEA agent searched the trunk and discovered one kilogram of cocaine. Smith and his passenger, Swindell, were arrested and were charged with conspiracy to possess cocaine with the intent to distribute it. Smith and Swindell's motions to suppress the cocaine were denied, and they were tried and convicted. *Id.* at 706.

The issue before the appellate court was whether the stop of Smith's car was reasonable. *Id.*[28] This is the same basic issue that will be before the *Campbell* court when it considers Campbell and Wright's motion to suppress. The *Smith* court held that the stop of Smith's car could not be upheld as a valid *Terry* stop, *id.* at 708, finding that "Trooper Vogel stopped the car because [Smith and Swindell][29] ... matched a few non-distinguishing characteristics contained on a drug courier profile and, additionally, because Vogel was bothered by the way the driver of the car chose not to look at him." *Id.* at 707.

Just as there was nothing in the *Campbell* drug courier profile to differentiate Campbell and Wright from other innocent college students returning from spring break in Florida, there was nothing in Vogel's drug courier profile to differentiate Smith and Swindell from other law-abiding motorists on I-95. It is usual to drive after dark to

27. This paragraph applies the facts in *Smith* to the facts in *Campbell*. Applying facts from one case to another case involves explaining the similarities and differences between the two sets of facts. Instead of simply stating that the facts from the two cases are very similar, the paragraph specifically states which facts are the same. Sometimes in the application you need to explain in what way the facts are similar if they are not identical. You can either apply the *Smith* facts to *Campbell* as done here, or you can wait until you have thoroughly discussed *Smith*. When you prepare your outline prior to starting to write the office memo, spend some time moving parts of your reasoning around to determine the best flow for your reasoning.

28. When you are referring to material from the same page as the material you referred to in the last citation, use just "*id.*" Note that *id.* is capitalized only at the beginning of a sentence.

29. "Smith and Swindell" are in brackets because this wording was inserted into the quotation by the person writing the memo. The ellipsis (...) shows that something was omitted from the original wording of the quotation. Your quotations must exactly match the wording and punctuation of the authority the quotation comes from. If you are sloppy in quoting and your reader discovers that you have taken "liberties" with the quotation, your reader may suspect that you are sloppy in other ways—perhaps even in your research. See Appendix C for an explanation of quoting correctly.

avoid heavy traffic and to complete an interstate trip.[30] Although many motorists speed on the highways, motorists driving "cautiously" at or near the speed limit are simply obeying traffic laws. Many people other than drug couriers drive large, late model cars with out-of-state tags. A motorist between the ages of twenty and forty is not unusual.

The contrast between the *Campbell* and *Smith* drug courier profiles, which do not support reasonable suspicion, and the *Sokolow* drug courier profile, which was held to support reasonable suspicion, is instructive. *Sokolow*, 490 U.S. at 3. In *Sokolow*, DEA agents found 1,063 grams of cocaine inside Sokolow's carry-on luggage when he was stopped in Honolulu International Airport based on the following profile:

1. He had paid $2,100 in cash for two airplane tickets from a roll of $20 bills that appeared to contain $4,000;
2. He was ticketed under a name other than his own;
3. He traveled to Miami, a known drug source, and back;
4. Although his round-trip flight lasted 20 hours, he stayed in Miami only 48 hours;
5. He appeared nervous;
6. He was about 25 years old;
7. He was dressed in a black jumpsuit and was wearing gold jewelry that he wore during both legs of the round trip flight; and
8. Neither he nor his companion checked any luggage.[31]

Id. at 3–5. The Court explained that the provided drug courier profile must be evaluated in light of "the totality of the circumstances—the whole picture." *Id.* at 8 (quoting *United States v. Cortez*, 449 U.S. 411, 417 (1981)).[32] "Any one of these factors [in the drug courier profile] is not by itself proof of any illegal conduct and is quite consistent with innocent travel. But we think taken together they amount to reasonable suspicion." *Id.* at 9. The *Sokolow* dissent would have found that all of the factors, even if "taken together," did not amount to reasonable suspicion. In criticizing the use of a drug courier profile to stop suspects, the dissent noted "the profile's 'chameleon-like way of adapting to any particular set of observations'" "subjecting innocent individuals to unwarranted police harassment and detention." *Id.* at 13 (Marshall, J., dissenting)[33] (quoting *Sokolow v. United States*, 831 F.2d 1413, 1418 (9th Cir. 1987), *rev'd*, 490 U.S. 1 (1989)[34]).

---

30. No page reference is needed when you have already given the facts in the cases you are using as authority and are referring to those cases in general.

31. Only those facts from *Sokolow* that are relevant to the discussion of *Smith* are given.

32. When you are quoting from a case that in turn quotes from another case, identify the second case by putting the citation to the second case in parentheses following the citation for the case you are quoting.

33. You must identify the type of opinion you are quoting from if it is other than the majority opinion.

34. Subsequent history must be given for the lower court decision in *Sokolow*.

As predicted in the *Sokolow* dissent, Smith, Swindell, Campbell, and Wright were subjected to "unwarranted police harassment and detention" even though the factors in the respective drug courier profiles, even if "taken together," did not amount to reasonable suspicion. In contrast, several of the *Sokolow* factors, such as carrying such a large amount of cash and traveling a long distance to stay a relatively short period of time, are unusual or even suspicious in and of themselves. Each of the *Smith* and *Campbell* factors was not at all out of the ordinary alone and certainly taken together did not amount to reasonable suspicion.

Conclusion[35] for Issue One

Because the drug courier profiles in *Smith* and *Campbell* are virtually identical and are in sharp contrast to the *Sokolow* drug courier profile, the *Campbell* court should find that there was not reasonable suspicion to stop Campbell and the stop on that ground was an unconstitutional violation of Campbell and Wright's constitutional guarantee against unreasonable search and seizure. Unless the agents had probable cause to investigate the alleged traffic violation, the *Campbell* court should suppress the cocaine as the fruit of an unconstitutional search and seizure.

Reasoning for Issue Two

An examination of *Whren v. United States* is necessary to answer the second issue. In *Whren*, Brown was driving a Pathfinder in which Whren was a passenger. Brown was stopped at a stop sign, looking down into Whren's lap. Plainclothes police officers were patrolling this "high drug area" of the District of Columbia in an unmarked patrol car. The Pathfinder caught the attention of the officers because Brown remained stopped at the stop sign for approximately twenty seconds. When the patrol car made a U-turn to follow the Pathfinder, Brown turned right without signaling and started off at an "unreasonable speed." The patrol car stopped the Pathfinder. When one of the officers approached Brown's window and peered in, he saw that Whren had two plastic bags of crack cocaine on his lap. The officers arrested Whren and Brown. 517 U.S. at 808, 809.

Justice Scalia phrased the issue as "whether the temporary detention of a motorist who the police have probable cause to believe has committed a civil traffic violation is inconsistent with the Fourth Amendment's prohibition against unreasonable seizures, unless a reasonable officer would have been motivated to stop the car by a desire to enforce the traffic laws." *Id.* at 808. The Court answered the question, "no." "[T]he district court found that the officers had probable cause to believe that petitioners had violated the traffic code. That rendered the stop reasonable under the Fourth Amendment, the evidence thereby discovered admissible, and the upholding

35. Your conclusion section at the end of a reasoning section ties together your previous discussion and reaches a conclusion. The difference between the conclusion section for issue one and answer one is that answer one is a more condensed one-sentence version of the conclusion section.

of the convictions by the Court of Appeals for the District of Columbia Circuit correct." *Id.* at 819.

Whren and Brown, both black, had urged the Court to apply the reasonable officer standard. They argued that, because of the multitude of traffic ordinances, an officer could almost invariably find some reason to stop a particular vehicle for an alleged traffic violation. This might allow an officer to target a particular vehicle to be stopped on the pretext of a traffic violation, when the real reason for stopping the vehicle was an impermissible factor such as the race of the persons in the vehicle. *Id.* at 810. The Court dismissed this argument. "We of course agree with petitioners that the Constitution prohibits selective enforcement of the law based on considerations such as race. But the constitutional basis for objecting to intentionally discriminatory application of laws is the Equal Protection Clause, not the Fourth Amendment." *Id.* at 813. The Court did not explain that an equal protection clause challenge is difficult to prove because it requires evidence of intentional discrimination.

Prior to *Whren*, some courts, including the court deciding *Smith*, had decided that a car stop for a traffic violation was unconstitutional unless a reasonable officer would have made the stop. The *Smith* court found that the cocaine should have been excluded from evidence because a reasonable officer would not have stopped Smith's car for the alleged traffic violation. 799 F.2d at 711. However, in *Whren*, the United States Supreme Court rejected the argument that the reasonable officer standard should apply. 517 U.S. at 813.

After *Whren*, it would be very difficult to convince a court that a stop for an alleged traffic violation is unconstitutional. However, if the court finds that the driver did not violate any traffic regulation, then the stop would be unconstitutional.

The applicable Florida motor vehicle statute states: "The driver of a motor vehicle shall not follow another vehicle more closely than is reasonable and prudent, having due regard for the speed of such vehicles and the traffic upon, and the condition of, the highway." Fla. Stat. Ch. 316.0895 (1) (2019). No simple test determines if Campbell violated the statute. The court must determine from any evidence presented whether the distance at which Campbell was following the car in front of him was reasonable and prudent.

Whren and *Campbell* are very similar in that, in both cases, the government claimed that the stop of a suspect car did not violate the driver's right against unreasonable search and seizure because there was some irregularity in the way the car was being driven that gave the officer reason to stop the car. The driving "irregularities" are similar in the failure to use a turn signal in changing lanes and speeding in *Whren* and the following too closely in *Campbell* are moving violations that can pose a severe safety hazard; under the circumstances, neither appeared to adversely impact any other vehicle's safety.

The alleged driving irregularities in *Whren* and *Campbell* are dissimilar in several respects. While it was clear that Brown committed a traffic violation, the Florida statute that Campbell allegedly violated does not apply to Campbell if he was following at a safe distance. Determining whether one vehicle is following another vehicle too closely involved much more of a judgment call than determining whether the Pathfinder in *Whren* failed to signal when turning right and exceeded the speed limit. The position of the vehicles on the highway and the weather and road conditions must all be considered to determine whether Campbell violated the statute by following the vehicle in front of him too closely.

Conclusion for Issue Two

Whren rejected the argument that a pretextual traffic stop is unconstitutional. *Whren* is binding on the *Campbell* court. Following the mandatory authority of *Whren*, the *Campbell* court should hold that the stop was constitutional if the agents had probable cause of a traffic violation; the court should hold that the stop was unconstitutional if there was no traffic violation. If the *Campbell* stop did not violate the Fourth Amendment, Campbell and Wright's motion to suppress would be denied. If the stop were unconstitutional, the cocaine would be suppressed.

SECOND SAMPLE OFFICE MEMO

To: legal research and writing classes
From: author of this memo
Re: whether drugs found in a car passenger's purse should be suppressed
Date: March 22, 2019

Facts

Cruz Estrada was riding with her friend, Luis Briones, when Luis's car was pulled over. They were traveling south on I-95 toward Miami to visit friends. The officer said he had stopped the car because they were speeding.

The officer stood at the window on the driver's side and asked for Luis's license and car registration. While Luis searched his wallet for the documents, the officer noticed a glass vial containing small kernels of an off-white substance in Luis's lap. Believing the vial to contain crack cocaine, the officer announced that he was seizing it. He asked Luis and Cruz to exit the car and asked Luis for his wallet.

Cruz got out of the car with her purse strap slung over her shoulder. The officer approached her and said, "You don't mind if I search this, do you?" Without giving her time to respond, the officer grabbed her purse and began to search it. Inside her purse, he found a brown paper envelope. Cruz claimed that someone had given it to her to give to a friend in Miami.

Still holding Cruz's purse and Luis's wallet, the officer asked them to wait in the patrol car while he searched Luis's car. Cruz and Luis nervously waited in the backseat of the patrol car. Cruz admitted to Luis that the envelope was hers and that it contained illegal drugs.

After Cruz and Luis were arrested, she discovered that the police officer had tape-recorded their conversation in the back of the patrol car. Luis told her that the reason the officer gave for stopping them must have been a pretext because, at the most, he was driving five miles over the speed limit. He said he suspected that he had been stopped for what is jokingly referred to as the offense of DWH or Driving While Hispanic.

She has been charged under the federal drug statutes.

Issues

1. Did the officer have probable cause to stop the Briones car for speeding when Luis was exceeding the speed limit by only a few miles and Luis suspects that his race (Hispanic) was the motivation for the stop?
2. When the officer grabbed Cruz's purse from her shoulder, did the officer's search of Cruz's purse violate her Fourth Amendment right against unreasonable search and seizure, and can the drugs found in her purse be suppressed?
3. When the officer tape-recorded Cruz and Luis's conversation while they were seated in the backseat of the patrol car, is the tape admissible as evidence?

Answers

1. Because an officer can stop the car for any traffic violation, no matter how minor, the stop did not violate Cruz's Fourth Amendment right against unreasonable search and seizure, and the drugs cannot be suppressed on that ground.
2. Because Cruz did not consent to the search of her purse, she may be able to have the drugs suppressed if the court views her purse as an outer layer of clothing.
3. Because Cruz and Luis had no reasonable expectation of privacy in the back of the patrol car, their conversation was not an "oral communication," suppressible under the federal eavesdropping statutes; however, the tape may be suppressed if the court decides that the search of Cruz's purse was unconstitutional and that the tape is derivative of the search.

Reasoning

The *Estrada* facts illustrate the tension between an individual's expectation of privacy and a federal law enforcement officer's duty to enforce the federal drug statutes. Car occupants usually feel that items they transport in a car will remain private; however, the Fourth Amendment allows a police officer to stop a car for a traffic violation and question the occupants. The officer may search the car if the occupants consent or if the officer has probable cause that the car contains illegal drugs. During the search, the officer may ask the car occupants to wait in the patrol car for their safety or comfort. Suspects seated in the rear seat of a patrol car may expect the same amount of privacy they would have were they in a private car. With the patrol car doors and windows closed, the officer outside the patrol car cannot hear the suspects' conversation. However, the officer might tape the suspects' conversation in the belief that the patrol car is similar to the officer's office in a police station.

Cruz can allege that her Fourth Amendment rights were violated when the officer stopped the car in which she was riding and searched her purse. She can also claim that her conversation in the backseat of the patrol car should have been protected against being tape-recorded under the federal eavesdropping statutes. The stop of the car for a traffic violation was constitutionally justifiable. Because Cruz did not consent to the search of her purse, she may be able to have the drugs suppressed if the court views her purse as similar to an outer layer of clothing. The conversation in the backseat of the patrol car will not be suppressed under the federal eavesdropping statutes because Cruz and Luis had no reasonable expectation of privacy; however, if the search of Cruz's purse was unconstitutional and the incriminating statements on the tape were the fruit of the search, then the tape could be suppressed as well.

General Reasoning for Issues One and Two

The Fourth Amendment to the United States Constitution guarantees "[t]he right of the people to be secure in their persons, houses, papers, and effects against unreasonable searches and seizures" and allows a search warrant to be issued only upon "probable cause." The Fourth Amendment does not prohibit all searches and seizures—just *unreasonable* searches and seizures. Although obtaining a search warrant before conducting a search is preferable, the courts have allowed a number of exceptions to the search warrant requirement over the years. At least two exceptions apply to a vehicle search. One exception is for the occupants to consent to a search of the vehicle. *Florida v. Jimeno*, 500 U.S. 248, 251 (1991). A second exception is that the officer can search the car if there is probable cause of criminal activity. Even without consent, the officer can search containers found in the car and suspected of holding the object of the officer's search, no matter who owns the container. *Wyoming v. Houghton*, 526 U.S. 295, 300–01 (1999). An officer may not search someone's person without probable cause. *Id.* at 303. These exceptions are the ones involved in *Estrada* and are discussed in detail in this memo.

Reasoning for Issue One

On June 10, 1996, the United States Supreme Court decided a landmark case in which the Court held that the Fourth Amendment allows a police officer to stop a vehicle for any type of traffic violation. *Whren v. United States*, 517 U.S. 806, 819 (1996). The facts of *Estrada* and *Whren* will be compared to determine if the *Estrada* vehicle stop was constitutional.

In *Whren*, plainclothes law enforcement officers were patrolling a high-drug area of the District of Columbia when they passed a Pathfinder truck stopped at a stop sign. The driver was looking into the lap of the passenger, and the truck paused an overly long period of time at the stop sign. As the patrol car made a U-turn to approach the truck, the truck turned right without signaling and started off at an "unreasonable" speed. The patrol car overtook the truck and stopped it. Whren was a passenger and Brown was the driver. When one officer looked through the driver's window, he saw plastic bags of something resembling crack cocaine in Whren's hands. *Id.* at 808.

In *Whren*, Justice Scalia phrased the issue as "whether the temporary detention of a motorist who the police have probable cause to believe has committed a civil traffic violation is inconsistent with the Fourth Amendment's prohibition against unreasonable seizures unless a reasonable officer would have been motivated to stop the car by a desire to enforce the traffic laws." *Id.* The Court answered the question, "no." "[T]he district court found that the officers had probable cause to believe that petitioners had violated the traffic code. That rendered the stop reasonable under the Fourth Amendment, the evidence thereby discovered admissible, and the upholding of the convictions by the Court of Appeals for the District of Columbia Circuit correct." *Id.* at 819.

Whren and Brown, both black, had urged the Court to apply the reasonable officer standard. They argued that, because of the multitude of traffic ordinances, an officer could almost invariably find some reason to stop a particular vehicle for an alleged traffic violation. This might allow an officer to target a particular vehicle to be stopped on the pretext of a traffic violation, when the real reason for stopping the vehicle was an impermissible factor such as the race of the persons in the vehicle. *Id.* at 810. The Court dismissed this argument. "We of course agree with petitioners that the Constitution prohibits selective enforcement of the law based on considerations such as race. But the constitutional basis for objecting to intentionally discriminatory application of laws is the Equal Protection Clause, not the Fourth Amendment." *Id.* at 813. The Court did not explain that an equal protection clause challenge is difficult to prove because it requires evidence of intentional discrimination.

After *Whren*, it would be very difficult to convince a court that a stop for an alleged traffic violation is unconstitutional. One instance is if the facts, which the officer states violate a traffic ordinance, are found by a court not to violate the ordinance. For example, an officer could stop a car because the officer believes that the windows are too heavily tinted. A court could find the stop unconstitutional if the tinting, although dark, did comply with the applicable traffic ordinance. Another instance is if the court finds that the officer lied; no facts existed that could support the alleged violation.

Whren and *Estrada* are very similar in that, in those cases, the government claimed that the stop of a suspect car did not violate the driver's right against unreasonable search and seizure because there was some irregularity in the way the car was being driven that gave the officer reason to stop the car. The driving "irregularities" are similar in that

Brown's failure to signal a right turn and speeding off and Briones' speeding did not appear to cause any imminent safety hazard. From the facts of the two cases, it appears that Brown exceeded the speed limit for only a short distance and Luis may have been traveling only a few miles over the speed limit. In each case, the reason articulated for the stop may have been a pretext for stopping the vehicle on account of the occupants' race.

Conclusion for Issue One

Whren rejected the argument that a pre-textual traffic stop is unconstitutional. *Whren* is binding on the *Estrada* court. Following the mandatory authority of *Whren*, the *Estrada* court should hold that the stop for speeding was constitutional because there was probable cause of a traffic violation. Because Cruz's Fourth Amendment right was not violated by the stop, the drugs would not be suppressed based on the Fourth Amendment.

Reasoning for Issue Two

The search of Cruz's purse is constitutional if she consented to the search or the container exception to the search warrant requirement extends to her purse. The United States Supreme Court has stated the standard for determining when an individual has consented to the search of a car. *Florida v. Jimeno*, 500 U.S. at 251. This portion of the office memo will examine whether the consent standard has been met. As far as the container exception is concerned, the United States Supreme Court recently held that "police officers with probable cause to search a car may inspect passengers' belongings found in the car that are capable of concealing the object of the search." *Wyoming v. Houghton*, 526 U.S. at 307. The facts of *Jimeno*, *Houghton*, and *Estrada* will be compared to determine if the search of Cruz's purse was constitutional.

In *Jimeno*, Officer Trujillo overheard a telephone call from a public telephone in which Jimeno was discussing a drug deal. Trujillo followed Jimeno's car and stopped Jimeno for failure to stop when turning right on red. After informing Jimeno about the traffic violation, Trujillo

> went on to say that he had reason to believe that respondent was carrying narcotics in his car, and asked permission to search the car. He explained that respondent did not have to consent to a search of the car. Respondent stated that he had nothing to hide, and gave Trujillo permission to search the automobile.

500 U.S. at 249–50. Trujillo found drugs in a brown paper bag on the car floorboard. *Id.* at 250.

The Court then set forth the test for determining whether consent was given. "The standard for measuring the scope of a suspect's consent under the Fourth Amendment is that of 'objective' reasonableness—what would the typical person have understood by the exchange between the officer and the suspect?" *Id.* at 251. Applying this standard, the Court found that Jimeno had consented to the search of the bag.

The facts of *Jimeno* and *Estrada* are similar in that the two cars were stopped for alleged traffic violations and the officers searched containers. The facts surrounding the consent issue differ greatly. Trujillo told Jimeno that the officer suspected that there were drugs in the car and explained that Jimeno did not have to consent to the search. When Trujillo asked Jimeno's permission, Jimeno claimed that he had nothing to hide and explicitly consented to the search. The officer in *Estrada* made a statement, "you don't mind if I search, do you?"; he did not ask Cruz for her consent. He gave Cruz no time to respond before snatching her purse. In *Jimeno*, the container was a brown paper bag located on the floor of the car. In *Estrada*, the container was Cruz's purse, hanging from her shoulder.

Applying the objective reasonableness standard, it would not be objectively reasonable to believe that Cruz had consented to the search of her purse. She did not verbally consent, and her actions did not imply consent. A woman's purse often contains objects of a personal nature that the individual wants to keep safe from prying eyes. A purse is often considered an extension of the individual's outer clothing. Because of the private nature of Cruz's purse, it presumably would take some overt action or response before it would be reasonable to believe that she had consented.

In *Houghton*, David Young was stopped for speeding and a faulty brake light. After the officer saw a hypodermic syringe in Young's pocket, Young admitted that he used it to take drugs. The officer asked the two female passengers seated in the front seat to exit the car, and the officer searched the car. The officer found Houghton's purse on the backseat of the car. Searching the purse, the officer found a brown pouch that contained drug paraphernalia and a syringe containing methamphetamine in a large enough quantity for a felony conviction. Houghton claimed that the brown pouch was not hers. The officer also found a black container that contained drug paraphernalia and a syringe containing a smaller amount of methamphetamine, insufficient for a felony conviction. Houghton's arms showed fresh needle marks. The officer arrested her. 526 U.S. at 297–98.

The issue in *Houghton* was "whether police officers violate the Fourth Amendment when they search a passenger's personal belongings inside an automobile that they have probable cause to believe contains contraband." *Id.* at 297. The Court held "that police officers with probable cause to search a car may inspect passengers' belongings found in the car that are capable of concealing the object of the search." *Id.* at 307. The Court first relied on a 1982 case in which the Court had found that, where there was probable cause to search a car, it was constitutionally permissible to search containers found in the car that might hold the object of the search. *Id.* at 301–02. The Court noted that an individual carrying a package in a vehicle traveling on public roads has a reduced expectation of privacy; however, the Court did note the "unique, significantly heightened protection afforded against searches of one's person." *Id.* at 303. The Court found no reason to afford more protection to a container owned by a passenger than a container owned by the driver. *Id.* at 305.

In *Houghton*, Justice Breyer joined in the majority opinion and wrote a separate concurring opinion. In the concurring opinion, he stated that *Houghton* should be limited to vehicle searches and to containers found in a vehicle. He was troubled by the fact that it was Houghton's purse that was searched.

> [A]lso important is the fact that the container here at issue, a woman's purse, was found at a considerable distance from its owner, who did not claim ownership until the officer discovered her identification while looking through it. Purses are special containers. They are repositories of especially personal items that people generally like to keep with them at all times. So I am tempted to say that a search of a purse involves an intrusion so similar to a search of one's person that the same rule should govern both. However, given this Court's prior cases, I cannot argue that the fact that the container was a purse automatically makes a legal difference.... But I can say that it would matter if a woman's purse, like a man's billfold, were attached to her person. It might then amount to a kind of "outer clothing," which under the Court's cases would properly receive increased protection.

Id. at 308 (Breyer, J. concurring) (citations omitted).

The facts of *Houghton* and *Estrada* are similar in that the two cars were stopped for alleged traffic violations, and the officers searched a passenger's purse. The facts of the two cases differ in that Houghton's purse was on the backseat of the car, Houghton had exited the car without taking the purse with her, and Houghton at first disclaimed ownership of the purse. In contrast, Cruz took her purse with her when she exited the car, and it was attached to her when the officer snatched it from her shoulder.

In dicta in *Houghton*, the Court draws a distinction between the permissible search of containers and the search of an individual. The officer would not have been permitted to search Houghton without probable cause that she was carrying drugs or a weapon on her person. In the concurrence, Justice Breyer struggles with the fact that the container being searched is Houghton's purse. Were *Estrada* before him, he would likely find that the search of Cruz's purse was unconstitutional. As a concurrence, Justice Breyer's opinion is not mandatory authority. In addition, his opinion requiring the search of a purse attached to an individual to be treated similarly to the search of an individual's outer clothing is based on hypothetical facts.

Conclusion for Issue Two

Applying the standard for consent enunciated in *Jimeno*, Cruz did not consent to the search of her purse. A reasonable person would not believe that Cruz's lack of response to the officer's statement, "you don't mind if I search, do you?", could be considered consent. Thus, the consent exception to the search warrant requirement does not exist in *Estrada*. Because Cruz did not consent to the search of her purse, the search on that ground was unconstitutional.

The comparison of *Houghton* and *Estrada* is more difficult. If the facts in the two cases are substantially similar, then the *Estrada* court should hold that the drugs found in Cruz's purse should not be suppressed. If the *Estrada* court finds that Cruz's purse can be likened to an item of clothing she was wearing, then the drugs found in her purse should be suppressed.

Although the facts in *Houghton* and *Estrada* are similar, they are different enough that a court could find that the drugs found in Cruz's purse should be suppressed. Because her purse was next to her body, Cruz had a heightened expectation of privacy in it. The officer could not have constitutionally searched Cruz without more evidence. Thus, the search of her purse should also be unconstitutional, and the drugs found in the purse should be suppressed.

Reasoning for Issue Three

To determine whether the audio recording of Cruz and Luis's conversation was permissible, the court must consider the federal eavesdropping statutes and their case law interpretation. The federal eavesdropping statutes protect certain types of face-to-face conversations against interception. To be protected, the conversation must qualify as an "oral communication." Under the statutes, an "'oral communication' means any oral communication uttered by a person exhibiting an expectation that such communication is not subject to interception under circumstances justifying such expectation...." 18 U.S.C.A. § 2510 (2) (West, Westlaw through P.L. 116-91). Thus, a conversation is not an oral communication unless the conversants expect that the conversation is private and an objective third party would consider that expectation reasonable.

It is illegal to intercept an oral communication. "[A]ny person who ... intentionally intercepts ... any oral communication ... shall be punished." 18 U.S.C.A. § 2511 (1) (West, Westlaw through P.L. 116-91). One exception to this prohibition involves a police officer; however, the police officer must be party to the conversation or one conversant must have consented to the taping for the exception to apply. "It shall not be unlawful under this chapter for a person acting under color of law to intercept [an] ... oral ... communication where such person is a party to the communication or one of the parties has given prior consent to the interception." 18 U.S.C.A. § 2511 (2)(c) (West, Westlaw through P.L. 116-91). If an oral communication is taped in violation of the eavesdropping statutes, the conversation cannot be used as evidence in court. "Whenever any ... oral communication has been intercepted, no part of the contents of such communication and no evidence derived therefrom may be received in evidence in any trial, hearing, or other proceeding ... before a court ... if the disclosure of that information would be in violation of this chapter." 18 U.S.C.A. § 2515 (West, Westlaw through P.L. 116-91).

Thus, if Cruz and Luis's conversation were an oral communication, it should be suppressed. Whether the conversation is an oral communication turns on whether Cruz and Luis had a reasonable expectation of privacy while seated in the rear seat of the patrol car. One prong of the two-prong test is satisfied; they appear to have had an expectation of privacy or they would not have made incriminating statements. The other prong of the test is whether their expectation was reasonable. On one hand, the conversation was not audible outside the patrol car. The only way the officer could have heard the conversation was by taping it. On the other hand, Cruz and Luis were not sitting in Luis's car. They were sitting in the officer's car. While an expectation of privacy in Luis's car would have been reasonable, it is unclear from the federal statutes whether an expectation of privacy in the officer's car was reasonable. Some might equate the officer's car to the officer's office. If Cruz and Luis were conversing in an office of a police station, it might not be reasonable to expect privacy.

In a case with similar facts, the issue before the United States Court of Appeals for the Eleventh Circuit was "whether the district court erred in denying the motion to suppress the tapes resulting from the secret recording of McKinnon's pre-arrest conversations while he sat in the back seat of the police car." *United States v. McKinnon*, 985 F.2d 525, 526 (11th Cir. 1993).

In *McKinnon*, police officers stopped a pickup truck for failure to travel in a single lane on the Florida Turnpike. Theodore Pressley was driving and Steve McKinnon was the passenger. Pressley consented to the search of his vehicle. While the officers were searching, McKinnon and Pressley waited in the rear seat of the patrol car. There they made incriminating statements that were secretly recorded by the officers. The officers arrested them after finding cocaine in the truck, and they were placed in the rear seat of the patrol car. The officers again recorded McKinnon and Pressley's incriminating statements. *Id.*

The *McKinnon* court considered the meaning of the term *oral communication* under the federal statutes. An oral communication is protected against taping. If a conversation is taped in violation of the statutes, the tape may be suppressed. A conversation is an oral communication only if the conversants exhibited a subjective expectation of privacy and the expectation of privacy was objectively reasonable. The court seemed to agree with the government's argument that a patrol car functions as the officer's office and the rear seat of the patrol car functions as a jail cell. The court held "that McKinnon did not have a reasonable or justifiable expectation of privacy for conversations he held while seated in the back seat area of a police car." *Id.* at 527.

In examining the facts of *McKinnon* and *Estrada*, the facts concerning the taping seem virtually identical. In each case, an officer asked two individuals to wait in the patrol car prior to their arrest. The officer taped their conversation in the rear seat of the patrol car; the conversation contained incriminating statements. One difference between the two cases is that the officer in *McKinnon* also taped McKinnon's conversation following his arrest. This difference is not significant because an arrestee held in the back of a patrol car would have a lesser expectation of privacy than a person not under arrest.

A number of state and a number of federal courts, other than the *McKinnon* court, have faced the issue of whether an officer may secretly tape a conversation of individuals seated in the rear seat of a patrol car. In each case the court has said that taping is permissible. *See United States v. Paxton*, 848 F.3d 803, 813 (7th Cir. 2017) ("because the defendants lacked an objectively reasonable expectation of privacy when placed into the marked police van, the interception and recording of their conversations did not constitute a search for purposes of their Fourth Amendment rights"); *United States v. Dunbar*, 553 F.3d 48, 58 (1st Cir. 2009) ("the police car was not a reasonably confidential place to talk"); *United States v. Clark*, 22 F.3d 799, 801 (8th Cir. 1994) (" defendant's expectation of privacy while seated in the police car was not reasonable").

Cruz could make the argument that the search of her purse tainted the tape recording. When a police officer obtains evidence in an unconstitutional manner, that evidence is excluded from use at trial. If that evidence leads the officer to other evidence, the other evidence is derivative of the first evidence. The derivative evidence is known as fruit of the poisonous tree and is also inadmissible. Generally, evidence that is tainted by the prior unconstitutional conduct is inadmissible; however, in some instances the second evidence is admissible because the connection between the unconstitutionally seized evidence and the subsequently obtained evidence is marginal.

Conclusion for Issue Three

Although persuasive authority in other circuits, *McKinnon* is mandatory authority in this circuit. The facts concerning the taping are virtually identical in *McKinnon* and *Estrada*. A number of other state and federal courts have also held that there is no reasonable expectation of privacy for persons seated in the back of a patrol car. Therefore, a court should find that Cruz and Luis had no reasonable expectation of privacy while they were seated in the rear seat of the patrol car. Because they did not have a reasonable expectation of privacy, their conversation was not protected against taping as an oral communication.

If the court rules that the search of Cruz's purse was unconstitutional, then the tape may be suppressed if the search led Cruz to make the incriminating statements. Standard police procedure is to place a car's occupants in the rear seat of the police car while the officer is conducting a search and to tape their conversation. After the search of her purse, Cruz may have been more likely to discuss the drugs found in her purse. Cruz may have made reference to the drugs even if the officer had not found them in her purse. She might have commented that she was glad the officer did not search her purse.

The court will have to decide from the evidence the likelihood of Cruz making some type of incriminating statement without the officer having searched her purse. The court would not suppress the tape if the court decides that Cruz would have made the incriminating statements without the search of her purse.

Summary

- The office memo records the results of legal research, explains how the researcher analyzed the law and applied it to the facts, and proposes a solution to the problem.
- The tone of the office memo is objective rather than persuasive.
- "IRAC" stands for issue, rule of law, application, and conclusion;
- "IGPAC" stands for issue, general rule, precedent, application, and conclusion; and "FIRAC" stands for facts, issue, rule of law, analysis, and conclusion.
- These three terms are acronyms for organizational schemes that are used to write legal arguments.
- Generally, the office memo contains a heading (to and from, re, and date), facts, issue(s) and answer(s), a thesis paragraph, the rule of law, the application of the law to the facts, and the conclusion.
- Refer to people by their names or terms such as suspect or officer instead of appellant, appellee, or similar terms.
- Each issue and each answer should be single sentences.
- Between the issue and the answer you should give your reader the most information possible.
- Usually there are the same number of answers as issues.
- If you refer to a constitutional or statutory provision in an issue or answer by number, also give your reader a short explanation of the provision's subject matter.
- A "thesis" is the central idea running through the entire memo.
- Quote only the relevant portion of constitutions or statutes.
- The first time you refer to a case by name, give the full citation; after that, use a short-form citation.

Key Terms

statement of the rule of law
thesis paragraph

Cyberlaw Exercises

1. Bryan Garner, a legal writing authority, has interviewed many judges and authors, many of whom give tips on legal writing that could be applicable to writing office memos. Go to http://www.lawprose.org/, watch videos of one or more of the judges, and identify three brief writing tips that you could use when you are asked to write an office memo.
2. A number of interesting videos are posted on https://www.youtube.com/, some of which are related to writing an effective office memo. Go to the

website and find a video providing legal writing tips on writing office memos. How do the legal writing tips add to your understanding of writing well? How do the tips differ from the legal writing advice provided in this chapter?

3. A sample office memo is accessible at https://www.law.cuny.edu/legal-writing/students/writing-sample/. Access a sample office memo from the website and compare it to the two sample office memos included in this chapter.

Discussion Points

1. Which footnotes in the first sample office memo seem to be helpful and why?
2. How does the second office memo differ from the first?
3. What changes would you make to the office memos to make them better?

Chapter 14

Memorandum of Law

Introduction

One of the standard legal documents written by a litigation attorney for submission to court is what will be referred to in this book as the "memorandum of law." (Some attorneys refer to it as a "trial brief," a "trial level brief," or a "memorandum of points and authorities.") This chapter explains the purpose, use, and format of the memorandum of law and includes two sample memoranda of law.

The first sample memorandum of law has been extensively footnoted to provide you with writing and citation tips. If the notes do not make much sense to you right now, read them again after you have gone over the rules for citations and quotations contained in Appendices B and C. It might also be helpful for you to refer to the notes again when you are writing your own memorandum of law.

Purpose and Use

In litigation, an attorney may be required by court rule, may be asked by the judge, or may feel the need to submit a written document called a "memorandum of law." For example, some United States district courts require any party filing a motion to also file a legal memorandum with citation of authorities in support of the relief requested. Certain rules give the party opposing the motion a time period to file a legal memorandum in opposition. As a court document, the memorandum of law is a matter of public record and a copy of it is delivered to opposing counsel. The purposes of the memorandum of law are to explain the client's position in a lawsuit and to convince the judge to rule in the client's favor.

Look for a moment at the first sample memorandum of law in this chapter, written by Mike Campbell's attorney. You may recall from prior chapters that Mike had been arrested for possession of cocaine. The cocaine was found in Mike's car after he was stopped on the interstate by DEA agents. Mike's position is that, because the stop of his car was unconstitutional, the cocaine should be suppressed as the fruit of an unconstitutional search and seizure. If Mike's attorney can convince the judge that the cocaine should be suppressed, the charge against Mike will have to be dropped for lack of evidence. Mike's attorney would formally request the judge to suppress the cocaine by filing a "motion to suppress" and, as required by local rule, a memorandum of law supporting the motion. Once Mike's attorney has filed the motion to suppress the cocaine and the supporting memorandum of law, the government attorney will file a "motion in opposition to the motion to suppress" and a memorandum of law supporting the government's motion in opposition.

The circumstances surrounding Mike's arrest can be viewed from two perspectives: Mike's perspective and the perspective of the DEA agents. Mike would argue that the agents singled him out on the hunch that because he is African American, he might be carrying illegal drugs. The agents then violated his constitutional right against unreasonable search and seizure by stopping and searching his car. The government would argue that the agents could have pulled Mike over either because of a traffic violation or because Mike fit a drug courier profile. In the agents' experience, persons who fit the drug courier profile often carry drugs. The drug courier profile, while not entirely accurate, has been one of the law enforcement officer's weapons in the war against the illegal drug trade.

The tone of the memorandum of law is persuasive. This is in contrast to the office memo, which is objective in tone. In her memorandum of law, Mike's attorney will try to persuade the judge that Mike's view of the facts is more accurate and is supported by case law interpretation of the Fourth Amendment. In the government's memorandum of law in opposition to Mike's motion to suppress, the government attorney will try to persuade the judge that Mike's motion to suppress should not be granted because the government's view of the facts is more accurate and applicable case law supports denial of the motion to suppress.

Although Mike's attorney has to represent Mike's best interests, this duty is tempered by the attorney's ethical duty as an officer of the court. Rule 4-3.3 of the Rules Regulating the Florida Bar states: "A lawyer shall not knowingly ... make a false statement of material fact or law to a tribunal ... [or] fail to disclose to the tribunal legal authority in the controlling jurisdiction known to the lawyer to be directly adverse to the position of the client and not disclosed by opposing counsel...." Attorney ethics rules in other states contain similar wording. Thus, Mike's attorney has a dual role. She is an advocate for Mike's best interests as well as an advisor to the court. Mike's attorney must present Mike's side of the story but may not invent or change facts. In presenting the law in support of Mike's position, the attorney may not intentionally mislead the court and must disclose law "directly adverse" to Mike's position that the government has failed to disclose.

Style

An attorney must work very hard to build credibility with the judge and must work just as hard not to lose this credibility. The writer must build credibility by making absolutely sure that the facts and the law in the memorandum of law are stated accurately. Choose words that emphasize the client's position but are not obviously biased. The memorandum will be more credible if you include adverse facts and law as well as facts and law in the client's favor. The judge will be comparing your memorandum with that of opposing counsel to see how you have dealt with adverse facts and law. Your failure to deal with adverse facts and law may make the judge think you are doing a sloppy job, and you will quickly lose your credibility. Of course, adverse facts and law need only be mentioned and should not be dwelled upon. A well-organized memorandum will emphasize favorable facts and law and downplay unfavorable ones. (See the next section of this chapter for tips on organization.)

The appearance of the memorandum should be inviting, with enough descriptive headings to allow the judge to glance through the memorandum and "see" the flow of your writing. When the first draft of the memorandum has been completed, review it critically. Does it appear reader-friendly? Are the pages broken up into a number of paragraphs? Is the print large enough to be easily read? Are the margins wide enough to give the reader's eyes a chance to rest? Can you make it easier to spot headings by putting them in bold type or underlining them? Make any necessary changes.

Organization

When you are having trouble writing a memorandum of law, picture yourself as a busy judge with a heavy caseload and ask yourself what you would find helpful in a memorandum of law. A busy judge does not have the luxury of time to pore over a lengthy, disorganized memorandum containing a convoluted legal argument. The judge will be more inclined to read a shorter memorandum that is straightforward, well-organized, and just long enough to get the point across. If you can squeeze the issues and short answers into the first two pages, you will have the judge's attention.

Remember that a reader will pay more attention to the beginning and the end than to the middle of sections within the memorandum. Put any information you want to emphasize either at the beginning or at the end of a section. For example, in the facts section, focus the reader's attention on the client by referring to the client first and retelling the facts from the client's perspective. Diffuse the opposing party's thunder by including any significant adverse facts but downplay them by briefly mentioning them in the light most favorable to the client midway through the facts section.

Do something similar with the argument section. If there is an easy way for the judge to dispose of the case in the client's favor, put the argument supporting that easy ruling first. Otherwise, put the strongest argument first. "Bury" any adverse law that must be disclosed in the middle of the argument section. A duty to disclose adverse law does not mean that it has to be discussed in detail. Refer to it, distinguish it, and move on. Do the same with the opposing party's counterarguments. Refer to them briefly and then focus on the client's argument. The best defense is a good offense.

The organizational tip for sections of the memorandum applies for sentences and paragraphs. If you want your reader to focus on particular words in a sentence, rearrange your sentence to put the words first or last in the sentence. The focus will be even greater if rearranging the sentence changes the grammatical structure from the typical subject-verb-object structure of English sentences. Be careful that you do not change from the typical structure too often or the atypical structure will become routine and lose its impact. In addition, sentences are harder for the reader to understand if they differ from the typical subject, verb, and object order.

The reader will pay more attention to the first and last sentences in a paragraph than to the middle of the paragraph. For that reason, make your topic sentence either the first or last sentence in the paragraph. Put any information you want to make sure the reader does not miss in the first or last sentences. If the important information is more than can fit in the first and last sentences of the paragraph, consider splitting the paragraph into a number of paragraphs. Put adverse information three-fourths of the way through the paragraph to de-emphasize it.

Format

Although there is no one right format for a memorandum of law, the format given in this chapter is fairly standard. The format should be modified to conform to any applicable court rules and to the format customarily used for a particular court. For example, applicable court rules may specify line spacing, paper size, margins, document length, and information concerning the attorney signing the document, including the attorney's name, bar identification number, firm name and address, and telephone number.

The balance of this section gives a brief explanation of the various parts of the memorandum of law. It might be helpful for you to read the rest of this section while comparing the explanation to the sample memorandums of law later in this chapter.

Caption

The caption contains the name of the court, the names of the parties, the case number, and the title of the pleading. After the title of the pleading and before the questions presented section, it is customary to include a sentence stating who is submitting the memorandum and why it is being submitted.

The following text box contains a caption for a Florida State trial court.

IN THE CIRCUIT COURT
OF THE NINTH JUDICIAL CIRCUIT
IN AND FOR ORANGE COUNTY, FLORIDA

JAKE CARSON, Plaintiff,	))	
	)	CIVIL ACTION
- vs -	)	No. 19-000-00
	)	
TOM HARRIS, Defendant.	))	

Questions Presented

The questions presented section contains several numbered questions for the judge to consider. The questions should be stated in the light most favorable to the client and should be worded so that the judge can easily reach an answer favorable to the client. Give as much information as possible in each question without sacrificing readability. There should be enough information so that the judge understands a question without having to refer to other sections of the memorandum.

Each question should contain a combination of law and facts and should ask how the law applies to the facts. Because the facts section of the memorandum follows rather than precedes the questions presented section, the judge will not have read the facts before reading the questions. Therefore, the most important facts should be included in the questions to familiarize them to the judge.

Facts

The writer should create empathy for the client by painting a picture of the facts from the client's perspective. Choose descriptive words and incorporate a fair amount of detail when recounting facts favorable to the client. State the facts as specifically as possible to make them memorable. If the picture is created in sufficient detail, your picture will come to the judge's mind when considering the case. Relevant adverse facts that opposing counsel is likely to rely on can be mentioned briefly, in broad terms and with little detail, using bland, uninteresting language.

Highlight your client's view of the facts. Focus the reader's attention on the client by referring to the client first and by calling the client by name. Try telling the facts in the order the client perceived them rather than in strict chronological order. This ordering of the facts will make it easier for the judge to understand the client's position.

Choose your words carefully. Words chosen should reflect favorably on the client without conveying an argumentative or adversarial tone. The writer's credibility may be lost if the language is too exaggerated or overly biased. Well-stated facts are so subtly persuasive that the judge can believe they are stated objectively.

Argument

The argument section is the longest and most complex portion of the memorandum of law. This section is divided into a number of subsections by headings called *point headings* that answer the questions presented. There may be an introductory portion of the argument section preceding the first main point heading. The introductory material contains a thesis paragraph and may explain the law that is applicable to all the point headings in the memorandum. Each subsection following a point heading should explain the applicable rule of law and apply the rule of law to the facts.

Even though the tone of the memorandum of law is persuasive and the tone of the office memo is objective, the basic structure of the argument section of the memorandum of law should be similar to the structure of the reasoning section of an office memo.

You should present one or more thesis paragraphs, you should set forth the rule of law, and you should apply the rule of law to the facts of the case. Refresh your memory of how to write the thesis paragraph(s), the rule of law, and the application of law to the facts by rereading those portions of the "Format" section of Chapter 13.

Although opposing counsel and others will read the memorandum of law, the intended and primary audience is the judge. The judge is not your adversary and may become your ally on the strength of the memorandum of law. Make the judge your ally by advising the judge as to why ruling in the client's favor is the correct solution to the problem. In most cases, the judge has some discretion in making decisions. If you can convince the judge that he or she is your ally, the judge may use this discretion in your client's favor. Therefore, although the tone of the memorandum of law is persuasive, it should be subtly persuasive. Shy away from an argumentative or demanding tone of voice that may prejudice the judge against the client.

Thesis Paragraph

If an introductory portion of the argument section precedes the first main point heading, it should begin with a thesis paragraph. Besides stating your thesis in your thesis paragraph, you may want to use this paragraph to state your final conclusion in simple terms. If your argument section begins with a point heading rather than with an introductory portion, you should either follow your first point heading with a thesis paragraph or include a short thesis paragraph after each of your point headings. For a more detailed explanation of how to write a thesis paragraph, reread the thesis paragraph portion of the "Format" section of Chapter 13.

Rule of Law

A busy judge does not have the time to do extensive independent research before ruling on a motion. A judge will appreciate a step-by-step explanation of the current status of applicable law—either to familiarize the judge with an unfamiliar area of the law or to update the judge's knowledge. Be careful to advise rather than to lecture the judge on the law. A judge will appreciate a clear explanation of the law, but a judge who is being "lectured" may take offense. For the judge's easy reference, you may want to provide copies of the cases you have cited in the memorandum. For a more detailed explanation of how to write the rule of law, reread the rule of law portion of the "Format" section of Chapter 13.

Application of Law to Facts

After stating the rule of law, you must carefully lead the reader step by step from the law to your conclusion. For a detailed explanation of how to apply the rule of law to the facts, reread the application of law to the facts portion of the "Format" section of Chapter 13.

Either your argument section or the conclusion section should contain one or more paragraphs summarizing your argument. This summary serves the same purpose as the conclusion section of an office memo; it ties the facts to the rule of law and reaches a conclusion. Customarily, this summary is part of the argument rather than the conclusion section. Look through some recent memoranda of law filed with the court to determine what the custom is in your area. If the summary is part of the argument section, you can either put a summary of the answers to all of the questions presented at the end of the argument section or have a summary paragraph at the end of each subsection within your argument.

Conclusion

The conclusion section of a memorandum of law specifically requests the judge to take a particular action or actions. The motion that accompanies Mike Campbell's memorandum of law is a motion to suppress the evidence found in Mike's car. If the evidence is suppressed, the government will be forced to drop the charge against Mike for lack of evidence. Therefore, the conclusion section of the memorandum of law should request the judge to suppress the evidence and to dismiss the charge against Mike.

As stated before, you should include a summary of your argument in the conclusion section if you have not included it in the argument section.

FIRST SAMPLE MEMORANDUM OF LAW

UNITED STATES DISTRICT COURT
MIDDLE DISTRICT OF FLORIDA
ORLANDO DIVISION

UNITED STATES OF AMERICA,
Plaintiff,
Case No. 6:19-CR-000-ORL-00MNN[1]
MICHAEL CAMPBELL and JOHN WRIGHT,
Defendants.

______________________/

MEMORANDUM IN SUPPORT OF DEFENDANT CAMPBELL'S MOTION TO SUPPRESS[2]

Defendant Michael Campbell submits this memorandum of law in support of defendant's motion to suppress the evidence seized from the defendant's car.[3]

Questions Presented:[4]

1. Did the law enforcement officer violate Mike Campbell's constitutional right against unreasonable search and seizure when the law enforcement

1. This is the docket number written as required by Rule 1.03(a) of the Local Rules of the United States District Court for the Middle District of Florida. The first part of the docket number, "6," is the division of the court, "19," is an abbreviation for "2019" (the year in which the case was filed). The third part of the docket number, "CR," indicates that this is a criminal rather than a civil case (abbreviated "CIV"). The fourth part of the docket number, "000," indicates the order in which the case was filed in 2019. Were this a real case, the number of the case would be substituted for "000." Cases in the Orlando division of the district are consecutively numbered, corresponding to the order in which they are filed. "ORL" indicates that this is an Orlando division case. The last two numbers give the number of the judge to whom the case is assigned, and the last three initials are the initials of the magistrate handling the case. As Middle District of Florida judges are appointed, they are numbered in sequence, and the numbers are used to identify which judge is handling a particular case.

2. Use a descriptive title to identify the type of document (a memorandum of law), why it is being filed (in support of a motion to suppress), and the party filing the document (defendant Campbell). From the title, the judge should learn at a glance important information about the document without having to read the text of the document.

3. Use a short introductory sentence to explain to the judge why the document is being submitted. It does not hurt to lay out the explanation like this in a full sentence even though it repeats information from the title of the document.

4. Each of these questions asks how the law applies to the facts. Notice the word choice. The questions are worded from Mike's perspective, and Mike is referred to by name. Specific facts are included in the questions for a number of reasons. The judge's decision to grant or deny the motion to suppress turns on whether the facts were sufficient to justify the stop, making the facts extremely important. Because the factors in the drug courier profile and the nature of the alleged traffic violation are generally favorable to Mike, they are detailed so they are easy to remember. The way the questions are worded, they "paint" a picture of the scene for the judge, which the judge can use as a framework when reading the rest of the memorandum. The most important facts need to be laid out in the questions, or the judge will not be familiar with them, because the facts section follows the questions presented section.

officer stopped Mike's out-of-state tagged Lincoln Continental that Mike was driving on I-95 in the early evening at the speed limit when the only other information the officer had was that Mike and his passenger were African American, in their twenties, and wore beach attire?

2. Did the officer violate Mike Campbell's constitutional right against unreasonable search and seizure when the officer followed the Campbell car for a distance and then pulled the car over, claiming that Mike was following the car in front of him too closely?

Facts:[5]

Mike Campbell and his best friend had decided, like thousands of other college students, to enjoy a Florida spring break. After Mike promised to drive carefully, Mike's father let Mike borrow his car, a brand-new Lincoln Continental. After arriving in Florida, Mike and his friend spent every waking moment of their break on the beach. In the early evening on the last day of vacation, they went straight from the beach to their car to begin the long trip back to school, calculating that they would have just enough driving time to make it back for their first class. Mike was driving north on I-95 thinking about the promise he had made to his father when he saw patrol cars parked in the median, one with its lights shining across the northbound lanes. Almost immediately after driving through the arc of the patrol car's headlights, Mike looked in the rearview mirror and saw the patrol car pull out behind him. The patrol car put on its flashing lights and pulled Mike over.

An officer got out of the patrol car, walked over to Mike's car, and asked for Mike's driver's license and car registration. As Mike handed over his license and the registration he noticed the officer eyeing Mike's beach attire suspiciously. When Mike told the officer they were heading back to school from spring break, the officer commented, "We don't see too many Blacks down here over spring break." The officer added, "I stopped you for following the car in front of you too closely." Still holding the license and registration, the officer asked Mike whether the officer could search the car and said, "You don't have anything to hide, do you?" Hoping that if he answered "no" they could be on their way, Mike answered, "No." The officer said, "Wait here," turned around, walked back to the patrol car, and got in. Mike could not have left even if the officer had not told him to wait because the officer still had Mike's license and car registration.

Forty-five minutes later, another patrol car pulled up and an officer got out with a dog. The officer led the dog around the car. The dog circled the car once and then

5. The facts are told from Mike's perspective and in the order he perceived them. Mike is referred to by name to create empathy, whereas the other persons are not. The wording was chosen to be subtly persuasive rather than obviously biased. Compare this statement of the facts with the facts contained in the office memo in Chapter 13.

stopped and pawed the car's trunk. The officer motioned Mike to roll down his window. The officer told Mike that the dog had detected drugs in the trunk of Mike's car. The officer told Mike that Mike could either open the car trunk or wait there for whatever time was necessary for the officer to obtain a search warrant. Mike, feeling that he had no choice, opened the trunk. Both officers started pulling Mike's and his friend's belongings out of the trunk and tossing them on the ground. One of the officers found a brown paper bag containing cocaine wedged in a bottom corner of the trunk. Mike and his friend were arrested and were charged with possession with intent to distribute.

Argument:[6]

The car driver and passengers expect that activities within the car will be private and not subject to the scrutiny of law enforcement officials. They may feel that their privacy is invaded if a law enforcement officer stops the car to investigate. A trained police officer may have a hunch that a car's occupants are engaged in illegal activity; however, a law enforcement officer may not constitutionally stop a car unless there is either a reasonable suspicion of illegal activity or there is a traffic violation. The stop of Mike's car to investigate for criminal activity was not permissible because the agents did not have a reasonable suspicion of illegal drug activity. The stop for a traffic violation was constitutionally justifiable only if Mike was following too closely.

The Fourth Amendment[7] to the United States Constitution guarantees "[t]he[8] right of the people to be secure in their persons, houses, papers, and effects against unreasonable searches and seizures" and allows a search warrant to be issued only upon "probable cause."[9] A search warrant requirement was spelled out in the Amendment to safeguard this important right. Over the more than two hundred years since the Amendment was adopted, the individual's right against unreasonable search and seizure has been jealously guarded.

Although the time and level of evidence needed to obtain a search warrant protects the individual's constitutional right, the courts have allowed two exceptions to the search warrant requirement, both of which the government argues are applicable here

---

6. You should begin the argument portion of your memorandum of law with a thesis paragraph. A well-written thesis paragraph provides the reader with a framework into which the balance of the memo can be placed. It also tells the reader your ultimate conclusion.

7. When quoting a constitutional or statutory provision, quote only the relevant portion. Set quotations of fifty words or more off from the rest of the text in a quotation block indented left and right but not enclosed in quotation marks. If the quoted passage contains a quotation, the internal quotation should be enclosed in quotation marks.

8. The brackets indicate a change in the quotation from the original. Here the "t" was upper case originally.

9. Periods and commas go inside quotation marks; other punctuation is placed outside quotation marks unless it is part of the quotation.

and allowed them to stop the Campbell car. The first exception[10] requires a minimum of "reasonable suspicion" of illegal activity to stop a car and question its occupants. *Terry v. Ohio*, 392 U.S. 1, 27 (1968).[11] The second exception allows an officer to stop a car to investigate a traffic violation. *Whren v. United States*, 517 U.S. 806, 818 (1996).

Defendant Campbell's motion to suppress should be granted because neither of the two exceptions to the search warrant requirement apply here. The officer stopped Campbell's car on a mere "hunch," and Campbell was following at a "reasonable and prudent" distance, as required by the Florida Statutes. Fla. Stat. Ch. 316.0895 (1) (2019). This memorandum will first explain why there was not enough evidence to justify an investigatory stop and then why there was no traffic violation.[12]

A. Because the information the officer relied on to stop the Campbell car was no more than a mere "hunch," the evidence should be suppressed unless the officer had probable cause to stop the car for a traffic violation.[13]

Terry[14] was the landmark case that lowered the burden of proof necessary for a stop from probable cause to "reasonable suspicion." Such stops made on reasonable suspicion are often referred to as "*Terry* stops," after *Terry*, and the definition of *Terry* stops has been broadened to apply to car stops. The new reasonable suspicion standard allows a police officer to stop and briefly question someone, but is still designed to protect the innocent traveler, singled out because of certain immutable personal characteristics, such as race, sex, and age, from being subjected to "overbearing or harassing" law enforcement tactics. 392 U.S. at 14–15 n.11. A stop made only on an "unparticularized suspicion or 'hunch'"[15] is unconstitutional. *Id.* at 27. Assuming the officer has the

---

10. Signposts are words used to guide the reader in a particular direction. "The first exception" and "the second exception" are signposts clearly identifying the two exceptions that are discussed in much more detail later in the memo.

11. The first time you are referring to a case by name you must give the full citation. After that you should use a short-form citation.

Citations in the sample office memo are given in *Bluebook* form. Your professor may require you to cite according to some other citation rule (perhaps your state's citation rule). If so, always check the appropriate citation rule to make sure you are citing correctly.

12. This introductory portion of the argument section contains four paragraphs. The first paragraph is the thesis paragraph. The second and third paragraphs lay out in general terms the law applicable to the rest of the memorandum. The fourth paragraph contains a statement of the conclusion. Do not leave the judge in suspense. Tell the judge your conclusion up front. The fourth paragraph also contains signposts. With these signposts, the reader will expect the portion of the memorandum following the first point heading to discuss the drug courier profile and the portion of the memorandum after the second point heading to discuss the alleged traffic violation.

13. This point heading answers the first question presented and is in bold to make it stand out.

14. Once you have given the full citation for a case and are referring to the case in general terms, you can refer to it by using one or two of the words from the name of the case and underlining or italicizing them. Be sure the words you select are not so common as to cause confusion. Here, for example, use *Terry* rather than *Ohio*.

15. To indicate quotes within quotes, alternate double and single quotation marks, with double quotations outermost.

requisite reasonable suspicion for a *Terry* stop, the officer would still need probable cause or consent to search a car.[16]

The United States Court of Appeals for the Eleventh Circuit decided a case that involved almost identical facts to those being considered here. *United States v. Smith*, 799 F.2d 704 (11th Cir. 1986). In *Smith*, the government argued that a highway stop was constitutionally permitted based either on a drug courier profile or on Smith's alleged commission of a traffic violation. 799 F.2d at 705.[17] Smith filed a motion to suppress, claiming that the evidence seized from his car should be suppressed because of the violation of his right against unreasonable search and seizure. *Id.* at 706.[18] The United States Court of Appeals for the Eleventh Circuit found that the *Smith* drug courier profile did not support reasonable suspicion, reversed the lower court's denial of Smith's motion to suppress, and vacated Smith's conviction. *Id.* at 712.

One night in June of 1985, Trooper Robert Vogel, a Florida Highway Patrol trooper, and a DEA agent were observing cars traveling in the northbound lanes of I-95 in hopes of intercepting drug couriers. When Smith's car passed through the arc of the patrol car headlights, Vogel noticed the following factors that matched his drug courier profile:

1. The car was traveling at 3:00 a.m.;
2. The car was a 1985 Mercury, a large, late model car;
3. The car had out-of-state tags;
4. There were two occupants of the car who were around thirty; and
5. The driver was driving cautiously and did not look at the patrol car as the Mercury passed through the arc of the patrol car headlights.

Id. at 705–06.[19]

---

16. This discussion of *Terry* is written to support Mike's motion and to convince the judge to rule in Mike's favor. Compare it with the discussion of *Terry* contained in the office memo in the preceding chapter. There, the *Terry* discussion was more balanced.

17. Once you have cited a case in full, you should use a short-form citation the next time you refer to material from the case. This short-form citation contains "*Id.*," "at," and the page on which the "government's argument" is found in *Smith*. You should use "*Id.*" here instead of repeating "799 F.2d" because this citation is to the same case cited in the immediately preceding citation. If *Smith* had been cited previously but not in the immediately preceding citation, the citation to *Smith* would have been "799 F.2d at 705" or "*Smith*, 799 F.2d at 705," with the short-form citation including the volume number and the abbreviation for the reporter in which *Smith* is printed. To learn more about short-form citations, refer to Appendix C, which explains short-form citations.

18. You should use "*Id.*" here instead of repeating "799 F.2d" because this citation refers to the same case cited in the immediately preceding citation. Retain "at 706" because the referenced material appears on page 706 instead of on page 705, the page of the previously referenced material.

19. When you need to give a citation for a block quote or other material set off from the rest of the text, as is the tabulation here, bring the citation back to the left margin. When citing inclusive pages with three or more digits, drop all but the last two digits of the second number and place a hyphen between the numbers.

This drug courier profile is almost identical to the *Campbell* profile.[20] In both *Smith* and this case, the cars were traveling after dark, the cars were large, late models with out-of-state tags, the cars were being driven "cautiously," and each car contained two passengers in their twenties or thirties. The differences between the two profiles are very minor. Campbell and his friend were dressed casually, while it is not known how Smith and Swindell were dressed. Smith and Swindell did not look at Vogel as they passed. It is not known whether Campbell looked in the agents' direction as Campbell drove past. Campbell claims that race was a factor in the stop even though it was not listed as such by the agents. Smith and Swindell's race is unknown.[21]

In *Smith*, Vogel followed the Mercury for a mile and a half and noticed that the Mercury "wove" several times, once as much as six inches into the emergency lane. Vogel pulled Smith over. When a drug dog alerted on the car, a DEA agent searched the trunk and discovered one kilogram of cocaine. Smith and his passenger, Swindell, were arrested and were charged with conspiracy to possess cocaine with the intent to distribute it. Smith and Swindell's motions to suppress the cocaine were denied and they were tried and convicted. *Id.* at 706.

The issue before the appellate court was whether the stop of Smith's car was reasonable. *Id.*[22] This is the same basic question to be answered by this court in determining whether Campbell's motion to suppress should be granted. The *Smith* court held that the stop of Smith's car could not be upheld as a valid *Terry* stop, *id.* at 708, finding that "Trooper Vogel stopped the car because [Smith and Swindell][23] ... matched a few non-distinguishing characteristics contained on a drug courier profile and, additionally,

20. This is an example of a topic sentence. A topic sentence contains one main idea summarizing the paragraph, with the rest of the paragraph developing the idea presented in the topic sentence. Most paragraphs should have topic sentences. The typical location of a topic sentence is the first sentence in the paragraph. Sometimes the topic sentence is the last sentence in the paragraph and pulls together the rest of the paragraph. Some paragraphs, typically narrative paragraphs like the preceding paragraph, do not have topic sentences.

If a paragraph sounds disjointed or unorganized, try pulling it together using a topic sentence. If a topic sentence does not help, think about breaking the paragraph into more than one paragraph.

21. This paragraph applies the facts in *Smith* to the facts in *Campbell*. Applying facts from one case to another case involves explaining the similarities and differences between the two sets of facts.

Instead of simply stating that the facts from the two cases are very similar, the paragraph specifically states which facts are the same. Sometimes in the application you need to explain in what way the facts are similar if they are not identical.

You can either apply the *Smith* facts to *Campbell* midway in discussing *Smith*, as done here, or you can wait until you have thoroughly discussed *Smith*. When you prepare your outline prior to starting to write the memorandum of law, spend some time moving parts of your "argument" section around to determine the best flow.

22. When you are referring to material from the same page as the material you referred to in the last citation, just use "*id.*" *Id.* is capitalized only when it begins a sentence.

23. "Smith and Swindell" are in brackets because this wording was inserted into the quotation by the person writing the memo. The ellipsis (...) shows that something was omitted from the original wording of the quotation. Your quotations must exactly match the wording and punctuation of the authority the quotation comes from. If you are sloppy in quoting and your reader discovers that you have taken liberties

because Vogel was bothered by the way the driver of the car chose not to look at him." *Id.* at 707.

Just as there was nothing in the *Campbell* drug courier profile to differentiate Campbell and his friend from other innocent college students returning from spring break in Florida, there was nothing in Vogel's drug courier profile to differentiate Smith and Swindell from other law-abiding motorists on I-95. It is usual to drive after dark to avoid heavy traffic or to complete an interstate trip.[24] Although many motorists speed on the highways, motorists driving "cautiously" at or near the speed limit are simply obeying traffic laws. Many people other than drug couriers drive large, late model cars with out-of-state tags. A motorist between the ages of twenty and forty is not unusual.

The contrast between the *Campbell* and *Smith* drug courier profiles, which do not support reasonable suspicion, and another courier profile that was held to support reasonable suspicion is marked. *United States v. Sokolow*, 490 U.S. 1, 3 (1989).[25] In *Sokolow*, DEA agents found 1,063 grams of cocaine inside Sokolow's carry-on luggage when he was stopped in Honolulu International Airport based on the following profile:

1. He had paid $2,100 in cash for two airplane tickets from a roll of $20s that appeared to contain $4,000;
2. He was ticketed under a name other than his own;
3. He traveled to Miami, a known drug source, and back;
4. Although his round trip flight lasted 20 hours, he stayed in Miami only 48 hours;
5. He appeared nervous;
6. He was about 25 years old;
7. He was dressed in a black jumpsuit and was wearing gold jewelry that he wore during both legs of the round-trip flight; and
8. Neither he nor his companion checked any luggage.[26]

Id. at 3–5. The Court held that the *Sokolow* drug courier profile did support reasonable suspicion. *Id.* at 11.

The *Sokolow* dissent would have found that all of the factors, even if "taken together," did not amount to reasonable suspicion. In criticizing the use of a drug courier profile to stop suspects, the dissent noted "the profile's 'chameleon-like way of adapting to any

with the quotation, your reader may suspect that you are sloppy in other ways—perhaps even in your research. See the *Bluebook* for an explanation of quoting correctly.

24. No page reference is needed if you have already given the facts in the cases you are using as authority and are referring to those cases in general.

25. To avoid including a full citation in a textual sentence, *Sokolow* is referred to in general terms, and the citation to *Sokolow* is given in a separate citation sentence. Including the full citation in a sentence makes the sentence harder to read and understand.

26. Only those facts from *Sokolow* that are relevant to the discussion of *Smith* are given.

particular set of observations'" "subjecting innocent individuals to unwarranted police harassment and detention." *Id.* at 13 (Marshall, J., dissenting)[27] (quoting *Sokolow v. United States*, 831 F.2d 1413, 1418 (9th Cir. 1987), *rev'd*, 490 U.S. 1 (1989)[28]).

As predicted in the *Sokolow* dissent, Smith, Swindell, Campbell, and Campbell's friend were subjected to "unwarranted police harassment and detention" even though the factors in the respective drug courier profiles, even if "taken together," did not amount to reasonable suspicion. In contrast, several of the *Sokolow* factors, such as carrying such a large amount of cash and traveling a long distance to stay a relatively short period of time, are unusual or even suspicious in and of themselves. Each of the *Smith* and *Campbell* factors alone was not at all out of the ordinary and certainly taken together did not amount to reasonable suspicion.

B. Because Mike Campbell did not commit the traffic violation alleged by the officer, the evidence found in the trunk of Mike Campbell's car should be suppressed as the fruit of an unconstitutional search and seizure.

In *Whren*, Brown was driving a Pathfinder in which Whren was a passenger. Brown had stopped the vehicle at a stop sign and was looking down into Whren's lap. Plainclothes police officers were patrolling this "high drug area" of the District of Columbia in an unmarked patrol car. The Pathfinder caught the attention of the officers because Brown remained stopped at the stop sign for approximately 20 seconds. When the patrol car made a U-turn to follow the Pathfinder, Brown turned right without signaling and started off at an "unreasonable speed." The patrol car stopped the Pathfinder. When one of the officers approached Brown's window and peered in, he saw that Whren had two plastic bags of crack cocaine on his lap. The officers arrested Whren and Brown. 517 U.S. at 808, 809.

Justice Scalia phrased the issue as:

> whether the temporary detention of a motorist who the police have probable cause to believe has committed a civil traffic violation is inconsistent with the Fourth Amendment's prohibition against unreasonable seizures unless a reasonable officer would have been motivated to stop the car by a desire to enforce the traffic laws.

Id. at 808. The Court answered the question, "No":

> [T]he district court found that the officers had probable cause to believe that petitioners had violated the traffic code. That rendered the stop reasonable under

27. You must identify the type of opinion you are quoting from if it is other than the majority opinion.

28. This explanatory parenthetical tells the reader that the material Marshall is quoting came from the lower court decision in *Sokolow*. If you are quoting something that in turn quotes another source, you should identify the original source as is done here. Subsequent history must be given for the lower court decision in *Sokolow*.

> the Fourth Amendment, the evidence thereby discovered admissible, and the upholding of the convictions by the Court of Appeals for the District of Columbia Circuit correct.

Id. at 819.

Prior to *Whren*, some courts, including the court deciding *Smith*, had decided that a car stop for a traffic violation was unconstitutional unless a reasonable officer would have made the stop. The *Smith* court found that the cocaine should have been excluded from evidence because a reasonable officer would not have stopped Smith's car for the alleged traffic violation. 799 F.2d at 711. However, in *Whren*, the United States Supreme Court rejected the argument that the reasonable officer standard should apply. 517 U.S. at 813.

After *Whren*, it would be very difficult to convince a court that a stop for an alleged traffic violation is unconstitutional. However, if the court finds that the driver did not violate any traffic regulation, then the stop would be unconstitutional.

The Florida motor vehicle statute identified by the *Campbell* officer states, "The driver of a motor vehicle shall not follow another vehicle more closely than is reasonable and prudent, having due regard for the speed of such vehicles and the traffic upon, and the condition of, the highway." Fla. Stat. Ch. 316.0895 (1) (2019). No simple test determines if Campbell violated the statute. The court must determine from any evidence presented whether the distance at which Campbell was following the car in front of him was reasonable and prudent.

The alleged driving irregularities in *Whren* and *Campbell* are dissimilar. While it was clear that Brown committed a traffic violation, the Florida statute cited in this case does not apply to Campbell. Determining whether one vehicle is following another vehicle too closely involved much more of a judgment call than determining whether the Pathfinder failed to signal when turning right and exceeded the speed limit. The position of the vehicles on the highway and the weather and road conditions must all be considered to determine if Campbell violated the statute.

The evidence that will be presented at the hearing on the motion to suppress will show that Fla. Stat. Ch. 316.0895 (1) does not apply to Campbell because Campbell was following the car in front of him at more than the appropriate distance given the vehicles' speed, the traffic, and the condition of the highway.

Following *Whren*, this court should find the stop of Campbell's car unconstitutional because there was no traffic violation. Because Campbell was following the car in front of him at a reasonable and prudent distance, the stop violated Campbell's right against unreasonable search and seizure. Because Campbell's Fourth Amendment right was violated by the stop and the agents would not have found the evidence if they had not first stopped the car on I-95, the evidence should be suppressed as the fruit of the poisonous tree.

Conclusion:

For the reasons set forth, defendant Campbell requests this court to grant his motion to suppress and to dismiss the charge against him for lack of evidence.

Respectfully submitted,

____

Florida Attorney, Esq.
Florida Bar Number 000000
Law Firm
Main Street
Anytown, Fla.

SECOND SAMPLE MEMORANDUM OF LAW

UNITED STATES DISTRICT COURT
MIDDLE DISTRICT OF FLORIDA
ORLANDO DIVISION

UNITED STATES OF AMERICA,
Plaintiff,
Case No. 6:11 - CR - 000 - ORL - 00CNN
LUIS BRIONES and CRUZ ESTRADA,
Defendants.

______________________/

MEMORANDUM IN OPPOSITION TO DEFENDANT'S MOTION TO SUPPRESS

Plaintiff, the United States of America, submits this memorandum of law in opposition to defendant's motion to suppress the methamphetamines seized from the defendant and the tape of her conversation.

Questions presented:

1. Was Officer Green's search of the defendant's purse permissible when the defendant consented to the search?
2. Was Officer Green's search of defendant's purse permissible when the officer had probable cause to search the car and the purse fell under the container exception to the search warrant requirement?
3. When Officer Green had the defendant wait in his patrol car while he searched the car in which she had been riding, was it permissible for him to tape-record any statements defendant made?

Facts:

Officer Green was patrolling the southbound lanes of I-95 when he observed a car traveling at an excessive rate of speed. The radar in the patrol car showed that the car was traveling 80 in a 65-mile-per-hour speed zone.

Officer Green approached the driver's side of the car and requested the driver's license and car registration. While the driver searched his wallet for the documents, Officer Green looked through the open window and noticed a glass vial containing small kernels of an off-white substance in the driver's lap. Believing the vial to contain crack cocaine, Officer Green announced that he was seizing it. He asked the driver and passenger to exit the car and asked the driver for his wallet. Officer Green identified the driver as Luis Briones from his driver's license.

As the passenger got out of the car, Officer Green struck up a conversation with her. She said that her name was Cruz Estrada. Officer Green explained that he would have to search their car but that they could wait in the patrol car for their comfort and safety. The defendant turned back to the car, explaining that she had to retrieve something. She reached into the car and pulled out her purse, which had fallen behind the front seat. As the defendant passed Officer Green on the way to the patrol car, Officer Green asked if he could search her purse. Without responding, the defendant held out her purse to him. Inside her purse, Officer Green found a brown paper envelope. When Officer Green asked her what was in the envelope, defendant claimed that she did not know, that someone had given it to her to give to a friend in Miami. When Officer Green opened the envelope, he found a quantity of white powder that he believed to be methamphetamines.

The two waited in the patrol car while Officer Green searched the car. The tape of their conversation contains several incriminating statements, including defendant's admission that the envelope was hers and that it contained illegal drugs.

Argument:

Over the years, courts have recognized a variety of exceptions to the search warrant requirement of the Fourth Amendment in recognition that exigent circumstances often do not allow an officer time to obtain a search warrant. This case illustrates the tension between the officer's duty to collect evidence of the illegal drug trade and the individual's privacy concerns. Consent has long enabled an officer to conduct a search, even without probable cause. Even without consent but upon probable cause, an officer may search a car and any containers within the car, without regard to their ownership. A standard law enforcement technique has been to ask suspects to wait in the officer's patrol car while the officer searches the suspects' car; to obtain evidence, the officer tape-records any statements the suspects unwisely make while in the patrol car.

The government argues that two exceptions to the search warrant requirement allowed Officer Green to search the defendant's purse. Defendant's motion to suppress the contents of her purse should be denied, either because the defendant consented to the search or because probable cause to search the car allows Officer Green to search containers found in the car. Defendant has argued that the tape containing her incriminating statements should be suppressed because the tape was made in violation of the federal eavesdropping statutes. There is no ground to suppress the tape under the statutes; the statutes prohibit taping only if there is a reasonable expectation that the conversation is private. Society would not recognize any conversation of suspects in a patrol car to be private. This memorandum will first explain why the methamphetamines found in defendant's purse should not be suppressed and then why the tape of defendant's incriminating statements should not be suppressed.

A. Because it was objectively reasonable for Officer Green to believe that defendant had consented to the search when she held out her purse to him, the methamphetamines found should not be suppressed.

Once a vehicle is stopped, the officer can search the car if there is probable cause of criminal activity. An occupant can consent to the search of the occupant's belongings. *Florida v. Jimeno*, 500 U.S. 248, 251 (1991). Even without consent, the officer can search containers found in the car and suspected of holding the object of the officer's search, no matter who owns the container. *Wyoming v. Houghton*, 526 U.S. 295, 300–01 (1999). An officer may not search someone's person without probable cause. *Id.* at 303.

The search of Cruz's purse is constitutional if she consented to the search or the container exception to the search warrant requirement extends to her purse. The United States Supreme Court has stated the standard for determining when an individual has consented to the search of a car. *Jimeno*, 500 U.S. at 251. This portion of the office memo will examine whether the consent standard has been met. As far as the container exception is concerned, the United States Supreme Court recently held that "police officers with probable cause to search a car may inspect passengers' belongings found in the car that are capable of concealing the object of the search." *Houghton*, 526 U.S. at 307. The facts of *Jimeno*, *Houghton*, and *Estrada* will be compared to determine if the search of Cruz's purse was constitutional.

In *Jimeno*, Officer Trujillo overheard a telephone call from a public telephone in which Jimeno was discussing a drug deal. Trujillo followed Jimeno's car and stopped Jimeno for failure to stop when turning right on red. After informing Jimeno about the traffic violation, Trujillo

> went on to say that he had reason to believe that respondent was carrying narcotics in his car, and asked permission to search the car. He explained that respondent did not have to consent to a search of the car. Respondent stated that he had nothing to hide, and gave Trujillo permission to search the automobile.

500 U.S. at 249–50. Trujillo found drugs in a brown paper bag on the car floorboard. *Id.* at 250.

The Court then set forth the test for determining whether consent was given. "The standard for measuring the scope of a suspect's consent under the Fourth Amendment is that of 'objective' reasonableness—what would the typical person have understood by the exchange between the officer and the suspect?" *Id.* at 251. Applying this standard, the Court found that Jimeno had consented to the search of the bag. *Id.*

The facts of *Jimeno* and *Estrada* are similar in that the two cars were stopped for alleged traffic violations, the two defendants consented to searches, and the officers searched containers. The facts surrounding the consent issue are substantially similar. Trujillo told Jimeno that he suspected that there were drugs in the car and explained that Jimeno did not have to consent to the search. When Trujillo asked Jimeno's permission, Jimeno claimed that he had nothing to hide and explicitly consented to the search. Officer Green made a statement, "You don't mind if I search, do you?" Officer Green did not have time to explain that the defendant did not have to consent before she held out her purse to him.

In *Jimeno*, the container was a brown paper bag located on the floor of the car. In *Estrada*, the container was defendant's purse, hanging from her shoulder. If anything, it was more objectively reasonable to believe that the defendant in this case had consented to the search of her purse than that Jimeno consented to the search of the brown paper bag. The defendant's implied consent of offering her purse to Officer Green made it clear that she was consenting to the search of that particular container. It was not as clear that Jimeno consented to the search of the brown paper bag when he consented to the search of the car. In *Jimeno*, the trial court had granted Jimeno's motion to suppress the contents of the brown paper bag. The Florida District Court of Appeal and the Florida Supreme Court affirmed. *Id.* at 250.

Applying the objective reasonableness standard, it is objectively reasonable to believe that the defendant in this case had consented to the search of her purse. Her overt action makes it objectively reasonable to believe that she consented.

B. Because the purse was found in a car that was searched upon probable cause that it contained illegal drugs, the container exception to the search warrant requirement applied and the methamphetamines should not be suppressed.

As far as the container exception is concerned, the United States Supreme Court in *Houghton* held that "police officers with probable cause to search a car may inspect passengers' belongings found in the car that are capable of concealing the object of the search." 526 U.S. at 307. The facts of *Houghton* and *Estrada* will be compared to determine if the search of the defendant's purse was constitutional.

In *Houghton*, David Young was stopped for speeding and a faulty brake light. After the officer saw a hypodermic syringe in Young's pocket, Young admitted that he used it to take drugs. The officer asked the two female passengers seated in the front seat to exit the car, and the officer searched the car. The officer found Houghton's purse on the backseat of the car. Searching the purse, the officer found a brown pouch that contained drug paraphernalia and a syringe containing methamphetamine in a large enough quantity for a felony conviction. Houghton claimed that the brown pouch was not hers. The officer also found a black container that contained drug paraphernalia and a syringe containing a smaller amount of methamphetamine, insufficient for a felony conviction. Houghton's arms showed fresh needle marks. The officer arrested her. 526 U.S. at 297–98.

The issue in *Houghton* was "whether police officers violate the Fourth Amendment when they search a passenger's personal belongings inside an automobile that they have probable cause to believe contains contraband." *Id.* at 297. The Court held "that police officers with probable cause to search a car may inspect passengers' belongings found in the car that are capable of concealing the object of the search." *Id.* at 307. The Court first relied on a 1982 case in which the Court had found that, where there was probable cause to search a car, it was constitutionally permissible to search containers found in the car that might hold the object of the search. *Id.* at 301–02.

The Court noted that an individual carrying a package in a vehicle traveling on the public roads has a reduced expectation of privacy. *Id.* at 303. The Court found no reason to afford more protection to a container owned by a passenger than a container owned by the driver. *Id.* at 305. The *Houghton* Court foresaw the circumstance in which law enforcement efforts "would be appreciably impaired without the ability to search the passenger's belongings" because a passenger "will often be engaged in a common enterprise with the driver, and have the same interest in concealing the fruits or evidence of their wrongdoing." *Id.* at 304–05. In addition, the driver "might be able to hide contraband in a passenger's belongings as readily as in other containers in the car." *Id.* at 305.

The facts of *Houghton* and this case are very similar in that the two cars were stopped for alleged traffic violations, the passengers exited the cars, leaving their purses in the backseat, and the officers searched a passenger's purse. The facts of the two cases differ slightly in that Houghton at first disclaimed ownership of the purse. In contrast, this defendant returned to the car to retrieve her purse and offered it to Officer Green.

Applying the holding in *Houghton* to *Estrada*, Officer Green's search of the defendant's purse was constitutional. When Officer Green discovered the vial containing what he believed to be crack cocaine in the driver's possession, that gave Officer Green probable cause to search the car and all containers in the car that might contain illegal drugs. Defendant's purse was of the size that it might contain illegal drugs, and it was initially found in the car. Either of the two occupants might have concealed illegal drugs in defendant's purse as Officer Green pulled them over. Because of the substantial similarities between *Houghton* and *Estrada*, this court should find that Officer Green's search was constitutional.

C. Because a patrol car is similar to an office in a police station, the defendant had no reasonable expectation of privacy while seated in the rear seat of a patrol car, and the motion to suppress the tape containing the defendant's incriminating statements should be denied.

The federal eavesdropping statutes protect certain types of face-to-face conversations against interception; however, to be protected, the conversation must qualify as an "oral communication." Under the statutes, an "'oral communication' means any oral communications uttered by a person exhibiting an expectation that such communication is not subject to interception under circumstances justifying such expectation...." 18 U.S.C.A. § 2510 (2) (West, Westlaw through P.L. 116-91). Thus, a conversation is not an oral communication unless the conversants expect that the conversation is private and an objective third party would consider that expectation reasonable.

It is illegal to intercept an oral communication. "[A]ny person who ... intentionally intercepts ... any oral communication ... shall be punished." 18 U.S.C.A. § 2511 (1) (West, Westlaw through P.L. 116-91). One exception to this prohibition involves a police officer; however, the police officer must be party to the conversation or one conversant must have consented to the taping for the exception to apply. "It shall not be unlawful under this chapter for a person acting under color of law to intercept [an] ... oral ... communication where such person is a party to the communication or one of the parties has given prior consent to the interception." 18 U.S.C.A. § 2511 (2)(c) (West, Westlaw through P.L. 116-91). If an oral communication is taped in violation of the eavesdropping statutes, the conversation cannot be used as evidence in court:

> Whenever any ... oral communication has been intercepted, no part of the contents of such communication and no evidence derived therefrom may be received in evidence in any trial, hearing, or other proceeding ... before any court ... if the disclosure of that information would be in violation of this chapter.

18 U.S.C.A. § 2515 (West, Westlaw through P.L. 116-91).

Thus, if defendant's conversation was an oral communication, it should be suppressed. Whether the conversation is an oral communication turns on whether the defendant had a reasonable expectation of privacy while seated in the rear seat of the patrol car. One prong of the two-prong test is satisfied; defendant and the driver appear to have had an expectation of privacy or they would not have made incriminating statements. The other prong of the test is whether their expectation was reasonable. On one hand, the conversation was not audible outside the patrol car. The only way the officer could have heard the conversation was by taping it. On the other hand, they were not sitting in a privately owned car. They were sitting in the officer's car. While an expectation of privacy in a privately owned car would have been reasonable, it is unclear whether an expectation of privacy in the officer's car was reasonable. Some might equate the officer's car to the officer's office. If defendant and the driver were conversing in an office of a police station, it might not be reasonable to expect privacy.

In a case with similar facts, the issue before the United States Court of Appeals for the Eleventh Circuit was "whether the district court erred in denying the motion to suppress the tapes resulting from the secret recording of McKinnon's pre-arrest conversations while he sat in the back seat of the police car." *United States v. McKinnon*, 985 F.2d 525, 526 (11th Cir. 1993).

In *McKinnon*, police officers stopped a pickup truck for failure to travel in a single lane on the Florida Turnpike. Theodore Pressley was driving and Steve McKinnon was the passenger. Pressley consented to the search of his vehicle. While the officers were searching, McKinnon and Pressley waited in the rear seat of the patrol car. There they made incriminating statements that were secretly recorded by the officers. The officers arrested them after finding cocaine in the truck, and they were placed in the rear seat of the patrol car. The officers again recorded McKinnon and Pressley's incriminating statements. *Id.*

The *McKinnon* court considered the meaning of the term "oral communication" under the federal statutes. An oral communication is protected against taping. If a conversation is taped in violation of the statutes, the tape may be suppressed. A conversation is an oral communication only if the conversants exhibited a subjective expectation of privacy and the expectation of privacy was objectively reasonable. The court seemed to agree with the government's argument that a patrol car functions as the officer's office and the rear seat of the patrol car functions as a jail cell. *Id.* at 527. The court held "that McKinnon did not have a reasonable or justifiable expectation of privacy for conversations he held while seated in the back seat area of a police car." *Id.* at 528.

In examining the facts of *McKinnon* and *Estrada*, the facts concerning the taping seem virtually identical. In each case, an officer asked two individuals to wait in the patrol car prior to their arrest. The officer taped their conversation in the rear seat of the patrol car; the conversation contained incriminating statements. One difference between the two cases is that the officer in *McKinnon* also taped McKinnon's conversation following his arrest. This difference is not significant because an arrestee held in the back of a patrol car would have a lesser expectation of privacy than a person not under arrest.

A number of state and a number of federal courts, other than the *McKinnon* court, have faced the issue of whether an officer may secretly tape a conversation of individuals seated in the rear seat of a patrol car. In each case the court has said that taping is permissible. *See United States v. Paxton*, 848 F.3d 803, 813 (7th Cir. 2017) ("because the defendants lacked an objectively reasonable expectation of privacy when placed into the marked police van, the interception and recording of their conversations did not constitute a search for purposes of their Fourth Amendment rights"); *United States v. Dunbar*, 553 F.3d 48, 58 (1st Cir. 2009) ("the police car was not a reasonably confidential place to talk"); *United States v. Clark*, 22 F.3d 799, 801 (8th Cir. 1994) ("defendant's expectation of privacy while seated in the police car was not reasonable").

Although persuasive authority in other circuits, *McKinnon* is mandatory authority in this circuit. The facts concerning the taping are virtually identical in *McKinnon* and *Estrada*. A number of other state and federal courts have also held that there is no reasonable expectation of privacy for persons seated in the back of a patrol car. Therefore, a court should find that the defendants had no reasonable expectation of privacy while they were seated in the rear seat of the patrol car. Because they did not have a reasonable expectation of privacy, their conversation was not protected against taping as an oral communication. Therefore, a court would not suppress the tape under the federal eavesdropping statutes.

Defendant has also made the argument that the search of her purse tainted the tape recording. Obviously, were the court to deny the defendant's motion to suppress the illegal drugs, there would be no taint that could attach to the tape. Even were the court to grant the defendant's motion to suppress the methamphetamines, the court should not grant the motion to suppress the tape. In all probability, defendant would have made the incriminating statements even if Officer Green had not searched her purse.

When a police officer obtains evidence in an unconstitutional manner, that evidence is excluded from use at trial. If that evidence leads the officer to other evidence, the other evidence is derivative of the first evidence. The derivative evidence is known as fruit of the poisonous tree and is also inadmissible. Generally, evidence that is tainted by the prior unconstitutional conduct is inadmissible; however, in some instances the second evidence is admissible because the connection between the unconstitutionally seized evidence and the subsequently obtained evidence is marginal.

The tape is not derivative of the evidence the officer discovered searching Estrada's purse. The tape should not be suppressed.

Conclusion:

For the reasons set forth, the United States requests this court to deny defendant's motion to suppress the methamphetamines and the tape of her incriminating statements.

Respectfully submitted,

____

Florida Attorney, Esq.
Florida Bar Number 000000
Law Firm
Main Street
Anytown, Fla.

Summary

- In litigation, an attorney may be required by court rule, may be asked by the judge, or may feel the need to submit a memorandum of law to court.
- The purposes of the memorandum of law are to explain the client's position in a lawsuit and to convince the judge to rule in the client's favor.

- The tone of the memorandum of law is persuasive.
- While the attorney has to represent the client's best interest, this duty is tempered by the attorney's ethical duty as "an officer of the court."
- Build your credibility by stating the facts and the law accurately.
- Use a format that makes your memorandum of law reader-friendly.
- Organize the document to highlight important information and to obscure adverse information that you feel obligated to include.
- Comply with any court rules and format customarily used for the particular court.
- The parts of a standard memorandum of law are the caption, the question presented, the facts, the argument, the thesis paragraph, the rule of law, the application of law to the facts, and the conclusion.

Discussion Points

1. Which footnotes in the first sample memorandum of law seem to be the most helpful and why?
2. How does the second sample memorandum of law differ from the first?
3. What changes would you make to either of the sample memoranda of law to make them better?

Cyberlaw Exercises

1. Bryan Garner, a legal writing authority, has interviewed many judges, many of whom give tips that might be helpful in making a good impression on a judge. Go to http://www.lawprose.org/, watch videos of one or more of the judges, and identify three tips that you could use when you are asked to write a memorandum of law.
2. A number of interesting videos are posted on https://www.youtube.com/, some of which are related to writing a memorandum of law. Go to the website and find a video providing legal writing tips on writing effective memoranda of law. How do the legal writing tips add to your understanding of writing well? How do the tips differ from the legal writing advice provided in this chapter?
3. The United States courts website, located at https://www.uscourts.gov/, offers access to federal court rules. The Legal Information Institute, located at https://www.law.cornell.edu/, offers access to federal and state court rules. See if you can access the various court rules for your state. Find local, federal, and state court rules that apply to the area in which you are located.

Chapter 15

Appellate Brief

"An ability to write clearly has become the most important prerequisite for an American appellate lawyer."

—William H. Rehnquist, Chief Justice of the United States Supreme Court, "From Webster to Word-Processing: The Ascendance of the Appellate Brief," 1 J. App. Prac. & Process 1, 3 (1999).

Introduction

When a case is appealed, the attorneys for the parties submit appellate briefs to the appellate court. This chapter explains the purpose, use, and format of the appellate brief and includes two sample appellate briefs.

Much of the substance of the sample appellate brief is similar to the sample memoranda of law from Chapter 14. To save space, the footnotes from the first memorandum of law are not repeated in the first appellate brief. You may want to go back later and reread the footnotes to the first sample memorandum of law from Chapter 14.

Because the appellate brief is so important in an appeals case, the substance of the appellate brief must be well researched. Sloppy research will cause the judge to lose faith in the argument presented. Research also includes being aware of court rules governing the format of the appellate brief. Although a judge usually will overlook minor failures to comply with requisite format, a judge may complain in writing about the attorney's failure to comply.

YOU BE THE JUDGE

What would you do if the presiding judge granted an attorney permission to exceed the page limitation but you felt that the attorney's brief was overly long?

In reaching your decision, consider the following information:

- The brief was 202 pages long.
- The attorney ignored the standard of review and misstated the record.
- The attorney failed to provide analysis to support arguments and failed to provide citation to relevant authority.

To see how a state court answered the question, *see In re S.C.*, 41 Cal. Rptr. 3d 453 (Cal. Ct. App. 2006).

Purpose and Use

When a party appeals a lower court ruling, the appellate court's job is to review what the lower court did to determine whether the lower court committed reversible error. In its review, the appellate court examines the "record" of the lower court proceedings and reads the appellate briefs. Once the record on appeal is transmitted to the appellate court and appellate briefs are filed, the appellate court may rule on the appeal solely on the strength of the documents filed with the appellate court, or the court may hear oral argument. During oral argument, the attorney for each party has an allotted period of time to argue the client's position in the case and to respond to questions posed by the appellate judges.

The appellate briefs play a major role in the appeal. You might think of the appellate briefs as guidebooks to the case. They contain the arguments of the parties, they assist the appellate court in determining the issues to be decided on appeal, and they explain the applicable law and facts. Of course, because the appellate briefs are designed to persuade the appellate court of the correctness of the respective parties' positions, the **appellant's brief** is written from the appellant's perspective and the **appellee's brief** is written from the appellee's perspective .

Appellant's Brief

A document filed by the appellant in an appellate court explaining why the lower court's decision was incorrect.

Appellee's Brief

A document filed by the appellee in an appellate court explaining why the lower court's decision was correct.

The appellant's brief is filed first and gives the appellant's reasons why the appellate court should reverse or otherwise modify the lower court decision. Court rules give the appellee a certain period of time after the appellant's brief is filed to file the appellee's brief. The appellee's brief gives the appellee's reasons why the lower court decision should be affirmed.

In reviewing a lower court decision, the appellate court must follow a standard of review. A standard of review is the nature and extent of the action the appellate court may take in reviewing the lower court decision. The standard is different depending on whether the appellate court is reviewing a finding of fact, a ruling of law, or a ruling on a question involving law and fact. Because the trial court was in the best position to judge the credibility of the witnesses, the trial court's **findings of fact** are given great deference.

Findings of Fact

Determinations of the facts in a case.

The appellate court is bound to follow the trial court's findings of fact unless a jury finding was unreasonable or a trial judge's finding was clearly erroneous. When deciding a question of law or a question involving law and fact, the appellate court is free to reach a ruling different from that of the trial court.

Keep in mind the standard of review when writing the appellate brief. If you represent the appellee and the question for review is one of fact, emphasize that the trial court's finding of fact must be deferred to unless unreasonable or clearly erroneous. Whether the issue is one purely of fact, purely of law, or of fact and law is rarely clear-cut. If you represent the appellant, try to characterize the issue as one of law or of fact and law so that the appellate court will not have to defer to the decision of the trial court.

If you represent the appellee, use the lower court decision in the appellee's favor to your advantage. Do not hesitate to rely on the reasoning of the lower court. You may even want to quote particularly well-worded passages of the lower court's opinion. Although an appellate court is not bound by the trial court's ruling on a question of law or a mixed question of fact and law, sometimes it helps to remind the appellate court that after studying the issue, the lower court ruled in the appellee's favor.

Compare the appellate brief with the memorandum of law. Of the legal documents covered in this book, the appellate brief is most similar to the memorandum of law. Because both the memorandum of law and the appellate brief are persuasive in tone and are designed to convince the reader of the correctness of the client's position, much of the substance of the two documents will be similar. Although similar in tone and purpose, the two documents differ in two respects. As explained, the appellate brief differs from the memorandum of law in the standard of review by the appellate court.

The different standard of review in the appellate court will probably dictate some change in the wording of the issues and argument of the appellate brief from the questions presented and argument of the memorandum of law. Another difference is format. Aside from complying with page size and other such mundane requirements, attorneys writing memoranda of law generally follow the format customary in their area rather than having to follow a certain detailed format specified by court rule. In contrast, the format for appellate briefs is usually specified in detail in the applicable court rules.

At this point, it would be well for you to reread the preceding chapter on the memorandum of law (Chapter 14). Except for differences in the standard of review and format, assume that the explanation of the memorandum of law from that chapter applies to the appellate brief.

The next section of this chapter discusses format for appellate briefs.

Format

The first step in writing an appellate brief is to check applicable court rules to determine the format required by the court. For a case being appealed to a federal circuit court you would check the Federal Rules of Appellate Procedure. The United States Supreme Court has its own set of rules that must be consulted for documents submitted to it. For a case being appealed to the intermediate appellate court of your state, check the rules of appellate procedure for your state. The court of last resort of your state may have its own set of rules that must be consulted for documents submitted to it, or it may use the same rules as the state intermediate appellate courts.

In addition to the rules referred to in the previous paragraph, many courts have local rules that must be complied with.

Failure to follow court rules for appellate briefs may have serious consequences. The least serious of the consequences is attorney embarrassment if the failure to comply is pointed out by the clerk of the court, by opposing counsel, or by a judge. A judge may impose monetary sanctions on an attorney who fails to comply with the rules. The most serious consequence is the clerk's office refusing to file an appellate brief that fails to comply with applicable appellate rules. Another consequence no less serious to the attorney's reputation in the legal community is for the judge to chastise the attorney, or even the attorney's firm, in writing as part of the court's opinion. This written admonishment in a published case or a case included in an electronic database exists in perpetuity.

YOU BE THE JUDGE

What action might you take where neither attorney in a case seems to feel obliged to follow court rules as to the content and format of appellate briefs?

In reaching your decision, consider the following information:

- The facts section of each brief contains arguments, some facts are misstated, and some facts are unsupported by the record.
- The briefs contain an excessive number of footnotes and a number of the footnotes contain arguments.
- The briefs exceed the page limits.
- The record was organized poorly, some of the documents made part of the record were illegible, and the manner in which the record was bound made it difficult to read.

One method of dealing with the attorneys' noncompliance would be to strike the briefs and dismiss the appeal.

Another way to deal with the attorneys' noncompliance would be to admonish the attorneys and their law firms in writing in a portion of the court opinion.

To see how a state court answered the question, see *Technology Solutions Company v. Northrup Grumman Corporation*, 826 N.E.2d 1220 (Ill. App. Ct. 2005).

The rules for appellate briefs cover a number of matters. They usually specify the major sections required to be included in the appellate brief and may specify their content. For example, Rule 28 of the Federal Rules of Appellate Procedure states the sections required for the appellate brief and gives a brief explanation of the information to be included in each section. The rules may also mandate certain more mundane matters such as paper size, type size, and maximum page length. Rule 32 requires appellate briefs to be double-spaced on eight-and-one-half by eleven-inch paper with at least one-inch margins. The rule specifies the minimum size typeface, limits a brief to thirty pages, and limits a reply brief to fifteen pages. (To save space, the sample appellate brief contained in this chapter is single- rather than double-spaced.) Rule 32 also specifies the information required on the cover of the appellate brief and the color of the cover.

The format used in this chapter complies with the Federal Rules of Appellate Procedure (except for being single-spaced rather than double-spaced). The following are the sections of an appellate brief required by Rule 28.

Table of Contents

The table of contents includes the titles of the sections of the brief and the wording of the point headings as well as the page references.

Table of Authorities

This table of cases, statutes, and other authorities contains references to the pages of the brief on which the listed authorities are cited.

Jurisdictional Statement

The statement must provide the basis for the trial court's or agency's subject matter jurisdiction, the basis for the appellate court's subject matter jurisdiction, the filing date indicating that the appeal is timely, and an assertion that the appeal is from a final order or there is other reason for the appellate court's jurisdiction.

Statement of the Issues Presented for Review

The issues are the questions you are suggesting the appellate court consider. Word the issues so the appellate court can easily reach the decision in your client's favor. Often the appellee will start an issue with the words, "Did the trial court properly find that" or "Did the trial court properly rule that." Such wording suggests that the trial court decision was correct. In contrast, the appellant would start the same issue with the words, "Did the trial court err in." That wording suggests that there was something wrong with the trial court's decision.

Statement of the Case and Statement of the Facts

Rule 28 requires "a concise statement of the case setting out the facts relevant to the issues submitted for review, describing the relevant procedural history, and identifying the rulings presented for review, with appropriate references to the record." For ease of reference, the appellant's brief usually has an appendix attached to it, containing copies of the parts of the record referenced in appellant's brief. The abbreviation "(A. 3)" would reference page three of the appendix.

Summary of the Argument

Rule 28 states that a summary of the argument, which precedes the argument, "must contain a succinct, clear, and accurate statement of the arguments made in the body of the brief, and which must not merely repeat the argument headings."

Argument

The argument must contain:

(A) "appellant's contentions and the reasons for them, with citations to the authorities and parts of the record on which the appellant relies"; and

(B) "for each issue, a concise statement of the applicable standard of review (which may appear in the discussion of the issue or under a separate heading placed before the discussion of the issues)[.]"

As in the memorandum of law, use point headings to make the brief reader-friendly. The brief should contain one or more major point headings for major sections and may contain subheadings within a major section to divide a major section into subsections. The major point headings should be equal in number to the issues presented, should answer the issues, and should appear in the same order as the issues presented.

Legal Conclusion

Rule 28 requires "a short conclusion stating the precise relief sought."

YOU BE THE JUDGE

What type of sanction would you impose for an attorney's failure to follow format or content of appellate briefs?

In reaching your decision, consider the following sanctions:

- The judge could impose monetary sanctions.
- The judge could chastise the attorney in writing.
- The judge could strike the noncomplying brief and dismiss the appeal.

To see how courts answered the question, see *In re McIntyre*, 181 B.R. 420 (B.A.P. 9th Cir. 1995); *N/S Corp. v. Liberty Mut. Ins. Co.*, 127 F.3d 1145 (9th Cir. 1997).

FIRST SAMPLE APPELLATE BRIEF

IN THE
UNITED STATES COURT OF APPEALS
FOR THE ELEVENTH CIRCUIT

CASE NO. 19-0000

UNITED STATES OF AMERICA,
Appellee,
v.
MICHAEL CAMPBELL and JOHN WRIGHT,
Appellants.

APPEAL OF A CRIMINAL CONVICTION FROM THE
UNITED STATES DISTRICT COURT
ORLANDO DIVISION

BRIEF FOR APPELLANT CAMPBELL

Florida Attorney, Esq.
Florida Bar Number 000000
Law Firm
Main Street
Anytown, Fla.

Table of Contents

Table of Authorities

Statement of Subject Matter Jurisdiction in the United States District Court

The defendant, Michael Campbell, was indicted in the United States District Court for the Middle District of Florida on April 5, 2019. The indictment charged him with violating 21 U.S.C.A. § 841 (a)(1) (West, Westlaw through P.L. 116-91) for possession with intent to distribute a quantity of cocaine. (A. 21). Defendant received a jury verdict of guilty on June 12, 2019, and was sentenced on June 14, 2019, to a term of three years. (A. 25).

Statement of Jurisdiction

This is an appeal from the final judgment of the United States District Court for the Middle District of Florida in a criminal case pursuant to a Motion under Rule 4(b) of the Federal Rules of Appellate Procedure. Jurisdiction in the United States Court of Appeals for the Eleventh Circuit is invoked under 28 U.S.C.A. § 1291 (West, Westlaw through P.L. 116-91), which provides that the Court of Appeals has jurisdiction from all final decisions of the United States District Court. Defendant was sentenced on June 14, 2019. On June 21, 2019, a timely Notice of Appeal was filed from which this appeal follows. (A. 25, 27).

Statement of the Issue

Did the trial court err in admitting evidence seized from defendant Mike Campbell's car where a law enforcement officer pursued the Campbell car after he observed Mike and his friend, two African American college students in their twenties in beach attire, traveling on I-95 in the early evening at the speed limit in an out-of-state tagged Lincoln Continental and where the law enforcement officer pulled the Campbell car over for following too closely? (A. 3–4).

Statement of the Case

On April 1, 2019, United States Drug Enforcement Agents stopped the defendant, Michael Campbell, on I-95 because he fit their drug courier profile and for following too closely. (A. 3–4). After the agents found cocaine in the trunk of Campbell's car, he was arrested and taken into custody. (A. 5). He was provided an initial detention hearing on April 2, 2019. (A. 20). On April 5, 2019, an indictment was filed charging him with a violation of 21 U.S.C.A. § 841 (a)(1) for possession with intent to distribute a quantity of cocaine. He was arraigned the same day, and he entered a plea of not guilty. (A. 21).

A trial date was set for June 10, 2019, for a jury trial. Prior to trial defendant filed a motion to suppress the cocaine found in the trunk of defendant's car. The district court denied the motion and the trial began on June 10, 2019. (A. 22). Defendant received a jury verdict of guilty on June 12, 2019. (A. 24). Defendant was sentenced on June 14, 2009, to a term of three years. (A. 25).

Statement of the Facts

Mike Campbell and his best friend, like thousands of other college students, had decided to enjoy a Florida spring break. After Mike promised to drive carefully, Mike's father let Mike borrow his car, a brand new Lincoln Continental. After arriving in Florida, they spent every waking moment of their break on the beach. In the early evening on the last day of vacation, they went straight from the beach to their car to begin the long trip back to school, calculating that they would have just enough driving time to make it back for their first class. (A. 1–2). Mike was driving north on I-95, thinking about the promise he had made to his father, when he saw patrol cars parked in the median, one with its lights shining across the northbound lanes. Almost immediately after driving through the arc of the patrol car's headlights, Mike looked in the rear view mirror and saw the patrol car pull out behind him. The patrol car followed Mike for a distance before pulling Mike over. (A. 3–4).

An officer got out of the patrol car, walked over to Mike's car and asked for Mike's driver's license and car registration. As Mike handed over his license and the registration he noticed the officer eyeing Mike's beach attire suspiciously. When Mike told the officer they were heading back to school from spring break, the officer commented, "We don't see too many blacks down here over spring break." The officer added, "I stopped you for following the car in front of you too closely." Still holding the license and registration, the officer asked Mike whether the officer could search the car and said, "You don't have anything to hide, do you?" Hoping that if he refused they could be on their way, Mike answered, "No." The officer said, "Wait here," turned around, walked back to the patrol car, and got in. Mike could not have left even if the officer had not told him to "wait" because the officer still had Mike's license and car registration. (A. 3–4).

Forty-five minutes later another patrol car pulled up and an officer got out with a dog. The officer led the dog around the car. The dog circled the car once and then stopped and pawed the car's trunk. The officer motioned Mike to roll down his window. The officer told him that the dog had detected drugs in the trunk of Mike's car. The officer told Mike that Mike could either open the car trunk or wait there for whatever time was necessary for the officer to obtain a search warrant. Feeling that he had no choice, Mike opened the trunk. Both officers started pulling Mike's and his friend's belongings out of the trunk and tossing them on the ground. One of the officers found a brown paper bag containing cocaine wedged in a bottom corner of the trunk. Mike and his friend were arrested and were charged with possession with intent to distribute. (A. 4–5).

Summary of Argument

The car driver and passengers expect that activities within the car will be private and not subject to the scrutiny of law enforcement officials. They may feel that their privacy is invaded if a law enforcement officer stops the car to investigate. A trained police officer may have a hunch that a car's occupants are engaged in illegal activity; however, a law enforcement officer may not constitutionally stop a car unless there is a reasonable suspicion of illegal activity or there is a traffic violation. The stop of Mike's car to investigate for criminal activity was not permissible because the agents did not have reasonable suspicion of illegal drug activity. The stop for a traffic violation was constitutionally justifiable only if Mike was following too closely.

The Fourth Amendment to the United States Constitution guarantees "[t]he right of the people to be secure in their persons, houses, papers, and effects against unreasonable searches and seizures" and allows a search warrant to be issued only upon "probable cause." A search warrant requirement was spelled out in the amendment to safeguard this important right. Over the more than two hundred years since the amendment was adopted, the individual's right against unreasonable search and seizure has been jealously guarded.

Although the time and level of evidence needed to obtain a search warrant protects the individual's constitutional right, the courts have allowed two exceptions to the search warrant requirement, either of which the government argues is applicable here and allowed the officer to stop the Campbell car. The first exception requires a minimum of "reasonable suspicion" of illegal activity to stop a car and question its occupants. *Terry v. Ohio*, 392 U.S. 1, 27 (1968). *United States v. Smith*, 799 F.2d 704, 707 (11th Cir. 1986). The second exception allows an officer to stop a car to investigate a traffic violation. *Whren v. United States*, 517 U.S. 806, 818 (1996).

Defendant Campbell's motion to suppress should be granted because neither of the two exceptions to the search warrant requirement apply here. The officer stopped Campbell's car on a mere "hunch," and Campbell was following at a "reasonable and prudent" distance, as required by the Florida Statutes. Fla. Stat. Ch. 316.0895 (1) (2019). The argument section of this brief will first explain why there was not enough evidence to justify an investigatory stop and then why the alleged traffic violation did not justify the stop.

Argument

THE EVIDENCE FOUND IN THE TRUNK OF DEFENDANT CAMPBELL'S CAR SHOULD HAVE BEEN SUPPRESSED AS THE FRUIT OF AN UNCONSTITUTIONAL SEARCH AND SEIZURE BECAUSE THE DRUG COURIER PROFILE DID NOT SUPPORT THE REASONABLE SUSPICION NECESSARY FOR AN INVESTIGATORY STOP, AND CAMPBELL DID NOT COMMIT A TRAFFIC VIOLATION.

A. Because the information the officer relied on to stop the Campbell car was no more than a mere "hunch," the evidence should be suppressed unless the officer had probable cause to stop the car for a traffic violation.

Terry was the landmark case that lowered the burden of proof necessary for a stop from probable cause to "reasonable suspicion." Such stops made on reasonable suspicion are often referred to as "*Terry* stops," after *Terry*, and the definition of *Terry* stops has been broadened to apply to car stops. The new reasonable suspicion standard allows a police officer to stop and briefly question someone but is still designed to protect the innocent traveler, singled out because of certain immutable personal characteristics such as race, sex, and age, from being subjected to "overbearing or harassing" law en forcement tactics. 392 U.S. at 14–15 n. 11. A stop made only on an "unparticularized suspicion or 'hunch'" is unconstitutional. *Id.* at 27. Assuming the officer has the requisite reasonable suspicion for a *Terry* stop, the officer would still need probable cause or consent to search a car.

Smith involved almost identical facts to those being considered here. In *Smith*, the government argued that a highway stop was constitutionally permitted based either on a drug courier profile or on Smith's alleged commission of a traffic violation. 799 F.2d at 705. Smith filed a motion to suppress, claiming that the evidence seized from his car should be suppressed because of the violation of his right against unreasonable search and seizure. *Id.* at 706. The United States Court of Appeals for the Eleventh Circuit found that the *Smith* drug courier profile did not support reasonable suspicion, reversed the lower court's denial of Smith's motion to suppress, and vacated Smith's conviction. *Id.* at 712.

The *Smith* facts are very similar to the *Campbell* facts. In *Smith*, one night in June of 1985, Trooper Robert Vogel, a Florida Highway Patrol trooper, and a DEA agent were observing cars traveling in the northbound lanes of I-95 with hopes of intercepting drug couriers. When Smith's car passed through the arc of the patrol car headlights, Vogel noticed the following factors that matched his drug courier profile:

1. The car was traveling at 3:00 a.m.;
2. The car was a 1985 Mercury, a large late-model car;
3. The car had out-of-state tags;
4. There were two occupants of the car who were around 30; and
5. The driver was driving cautiously and did not look at the patrol car as the Mercury passed through the arc of the patrol car headlights.

Id. at 705–06.

The *Smith* drug courier profile is almost identical to the profile in this case. In both *Smith* and this case, the cars were traveling after dark; the cars were large late models with out-of-state tags; the cars were being driven "cautiously"; and each car contained two passengers in their twenties or thirties. The differences between the two profiles are very minor. Campbell and his friend were dressed casually while it is not known how Smith and Swindell were dressed. Smith and Swindell did not look at Vogel as they passed. It is not known whether Campbell looked in the agents' direction as Campbell drove past. Campbell claims that race was a factor in the stop even though it was not listed as such by the agents. (A. 3–4). Smith and Swindell's race is unknown.

In *Smith*, Vogel followed the Mercury for a mile and a half and noticed that the Mercury "wove" several times, once as much as six inches into the emergency lane. Vogel pulled Smith over. When a drug dog alerted on the car, a DEA agent searched the trunk and discovered one kilogram of cocaine. Smith and his passenger, Swindell, were arrested and were charged with conspiracy to possess cocaine with the intent to distribute it. Smith and Swindell's motions to suppress the cocaine were denied, and they were tried and convicted. *Id.* at 706.

The issue before the appellate court was whether the stop of Smith's car was reasonable. *Id.* This is the same basic question to be answered by this court in determining whether Campbell's motion to suppress should be granted. The *Smith* court held that the stop of Smith's car could not be upheld as a valid *Terry* stop, *id.* at 708, finding that "Trooper Vogel stopped the car because [Smith and Swindell] ... matched a few nondistinguishing characteristics contained on a drug courier profile and, additionally, because Vogel was bothered by the way the driver of the car chose not to look at him." *Id.* at 707.

Just as there was nothing in the *Campbell* drug courier profile to differentiate Campbell and his friend from other innocent college students returning from spring break in Florida, there was nothing in Vogel's drug courier profile to differentiate Smith and Swindell from other law-abiding motorists on I-95. (A. 3–4). It is usual to drive after dark to avoid heavy traffic or to complete an interstate trip. Although many motorists speed on the highways, motorists driving "cautiously" at or near the speed limit are simply obeying traffic laws. Many people other than drug couriers drive large late model cars with out-of-state tags. A motorist between the ages of twenty and forty is not unusual.

The contrast between the *Campbell* and *Smith* drug courier profiles, which do not support reasonable suspicion, and another courier profile which was held to support reasonable suspicion, is marked. *United States v. Sokolow*, 490 U.S. 1, 3 (1989). In *Sokolow*, DEA agents found 1,063 grams of cocaine inside Sokolow's carry-on luggage when he was stopped in Honolulu International Airport based on the following profile:

1. He had paid $2,100 in cash for two airplane tickets from a roll of $20 which appeared to contain $4,000;
2. He was ticketed under a name other than his own;
3. He traveled to Miami, a known drug source, and back;
4. Although his round trip flight lasted 20 hours, he stayed in Miami only 48 hours;
5. He appeared nervous;
6. He was about 25 years old;
7. He was dressed in a black jumpsuit and was wearing gold jewelry which he wore during both legs of the round-trip flight; and
8. Neither he nor his companion checked any luggage.

Id. at 3–5. The Court held that the *Sokolow* drug courier profile did support reasonable suspicion. *Id.* at 11.

The *Sokolow* dissent would have found that all of the factors even if "taken together" did not amount to reasonable suspicion. In criticizing the use of a drug courier profile to stop suspects, the dissent noted "the profile's 'chameleon-like way of adapting to any particular set of observations'" "subjecting innocent individuals to unwarranted police harassment and detention." *Id.* at 13 (Marshall, J., dissenting) (quoting *Sokolow v. United States*, 831 F.2d 1413, 1418 (9th Cir. 1987), *rev'd*, 490 U.S. 1 (1989)).

As predicted in the *Sokolow* dissent, Smith, Swindell, Campbell, and Campbell's friend were subjected to "unwarranted police harassment and detention" even though the factors in the respective drug courier profiles, even if "taken together" did not amount to reasonable suspicion. In contrast, several of the *Sokolow* factors, such as carrying such a large amount of cash and traveling a long distance to stay a relatively short period of time, are unusual or even suspicious in and of themselves. Each of the *Smith* and *Campbell* factors was not at all out of the ordinary alone and certainly taken together did not amount to reasonable suspicion. (A. 3–4).

B. Because Mike Campbell did not commit the traffic violation alleged by the officer, the evidence found in the trunk of Mike Campbell's car should be suppressed as the fruit of an unconstitutional search and seizure.

An examination of *Whren v. United States* is necessary to answer the question of whether the officer stopping Campbell on an alleged traffic violation was constitutional. In *Whren*, Brown was driving a Pathfinder in which Whren was a passenger. Brown stopped at a stop sign and looked down into Whren's lap. Plain clothes police officers were patrolling this "high drug area" of the District of Columbia in an unmarked patrol car. The Pathfinder caught the attention of the officers because Brown remained stopped at the stop sign for approximately twenty seconds. When the patrol car made a U-turn to follow the Pathfinder, Brown turned right without signaling and started off at an "unreasonable speed." The patrol car stopped the Pathfinder. When one of the officers approached Brown's window and peered in, he saw that Whren had two plastic bags of crack cocaine on his lap. The officers arrested Whren and Brown. 517 U.S. at 808, 809.

Justice Scalia phrased the issue as:

> whether the temporary detention of a motorist who the police have probable cause to believe has committed a civil traffic violation is inconsistent with the Fourth Amendment's prohibition against unreasonable seizures unless a reasonable officer would have been motivated to stop the car by a desire to enforce the traffic laws.

Id. at 808. The Court answered the question, "no":

> [T]he district court found that the officers had probable cause to believe that petitioners had violated the traffic code. That rendered the stop reasonable under the Fourth Amendment, the evidence thereby discovered admissible, and the up

holding of the convictions by the Court of Appeals for the District of Columbia Circuit correct.

Id. at 819.

Prior to *Whren*, some courts, including the court deciding *Smith*, had decided that a car stop for a traffic violation was unconstitutional unless a reasonable officer would have made the stop. The *Smith* court found that the cocaine should have been excluded from evidence because a reasonable officer would not have stopped Smith's car for the alleged traffic violation. 799 F.2d at 711. However, in *Whren*, the United States Supreme Court rejected the argument that the reasonable officer standard should apply. 517 U.S. at 813.

After *Whren*, it would be very difficult to convince a court that a stop for an alleged traffic violation is unconstitutional. However, if the court finds that the driver did not violate any traffic regulation, then the stop would be unconstitutional.

The Florida motor vehicle statute identified by the *Campbell* officer states, "The driver of a motor vehicle shall not follow another vehicle more closely than is reasonable and prudent, having due regard for the speed of such vehicles and the traffic upon, and the condition of, the highway." Fla. Stat. Ch. 316.0895 (1) (2019). No simple test determines if Campbell violated the statute. The court must determine from any evidence presented whether the distance at which Campbell was following the car in front of him was reasonable and prudent.

The alleged driving irregularities in *Whren* and *Campbell* are dissimilar. While it was clear that Brown committed a traffic violation, the Florida statute cited in this case does not apply to Campbell. Determining whether one vehicle is following another vehicle too closely involved much more of a judgment call than determining whether the Pathfinder failed to signal when turning right and exceeded the speed limit. The position of the vehicles on the highway and the weather and road conditions must all be considered to determine if Campbell violated the statute.

The evidence presented at the hearing on the motion to suppress showed that Fla. Stat. Ch. 316.0895 (1) did not apply to Campbell because Campbell was following the car in front of him at more than the appropriate distance given the vehicles' speed, the traffic, and the condition of the highway.

Following *Whren*, this court should find the stop of Campbell's car unconstitutional because there was no traffic violation. Because Campbell was following the car in front of him at a reasonable and prudent distance, the stop violated Campbell's right against unreasonable search and seizure. Because Campbell's fourth amendment right was violated by the stop, and the agents would not have found the evidence if they had not first stopped the car on I-95, the evidence should be suppressed as the fruit of the poisonous tree.

Conclusion

For the reasons set forth above, defendant Campbell requests this court to reverse the district court's denial of his motion to suppress, vacate his conviction, and remand the case to the district court.

Respectfully submitted,

____

Florida Attorney, Esq.
Florida Bar Number 000000
Law Firm
Main Street
Anytown, Fla.

8

SECOND SAMPLE APPELLATE BRIEF

In The
United States Court of Appeals
For The Eleventh Circuit

Case No. 19-0000

United States of America,
Appellant,
v.
Cruz Estrada,
Appellee.

Appeal of a Suppression Order From The
United States District Court
Orlando Division

Brief For Appellant The United States Of America

Florida Attorney, Esq.
Florida Bar Number 000000
Law Firm
Main Street
Anytown, Fla.

Table of Contents

Table of Authorities

Cases

Federal Rules of Appellate Procedure

United States Code

United States Constitution

Statement of Subject Matter Jurisdiction in the United States District Court

The defendant was indicted in the United States District Court for the Middle District of Florida on March 15, 2019. The indictment charged her with violating 21 U.S.C.A. § 841 (a)(1) (West, Westlaw through P.L. 116-91) for possession with intent to distribute a quantity of methamphetamines. (A. 21). On May 16, 2019, the trial court granted the defendant's motion to suppress the methamphetamines found in her possession and the tape recording of her incriminating statements. (A. 25).

Statement of Jurisdiction

This is an appeal from a suppression order of the United States District Court for the Middle District of Florida in a criminal case pursuant to a Motion under Rule 4(b) of the Federal Rules of Appellate Procedure. Jurisdiction in the United States Court of Appeals for the Eleventh Circuit is invoked under 28 U.S.C.A. § 1291 (West, Westlaw through P.L. 116-91), which provides that the Court of Appeals has jurisdiction from all final decisions of the United States District Court. Defendant's motion to suppress was granted on May 16, 2019. On May 20, 2019, a timely Notice of Appeal was filed from which this appeal follows. (A. 25, 27).

Statement of the Issues

1. Did the trial court err in granting the motion to suppress methamphetamines seized from defendant Estrada's purse after she gave the officer consent to search her purse? (A. 3–4).
2. Did the trial court err in granting the motion to suppress the tape recording of the defendants' conversation made while the defendants were seated in the rear seat of the patrol car? (A. 4).

Statement of the Case

On March 13, 2019, a highway patrol officer stopped the defendant and her driver on I-95 because the car was travelling 15 miles per hour over the speed limit. (A. 3–4). After the officer saw glass vials containing crack cocaine in the driver's lap, the officer asked them to wait in the patrol car while the officer searched the car. As she was walking toward the patrol car, defendant consented to a search of her purse. The officer found methamphetamine powder in a brown envelope in her purse. The officer recorded the defendant's statements while she was seated in the patrol car with the driver. The defendant was arrested and taken into custody. (A. 5). She was provided an initial detention hearing on March 14, 2019. (A. 20). On March 15, 2019, an indictment was filed charging her with a violation of 21 U.S.C.A. § 841 (a)(1) for possession with intent to distribute a quantity of methamphetamines. She was arraigned the same day and entered a not guilty plea. (A. 21).

A trial date was set for May 20, 2019, for a jury trial. Prior to trial defendant Estrada filed a motion to suppress the methamphetamines found in her purse, and the defendants filed a motion to suppress the tape recording. The district court granted both motions at a suppression hearing on May 16, 2019. (A. 22).

Statement of the Facts

Officer Green was patrolling the southbound lanes of I-95 when he observed a car travelling at an excessive rate of speed. The radar in the patrol car showed that the car was travelling 80 in a 65-mile-per-hour speed zone. (A. 1–2).

After stopping the car, Officer Green approached the driver's side of the car and requested the driver's license and car registration. While the driver searched his wallet for the documents, Officer Green looked through the open window and noticed a glass vial containing small kernels of an off-white substance in the driver's lap. Believing the vial to contain crack cocaine, Officer Green announced that he was seizing it. He asked the driver and passenger to exit the car and asked the driver for his wallet. Officer Green identified the driver as Luis Briones from his driver's license. (A. 3–4).

As the passenger got out of the car, Officer Green struck up a conversation with her. She said that her name was Cruz Estrada. Officer Green explained that he would have to search their car but that they could wait in the patrol car for their comfort and safety. The defendant turned back to the car, explaining that she had to retrieve something. She reached into the car and pulled out her purse, which had fallen behind the front seat. As the defendant passed him on the way to the patrol car, Officer Green asked if he could search her purse. Without responding, the defendant held out her purse to him. Inside her purse, Officer Green found a brown paper envelope. When Officer Green asked her what was in the envelope, defendant claimed that she did not know, that someone had given it to her to give to a friend in Miami. When Officer Green opened the envelope, he found a quantity of white powder that he believed to be methamphetamines. (A. 4).

The two waited in the patrol car while Officer Green searched the car. The tape of their conversation contains several incriminating statements, including defendant's admission that the envelope was hers and that it contained illegal drugs. (A. 4–5).

Summary of Argument

Over the years, courts have recognized a variety of exceptions to the search warrant requirement of the Fourth Amendment in recognition that exigent circumstances often do not allow an officer time to obtain a search warrant. This case illustrates the tension between the officer's duty to collect evidence of the illegal drug trade and the individual's privacy concerns. Consent has long enabled an officer to conduct a search, even without probable cause. Even without consent but upon probable cause, an officer may search a car and any containers within the car, without regard to their ownership. A standard law enforcement technique has been to ask suspects to wait in the officer's patrol car while the officer searches the suspects' car; to obtain evidence, the officer tape records any statements the suspects unwisely make while in the patrol car.

The government argues that two exceptions to the search warrant requirement allowed Officer Green to search the defendant's purse. Defendant's motion to suppress the contents of her purse should be denied either because defendant consented to the search or because probable cause to search the car allows Officer Green to search containers found in the car. Defendant has argued that the tape containing her incriminating statements should be suppressed because the tape was made in violation of the federal eavesdropping statutes. There is no ground to suppress the tape under the statutes; the statutes prohibit taping only if there is a reasonable expectation that the conversation is private. Society would not recognize any conversation of suspects in a patrol car to be private.

Argument

I. THE MOTION TO SUPPRESS THE METHAMPHETAMINES FOUND IN DEFENDANT'S PURSE SHOULD HAVE BEEN DENIED EITHER BECAUSE DEFENDANT CONSENTED TO THE SEARCH OR THE PURSE FELL UNDER THE CONTAINER EXCEPTION TO THE SEARCH WARRANT REQUIREMENT.

A. Because it was objectively reasonable to believe that Defendant consented to the search of her purse, the motion to suppress the methamphetamines found in her purse should have been denied.

Once a vehicle is stopped, the officer can search the car with consent. An occupant can consent to the search of the occupant's belongings. *Florida v. Jimeno*, 500 U.S. 248, 251 (1991). Even without consent, the officer can search the car if there is probable cause of criminal activity. The officer is entitled to search containers found in the car and suspected of holding the object of the officer's search, no matter who owns the container. *Wyoming v. Houghton*, 526 U.S. 295, 300–01 (1999). An officer may not search someone's person without probable cause. *Id.* at 303.

The search of defendant's purse is constitutional if she consented to the search or the container exception to the search warrant requirement extends to her purse. The United States Supreme Court has stated the standard for determining when an individual has consented to the search of a car. *Jimeno*, 500 U.S. at 251. This portion of this brief will explain why the consent standard has been met. As far as the container exception is concerned, the United States Supreme Court held that "police officers with probable cause to search a car may inspect passengers' belongings found in the car that are capable of concealing the object of the search." *Houghton*, 526 U.S. at 307. The facts of *Jimeno*, *Houghton*, and *Estrada* will be compared to show that the search of the defendant's purse was constitutional.

In *Jimeno*, Officer Trujillo overheard a telephone call from a public telephone in which Jimeno was discussing a drug deal. Trujillo followed Jimeno's car and stopped Jimeno for failure to stop when turning right on red. After informing Jimeno about the traffic violation, Trujillo went on to say that he had reason to believe that respondent was carrying narcotics in his car and asked permission to search the car. He explained that respondent did not have to consent to a search of the car. Respondent stated that he had nothing to hide and gave Trujillo permission to search the automobile. 500 U.S. at 249–50. Trujillo found drugs in a brown paper bag on the car floorboard. *Id.* at 250.

The Court then set forth the test for determining whether consent was given. "The standard for measuring the scope of a suspect's consent under the Fourth Amendment is that of 'objective' reasonableness—what would the typical person have understood by the exchange between the officer and the suspect?" *Id.* at 251. Applying this standard, the Court found that Jimeno had consented to the search of the bag.

The facts of *Jimeno* and *Estrada* are similar in that the two cars were stopped for alleged traffic violations, the two defendants consented to searches, and the officers searched containers. The facts surrounding the consent issue are substantially similar. Trujillo told Jimeno that the officer suspected that there were drugs in the car and explained that Jimeno did not have to consent to the search. When Trujillo asked Jimeno's permission, Jimeno claimed that he had nothing to hide and explicitly consented to the search. Officer Green made a statement, "you don't mind if I search, do you?" Officer Green did not have time to explain that the defendant did not have to consent before she held out her purse to him.

In *Jimeno*, the container was a brown paper bag located on the floor of the car. In *Estrada*, the container was defendant's purse, hanging from her shoulder. If anything, it was more objectively reasonable to believe that the defendant in this case had consented to the search of her purse than that Jimeno consented to the search of the brown paper bag. The defendant's implied consent of offering her purse to Officer Green made it clear that she was consenting to the search of that particular container. It was not as clear that Jimeno consented to the search of the brown paper bag when he consented to the search of the car. In *Jimeno*, the trial court had granted Jimeno's motion to suppress the contents of the brown paper bag. The Florida District Court of Appeals and the Florida Supreme Court affirmed. *Id.* at 250.

Applying the objective reasonableness standard, it is objectively reasonable to believe that the defendant in this case had consented to the search of her purse. Her overt action makes it objectively reasonable to believe that she consented.

B. Because the purse was found in a car that was searched upon probable cause that it contained illegal drugs, the container exception to the search warrant requirement applied, and the methamphetamines should not have been suppressed.

As far as the container exception is concerned, the United States Supreme Court held that "police officers with probable cause to search a car may inspect passengers' belongings found in the car that are capable of concealing the object of the search."

Houghton, 526 U.S. at 307. The facts of *Houghton* and *Estrada* will be compared to determine that the search of Cruz' purse was constitutional.

In *Houghton*, David Young was stopped for speeding and a faulty brake light. After the officer saw a hypodermic syringe in Young's pocket, Young admitted that he used it to take drugs. The officer asked the two female passengers seated in the front seat to exit the car and the officer searched the car. The officer found Houghton's purse on the backseat of the car. Searching the purse, the officer found a brown pouch that contained drug paraphernalia and a syringe containing methamphetamine in a large enough quantity for a felony conviction. Houghton claimed that the brown pouch was not hers. The officer also found a black container that contained drug paraphernalia and a syringe containing a smaller amount of methamphetamine, insufficient for a felony conviction. Houghton's arms showed fresh needle-marks. The officer arrested her. 526 U.S. at 297–98.

The issue in *Houghton* was "whether police officers violate the Fourth Amendment when they search a passenger's personal belongings inside an automobile that they have probable cause to believe contains contraband." *Id.* at 297. The Court held "that police officers with probable cause to search a car may inspect passengers' belongings found in the car that are capable of concealing the object of the search." *Id.* at 307. The Court first relied on a 1982 case in which the Court had found that, where there was probable cause to search a car, it was constitutionally permissible to search containers found in the car that might hold the object of the search. *Id.* at 301–02. The Court noted that an individual carrying a package in a vehicle travelling on the public roads has a reduced expectation of privacy. *Id.* at 303. The Court found no reason to afford more protection to a container owned by a passenger than a container owned by the driver. *Id.* at 305.

The facts of *Houghton* and this case are very similar in that the two cars were stopped for alleged traffic violations, the passengers exited the cars, leaving their purses in the backseat, and the officers searched a passenger's purse. The facts of the two cases differ slightly in that Houghton at first disclaimed ownership of the purse. In contrast, this defendant returned to the car to retrieve her purse and offered it to Officer Green.

Applying the holding in *Houghton* to *Estrada*, Officer Green's search of defendant's purse was constitutional. When Officer Green discovered the vial containing what he believed to be crack cocaine in the driver's possession, that gave Officer Green probable cause to search the car and all containers in the car that might contain illegal drugs. Defendant's purse was of the size that it might contain illegal drugs, and it was initially found in the car. Either of the two occupants might have concealed illegal drugs in defendant's purse as Officer Green pulled them over. Because of the substantial similarities between *Houghton* and *Estrada*, this court should find that Officer Green's search was constitutional.

II. The Motion to Suppress the Defendant's Conversation Taped in the Rear Seat of the Patrol Car Should Have Been Denied Because the

CONVERSATION WAS NOT PROTECTED AS AN ORAL COMMUNICATION UNDER 18 U.S.C.A. §§2510–2515 (West, Westlaw through P.L. 116-91).

A. Because Defendant had no reasonable expectation of privacy while seated in the rear seat of a patrol car, the motion to suppress the tape containing Defendant's incriminating statements should have been denied.

The federal eavesdropping statutes protect certain types of face-to-face conversations against interception; however, to be protected, the conversation must qualify as an "oral communication." Under the statutes, an "'oral communication' means any oral communication uttered by a person exhibiting an expectation that such communication is not subject to interception under circumstances justifying such expectation ...." 18 U.S.C.A. §2510 (2) (West, Westlaw through P.L. 116-91). Thus, a conversation is not an oral communication unless the conversants expect that the conversation is private and an objective third party would consider that expectation reasonable.

It is illegal to intercept an oral communication. "[A]ny person who ... intentionally intercepts ... any oral communication ... shall be punished." 18 U.S.C.A. §2511 (1) (West, Westlaw through P.L. 116-91). One exception to this prohibition involves a police officer; however, the police officer must be party to the conversation or one conversant must have consented to the taping for the exception to apply. "It shall not be unlawful under this chapter for a person acting under color of law to intercept [an] ... oral ... communication where such person is a party to the communication or one of the parties has given prior consent to the interception." 18 U.S.C.A. §2511 (2)(c) (West, Westlaw through P.L. 116-91). If an oral communication is taped in violation of the eavesdropping statutes, the conversation cannot be used as evidence in court:

> Whenever any ... oral communication has been intercepted, no part of the contents of such communication and no evidence derived therefrom may be received in evidence in any trial, hearing, or other proceeding ... before any court ... if the disclosure of that information would be in violation of this chapter.

18 U.S.C.A. §2515 (West, Westlaw through P.L. 116-91).

Thus, if defendant's conversation was an oral communication, it should be suppressed. Whether the conversation is an oral communication turns on whether the defendant had a reasonable expectation of privacy while seated in the rear seat of the patrol car. One prong of the two-prong test is satisfied; defendant and the driver appear to have had an expectation of privacy, or they would not have made incriminating statements. The other prong of the test is whether their expectation was reasonable. They were not sitting in a privately owned car. They were sitting in the officer's car. While an expectation of privacy in a privately owned car would have been reasonable, an expectation of privacy in the officer's car was not reasonable. The officer's car is equivalent to the officer's office. If defendant and the driver were conversing in an office of a police station, it would not be reasonable to expect privacy.

In a case with similar facts, the issue before the United States Court of Appeals for the Eleventh Circuit was "whether the district court erred in denying the motion to suppress the tapes resulting from the secret recording of McKinnon's pre-arrest conversations while he sat in the back seat of the police car." *United States v. McKinnon*, 985 F.2d 525, 526 (11th Cir. 1993).

In *McKinnon*, police officers stopped a pick-up truck for failure to travel in a single lane on the Florida Turnpike. Theodore Pressley was driving and Steve McKinnon was the passenger. Pressley consented to the search of his vehicle. While the officers were searching, McKinnon and Pressley waited in the rear seat of the patrol car. There they made incriminating statements that were secretly recorded by the officers. The officers arrested them after finding cocaine in the truck, and they were placed in the rear seat of the patrol car. The officers again recorded McKinnon's and Pressley's incriminating statements. *Id.*

The *McKinnon* court considered the meaning of the term "oral communication" under the federal statutes. An oral communication is protected against taping. If a conversation is taped in violation of the statutes, the tape may be suppressed. A conversation is an oral communication only if the conversants exhibited a subjective expectation of privacy and the expectation of privacy was objectively reasonable. The court seemed to agree with the government's argument that a patrol car functions as the officer's office, and the rear seat of the patrol car functions as a jail cell. *Id.* at 527. The court held "that McKinnon did not have a reasonable or justifiable expectation of privacy for conversations he held while seated in the backseat area of a police car." *Id.* at 528.

In examining the facts of *McKinnon* and *Estrada*, the facts concerning the taping seem virtually identical. In each case, an officer asked two individuals to wait in the patrol car prior to their arrest. The officer taped their conversation in the rear seat of the patrol car; the conversation contained incriminating statements. One difference between the two cases is that the officer in *McKinnon* also taped McKinnon's conversation following his arrest. This difference is not significant because an arrestee held in the back of a patrol car would have a lesser expectation of privacy than a person not under arrest.

A number of state and a number of federal courts, other than the *McKinnon* court, have faced the issue of whether an officer may secretly tape a conversation of individuals seated in the rear seat of a patrol car. In each case the court has said that taping is permissible. *See United States v. Paxton*, 848 F.3d 803, 813 (7th Cir. 2017) ("because the defendants lacked an objectively reasonable expectation of privacy when placed into the marked police van, the interception and recording of their conversations did not constitute a search for purposes of their Fourth Amendment rights"); *United States v. Dunbar*, 553 F.3d 48, 58 (1st Cir. 2009) ("the police car was not a reasonably confidential place to talk"); *United States v. Clark*, 22 F.3d 799, 801 (8th Cir. 1994) (" defendant's expectation of privacy while seated in the police car was not reasonable").

Although persuasive authority in other circuits, *McKinnon* is mandatory authority in this circuit. The facts concerning the taping are virtually identical in *McKinnon* and *Estrada*. A number of other state and federal courts have also held that there is no reasonable expectation of privacy for persons seated in the back of a patrol car. Therefore, a court should find that Cruz and Luis had no reasonable expectation of privacy while they were seated in the rear seat of the patrol car. Because they did not have a reasonable expectation of privacy, their conversation was not protected against taping as an oral communication. Therefore, a court would not suppress the tape under the federal eavesdropping statutes.

Defendant has also made the argument that the search of her purse tainted the tape recording. Obviously, were the court to deny the defendant's motion to suppress the illegal drugs, there would be no taint that could attach to the tape. Even were the court to grant the defendant's motion to suppress the methamphetamines, the court should not grant the motion to suppress the tape. In all probability, defendant would have made the incriminating statements even if Officer Green had not searched her purse.

B. Because the officer followed standard procedure in requesting the defendants to wait in the patrol car, the defendants' incriminating statements were not related to the prior search of the car, and the tape containing defendant's incriminating statements should not have been suppressed.

Where a police officer obtains evidence in an unconstitutional manner, that evidence is excluded from use at trial. If that evidence leads the officer to other evidence, the other evidence is derivative of the first evidence. The derivative evidence is known as fruit of the poisonous tree and is also inadmissible. Generally, evidence that is tainted by the prior unconstitutional conduct is inadmissible; however, in some instances the second evidence is admissible because the connection between the unconstitutionally seized evidence and the subsequently obtained evidence is marginal.

The tape is not derivative of the evidence the officer discovered searching Estrada's purse. The tape should not have been suppressed.

Conclusion

For the reasons set forth above, the government requests this court to reverse the district court's order suppressing the methamphetamines and the tape recording and remand the case to the district court for trial.

Respectfully submitted,

____

Florida Attorney, Esq.
Florida Bar Number 000000
Law Firm
Main Street
Anytown, Fla.

8

Summary

- The appellate brief is a written statement submitted to an appellate court to persuade it of the correctness of one's position.
- When a party appeals, the appellate court's job is to review what the lower court did to determine whether the lower court committed reversible error.
- The standard of review is different depending on whether the appellate court is reviewing a finding of fact, a ruling of law, or a ruling on a question involving law and fact.
- The appellate court is bound to follow the trial court's finding of fact unless a jury finding was unreasonable or a trial judge's finding was clearly erroneous.
- When deciding a question of law or a question involving law and fact, the appellate court is free to reach a ruling different from that of the trial court.
- The appellate brief is persuasive in tone.
- Follow any applicable court rules (including local rules) governing the appellate brief.
- Rule 28 of the Federal Rules of Appellate Procedure requires:
    - A table of contents;
    - A table of authorities;
    - A statement of jurisdiction;
    - A statement of the issues;
    - A statement of the case;
    - A statement of the facts;
    - A summary of the argument;
    - An argument; and
    - A conclusion.

Key Terms

appellant's brief
appellee's brief
findings of fact

Exercises

1. Pick one of the research problems from Appendix E.
2. Research the problem you have chosen.
3. Write an appellate brief using your research.

Cyberlaw Exercises

1. Bryan Garner is an authority on legal writing, and his company's website is located at http://www.lawprose.org/. He has interviewed a number of the Jus-

tices on the United States Supreme Court concerning legal writing and posted the video interviews linked to the website. Go to the website, watch the video of one of the Justices, and list three legal writing tips the Justice provides.

2. Bryan Garner, a legal writing authority, has interviewed many judges, many of whom give tips on writing briefs. Go to http://www.lawprose.org/, watch videos of one or more of the judges, and identify three brief writing tips that you could use when you are asked to write an appellate brief.
3. A number of interesting videos are posted on https://www.youtube.com/, some of which are related to writing an appellate brief. Go to the website and find a video providing legal writing tips on writing effective appellate briefs. How do the legal writing tips add to your understanding of writing well? How do the tips differ from the legal writing advice provided in this chapter?
4. The briefs filed by the Department of Justice in the United States Supreme Court are accessible at https://www.justice.gov/osg/supreme-court-briefs. Go to the website, and access several briefs. How do they compare with the two sample appellate briefs included in this chapter?
5. In a written opinion, a judge may commend an attorney for the quality of the attorney's appellate brief, and you may be able to access the brief on an online database. Search for quality briefs using terms such as "commend," "quality," and "brief" within the same sentence.
6. The United States courts website, located at https://www.uscourts.gov/, offers access to federal court rules. The Legal Information Institute, located at https://www.law.cornell.edu/, offers access to federal and state court rules. See if you can access the various court rules for your state. Find local federal and state court rules that apply to the area in which you are located.
7. Access several appellate briefs from your state on an online database, and compare them to the examples in this chapter.
8. Several **You Be the Judge** boxes providing information on selected cases are included in this chapter. At the end of each box, there is a citation to the referenced case. Use a portion of the case citation, such as the case name or the volume number, abbreviation for the reporter, and the first page of the case to find the case online. Read the case to determine why it was included in this chapter.

Discussion Points

1. Locate an appellate brief, and compare it in substance and format to the two sample appellate briefs in this chapter. How do the documents differ?
2. What is the purpose of the table of contents and the table of authorities?
3. Why do court rules govern appellate briefs in detail?

Appendix A

Search and Seizure

Introduction

You were introduced to Joshua Smeek in Chapter 2. He had accepted a ride back to college with two acquaintances. During the drive, they were pulled over by a police officer who claimed the window tinting on their car was too dark. After the driver consented to a search of the car, the officer discovered illegal drugs. While the search was proceeding, the three college students were seated in the back seat of the patrol car, where their conversation was recorded. The three were arrested after the officer found the drugs. Joshua knew nothing about the drugs and wants to defend himself against the pending federal charges of possession of illegal drugs.

Joshua wondered whether the car stop was constitutional because no violation of any traffic ordinance supported the stop. He wanted to know if the federal statute imposing a ten-year minimum prison term for certain drug offenses applies to the non-crack substance found in the car. Joshua was unsure whether the police officer had the right to tape what he said in the back of the patrol car.

If you were to research Joshua's case, you might discover primary sources such as *United States v. Chanthasouxat*, 342 F.3d 1271 (11th Cir. 2003), a federal case discussing the constitutionality of a traffic stop unsupported by a traffic violation, *DePierre v. United States*, 564 U.S. 70 (2011), and federal eavesdropping statutes. In your research, you might also discovered information from secondary sources concerning search and seizure.

Chanthasouxat discusses the constitutionality of an officer stopping a vehicle on the misimpression that the driver violated a traffic ordinance and whether the federal eavesdropping statutes allow a police officer to tape-record suspects' conversations while seated in the back of a patrol car. The issue in *DePierre* was whether the federal statute imposing a minimum ten-year prison term should be applied to DePierre. DePierre argued that the statute was limited to offenses involving crack cocaine and could not be applied to a suspect possessing cocaine in its basic form.

As stated above, Chapter 2 contains the Joshua Smeek Search and Seizure Problem; Chapter 2 also contains a discussion of whether the federal eavesdropping statutes and federal case law allow a police officer to tape-record suspects' conversations while seated in the back of a patrol car. Chapter 5 contains an explanation of the eavesdropping statutes, and Appendix F contains the text of the statutes.

Relevant Primary Sources

The following are potentially relevant primary sources for resolving the Joshua Smeek search and seizure problem:

1. U.S. Const. amend. IV.
2. *DePierre v. United States*, 564 U.S. 70 (2011).
3. 18 U.S.C.A. § 2510 (West, Westlaw through P.L. 116-91).
4. 18 U.S.C.A. § 2511 (West, Westlaw through P.L. 116-91).
5. 18 U.S.C.A. § 2515 (West, Westlaw through P.L. 116-91).
6. *United States v. Chanthasouxat*, 342 F.3d 1271 (11th Cir. 2003).

Research and Writing Exercises

1. Read *Chanthasouxat*, and write a case brief of the case.
2. Use a citator to determine whether *Chanthasouxat* is still good law and whether there is any more recent case law on an officer's mistake of law and an officer's mistake of fact concerning the driver's alleged violation of a traffic ordinance.
3. Research to find the most recent case law in your federal circuit deciding how a court would treat an officer's mistake of law and an officer's mistake of fact concerning whether the driver violated a traffic ordinance. Write a case brief of the case.
4. Write a client opinion letter to Joshua Smeek explaining his chances of prevailing in the lawsuit. You might find the second sample client opinion letter of Chapter 11 helpful in writing your client opinion letter.
5. Write a law office memo concerning Joshua Smeek and his chances of prevailing in the lawsuit. You might find the second sample law office memo of Chapter 13 helpful in writing your client opinion letter.
6. Write a memorandum of law either in support of or in opposition to Joshua Smeek's motion to suppress the evidence found in the car. You might find the second sample memorandum of law of Chapter 14 helpful in writing your memorandum of law.
7. Imagine that the trial court judge suppressed the evidence found in the car, and the government is appealing the decision. Write either the appellant's or the appellee's brief in the case. You might find the second appellate brief of Chapter 15 helpful in writing your appellate brief.

Appendix B

Locating and Citing to Cases

This appendix gives you a summary of basic citation rules. For a more detailed explanation of the citation rule for a particular authority, refer back to the chapter in which the authority was discussed.

Location of Cases

Cases are generally found in the law library in **looseleaf publications**, **advance sheets**, or **reporters**. Libraries designated as government depositories may also have cases in slip opinion form. For the names of the looseleaf publications and reporters for federal court cases (with their abbreviations included in parentheses), refer to the following chart. You will need to obtain the names of the looseleaf publication (if any) and reporters for your state's cases from your professor or from your own research.

Loose-Leaf Publications The legal sources appearing in loose-leaf publication format include state annotated codes, state administrative codes, formbooks, and services providing a collection of source material in a particular subject area. The information in loose-leaf services is stored in binders rather than formatted as hardbound volumes and paper pamphlet supplements.

Advance Sheets "Hot off the press" unbound copies of case decisions that will later be printed with other cases in bound form.

Reporters Sets of books containing published court decisions.

Reporters and Looseleaf Services

Federal

United States Supreme Court

United States Law Week (looseleaf) (U.S.L.W.)

United States Reports (official) (U.S.)

Supreme Court Reporter (unofficial—West) (S. Ct.)

United States Supreme Court Reports, Lawyers' Edition (unofficial—LexisNexis) (L. Ed. or L. Ed. 2d)

United States Circuit Courts of Appeal

Federal Reporter (unofficial—West) (F., F.2d, or F.3d)

Federal Appendix (unofficial—West) (F. App'x)

United States District Courts

Federal Supplement (unofficial—West) (F. Supp., F. Supp. 2d, or F. Supp. 3d)

Federal Rules Decisions (unofficial—West) (F.R.D.)

State

(fill in for your state)

Court of last resort

Intermediate appellate court

Trial court(s)

You would use the looseleaf publication to read recently announced cases that are not yet contained in the advance sheets or reporters. Once a case is available in the advance sheets or the reporters, you would cite to the reporter rather than to the looseleaf publication. Cases in looseleaf publications, advance sheets, and reporters are organized chronologically.

Cases from a particular court may be printed in more than one reporter. Where a case is published in more than one reporter, parallel citations are citations to the various reporters containing the authority being cited. For example, United States Supreme Court opinions are printed in three different reporters: *United States Reports*, *Supreme Court Reporter*, and *United States Supreme Court Reports, Lawyers' Edition*. The text of the court opinion is identical in each of the three reporters, but the material preceding the case, which is prepared by the publisher, is different. The reporter prepared by the government or under authority of the government is referred to as the "official reporter." The official reporter for United States Supreme Court opinions is *United States Reports*. Although *United States Reports* is considered the official reporter, many law libraries may only have one of the other two reporters. Because *United States Reports* is a government publication, it lags considerably behind the other two reporters in publication date and does not contain the headnotes and other material prepared by the commercial publisher of the other two reporters.

As shown in the box below, West publishes seven different regional reporters. A particular regional reporter will contain state cases from courts in a particular region of the country. For example, *North Eastern Reporter* contains cases from Illinois, Indiana, Ohio, New York, and Massachusetts. With the wide availability of the regional reporters, many states that used to have official reporters in addition to the regional reporters no longer publish official reporters.

Although not shown in the chart below, West publishes a number of state reporters that contain cases from court in a particular state.

The West regional reporters, their abbreviations, and the states covered are:

Atlantic Reporter (A., A.2d, or A.3d)	Maine, New Hampshire, Rhode Island, Connecticut, New Jersey, Delaware, District of Columbia, Vermont, Pennsylvania, Maryland
North Eastern Reporter (N.E., N.E.2d, or N.E.3d)	Illinois, Indiana, Ohio, New York, Massachusetts
North Western Reporter (N.W. or N.W.2d)	North Dakota, South Dakota, Nebraska, Minnesota, Iowa, Wisconsin, Michigan
Pacific Reporter (P., P.2d, or P.3d)	Alaska, Hawaii, Washington, Oregon, Nevada, California, Montana, Idaho, Wyoming, Utah, Arizona, New Mexico, Colorado, Kansas, Oklahoma
South Eastern Reporter (S.E. or S.E.2d)	Georgia, South Carolina, North Carolina, Virginia, West Virginia
South Western Reporter (S.W., S.W.2d, or S.W.3d)	Texas, Arkansas, Missouri, Kentucky, Tennessee
Southern Reporter (So., So. 2d, or So. 3d)	Louisiana, Mississippi, Alabama, Florida

There are three important pieces of information you need to find a case. First, you need to know what series of what reporter contains the case. You will find that many law books with multiple volumes are published in series. When the volume numbers of a reporter are so large that they become unmanageable, the publisher will start a new series of reporter beginning with volume 1. The series are designated by ordinal numbers with the highest series number containing the most recent information. For example, the most recent United States Supreme Court opinions are published in *United States Supreme Court Reports, Lawyers' Edition, Second Series*, abbreviated "L. Ed. 2d." Assume you wanted to find *Brown v. Board of Education* and you know the partial citation in *Lawyers' Edition* is "98 L. Ed. 873." First of all, "L. Ed." tells you that you would need to look in the first series rather than the second series of the reporter. Each time you write a citation or pull a case, make sure you have the correct series.

The second and third things you need to know are the volume number and the page on which the case begins. In a citation, the volume number precedes the abbreviation for the reporter and the page number follows it. In the citation for *Brown*, "98" is the volume number and "873" is the first page of the case.

Published and Unpublished Cases

Some courts differentiate between "published" and "unpublished" cases. Reasons for designating an opinion as unpublished include limiting the number of opinions produced, encouraging a more cohesive body of law, and conserving judicial time and resources. If a court deciding a case designates it as published, this means that the case will be published in a print reporter, and the case is precedential.

If a court designates a case as unpublished, the court is indicating that the case is binding on the parties to the case but does not serve as precedent for other cases; however, designating a case as unpublished does not necessarily mean that it is unavailable as a print or digital publication, or both. A case designated as unpublished would not be printed in an official reporter but might be available in a reporter produced by a commercial publisher or online. An unpublished case is not considered binding authority except by the parties to the case, and an attorney might choose to cite to an unpublished decision as persuasive authority.

Beginning in 2001, West differentiated published and unpublished opinions of the federal courts of appeals by publishing the two types of cases in different reporters. *Federal Reporter* contains cases that the federal courts of appeals designated as published, while *Federal Appendix* contains cases that the federal courts of appeals designated as unpublished. For example, a federal court of appeals might designate one case as published and a second case as unpublished. The court would make the first case available to West, which would publish the case in *Federal Reporter*. The court could also make the second case available to West, which would publish the case in *Federal Appendix*.

Some courts have court rules prohibiting an attorney from citing to an unpublished opinion. Until 2007, the federal courts of appeals were inconsistent in their treatment of unpublished cases and the restrictions on their use by attorneys. Rule 32.1 of the Federal Rules of Appellate Procedure was adopted to ensure consistency among the circuits. Under the rule, a court may not prohibit an attorney from citing to an unpublished opinion decided on or after January 1, 2007, and an attorney citing to a case not readily available online must file a copy of the case with the document in which the case is cited.

Case Citations

A citation is an abbreviation used to refer to a legal authority that allows the reader to find the legal authority in the law library. When you answer a research question or perform legal analysis, it is expected that your answer or analysis be backed up by a citation to your legal authority. It is important for you to learn correct citation form because that form allows legal professionals to speak the same language. Correct usage is a sign of excellence.

Citations are integral to formal legal documents. Legal citations have several purposes. Legal writers use them to identify the source of a quotation or the authority for a statement. A legal researcher uses them to locate the cited source. The reader uses them to obtain information concerning the source. For example, case citations indicate the precedential authority by identifying the level of the deciding court and the year of the decision. A final purpose, perhaps more aspirational than realistic, is to allow the layperson access to the law.

Citation Manuals

For years, ***The Bluebook: A Uniform System of Citation***, published by several prominent law reviews, has been the standard for citation. The twenty-first edition of *The Bluebook* was published in 2020. *The Bluebook* has been criticized for being too detailed and hard to learn; *The Bluebook* is over 360 pages long, with 57 pages of introductory materials to legal citation called "Bluepages," 21 multipart citation rules, and 101 pages of tables and lists of abbreviations.

> ***The Bluebook: A Uniform System of Citation*** The style guide for legal citation published by the *Columbia Law Review*, the *Harvard Law Review*, the *University of Pennsylvania Law Review*, and the *Yale Law Journal*.

Many states have their own citation rules, which may be found in state statutes or court rules; law school students usually do not study the state-specific citation rules and must learn them on their own after law school.

The ***ALWD Guide to Legal Citation***, formerly the *ALWD Citation Manual*, first published in 2000, is now in its sixth edition, published in 2017. Although longer than *The Bluebook*, the *ALWD Guide to Legal Citation* is considerably more reader-friendly and is more easily used in the classroom as a teaching tool. The Association of Legal Writing Directors hoped that the *ALWD Guide to Legal Citation* would be adopted by enough law schools and practicing attorneys that the *ALWD Guide to Legal Citation* would gradually supplant *The Bluebook*. Information concerning the *ALWD Citation Manual* is accessible via the Association of Legal Writing Directors website under publications at http://www.alwd.org.

ALWD Guide to Legal Citation The style guide for legal citation produced by the Association of Legal Writing Directors.

There is also a movement toward universal citation form. Traditional case citation form is tied to the print medium; it references a particular volume and page number. In addition, traditional citation form references the product of a particular publisher. Universal citation form is both medium and publisher neutral; it can be used with the online or print version of a case and does not reference any particular publisher's product.

The American Association of Law Libraries published its ***Universal Citation Guide*** in 1999, with a third edition in 2014. The *Universal Citation Guide* gives the recommended universal citation form for federal and state cases, constitutions, statutes, and administrative regulations. Public domain citation form had been adopted by a number of states prior to the publication of the *Universal Citation Guide.* Over one-quarter of the states have adopted public domain citation form.

Universal Citation Guide The style guide for legal citations published by the American Association of Law Libraries. The legal citations in this guide are medium and publisher neutral.

Basic Citation Form

CITATION TIP

Citation Form

Do not assume that the legal citations found when researching are in correct citation form. Citations, even those included in cases, may or may not comply with the citation rules your professor has asked you to use. Always check your citations against the appropriate citation rule for correct form.

This section explains the basics of citation form for cases and then gives you sample citations for federal and state cases. The sample citation forms in this book approximate *Bluebook* form. The suggestion is to either learn citation forms from this book or learn the citation forms contained in your state's citation rule. Your professor can tell you which he or she prefers. Those citation forms will be the only ones you will need much of the time. If the form for something you need to cite is not in this book or in your state's citation rule, you can refer to *The Bluebook*.

There is a certain framework for case citations that is fairly consistent for cases from all courts. Look at the following citation and analyze its components:

Citation for *Procopio v. Secretary of Veterans Affairs* *Procopio v. Secretary of Veterans Affairs*, 943 F.3d 1376 (Fed. Cir. 2019).

Analysis of Citation for *Procopio v. Secretary of Veterans Affairs* *Procopio v. Secretary of Veterans Affairs* [Case name], 943 [Volume] F.3d [Abbreviation for *Federal Reporter, Third Series*] 1376 [Initial page] (Fed. Cir. [Abbreviation for the United States Court of Appeals for the Federal Circuit] 2019 [Year in which case was decided]).

The name of the case comes first, is italicized (or underlined), and is followed by a comma. Only the name of the first party on each side is given, with "v." (for versus) in between. "Procopio" is the last name of the first of six petitioners. When a party is an individual, the case name contains only the party's last name, and the case name contains only one party even if there are multiple persons and entities who are parties.

CITATION TIP

Case Names

In a reporter, a case begins with the full name of the case, a portion of the name appearing in all capital letters. Unless your reader requires *Bluebook* form for case names, use that portion of the case name that appears in all capitals, with the further modifications explained in this citation tip as the case name in your citation; in the citation, only the initial letter of the various words comprising the case name would be capitalized, and the balance of the word would be in lower case. You will have a very close approximation of *Bluebook* form without having to master a very complicated *Bluebook* rule.

Caveat: This does not give you an excuse not to follow the *Bluebook* if your instructor or your reader requires conformance with the *Bluebook*.

For case names, individuals are referred to only by their surnames. When the United States of America is a party to a case, the citation needs to show "United States" rather than "United States of America" or "U.S." If a state is a party to the case and the case is being decided by a court of the state, the citation should contain only "State," "Commonwealth," or "People." If a state is a party to the case but the case is being decided by a court other than a court of the state, then the citation should contain only the name of the state, for example "Minnesota," not "State of Minnesota."

"Secretary of Veterans Affairs" is the name of the respondent. The number "943" is the volume number, "F.3d" is the abbreviation for *Federal Reporter, Third Series*, and "1376" is the page on which the case begins. If needed, the first information within the parentheses identifies the court deciding the case. *Procopio* was decided by the United States Court of Appeals for the Federal Circuit, but only the abbreviation for the circuit is stated in the citation. You know it is a United States court of appeals case because the *Federal Reporter* contains only United States court of appeals cases. The year within the parentheses is the year in which the case was decided. Make sure you put the year of the decision in your citation rather than the year in which the case was argued.

CITATION TIP

Italics

A certain portion of a case citation calls for the use of italics. For example, in a case citation, the name of the case is in italics. You may substitute underlining for italics. Choose either italics or underlining; do not both underline and italicize.

CITATION TIP

Ordinal Numbers

In legal citations the ordinal numbers "second" and "third" are abbreviated to "2d" and "3d." For all other ordinal numbers, use the standard abbreviations.

CITATION TIP

Citations Contained in Hyperlinks

In an online database such as Westlaw or LexisNexis, many citations are underlined and are presented in color. The underlining and color indicate that the citation is hyperlinked to the source referenced by the citation. The color is not part of the citation, nor is the underlining unless indicated by your citation rules. A good practice is to remove the hyperlink when citing to a case.

Subsequent History

The following case citation illustrates subsequent history:

Jam v. International Finance Corporation, 172 F. Supp. 3d 104 (D.D.C. 2016), *aff'd*, 860 F.3d 703 (D.C. Cir. 2017), *rev'd*, 139 S. Ct. 759 (2019).

Jam was decided by the United States District Court for the District of Columbia, the United States Court of Appeals for the District of Columbia affirmed the lower court decision, and the United States Supreme Court reversed the intermediate appellate decision.

The decisions of the federal intermediate appellate court and the United States Supreme Court are called subsequent history because they happened subsequent to (after) the District of Columbia District's decision in *Jam*.

When citing to a case, you must generally give your reader all subsequent history. Where an intermediate appellate court issued an opinion and the intermediate appellate court en banc issued an opinion, subsequent history would include both opinions; the italics preceding the en banc decision should identify the decision as an en banc decision, for example "*aff'd en banc*" or "*rev'd en banc*." Exceptions to this general rule include:

- a withdrawn opinion;
- history on remand;
- denial of a rehearing;
- denial of certiorari or denial of review by a court with discretionary review unless the case for which certiorari or review is sought is less than two years old;
- the United States Supreme Court granting certiorari unless the Court has granted certiorari, but has not yet reached a decision in the case; and
- an appellate court granting review or a rehearing unless the court has granted review or a rehearing, but has not yet reached a decision in the case.

CITATION TIP

Subsequent History

Connect subsequent history to the end of the citation of the lower court decision by explaining what the higher court did, underlining the explanation, and setting it off by commas. "Certiorari denied" should be abbreviated to "*cert. denied*," "affirmed" should be abbreviated to "*aff'd*," and "reversed" should be abbreviated to "*rev'd*." Otherwise the explanation should be written out, for example, "*vacated*." *The Bluebook* instructs you to omit information on denial of certiorari unless the case is less than two years old or there is a particular reason to include the information.

Sometimes a court issues an opinion, but later decides to modify the opinion. Rather than have two published opinions that might conflict, the court withdraws the first opinion. In essence, the court treats the first opinion as if it were never issued. Because the withdrawn opinion is of no force and effect, the withdrawn opinion is not included in subsequent history.

When an appellate court remands a case, it sends it back to the lower court to redo something the lower court did incorrectly before. The appellate decision in which the appellate court lays down the rule of law to be followed by the lower court on remand, and not the lower court decision in which the rule of law is carried out, is more important for its precedential value. For that reason, history on remand is not usually cited in subsequent history.

The reason you would not give the citation for the denial of a rehearing is that many parties routinely petition for a rehearing and the rehearing is routinely denied. A denial of a rehearing is different from a court denying review or the United States Supreme Court denying a petition for certiorari. A rehearing is denied by the same court that has already rendered a decision.

In contrast, only a higher court can deny review or deny a petition for certiorari. Therefore, a denial of review or a denial of a petition for certiorari is important enough to be given as subsequent history for two years after the case has been decided, whereas denial of rehearing is not. The two-year period was selected because the appeal of a case to a higher court is generally concluded within two years of the lower court decision. Subsequent history indicating denial of certiorari or denial of review within the two-year period tells the reader the lower court decision is final.

When citing to a case, you would not give subsequent history for the United States Supreme Court granting certiorari unless the Court has granted certiorari, but has not yet reached a decision in the case. The reason that you would not include the grant of certiorari is because it is obvious that the Court granted certiorari if the Court issued a decision in the case.

By the same token, when citing to a case, you would not give subsequent history for an appellate court granting review or a rehearing unless the court has granted review or a rehearing but has not yet reached a decision in the case. The reason that you would not include the grant of review or rehearing is because it is obvious that the court granted review or rehearing if the court issued a decision in the case.

The following is the full citation of *Jam*:

Jam v. International Finance Corporation, 172 F. Supp. 3d 104 (D.D.C. 2016), *aff'd*, 860 F.3d 703 (D.C. Cir. 2017), *rev'd*, 139 S. Ct. 759 (2019).

The analysis of this citation is shown in the following box.

Analysis of the Full Citation of *Jam v. International Finance Corporation*

Jam v. International Finance Corporation [Case name], 172 [Volume] F. Supp. 3d [Abbreviation for Federal Supplement, Third Series] 104 [Page] (D.D.C. [Abbreviation for the United States District Court for the District of Columbia] 2016 [Year in which the case was decided]), *aff'd* [Abbreviation for affirmed], 860 [Volume] F.3d [Abbreviation for *Federal Reporter, Third Series*] 703 [Page] (D.C. Cir. [Abbreviation for the United States Court of Appeals for the District of Columbia Circuit] 2017 [Year in which the case was decided]), *rev'd* [Abbreviation for reversed], 139 [Volume] S. Ct. [Abbreviation for *Supreme Court Reporter*] 759 [Page] (2019 [Year in which the case was decided]).

Notice that you place a comma after the first parentheses; italicize (or underline) the explanation of what happened in subsequent history ("*aff'd*" explains that the district court decision was affirmed); add a comma; identify the volume, reporter, and page at which the district court decision was affirmed; identify the court deciding the case; and give the year of the decision. You would continue with the same pattern for the balance of the subsequent history. In other words, place a comma after the second parentheses;

italicize (or underline) the explanation of what happened in subsequent history ("*rev'd*" explains that the intermediate appellate court decision was reversed); add a comma; identify the volume, reporter, and page at which the United States Supreme Court reversed the intermediate appellate court decision; and give the year of the decision. Note that the United States Supreme Court is not identified in the parentheses because a knowledgeable reader knows that the *Supreme Court Reporter* only contains decisions of the United States Supreme Court.

Different Case Name on Appeal

The case name may be different on appeal and, when providing subsequent history, the different case name should be included. The new case name should be introduced by adding "*sub nom*" to the end of the italicized explanation of what the higher court did and providing the new case name. An example of this citation tip is shown in the following box.

Example of a Case with a Different Name on Appeal

Mensing v. Wyeth, Inc., 562 F. Supp.2d 1056 (D.Minn. 2008), *rev'd*, 588 F.3d 603 (8th Cir. 2009), *rev'd sub nom, PLIVA, Inc. v. Mensing*, 131 S. Ct. 2567 (2011).

Page Numbers

When you are referring to specific information from a case or you are quoting from a case, you need to give a *pinpoint*, *locus*, or *jumpcite* page reference to the page or pages on which the material was found. Page references to material within a case can be made part of your full citation as shown in the following citation:

Procopio v. Secretary of Veterans Affairs, 943 F.3d 1376, 1382 (Fed. Cir. 2019).

You could use this citation if you had not cited to *Procopio* previously and you are referencing the holding of the case, which is found on page 1382. The page numbers in this citation mean that 1376 is the first page of the case, and the material you are referring to is found on page 1382. If you wanted to refer to material on the first page of the opinion, you would repeat the number of the first page and separate the numbers by a comma.

Analysis of Page Reference within *Procopio*

Procopio v. Secretary of Veterans Affairs, 943 F.3d 1376 [First page of case], 1382 [Material referred to found on page 1382] (Fed. Cir. 2019).

CITATION TIP

Pages

When citing to consecutive pages, give the first and the last page numbers joined by a hyphen. When citing to non-consecutive pages, separate the pages by commas. The first example illustrates the use of hyphens for consecutive pages (14 through 15). The second example illustrates the use of a comma for non-consecutive pages (249 and 251).

Terry v. Ohio, 392 U.S. 1, 14–15 (1968).

Florida v. Jimeno, 500 U.S. 248, 249, 251 (1991).

United States Supreme Court Cases

Cases appear in *United States Law Week* before they are printed in the reporters. The following box contains the citation for *Wyoming v. Houghton* in *United States Law Week*. The citation to *United States Law Week* is used only until the case is published in one of the three reporters containing decisions of the United States Supreme Court.

Citation to *Wyoming v. Houghton* in *United States Law Week*

Wyoming v. Houghton, 67 U.S.L.W. 4225 (1999).

If the case has been printed in a reporter you should give the citation to a reporter rather than to the looseleaf service. *The Bluebook* requires a citation to *United States Reports*, *Supreme Court Reporter*, or *United States Supreme Court Reports, Lawyers' Edition*, in that order of preference. At the time this book was being written, *Wyoming v. Houghton* was published in *United States Reports*, *Supreme Court Reporter*, and *United States Supreme Court Reports, Lawyers' Edition*. Because *The Bluebook* prefers *United States Reports* over *Supreme Court Reporter* and *United States Supreme Court Reports, Lawyers' Edition*, the citation would be to *United States Reports*. The following box shows *The Bluebook*-required citation to *United States Reports*.

Citation to *Wyoming v. Houghton* in *Bluebook* Form

Wyoming v. Houghton, 526 U.S. 295 (1999).

Although *The Bluebook* does not require you to give parallel citations to United States Supreme Court cases, you may give parallel citations to those cases if permitted by the governing court rule, as shown in the following box; parallel citations are often helpful to readers with more limited library resources.

Citation to *Wyoming v. Houghton* with Parallel Citations

Wyoming v. Houghton, 526 U.S. 295, 119 S. Ct. 1297, 143 L. Ed. 2d 408 (1999).

If you are citing to only one reporter, cite to *United States Reports*, if the case is contained in it. If the case has not yet appeared in *United States Reports*, cite to *Supreme Court Reporter*. If the case has not yet appeared in *United States Reports* or *Supreme Court Reporter*, cite to *United States Supreme Court Reports, Lawyers' Edition*.

United States Court of Appeals Cases

Federal Reporter contains cases decided by the United States courts of appeals that have been designated by the courts for publication. *Federal Appendix*, which started publication on September 1, 2001, for those cases decided after January 1, 2001, contains cases decided by the United States courts of appeals not designated for publication. The abbreviation for *Federal Appendix* is "F. App'x."

The following box shows a citation to a case reported in *Federal Reporter* from a United States court of appeals. A citation to a case in *Federal Appendix* would follow the same format, except for substituting "F. App'x" for "F.2d."

Citation to *Procopio v. Secretary of Veterans Affairs*

Procopio v. Secretary of Veterans Affairs, 943 F.3d 1376, 1382 (Fed. Cir. 2019).

United States District Court Cases

The following box contains a citation to a case from the United States District Court for the Northern District of California. Notice that "Northern District of California" has been abbreviated to "N.D. Cal." You know from this citation that California has more than one federal district. In the federal district court system, many states are divided into districts and further divided into divisions. The parenthetical information should identify the district, but not the division within the district. Some of the less populous or smaller states, such as New Jersey, have only one United States district court to cover the whole state. The abbreviation for the United States District Court for the District of New Jersey would be "D.N.J."

Citation to *In re National Security Letter*

In re National Security Letter, 930 F. Supp. 2d 1064 (N.D. Cal. 2013).

State Courts

In many states, decisions of the state courts are reported in more than one reporter. Often, one reporter is the official state reporter and the other reporter is a regional reporter prepared by West, a commercial publisher. As explained earlier in this appendix, the regional reporter contains state court decisions of a number of states. A state court rule or a local court rule may require a distinction in citation form between a state case cited in a document filed in a court of the state and a state case from another state filed in state court. In many states, when citing to a case decided by a state court of the same state, the citation includes parallel citations, with the reference to the official reporter preceding the reference to the regional reporter; this information allows a researcher to easily locate the case in both reporters. In many states, when citing to a case decided by a state court of another state, the citation includes only the information allowing the researcher to locate the case in the regional reporter.

The following box contains two citations to a case decided by the Supreme Court of Utah. The first citation would be used in a document filed in a Utah state court, and the second citation would be used in a document filed in a state court other than Utah.

Citation to *Peters v. Pine Meadow Ranch Home Ass'n*

Peters v. Pine Meadow Ranch Home Ass'n, 2007 UT 2, 151 P.3d 962.
Peters v. Pine Meadow Ranch Home Ass'n, 151 P.3d 962 (Utah 2007).

Notice that Utah uses public domain citation format, with "2007" identifying the year of the decision, "UT" identifying the Supreme Court of Utah, and "2" identifying the second decision of the year. Paragraphs within the decision are numbered consecutively, allowing the researcher to easily locate material referenced by pinpoint citation to the paragraph. Notice that the second citation is to a regional reporter. Because *Pacific Reporter* contains cases from a number of the states, the parenthetical information must identify that this is a case from Utah. You know that the case is from the highest court in the state, the Supreme Court of Utah, because there is no further identification of the court. If the case were from the Utah Court of Appeals, "Utah Ct. App." would appear in the parentheses preceding the year of the decision.

Key Terms

advance sheets
ALWD Citation Manual
looseleaf publications
reporters
The Bluebook: A Uniform System of Citation
Universal Citation Guide

Appendix C

Rules for Quotations and Short-Form Citations

Introduction

Many students have a mental block about using quotations and short-form citations in their legal writing. They have so convinced themselves that they will never master the rules of quotations and short-form citations that they structure their writing to avoid having to deal with quotations and short-form citations at all. This appendix is designed to help you through this "writer's block." First, it gives you the most basic rules for quotations and short-form citations, and then it lets you practice applying the rules by working through some exercises. These basic rules should be sufficient for your writing assignments in a legal writing class. If you have questions not covered by the rules, refer to the *Bluebook* or the *ALWD Guide to Legal Citation.*

The *Bluebook* rules for law review articles differ in many respects from rules used in the other types of legal writing you will be doing. The rules discussed in this appendix can be used for all types of legal writing other than law review articles. If you have the occasion to write a law review article, you will need to follow either the *Bluebook* or the *ALWD Guide to Legal Citation.*

Quotations

To Quote or Not to Quote

When your authority is constitutional or statutory provisions, it is a good idea to quote the relevant portions of those provisions. The reason is that each word in those provisions has been carefully selected and a court interpreting those provisions will use the wording of those provisions as a starting point. Focus your reader's attention by quoting only those portions that are relevant. You may want to make sure your reader understands a complicated provision you have quoted by pairing the quotation with a summary of the provision in your own words.

For example, if you are discussing several federal statutes, you would want to quote the relevant portion of the statutes. Because the statutory language would be difficult for your reader to understand, you might also summarize several of the quoted portions of the statutes in your own words. The following passage illustrates a summary explanation of the statutes, with potentially relevant language of the statutes inserted as quotations.

> It is illegal to intercept an oral communication. "[A]ny person who ... intentionally intercepts ... any oral communication ... shall be punished." 18 U.S.C.A. § 2511 (1) (West, Westlaw through P.L. 116-91). One exception to this prohibition involves a police officer; however, the police officer must be party to the conversation or one conversant must have consented to the taping for the exception to apply. "It shall not be unlawful under this chapter for a person acting under color of law to intercept [an] ... oral ... communication where such person is a party to the communication or one of the parties has given prior consent to the interception." 18 U.S.C.A. § 2511 (2)(c) (West, Westlaw through P.L. 116-91). If an oral communication is taped in violation of the eavesdropping statutes, the conversation cannot be used as evidence in court, as provided by statute.
>
>> Whenever any ... oral communication has been intercepted, no part of the contents of such communication and no evidence derived therefrom may be received in evidence in any trial, hearing, or other proceeding ... before any court ... if the disclosure of that information would be in violation of this chapter."
>
> 18 U.S.C.A. § 2515 (West, Westlaw through P.L. 116-91).

The passage above uses ellipses (...) and brackets ([ ]). The use of ellipses and brackets is explained later in this appendix.

Quoting from cases is a little different from quoting from constitutions or statutes. Your own personal writing style determines to a great extent whether you use quotations in your legal writing and how many you use. You do not have to use any quotations at all if you can state everything in your own words. On the other hand, if you like to quote, do not use so many quotations that your writing is mostly quotations with very little in between. A reader who is faced with a number of long block quotes may be tempted to skip over the block quotes and read only what is between the quotes. Your goal is to keep your reader interested in what you have written. Quotations should be reserved for well-stated passages that you would have trouble stating in your own words. You may want to quote a portion of the issues, the holdings, and the reasoning. Usually you would not quote the facts, the case history, or the results because you can state those portions of the case better yourself.

Quote Accurately

When you quote, your quote must be accurate down to punctuation and case of letters. (An "uppercase" letter means a capital letter and a "lowercase" letter means a small letter.) If your reader happens to check your quotation against the original source and finds differences, the reader will know you have been sloppy. Then the reader will wonder how far the sloppiness extended. If the writer did not take the time to quote accurately, perhaps the writer did not take the time to research thoroughly. You will quickly lose your credibility and the reader's confidence by not quoting accurately.

Avoid Plagiarism

Be wary of the possibility of plagiarism. Plagiarism occurs when you use portions of someone else's writing without indicating that you are quoting. It also occurs when your paraphrasing of portions of a case differs little from the wording of the case except for word order. One way to avoid this is to quote. A second way is to spend enough time with the case that you know it intimately ("internalize" it) and can write about it as if you were telling someone a story. Test yourself to see whether you understand a case by explaining it out loud to someone else. If you have trouble, go back and read the case again until you understand it.

Basic Quotation Rules

1. **Use of ellipses.** Delete any unnecessary wording. If the wording is in the middle of a quoted passage, indicate the deletion by using an ellipsis. Do not use an ellipsis when you are omitting something at the beginning of a quoted passage. Whether you use an ellipsis at the end of a quoted passage depends on whether you are quoting a complete sentence or a phrase used as part of your sentence. When quoting a complete sentence and omitting something at the end of the sentence, insert an ellipsis before the final punctuation of the sentence. When quoting a phrase, do not use an ellipsis at the end of the phrase.
2. **Use of brackets.** Add your own words to make the quotations easier to understand and place your words inside brackets. When you are changing a letter from upper to lowercase or from lower to uppercase, place the changed letter in brackets. You can replace a word in the quoted material with one of your own, so long as you bracket the word substituted for the original. Where a word is altered in this way, there is no need to include an ellipsis to indicate the omission.
3. **Omission of citations.** When you omit a citation, you do not need to replace it with an ellipsis if you use an explanatory parenthetical explaining this. (See 8 below.)
4. **Adding emphasis.** Add emphasis to quoted words by italicizing or underlining them and indicate this change in an explanatory parenthetical. (See 8 below.)
5. **Placement of punctuation and quotation marks.** Place periods and commas inside quotation marks and other punctuation outside the quotation marks unless the punctuation was part of the original quotation.
6. **Use of quotation marks.** Do not use quotation marks at the beginning and the end of a block quote; but do use quotation marks in block quotes when the passage you are quoting in turn quotes something else. For quotes other than block quotes, precede and follow the quoted language with quotation marks. Quotation marks for quotations within quotations use both double and single quotation marks with the outermost quotation marks double.

7. **Placement of the citation to the quoted passage.** The citation to the quoted passage should be fairly close to the passage and may precede or follow it. The citation may appear in a textual sentence or in a citation sentence. A citation following a block quote should be placed at the left-hand margin.
8. **Use of explanatory parentheticals.** When the case you are quoting in turn quotes a second case, identify the second case, including a page reference to the quoted material, by using an explanatory parenthetical. Explain you have underlined something or omitted citations by using an explanatory parenthetical: (emphasis added), (citations omitted).
9. **Paragraph structure.** In block quotes, indicate the paragraph structure by indenting the beginning of paragraphs; however, indent the beginning of the first paragraph only if there were no words omitted from the beginning of the paragraph. Indicate the omission of language from the beginning of subsequent paragraphs by an indented ellipse (. . .). Within the block quote, indicate the omission of one or more entire paragraphs from the quoted language by indented four periods (. . . .).

Types of Quotations

Quotations can appear:

1. as block quotations;
2. as complete sentences within your paragraph; or
3. as phrases within your sentence.

The following sections of this appendix will discuss block quotations, quoted sentences, and quoted phrases.

Block Quotations

A "block quotation" is a long quotation that looks like a "block" on the page. It is set off from the rest of your writing by double-spacing and is indented left and right. Do not use quotation marks around the outside of the block quote. You may use quotation marks inside the block quote if the passage you are quoting in turn quotes something else. If your citation follows the block quote, place your citation back at the left-hand margin. The *Bluebook* tells you to use a block quote if the quotation contains at least fifty words. This is a good rule of thumb that is frequently violated by block quoting shorter passages. Unless your professor wants you to adhere strictly to this rule, use a block quote when the block quote format makes the quotation easier to understand.

Rules for Block Quotations

1. Use if quotation is fifty words or more.
2. Indent left and right.
3. Do not enclose in quotation marks.
4. Place citation at left-hand margin.

Sample Block Quotation

The following is a sample block quotation passage from *United States v. McKinnon*, 985 F.2d 525, 527 (11th Cir. 1993), edited to include significant information. The superscript numbers, which indicate editing changes, correspond to the numbered basic quotation rules and appear in the example to help you understand the changes from the original text.

> [9]McKinnon asserts that the tape recording of his pre-arrest conversations violates Title III and his Fourth Amendment right to privacy....[1] The government argues that the recording of McKinnon's conversation does not constitute the recording of an "oral communication" as defined in 18 U.S.C. § 2510(2)....[1]
>
> The legislative history of Title III directs that we consider "oral communication"[6] in light of ...[1] constitutional standards ....[1] The constitutional question is "whether the person invoking its [Fourth Amendment] protection can claim a 'justifiable,' a 'reasonable,'[6] or a 'legitimate expectation of privacy' that has been invaded by government action."[6] Hence, the statutory and constitutional test is whether a *reasonable or justifiable*[4] expectation of privacy exists.
>
> This test has two prongs. First, whether McKinnon's conduct exhibited a subjective expectation of privacy; second, whether McKinnon's subjective expectation of privacy is one that society is willing to recognize as reasonable.

United States v. McKinnon, 985 F.2d 525, 527 (11th Cir. 1993)[2] (quoting *Smith v. Maryland*, 442 U.S. 735, 740 (1979)[8] (referring to *Katz*)) (emphasis added)[4] (citations omitted).[3]

Now compare the block quote with the original case text:

> McKinnon asserts that the tape recording of his pre-arrest conversations violates Title III and his Fourth Amendment right to privacy. Title III prohibits unauthorized interception and disclosure of oral communications. 18 U.S.C. § 2511. The government argues that the recording of McKinnon's conversation does not constitute the recording of an "oral communication" as defined in 18 U.S.C. § 2510(2). Title III defines "oral communication" as "any oral communication uttered by a person exhibiting an expectation that such communication is not subject to interception under circumstances justifying such exception, but such term does not include any electronic communication." 18 U.S.C. § 2510(2). Thus, we must decide the statutory question gleaned from Title III's language and the legislative

history. That is, whether the person uttering the words has a reasonable or justifiable expectation of privacy. See 18 U.S.C. § 2510(2); S.Rep. No. 541, 99th Cong., 2d Sess. (1986), reprinted in 1986 U.S.C.C.A.N. 3555, 3567; *United States v. Harrelson*, 754 F.2d 1153, 1169 (5th Cir.), cert. denied, 474 U.S. 908, 106 S.Ct. 277, 88 L.Ed.2d 241 (1985) (framing the question as whether a reasonable expectation of privacy existed).

The legislative history of Title III directs that we consider "oral communication" in light of the constitutional standards expressed in *Katz v. United States*, 389 U.S. 347, 88 S.Ct. 507, 19 L.Ed.2d 576 (1967). S.Rep. No. 1097, 90th Cong., 2d Sess. (1968), reprinted in 1968 U.S.C.C.A.N. 2112, 2178. The constitutional question is "whether the person invoking its [Fourth Amendment] protection can claim a 'justifiable,' a 'reasonable,' or a 'legitimate expectation of privacy' that has been invaded by government action." *Smith v. Maryland*, 442 U.S. 735, 740, 99 S.Ct. 2577, 2580, 61 L.Ed.2d 220 (1979) (referring to *Katz*); accord *United States v. Shields*, 675 F.2d 1152, 1158 (11th Cir.), *cert. denied*, 459 U.S. 858, 103 S.Ct. 130, 74 L.Ed.2d 112 (1982) (citing *Katz*, 389 U.S. at 353, 88 S.Ct. at 512 and *United States v. White*, 401 U.S. 745, 752, 91 S.Ct. 1122, 1126, 28 L.Ed.2d 453 (1971)). Hence, the statutory and constitutional test is whether a reasonable or justifiable expectation of privacy exists.

This test has two prongs. First, whether McKinnon's conduct exhibited a subjective expectation of privacy; second, whether McKinnon's subjective expectation of privacy is one that society is willing to recognize as reasonable. *Smith*, 442 U.S. at 740, 99 S.Ct. at 2580 (citing *Katz*, 389 U.S. at 361, 88 S.Ct. at 516).

Show Your Readers Changes from the Original Text

The edited first block quote passage above, which includes significant information from the case, is much more "reader-friendly" because it is not clogged with citations and unnecessary words. Omitting citations and unnecessary words allows the reader to focus on what the court was trying to communicate. The rules on the preceding page explain how to indicate any editing of quotations by using ellipses (...), brackets ([ ]), and explanatory parentheticals (explanations within parentheses). The rules apply to all types of quotations, not just block quotations. The rule numbers coincide with the superscript numbers in the first sample block quotation.

Quoting Complete Sentences and Quoting Phrases

When the passage you are quoting contains fewer than fifty words and can stand alone as one or more complete sentences, the passage should be part of a paragraph rather than being set apart as a block quote. Capitalize the first letter of the quoted passage and bracket the capital letter if this is a change. When the passage you are quoting is not a complete sentence, use it as a phrase in your sentence without capitalizing the first letter of the quoted phrase unless it begins your sentence. Remember to use the first eight basic quotation rules when quoting complete sentences and phrases.

The following example, which contains information from *Jimeno*, illustrates what one might write when providing the reader significant information from *Jimeno*. The example contains both types of quotations—complete sentences and phrases. The superscript numbers appear in the example to help you understand the changes from the original text. The block-quoted passage from which the quotations were taken follows the explanation of the superscript numbers appearing in the example.

In *Florida v. Jimeno*, 500 U.S. 248, 251 (1991),[1] the United States Supreme Court looked at the "expressed object"[2] of a search to determine "[t]he[3] scope of a search."[2] After the officer told the suspect that the officer suspected there were drugs in the suspect's car, the suspect consented to the search.[4] "[I]t[5] was objectively reasonable for the police to conclude that the general consent to search [the suspect's][6] car included consent to search containers within that car which might bear drugs. . . .[7] The authorization to search in this case therefore, extended beyond the surfaces of the car's interior to the paper bag . . .[8]." *Id.*[9]

This is an explanation of the superscript numbers included in the example above:

1. The citation to two quoted phrases from *Jimeno* precedes the phrases and gives the page reference to those phrases.
2. The quoted phrases are enclosed in quotation marks. Following basic quotation rule 1, because these are phrases, no ellipsis is needed to indicate omission of words preceding or following the phrases.
3. The "t" is changed from upper to lowercase because the phrase is in the middle of the author's sentence and the change is bracketed.
4. This sentence does not need quotation marks because it is stated in the author's own words. Even though the sentence is not a direct quote, it does need a page reference because the substance of the sentence is taken from the case. In this paragraph, the two citations, one at the beginning and one at the end, give the page reference and are close enough to this sentence so that no additional citation is needed. If the sentence were not so near the two citations, a reference to page 251 should have been given.
5. Following basic quotation rule 1, no ellipsis is needed to indicate omission of words at the beginning of the quoted complete sentence and the "i" is bracketed to indicate the letter was changed from lower- to uppercase.
6. The brackets indicate that the words "the suspect's" are added. "Suspect" is used instead of "respondent" because this reference makes it easier for the reader to understand who is being identified. There is no need to indicate

the omission of "respondent" by inserting an ellipsis where the substituted wording is bracketed.

7. Following basic quotation rule 1, the ellipsis indicates that wording has been omitted. Here a textual sentence and a citation sentence were omitted.
8. Following basic quotation rule 1, the ellipsis indicates that wording was omitted from the end of this quoted sentence, and the ellipsis is followed by the final punctuation (a period).
9. Here the citation follows the quoted complete sentences and is placed in a citation sentence.

Now compare the quotations contained in the preceding example with the text from which the quotations were taken:

> The scope of a search is generally defined by its expressed object. *United States v. Ross*, 456 U.S. 798, 102 S. Ct. 2157, 72 L. Ed. 2d 572 (1982). In this case, the terms of the search's authorization were simple. Respondent granted Officer Trujillo permission to search his car, and did not place any explicit limitation on the scope of the search. Trujillo had informed respondent that he believed respondent was carrying narcotics, and that he would be looking for narcotics in the car. We think it was objectively reasonable for the police to conclude that the general consent to search respondent's car included consent to search containers within that car which might bear drugs. A reasonable person may be expected to know that narcotics are generally carried in some form of a container. "Contraband goods rarely are strewn across the trunk or floor of a car." *Id.*, at 820, 102 S. Ct., at 2170. The authorization to search in this case therefore, extended beyond the surfaces of the car's interior to the paper bag lying on the car's floor.

Florida v. Jimeno, 500 U.S. 248, 251 (1991).

Exercises on Quotations

A. Review a sample document from Chapters 13, 14, or 15, noting the use of quotations.

B. Select a statute you might use in a legal document. Distinguish the relevant wording of the statute from the wording that is not potentially relevant. Rewrite the statute to include only the relevant wording, showing alterations from the original statutory wording. Write a paragraph containing the quoted statute.

C. Select a case you might use in a legal document. Identify significant wording, such as the issue, the holding, or a portion of the reasoning, that you might quote in your document. Imagine how you would show the alterations from the original passages. Write several paragraphs containing the quoted passages.

Short-Form Citations

The first time you refer to a case, you must give its full citation. If you refer to the case again, you should use an abbreviation to the citation rather than give the full citation. This abbreviated citation is called a "short-form citation." This section of the appendix uses the following citations in the examples and exercises:

Florida v. Jimeno, 500 U.S. 248 (1991).

Wyoming v. Houghton, 526 U.S. 295 (1999).

Whren v. United States, 517 U.S. 806 (1996).

United States v. McKinnon, 985 F.2d 525 (1993).

This section of the appendix reviews examples of full- and short-form citations. In the examples, the citations are all followed by periods as they would be in citation sentences. If you are using the citations in textual sentences, you would not need a period at the end of a citation unless it is the end of the sentence.

Suppose in an office memo you first cite to the holding in *Whren* on page 819 of the case. You must give the full citation to *Whren* because you have not cited the case before. In the full citation, you can indicate the page of the case holding by adding a comma and the page of the holding after the first page of the case:

Whren v. United States, 517 U.S. 806, 819 (1996).

Suppose you now want to give another citation to *Whren*, this time to the facts on pages 808 and 809. Use "*id.*" to indicate that you are citing to the immediately preceding authority. "*Id.*" is always italicized or underlined, including the period. It is capitalized when it begins a sentence, but is not when it appears in the middle of a sentence. If you were referring to the same page again, page 819, the complete citation would be "*Id.*" Because you are referring to different pages, you must indicate the new page numbers by adding "at" and the new page numbers:

Id. at 808, 809.

> **WRITING TIP**
>
> ***Distinguishing Textual Sentences from Citation Sentences***
>
> The two types of sentences in legal writing are textual sentences and citation sentences. A textual sentence is the type of sentence you have been writing all your life. It is a complete grammatical sentence with a subject and a verb. A citation sentence contains only citations. The four citations listed above are written as citation sentences. Each is appropriately ended with a period.

Suppose now you give the following string cite to *Jimeno* and *Houghton* (a string cite is a citation to more than one case with the cases separated by a semicolon):

Florida v. Jimeno, 500 U.S. 248 (1991); *Wyoming v. Houghton*, 526 U.S. 295 (1999).

Then you want to cite to *Houghton* again, this time to page 1304. You might think that you could use *id.* as a short-form citation for *Houghton* because you just cited it. However, if you used *id.*, you would be referring your reader back to the immediately preceding citation which is your string cite. Unless you want to refer to all the cases in the string cite, you must use another short-form citation to cite to *Houghton*. Any one of the following three short citation forms for *Houghton* is acceptable:

Wyoming v. Houghton, 526 U.S. at 307.

Houghton, 526 U.S. at 307.

526 U.S. at 307.

When using short-form citations, try to use the shortest form possible so long as there is no confusion. If you had cited *Houghton* within the last few pages and there is no other United States Supreme Court case you had cited that is in volume 526 of *United States Reports*, use the third type of short citation form. If it had been several pages since you last cited *Houghton* or the reader might confuse *Houghton* with another case in the same volume of the reporter, use either the first or second versions of short form citations. When you are referring to a case by the name of only one of the parties, select a name that easily distinguishes the case from other cases. Because there are numerous case names that contain "*Wyoming*" but many fewer that contain "*Houghton*," you would use "*Houghton*" rather than "*Wyoming*."

If you wanted to refer to page 307 of *Houghton* again use:

Id.

If you want to refer to footnote 1 on page 303 of *Houghton*, use:

Id. at 303 n.1.

If you then wanted to refer to page 310 of *Houghton*, use:

Id. at 310 (Stevens, J., dissenting).

You must indicate the page number because it is not the same one referred to before. The explanatory parenthetical is needed because you are referring to something other than the majority opinion.

If you want to refer to pages 249 through 250 and 252 of *Jimeno*, you cannot use "*id.*" because *Jimeno* is not the immediately preceding citation. If you have recently cited *Jimeno*, use:

500 U.S. at 249–50, 252.

If you have not referred to *Jimeno* recently, precede the above short-form citation by either "*Florida v. Jimeno*" or by "*Jimeno*." Where material referred to spans more than one page, give the numbers of the first and last pages, joined by a hyphen. Retain only the last two digits of the second number. Where material appears on more than one page but does not span pages, separate the page numbers by a comma.

If you want to refer to *Jimeno* in general rather than to any specific material from *Jimeno*, use:

Jimeno.

When you are using *Jimeno* as an abbreviation to refer to the case, "*Jimeno*" is italicized or underlined. "Jimeno" would not be italicized or underlined if you are referring to the individual.

If you want to refer to pages 525 (the first page of the case), 526, and 528 of *McKinnon* and you had not given the full citation of *McKinnon* before, use:

United States v. McKinnon, 985 F.2d 525, 525, 526, 528 (1993).

Because you wanted to refer to the first page of the case in the full citation, the number "525" must be written twice, with the two numbers separated by a comma.

Afterwards, if you want to refer to pages 526 through 527 of *McKinnon*, use:

Id. at 526–27.

Short-Form Citations for Statutes

Just as for cases, you must use the complete citation the first time you cite to a statute. For example, you may cite to a federal wiretapping statute as follows:

18 U.S.C.A. § 2511 (West, Westlaw through P.L. 116-91).

Later, if you cite to the same statute you should use a short-form citation. If you are citing to the immediately preceding statute, you use "*id.*" If you are citing to a statute you cited to previously, but it is not the immediately preceding statute, use a short citation that sufficiently identifies the statute for your reader. For a federal statute, you can either give the title and section number of the United States Code ("18 U.S.C.A. § 2511"), or just the section number ("§ 2511").

Exercises on Short-Form Citations

A. Review a sample document from Chapters 13, 14, or 15, noting the use of short-form citations.

B. Using the citations to 18 U.S.C.A. § 2511, *Jimeno*, *Houghton*, *Whren*, and *McKinnon*, give the correct citations called for by the following descriptions:

1. String cite to *Jimeno*, *Houghton*, and *Whren*.
2. Cite to pages 1302 and 1304 of *Houghton*.
3. Cite to pages 1299 through 1300 of *Houghton*.
4. Refer to *Jimeno* in general terms.
5. Cite to pages 1772 through 1773 of *Whren*.
6. Cite to page 251 of *Jimeno*.
7. Cite to page 252 of *Jimeno*.
8. Cite to note 1 on page 1302 of *Houghton*.
9. Cite to pages 526 and 528 of *McKinnon*.
10. Cite to 18 U.S.C.A. § 2511.
11. Cite to 18 U.S.C.A. § 2511.
12. Cite to pages 526 and 528 of *McKinnon*.
13. Cite to 18 U.S.C.A. § 2511.

C. If you have completed either of the exercises at the end of this appendix's section on quotations, insert citations as necessary.

Appendix D

Mechanical Errors

Introduction

Elimination of mechanical errors is the tedious, though necessary, part of writing. You need to do your best to eliminate mechanical errors for two reasons. The first reason is that you want your reader to concentrate on your message and not be distracted by mechanical errors. The second reason is that a reader who spots a number of mechanical errors will begin to wonder if the writer is sloppy. If the writer failed to proof for typographical and spelling errors, perhaps the writer's sloppiness extended to legal research, too. Do not lose your credibility over a few easily eliminated mechanical errors.

You know your own writing and you probably know from past experience what types of mechanical errors give you problems. Keep in mind those types of mechanical errors that have given you problems in the past so you can eliminate them when editing and proofing your legal writing. If you have trouble spotting them yourself, ask a fellow student to help you proof your writing. Do the same for that student in return.

This appendix gives you practice in rewriting sentences containing the mechanical errors discussed in Chapter 9.

Excess Words

Rewrite the following sentences to eliminate excess words:

1. These cases are similar to each other in many ways.

2. The expectation of privacy within the police car is not one society would consider as a reasonable expectation of privacy.

3. In the case of *Inciarrano v. State*, Inciarrano went to the office of the victim over a business deal between the two that had gone bad.

4. The case against Jane Doe and the case of *Inciarrano* are of similar nature.

5. In both of the cases there is a tape recorder involved that captured the murders on audiotape.

6. The taped conversation in the *Inciarrano* case was admissible as evidence.

7. The conversation taped in Jane Doe's home will not be suppressed as evidence due to the fact that Jane Doe had no reasonable expectation of privacy because she taped the conversation herself.

8. The judge will suppress the conversation based on the laws found in sections 934.02(2), 934.03(1), and 934.06, and the case law found in *Smith.*

9. The statute says that there are two requirements that must be true in order for the taped conversation to be inadmissible as evidence in court.

10. The court found that the tape recording in the *Inciarrano* case should not be suppressed.

11. The tape revealed a business deal between the victim and Inciarrano, in which the victim no longer wanted to be a part of the business deal.

12. The two cases also differ, too.

13. In the case of *Astaire*, there was probable cause to search the automobile for contraband.

14. The evidence against Dealer should be suppressed and not be allowed to be used against him.

15. People at home expect an expectation of privacy when having an intimate party with family and friends.

16. The courts in the *Stevenson* and *Brandin* cases did not suppress the evidence.

17. Under section 934.06, it states that a taped private conversation may not be used as evidence if playing the tape would violate Chapter 934.

18. In the *Blackheart* case, Laura taped a conversation without her husband's knowledge.

19. Inciarrano was a participant in a taped conversation in which a conversation between him and a murder victim was surreptitiously recorded.

20. Smith filed a motion with the court to suppress the tape from evidence.

21. They were having a private conversation of a business transaction involving drugs.

22. Did the detectives violate Bryce Cannon's constitutional right to privacy under sections 12 and 13 of the Florida Constitution when they intercepted phone calls of Bryce?

23. This particular stop was unconstitutional, and any evidence seized as a product of this stop is deemed to be regarded as inadmissible in court.

24. The court will apply the exclusionary rule, which prohibits the court from using at trial any evidence which was obtained through an unconstitutional search and seizure to be used.

25. According to the Fourth Amendment to the United States Constitution, individuals are guaranteed protection against unreasonable search and seizure.

26. Vogel proceeded to confiscate the amount of $6,003.00.

Use of Apostrophes

Rewrite the following sentences using the rules you read in Chapter 9:

1. Should the tape seized from Jane Does home be suppressed?

2. In this case, and in the Jane Doe case, both defendant's were asked to sit in the back of a patrol car for "safety and comfort reasons."

3. Prior to her husbands arrival, Jane Doe decides to tape-record the meeting.

4. According to the courts ruling in *Smith*, there is no reasonable expectation of privacy in the back of a police car.

5. Carducci privacy rights were violated because her conversation was tape-recorded and later broadcast on television.

6. The Court gave three reasons why a strangers illegal conduct does not suffice to remove the First Amendment shield from speech.

7. The defendant's in both cases were not the ones who illegally taped the conversations.

8. Defendants General News and Chimino submit this memorandum of law in support of defendant's motion for summary judgment.

9. Without the parties awareness, an unidentified person recorded the call between Tine and Carducci.

10. For the reasons set forth above, defendants' request this court to grant their motion for summary judgment.

11. Officer Pyle instructed the defendants' to sit in the back of the patrol car.

12. The trial court denied Miss Houghton motion to suppress the evidence obtained from her purse.

13. Can the conversation in the back of the police car, recorded without the parties consent, be suppressed?

14. It was Officer Pyle right to ensure that these young adults were not breaking any other laws.

15. Officer Pyle discovered the presence of cocaine in the defendants purse.

16. The court held that anything seized during the search of a passengers property was legal.

17. Because Rogers Fourth Amendment rights were not violated, her taped conversation should not be suppressed.

18. An officer who has probable cause can search a car and it's contents without consent.

19. We have laws that protect us from illegal invasions of privacy, such as occurred in James situation.

20. This memorandum of law is submitted in support of James Dealer motion to suppress.

21. The police officers illegally taped a private conversation because the tape was made with a bionic ear at the small gathering in a close friends residence.

22. The court would find that Dealer conversation at a wild party could not have been made with a reasonable expectation of privacy.

23. James Dealer was in an enclosed and secluded area of a close friends' home.

24. The state is trying to safeguard it's citizens from police officers illegally taping private conversations.

25. The police officers were listening to the conversation using a bionic ear, a device used to hear all conversations within it's range.

26. When they reached the jail, Laura met with her attorney's and began to ask many questions.

Sentence Fragments

Rewrite the following sentences by correcting any sentence fragments.

1. Also that she was seeing the neighbor.

2. Because Jane Doe and Joe did not have a reasonable expectation of privacy; the tape recording made by the officers in the patrol car would not be suppressed.

3. Which means anyone who knowingly tapes or discloses an illegally taped conversation is doing something illegal.

4. Because the tape contained information about marijuana and an extramarital affair of a public figure.

5. Whereas, in *Carducci*, the tape was played on the news and because Carducci was running for re-election, it affected the outcome.

6. The facts in *Houghton* and *Rogers* are similar; yet there are many differences.

7. Whereas, the officer only searched Ginger's purse.

8. Because the defendant was subject to reasonable suspicion.

9. That the recording came from the illegal search of her purse.

10. Although many types of drug paraphernalia could have reasonably been located in her purse.

11. Section 934.03(1). Prohibits the taping of private conversations.

12. If the conversation is not private; section 934.06 does not apply.

13. Which means that any conversation taped in a patrol car is not a private conversation.

14. Whereas in *Smith* a traffic violation never occurred.

15. Because we are protected by the Fourth Amendment to the United States Constitution.

16. A *Terry* stop based on an Ohio case which eventually went to the United States Supreme Court.

17. The Court reasoned that the totality of the circumstances must be considered in evaluating the stop and that any one of the factors by itself was not proof of any illegal conduct. But when taken together they amount to a reasonable suspicion.

18. In *United States v. Sokolow*, 490 U.S. 1 (1989). Andrew Sokolow was stopped by DEA agents while trying to leave Honolulu International Airport.

Run-On Sentences

Analyze the following passages, and rewrite them to eliminate run-on sentences.

1. These issues and answers are based on reasoning, the reasoning comes from the cases.

2. There was no oral communication therefore there was no felony committed.

3. Society would not believe the expectation was reasonable, therefore under this statute the tape recording would not be suppressed.

4. The officer asks if he can search Clark's house, she agrees.

5. Carducci can sue for civil remedies, she would have to sue the person who illegally taped her conversation.

6. Carducci's duty as a congresswoman is of public importance, therefore, if she participated in illegal activities, the public has the right to be informed.

7. There is no bright-line test to determine what is protected as private in a public setting, the individual must determine what is appropriate to say.

8. Officer Pyle ran Fred's license and it came back suspended, therefore, the officer told Fred that his car was being impounded for violating the Florida Contraband Act.

9. The Florida Supreme Court found that the motorist and his passenger upon being placed in the rear of a patrol car had no reasonable expectation of privacy, therefore, the taped conversation was admissible.

10. Florida Statutes section 934.06 prohibits the use of taped private conversations as evidence, however, this statute does not apply because conversations taped in the back of a patrol car are not considered private.

11. The recorded conversation was the fruit of an unconstitutional search and seizure, therefore it should be suppressed.

12. *Smith* illustrates that persons in the back of a patrol car do not have a

reasonable expectation of privacy, therefore conversations within the patrol car are not protected against being taped.

13. Rogers' Fourth Amendment right against unreasonable search and seizure was violated, therefore, the incriminating conversation must be excluded as the fruit of an unlawful search and seizure.

14. James had certain expectations of privacy, knowing that what he said could be taken out of context, he never would have told such false stories.

15. According to section 934.06 provides that a private conversation that has been illegally taped cannot be used as evidence.

16. The defendant did not exhibit an expectation of privacy, he was outside, boasting loudly, and was heard over all the other people at the party.

17. The deputy then radioed another deputy who then pulled over Brandin and had a canine who circled the vehicle alerted and the vehicle was searched and Brandin was subsequently arrested.

18. In *Inciarrano*, the taped conversation and the murder took place in a business office open to the public, therefore there was no reasonable expectation of privacy.

19. The taped conversation occurred in the privacy of Laura's home and she was aware of the taping, therefore she relinquished her expectation of privacy.

20. She threatened her husband with a gun and told him that she would get custody, then she shot him.

Parallel Construction

Rewrite the following sentences by correcting any errors in parallel construction:

1. The issue is whether the utterances made by the defendant were made with a reasonable expectation of privacy and therefore inadmissible.

2. Accordingly, we are again confronted with a two-part analysis of the Fourth Amendment right to privacy, which requires the person to (1)

have a subjective expectation of privacy; and (2) that the expectation must be one that society recognizes as reasonable.

3. Both cases include a cellular phone conversation taped by unknown persons, the media playing this conversation, a conversation that is of great public concern, and statutes that allow the persons whose conversations were taped to sue for civil remedies.

4. The newscaster wanted to inform citizens about the person whom they trusted and received their vote to fulfill an important position.

5. Defendants submit this memorandum of law in support of their motion for summary judgment because they played no part in the illegal taping, that their access to the information was obtained lawfully, and that the conversation was a matter of public concern.

6. This memorandum will cover if the defendants took part in the illegal taping of the conversation, the way the information was obtained, if the subject matter is of public concern, and if the First Amendment protects defendant's right to publish the taped information.

7. Laura decided to tape the conversation in case her husband created a problem or to use against him at a later date.

8. *Van Halen* and *Stevenson* both deal with the use of bionic ears, drugs, both defendants were stopped by the police, and taping a conversation.

9. These statutes are intended to protect the private conversations of citizens, to allow for the government's taping of conversations after obtaining a court order, and inhibit the growth of organized crime.

10. She was a female basketball coach who worked the same hours, same season, and had the same amount of responsibility as the male coach.

11. Plaintiff engaged in a protected activity, suffered an adverse employment action, and there is a causal connection between the protected activity and the adverse employment action; therefore, plaintiff established a *prima facie* case.

12. The conversation taped on an answering machine was admitted because

the taping was accidental, the taping was done by a child, and the child's unfamiliarity with the answering machine.

13. The officer asked Lyn whether she had been drinking because the officer noticed her stumbling, her eyes were bloodshot, and the smell of alcohol.

14. The statute states that an individual must display the license plate on the rear of the vehicle and must be visible within one hundred feet.

15. They were in her office, they were having a face-to-face conversation, and it was her home.

16. The order denying the motion to suppress reversed, the judgments of conviction were vacated, and the cases remanded to the district court.

17. For the reasons stated above, Defendant Canyon requests that his motion to suppress be granted and to dismiss the charge against him for lack of evidence.

18. Trooper Vogel had developed a reasonable suspicion of illegal activity based on the fact that the suspect, a thirty-year-old man, was driving at 3:00 a.m. on a known drug corridor highway and being very cautious by driving 50 miles per hour and did not look at the marked patrol car as the car went past.

19. The employer had told its employees to attend the trade show because of the business benefits, paid for and deducted the employees' expenses, and reimbursed the employee for mileage.

20. Such steps shall include: use of an alternative entrance for construction vehicles and equipment, requiring that all construction vehicles be cleaned of loose mud, gravel, dirt, and other debris prior to traversing the access road, and cleaning up any dirt gravel, construction materials, and other debris deposited on the road.

21. The profile consists of a late-model car, Florida rental tag, two persons about 35 years old, driver-male, car going northbound on I-95, driving in a cautious manner, and not looking at the trooper while passing.

22. Did Vogel have reasonable suspicion that the suspects were committing, has committed, or is about to commit a crime?

Antecedents

Rewrite the following sentences by correcting any antecedent problems:

1. Smith consented to be seated in the back of the officer's patrol car for safety reasons while the officer searched his car.

2. A person has a reasonable expectation of privacy in their house.

3. In *Inciarrano*, Inciarrano went to the victim's office building with the initial intention of informing him that he no longer wished to participate in a business deal and thus, was an invitee as he had initially entered for a lawful purpose.

4. The officers then placed the client and her neighbor in the police car while they searched the house.

5. A while after, the officers came out and told the suspects that they had just found the recording and had them on tape with everything they had just said in the back of the squad car.

6. The police officer placed her and Joe in the patrol car for comfort and safety while he searched the house.

7. Because General News disclosed information on the tape, they could be liable for civil damages.

8. Any person is capable of making this distinction and should conduct their conversations accordingly.

9. They both claim the drugs belonged to a friend and that it was not theirs.

10. The state believes that even without the evidence obtained from the search, they have the tape of the incriminating conversation between Ginger and Fred.

11. Inciarrano had every intention of murdering the victim when he chose to bring a gun to the meeting.

12. The legislature surely did not intend for the person who conducted the taping to use the statute to their benefit by having the taped conversation suppressed.

13. The court will distinguish between what they deem a private conversation and what can be used as evidence.

14. Smith appealed and the appellate court reversed and remanded the case. They found that the trial court erred when they failed to suppress the taped conversation.

15. Inciarrano had the intent to kill Phillips when he brought the gun to the meeting.

16. The police officer requested the driver and the passenger to sit in the back seat of the patrol car while he searched the automobile.

17. There was no consent by the two defendants to allow the police officers to record their conversation.

18. A person asked to sit in the back of a patrol car should not expect privacy because they are in a patrol car, an extension of a police station.

19. Society would agree that a person can reasonably expect privacy in their home and any conversation will not be subject to taping.

20. State statutes protect a person's right to privacy while talking on their cellular telephone.

21. The radio station had nothing to do with the taping of the conversation. They only broadcast what they were given.

22. The individual should feel free to speak to whomever they want with a reasonable expectation of privacy.

Active versus Passive Voice

Rewrite the following sentences in active voice:

1. A conversation between Inciarrano and the murder victim was surreptitiously recorded by the victim.

2. The vehicle was searched, and Brandin was subsequently arrested.

3. The decision to deny his motion to suppress was affirmed by the appellate court.

4. The defendant was charged with possession of cocaine.

5. The defendant's motion to suppress the taped conversation was denied by the trial court.

6. Defendant's car was stopped and searched by a canine, and he was subsequently arrested.

7. Brandin stopped his vehicle in the middle of the street and was approached by two men.

8. Brandin was observed by a deputy of the Street Crimes Unit around 9:15 p.m. in a known narcotics area.

9. The defendant was heard discussing a drug deal and was searched and arrested based on the conversation.

10. The suspect was arrested.

11. The conversation was intercepted and taped illegally by the police officer.

12. The suspect's conversation was recorded by the police officer.

13. The defendant filed a motion to suppress the drugs but the motion was denied.

14. A warrant is issued by a judge only upon probable cause.

15. In *Sokolow*, it was held that all the factors as a whole were enough for reasonable suspicion.

16. The order denying the motion to suppress reversed, the judgments of conviction were vacated, and the cases remanded to district court.

17. The canine alerted, the vehicle was searched, and Brandin was subsequently arrested.

18. The Longs were informed by the Browns that they wanted to build a small toy store on the commercial lot and live in the residence next door.

19. All profits of the joint venture will be split evenly between Arctic and Marine.

20. It is the intention of each party to protect its confidential and proprietary information.

Change in Tenses

Rewrite the following sentences to keep the verb tense consistent:

1. Not remembering that the tape recorder was still on, she went next door and gets her neighbor.

2. They went back to Doe's house and begin to come up with a cover up story.

3. The police arrived and Jane and Joe tell the officer that there was a robbery and when Jane came in the house, she saw her husband dead.

4. An anonymous person taped a conversation between Congresswoman Carducci and her intern, Nico. In the conversation, they talk about Carducci's addiction to illegal drugs.

5. Congresswoman Carducci was unaware that her conversation was being taped. Nico tells Carducci that he is afraid that he will be exposed and he wanted to end their affair.

6. This information was being conveyed at a very crowded, wild party. A reasonable expectation of privacy cannot exist when Dealer took no precautions to keep this information private.

7. Because the conversation in *Inciarrano* took place in a business office open to the public, there is no reasonable expectation of privacy.

8. The victim was aware of Inciarrano's dark nature and had some suspicion that the meeting may turn violent.

9. The police found the tape recorder, which was still on at the time the police entered the house. In the patrol car the defendant tells Joe that she forgot to turn off the tape recorder.

10. Smith was not under arrest but was asked to sit in the patrol car for his safety and comfort. Smith expects that conversations within the patrol car will remain private.

11. Assuming that Inciarrano had a subjective expectation of privacy, the court concludes that once Inciarrano entered the business office with the intent to do harm, Inciarrano became a trespasser.

12. Nico no longer wanted to supply Carducci with drugs. Carducci threatens Nico, stating that she could take him down and ruin his career.

13. Carducci threatened Nico by telling him that if she goes down he will come with her. This conversation was taped by an unknown individual.

14. An unknown person using a scanner recognizes Carducci's voice. Knowing that it was an election year, the unknown person recorded the conversation between Carducci and her intern.

15. The wife filed a motion to suppress the taped telephone conversation. The court held that the husband does not have the right to invade his wife's right of privacy by taping the wife's telephone conversations.

16. Laura and Joe agree to meet at her home to discuss a private matter. Three days later Joe was found dead in his car.

17. Her husband secretly records this conversation and therefore violated these statutes.

18. Ms. Harker established a *prima facie* case; however, she fails to prove that the defendant's decision not to renew her contract was unrelated to her complaints.

19. The court denied the motion to suppress because the statutory exception does not apply.

20. In the majority opinion, the court held that cordless telephone conversations were not protected against recording at the time. The Chief Justice concurs in the result, yet not with the reasoning of the majority.

Appendix E

Problems

The following four problems were designed to give students practice in research and writing. Students can be assigned one or more of the problems to research. Writing assignments on the problems can include:

1. A client opinion letter (written to one of the persons named in a problem).
2. An office memo to a senior partner concerning one of the problems.
3. A memorandum of law in support of a motion for summary judgment or other litigation motion filed in a lawsuit concerning one of the problems.
4. An appellate brief filed after a judgment was reached in a lawsuit concerning one of the problems.

Was Swimming Pool an Attractive Nuisance?

John and Mary Cooke own a home in Anytown, Your State, with a private swimming pool in their backyard. Pursuant to local ordinances, their backyard is completely fenced by a five-foot wooden fence and the gate is kept closed with a latch at the top of the fence.

The Cookes live next door to the Andersons, a family with a two-year-old son, Joseph. Joseph loved water and the Andersons had joined the Cookes swimming in the Cookes' pool on numerous occasions. Although not yet "swimming" on his own, Joseph greatly enjoyed splashing in the pool and looked forward to playing with the Cookes' dog, Rover. From the moment Joseph woke up in the morning until he went to bed at night, his favorite topics were "pool" and "dog." Rover spent most of his days in the pool enclosure, relaxing on the pool deck or swimming. Joseph would become extremely excited anytime he heard Rover bark from next door.

One Saturday morning Joseph was playing on the screened-in porch of his home. He seemed quite content playing with his toys while his parents completed some odd jobs around the house. Once, when his mother checked on him, he was gazing toward the Cookes' house and listening for Rover's bark. His mother told Joseph that they could go swimming and visit Rover later in the day.

The parents lost track of time, each assuming that the other had been checking on Joseph. All of a sudden, the Andersons realized that neither one of them had checked on Joseph for a while. When they went to the screened-in porch Joseph was nowhere to be found and the outside screen door was slightly ajar. They called to Joseph, but he didn't answer, even though he was usually very good about coming when called.

The Andersons immediately started looking outside for Joseph. He was not in the Anderson's yard. At that moment, they noticed that the gate to the Cookes' pool fence was wide open. Fearing the worst, they rushed through the gate calling for Joseph. Initially nothing appeared out of the ordinary except that Rover was dashing around the outside of the pool and barking as if to attract someone's attention. Then they noticed the pool blanket was slightly pulled back from the side of the pool at the deep end.

The Cookes always kept the pool covered with a pool blanket when the pool was not in use. The blanket kept the water from losing heat during the night and kept debris from falling into the water. The pool blanket was constructed of two layers of blue plastic material with small air pockets between the layers. The blanket, floating on the surface of the water, covered the entire pool surface except for a small area left open so Rover could swim.

When the Cookes heard the Andersons yelling, they rushed out to the pool to find out what was the matter. When they heard that Joseph was missing, the Cookes' first thought was that he might have fallen into the pool while following Rover. John Cooke called for Phil Smith so Phil could help remove the pool blanket. Phil was a fifteen-year-old neighbor who often came to play with Rover. Phil had been playing with Rover inside the pool fence that morning. Phil did not answer so the Cookes and the Andersons together started pulling back the pool blanket.

To their horror, they saw two bodies in the deep end of the pool. They all jumped into the pool and pulled out the bodies. The two women tried to revive Joseph and Phil while the two men called the police and fire departments. When they arrived, the police and firefighters joined the Andersons and the Cookes in trying to revive the two boys. The two boys were rushed to the hospital but died a few hours later.

The police report of the incident showed that Mr. Cooke remembered opening the gate early in the morning while he was doing work around the pool. Joseph must have opened the outside screened door to his house and entered the pool enclosure looking for Rover. He may have fallen into the deep end of the pool while chasing Rover. The pool blanket would have parted enough from the side of the pool to allow Joseph to fall into the water. Although not a very good swimmer, Phil apparently jumped in to rescue Joseph at the same place Joseph had fallen in. The police theorized that Phil became disoriented while trying to rescue Joseph and couldn't get out from under the pool blanket.

The Cookes have just been told that their neighbors are planning to file suit against them, holding them responsible for Joseph and Phil's deaths. The Cookes hired your firm to represent them. The senior partner in your firm has asked you to research the law of your state and answer the following questions:

1. Does your state follow the attractive nuisance doctrine and, if so, how does it apply to private swimming pools?
2. Can the Andersons hold the Cookes responsible for Joseph's death?
3. What duty did the Cookes owe Phil, and can the Smiths hold the Cookes liable for Phil's death?

Defamation

Tom Harris and Jake Carson had been sports and political leaders and rivals ever since high school. They competed on the same sports teams and were of equal physical ability. In track and swimming races Tom would come in first in one race, Jake would come in first in the next race, and then they would tie each other for first in a third race. Either Tom or Jake had been class president each of four years in high school. Jake had been class president of his freshman and senior classes while Tom had been class president of his sophomore and junior classes.

Their friends speculated that the rivalry would continue in college. They both were to attend Collegiate University in nearby University Town. As freshmen they pledged two rival fraternities. Tom pledged Collegiate Alphas and Jake pledged Collegiate Betas. What had been friendly rivalry in high school gradually turned nasty during their years at the University. The Alphas pulled all sorts of pranks on the Betas and tried to discredit the Betas in the university community. The Betas did the same to the Alphas.

In the fall of their senior year at the University, Tom and Jake both decided to run for student body president. There was a lot of mudslinging during the campaign. At one point in the campaign, it was rumored that Jake was gay. The rumors were traced back to the Alphas. Although no one seemed to believe the rumor, Jake and his fraternity brothers were very upset about it.

The night before the election, the candidates participated in skits in the football stadium. Everyone eagerly looked forward to the skits each year, with most of the students and faculty of Collegiate University attending. The skits were usually half serious and half in jest. On skit night, the crowd in the stadium enjoyed the first skits while they speculated about Tom and Jake's skits. Jake's skit was the next-to-the-last and Tom's was the last of the evening. In Jake's skit, Jake neatly poked fun at Tom and emphasized how he, Jake, was the better candidate.

Then came time for Tom's skit. The scene was Jake's doctor's office. Tom played Jake's doctor and one of the Alphas played Jake. In the skit "Jake" walked into the doctor's office and said, "Well, doctor, now that I've completed my executive physical, I feel ready to complete my duties as Collegiate University student body president and lead the University to great achievements. How did my tests come out?" The "doctor" replied, "Well, Jake, you better sit down. I have good news and bad news for you. The good news is that most of your tests came back negative and you should make a fine student body president. The bad news is that you and Magic Johnson have something in common. Both of you tested HIV-positive."

Those words were barely out of Tom's mouth when the stadium crowd gasped. A fight immediately broke out between the Alphas and Betas sitting near each other and the police were called in to clear the stands.

Although the student body president race had seemed almost even before the skits, Tom won with two-thirds of the vote. Jake was so outraged by Tom's skit that he hired your law firm to represent him. The senior partner in your firm has asked you to research the law of your state and answer the following questions:

1. Is it actionable per se as slander to announce that a person has tested HIV-positive where the statement is not true?
2. Although Tom claims that his statement that Jake was HIV-positive was made in jest, would the words give rise to an action for slander?
3. Could Jake be considered a public official or public figure in a slander action brought by him, and, if he is considered a public official or public figure, will it make any difference in the lawsuit?

The Nightmare Property

The Longs had purchased two adjoining lots on Nice Street in Anytown, Your State, as investment property. One of the lots was zoned residential and contained a three-bedroom, two-bathroom house that the Longs rented out. The other lot, zoned commercial, was vacant.

In September of 1988, the Longs rented the house to a 30-year-old businesswoman. Barely a month later the police called the Longs. A neighbor of the businesswoman had asked the police to investigate the Longs' Nice Street house. The neighbor reported he had heard a lot of yelling at the house and then a gun shot. The police found the front door open and the businesswoman dead, apparently shot by an intruder.

The Longs next rented the Nice Street house to a family. As soon as the family moved in, they reported that their television set repeatedly turned on and off, often in the middle of the night. The children claimed they had seen the ghost of the dead woman and were too terrified to sleep in their rooms. The neighborhood children started calling the Nice Street house the "haunted house" and refused to play with the children of the family renting the house. A few months later the family moved out complaining that they did not want to live with a ghost.

After that the Longs tried without success to rent the Nice Street house. At the same time the Longs posted a "For Sale" sign on the two lots. The Longs wanted to sell them for $250,000, the price at which the Longs had purchased them ten years earlier. The Longs received no offers until almost a year later. A retired couple, the Browns, called the Longs to ask the sale price on the two lots. The couple was looking to move to a warmer climate and open a small toy store. When the Browns heard the asking price of $250,000, they said they might be interested in purchasing the lots.

The Longs met the Browns at the lots and gave them a tour of the house. The Browns explained to the Longs that they wanted to build a small toy store on the vacant commercial property and live next door in the house. They said that they were attracted to the lots because of their location and because the asking price seemed reasonable. The Longs told the Browns that the only reason they had put such a low price on the property was because it had been on the market for a while. The Longs needed to sell the property quickly because they were in need of cash to pay for unexpected expenses.

The sale went through sixty days later and the Browns immediately started construction on the vacant lot. They hoped to have the construction finished by the time they moved to Anytown. Six months later the Browns moved into the Nice Street house and opened the then completed toy store. Business at the toy store seemed very slow. The Longs noticed that none of the children from the neighborhood came into the store. They did get some business from people vacationing in Anytown.

A week after the Browns moved into the house, their television turned on in the middle of the night. They didn't think anything of it until it happened the next two nights in a row. When Mr. Brown got up to turn off the television, he thought he saw something white and filmy at the other end of the room. Then the same thing started happening to the small television in the toy store. The Browns made sure they had turned off the television before locking the store for the evening but they found the television turned on when they opened the store the next morning. Before they turned on the store lights in the morning, the Browns thought they glimpsed something white moving at the other end of the store. They didn't see anything out of the ordinary when they turned the lights on.

A few days later Mr. Brown struck up a conversation with the teenage clerk at the local grocery store. The clerk asked Mr. Brown whether he had just moved to town. When Mr. Brown told him he owned the new toy store and lived next door, the clerk said, "I didn't think the Longs would ever sell the haunted house." Mr. Brown said, "What do you mean?" The clerk said, "Everybody around here knows the house is haunted. Why do you think you paid such a low price for it?"

Understandably shaken, Mr. Brown went home and told his wife the news. They immediately called the Longs and accused them of tricking the retired couple. The Browns demanded their money back and demanded to be reimbursed for the cost of construction of the toy store. When the Longs refused, the Browns hired your law firm to represent them. The senior partner in your firm has asked you to research the law of your state and answer the following questions:

1. Did the Longs have a duty to disclose that the two lots were "haunted"?
2. What are the elements of fraud concerning the sale of real property?
3. Are there enough facts for the Browns to win if they sue the Longs for fraud?

I Wonder What Was in the Package

Margie and Floyd Walker had been happily married for forty-five years. Even though past retirement age, Floyd continued to work for the railroad as a porter on its passenger trains. Margie was worried about Floyd's health and had been trying to get him to stop working for some time. She was concerned that the porter's job was too physically taxing for someone of Floyd's age.

One Monday morning as Floyd was getting ready for work, Margie had the uncomfortable feeling that something would happen to Floyd at work. Margie pleaded with Floyd to call in sick. Floyd said, "I feel fine. Why should I call in sick if I feel fine?" Floyd reported for work as usual. Margie tried to convince herself that she was worrying for nothing, but to no avail. She wandered through the house all day, not able to get anything done except worry.

At three o'clock in the afternoon the telephone rang. Margie was so frightened that her hand shook as she answered the telephone. Floyd's supervisor at the railroad said, "Margie, I think you better sit down. I have bad news for you. Floyd fell from the train as it was going full speed and was killed. It appears he became disoriented, opened the outside door of the train, and was pulled off the train step by a sudden gust of wind. Floyd's body is at the Near Town Funeral Home. I'll make arrangements if you'd like to have the body transferred to a funeral home in Any Town." Margie felt like she had been hit by a truck. She was glad that she was sitting down or she very likely would have fainted. She responded, "Please make the arrangements with Webury Funeral Home."

Margie's worst fear had come true. Somehow she made it through the funeral. She kept feeling that it must all be a bad dream. She kept imagining that she would wake up one morning with Floyd still alive. She did remember having to call the Near Town Funeral Home several times to have Floyd's personal effects forwarded to Webury. Webury delivered the personal effects to her the day after the funeral.

It was not until almost a week after Floyd's death when Margie went through Floyd's personal effects. To her horror, in a plastic bag labeled "personal effects" she found a kidney, teeth, and fingers. At the sight of her dead husband's body parts she fainted. A neighbor lady friend found Margie an hour later collapsed on the floor. She was hospitalized for extreme exhaustion for two days and her doctor put her on antidepressant medication.

When she had recovered sufficiently, she called Webury to complain. Webury's owner disclaimed all responsibility. The owner said that Webury had simply forwarded the plastic bag, at Margie's insistence, from the Near Town Funeral Home. The owner added that the Webury employees had no reason to check what was in the bag.

Margie still suffers from depression and has not had a good night's sleep since she opened the plastic bag. She keeps having nightmares about the employees of Near Town Funeral Home placing Floyd's body parts in the plastic bag and imagines them laughing as they labeled the bag "personal effects." It also makes her angry that Webury seemed so unconcerned and did not even offer an apology. Margie has hired your law firm to represent her in a possible lawsuit against the funeral homes. The senior partner in your firm has asked you to research the law of your state and answer the following questions:

1. What would Margie Walker have to prove to recover damages for the tort of interference with a dead body?
2. What are the elements of the tort of intentional infliction of emotional distress, sometimes called the "tort of outrage"?
3. Will Margie Walker be able to hold Near Town Funeral Home and Webury Funeral Home liable for the torts of interference with a dead body and intentional infliction of emotional distress?

Appendix F

Wiretapping Statutes

The following are relevant federal wiretapping statutes (sections 2510, 2511, and 2515 of title 18 of the United States Code) found when researching the Joshua Smeek problem:

Title 18 United States Code

§ 2510. Definitions

As used in this chapter—

(1) "wire communication" means any aural transfer made in whole or in part through the use of facilities for the transmission of communications by the aid of wire, cable, or other like connection between the point of origin and the point of reception (including the use of such connection in a switching station) furnished or operated by any person engaged in providing or operating such facilities for the transmission of interstate or foreign communications or communications affecting interstate or foreign commerce;

(2) "oral communication" means any oral communication uttered by a person exhibiting an expectation that such communication is not subject to interception under circumstances justifying such expectation, but such term does not include any electronic communication;

(3) "State" means any State of the United States, the District of Columbia, the Commonwealth of Puerto Rico, and any territory or possession of the United States;

(4) "intercept" means the aural or other acquisition of the contents of any wire, electronic, or oral communication through the use of any electronic, mechanical, or other device;

(5) "electronic, mechanical, or other device" means any device or apparatus which can be used to intercept a wire, oral, or electronic communication other than—

(a) any telephone or telegraph instrument, equipment or facility, or any component thereof, (i) furnished to the subscriber or user by a provider of wire or electronic communication service in the ordinary course of its business and being used by the subscriber or user in the ordinary course of its business or furnished by such subscriber or user for connection to the facilities of such service and used in the ordinary course of its business; or (ii) being used by a provider of wire or electronic communication service in the ordinary course of its business, or by an investigative or law enforcement officer in the ordinary course of his duties;

(b) a hearing aid or similar device being used to correct subnormal hearing to not better than normal;

(6) "person" means any employee, or agent of the United States or any State or political subdivision thereof, and any individual, partnership, association, joint stock company, trust, or corporation;

(7) "Investigative or law enforcement officer" means any officer of the United States or of a State or political subdivision thereof, who is empowered by law to conduct investigations of or to make arrests for offenses enumerated in this chapter, and any attorney authorized by law to prosecute or participate in the prosecution of such offenses;

(8) "contents," when used with respect to any wire, oral, or electronic communication, includes any information concerning the substance, purport, or meaning of that communication;

(9) "Judge of competent jurisdiction" means—

(a) a judge of a United States district court or a United States court of appeals; and

(b) a judge of any court of general criminal jurisdiction of a State who is authorized by a statute of that State to enter orders authorizing interceptions of wire, oral, or electronic communications;

(10) "communication common carrier" has the meaning given that term in section 3 of the Communications Act of 1934;

(11) "aggrieved person" means a person who was a party to any intercepted wire, oral, or electronic communication or a person against whom the interception was directed;

(12) "electronic communication" means any transfer of signs, signals, writing, images, sounds, data, or intelligence of any nature transmitted in whole or in part by a wire, radio, electromagnetic, photoelectronic or photooptical system that affects interstate or foreign commerce, but does not include—

(A) any wire or oral communication;

(B) any communication made through a tone-only paging device;

(C) any communication from a tracking device (as defined in section 3117 of this title); or

(D) electronic funds transfer information stored by a financial institution in a communications system used for the electronic storage and transfer of funds;

(13) "user" means any person or entity who—

(A) uses an electronic communication service; and

(B) is duly authorized by the provider of such service to engage in such use;

(14) "electronic communications system" means any wire, radio, electromagnetic, photooptical or photoelectronic facilities for the transmission of wire or electronic communications, and any computer facilities or related electronic equipment for the electronic storage of such communications;

(15) "electronic communication service" means any service which provides to users thereof the ability to send or receive wire or electronic communications;

(16) "readily accessible to the general public" means, with respect to a radio communication, that such communication is not—

(A) scrambled or encrypted;

(B) transmitted using modulation techniques whose essential parameters have been withheld from the public with the intention of preserving the privacy of such communication;

(C) carried on a subcarrier or other signal subsidiary to a radio transmission;

(D) transmitted over a communication system provided by a common carrier, unless the communication is a tone only paging system communication; or

(E) transmitted on frequencies allocated under part 25, subpart D, E, or F of part 74, or part 94 of the Rules of the Federal Communications Commission, unless, in the case of a communication transmitted on a frequency allocated under part 74 that is not exclusively allocated to broadcast auxiliary services, the communication is a two-way voice communication by radio;

(17) "electronic storage" means—

(A) any temporary, intermediate storage of a wire or electronic communication incidental to the electronic transmission thereof; and

(B) any storage of such communication by an electronic communication service for purposes of backup protection of such communication;

(18) "aural transfer" means a transfer containing the human voice at any point between and including the point of origin and the point of reception;

(19) "foreign intelligence information," for purposes of section 2517(6) of this title, means—

(A) information, whether or not concerning a United States person, that relates to the ability of the United States to protect against—

(i) actual or potential attack or other grave hostile acts of a foreign power or an agent of a foreign power;

(ii) sabotage or international terrorism by a foreign power or an agent of a foreign power; or

(iii) clandestine intelligence activities by an intelligence service or network of a foreign power or by an agent of a foreign power; or

(B) information, whether or not concerning a United States person, with respect to a foreign power or foreign territory that relates to—

(i) the national defense or the security of the United States; or

(ii) the conduct of the foreign affairs of the United States;

(20) "protected computer" has the meaning set forth in section 1030; and

(21) "computer trespasser"—

(A) means a person who accesses a protected computer without authorization and thus has no reasonable expectation of privacy in any communication transmitted to, through, or from the protected computer; and

(B) does not include a person known by the owner or operator of the protected computer to have an existing contractual relationship with the owner or operator of the protected computer for access to all or part of the protected computer.

§2511. Interception and disclosure of wire, oral, or electronic communications prohibited

(1) Except as otherwise specifically provided in this chapter any person who—

(a) intentionally intercepts, endeavors to intercept, or procures any other person to intercept or endeavor to intercept, any wire, oral, or electronic communication;

(b) intentionally uses, endeavors to use, or procures any other person to use or endeavor to use any electronic, mechanical, or other device to intercept any oral communication when—

(i) such device is affixed to, or otherwise transmits a signal through, a wire, cable, or other like connection used in wire communication; or

(ii) such device transmits communications by radio, or interferes with the transmission of such communication; or

(iii) such person knows, or has reason to know, that such device or any component thereof has been sent through the mail or transported in interstate or foreign commerce; or

(iv) such use or endeavor to use (A) takes place on the premises of any business or other commercial establishment the operations of which affect interstate or foreign commerce; or (B) obtains or is for the purpose of obtaining information relating to the operations of any business or other commercial establishment the operations of which affect interstate or foreign commerce; or

(v) such person acts in the District of Columbia, the Commonwealth of Puerto Rico, or any territory or possession of the United States;

(c) intentionally discloses, or endeavors to disclose, to any other person the contents of any wire, oral, or electronic communication, knowing or having reason to know that the information was obtained through the interception of a wire, oral, or electronic communication in violation of this subsection;

(d) intentionally uses, or endeavors to use, the contents of any wire, oral, or electronic communication, knowing or having reason to know that the information was obtained through the interception of a wire, oral, or electronic communication in violation of this subsection; or

(e)

(i) intentionally discloses, or endeavors to disclose, to any other person the contents of any wire, oral, or electronic communication, intercepted by means authorized by sections 2511(2)(a)(ii), 2511(2)(b)-(c), 2511(2)(e), 2516, and 2518 of this chapter, (ii) knowing or having reason to know that the information was obtained through the interception of such a communication in connection with a criminal investigation, (iii) having obtained or received the information in connection with a criminal investigation, and (iv) with intent to improperly obstruct, impede, or interfere with a duly authorized criminal investigation, shall be punished as provided in subsection (4) or shall be subject to suit as provided in subsection (5).

(2)

(a)

(i) It shall not be unlawful under this chapter for an operator of a switchboard, or an officer, employee, or agent of a provider of wire or electronic communication service, whose facilities are used in the transmission of a wire or electronic communication, to intercept, disclose, or use that communication in the normal course of his employment while engaged in any activity which is a necessary incident to the rendition of his service or to the protection of the rights or property of the provider of that service, except that a provider of wire communication service to the public shall not utilize service observing or random monitoring except for mechanical or service quality control checks.

(ii) Notwithstanding any other law, providers of wire or electronic communication service, their officers, employees, and agents, landlords, custodians, or other persons, are authorized to provide information, facilities, or technical assistance to persons authorized by law to intercept wire, oral, or electronic communications or to conduct electronic surveillance, as defined in section 101 of the Foreign Intelligence Surveillance Act of 1978, if such provider, its officers, employees, or agents, landlord, custodian, or other specified person, has been provided with—

(A) a court order directing such assistance or a court order pursuant to section 704 of the Foreign Intelligence Surveillance Act of 1978 signed by the authorizing judge, or

(B) a certification in writing by a person specified in section 2518(7) of this title or the Attorney General of the United States that no warrant or court order is required by law, that all statutory requirements have been met, and that the specified assistance is required, setting forth the period of time during which the provision of the information, facilities, or technical assistance is authorized and specifying the information, facilities, or technical assistance required. No provider of wire or electronic communication service, officer, employee, or agent thereof, or landlord, custodian, or other specified person shall disclose the existence of any interception or surveillance or the device used to accomplish the interception or surveillance with respect to which the person has been furnished a court order or certification under this chapter, except as may otherwise be required by legal process and then only after prior notification to the Attorney General or to the principal prosecuting attorney of a State or any political subdivision of a State, as may be appropriate. Any such disclosure shall render such person liable for the civil damages provided for in section 2520. No cause of action shall lie in any court against any provider of wire or electronic communication service, its officers, employees, or agents, landlord, custodian, or other specified person for providing information, facilities, or assistance in accordance with the terms of a court order, statutory authorization, or certification under this chapter.

(iii) If a certification under subparagraph (ii)(B) for assistance to obtain foreign intelligence information is based on statutory authority, the certification shall identify the specific statutory provision and shall certify that the statutory requirements have been met.

(b) It shall not be unlawful under this chapter for an officer, employee, or agent of the Federal Communications Commission, in the normal course of his employment and in discharge of the monitoring responsibilities exercised by the Commission in the enforcement of Chapter 5 of title 47 of the United States Code, to intercept a wire or electronic communication, or oral communication transmitted by radio, or to disclose or use the information thereby obtained.

(c) It shall not be unlawful under this chapter for a person acting under color of law to intercept a wire, oral, or electronic communication, where such person is a party to the communication or one of the parties to the communication has given prior consent to such interception.

(d) It shall not be unlawful under this chapter for a person not acting under color of law to intercept a wire, oral, or electronic communication where such person is a party to the communication or where one of the parties to the communication has given prior consent to such interception unless such communication is intercepted for the purpose of committing any criminal or tortious act in violation of the Constitution or laws of the United States or of any State.

(e) Notwithstanding any other provision of this title or section 705 or 706 of the Communications Act of 1934, it shall not be unlawful for an officer, employee, or agent of the United States in the normal course of his official duty to conduct electronic surveillance, as defined in section 101 of the Foreign Intelligence Surveillance Act of 1978, as authorized by that Act.

(f) Nothing contained in this chapter or Chapter 121 or 206 of this title, or section 705 of the Communications Act of 1934, shall be deemed to affect the acquisition by the United States Government of foreign intelligence information from international or foreign communications, or foreign intelligence activities conducted in accordance with otherwise applicable Federal law involving a foreign electronic communications system, utilizing a means other than electronic surveillance as defined in section 101 of the Foreign Intelligence Surveillance Act of 1978, and procedures in this chapter or chapter 121 and the Foreign Intelligence Surveillance Act of 1978 shall be the exclusive means by which electronic surveillance, as defined in section 101 of such Act, and the interception of domestic wire, oral, and electronic communications may be conducted.

(g) It shall not be unlawful under this chapter or Chapter 121 of this title for any person—

  (i) to intercept or access an electronic communication made through an electronic communication system that is configured so that such electronic communication is readily accessible to the general public;

(ii) to intercept any radio communication which is transmitted—

(I) by any station for the use of the general public, or that relates to ships, aircraft, vehicles, or persons in distress;

(II) by any governmental, law enforcement, civil defense, private land mobile, or public safety communications system, including police and fire, readily accessible to the general public;

(III) by a station operating on an authorized frequency within the bands allocated to the amateur, citizens band, or general mobile radio services; or

(IV) by any marine or aeronautical communications system;

(iii) to engage in any conduct which—

(I) is prohibited by section 633 of the Communications Act of 1934; or

(II) is excepted from the application of section 705(a) of the Communications Act of 1934 by section 705(b) of that Act;

(iv) to intercept any wire or electronic communication the transmission of which is causing harmful interference to any lawfully operating station or consumer electronic equipment, to the extent necessary to identify the source of such interference; or

(v) for other users of the same frequency to intercept any radio communication made through a system that utilizes frequencies monitored by individuals engaged in the provision or the use of such system, if such communication is not scrambled or encrypted.

(h) It shall not be unlawful under this chapter—

(i) to use a pen register or a trap and trace device (as those terms are defined for the purposes of Chapter 206 (relating to pen registers and trap and trace devices) of this title); or

(ii) for a provider of electronic communication service to record the fact that a wire or electronic communication was initiated or completed in order to protect such provider, another provider furnishing service toward the completion of the wire or electronic communication, or a user of that service, from fraudulent, unlawful or abusive use of such service.

(i) It shall not be unlawful under this chapter for a person acting under color of law to intercept the wire or electronic communications of a computer trespasser transmitted to, through, or from the protected computer, if—

(I) the owner or operator of the protected computer authorizes the interception of the computer trespasser's communications on the protected computer;

(II) the person acting under color of law is lawfully engaged in an investigation;

(III) the person acting under color of law has reasonable grounds to believe that the contents of the computer trespasser's communications will be relevant to the investigation; and

(IV) such interception does not acquire communications other than those transmitted to or from the computer trespasser.

(j) It shall not be unlawful under this chapter for a provider of electronic communication service to the public or remote computing service to intercept or disclose the contents of a wire or electronic communication in response to an order from a foreign government that is subject to an executive agreement that the Attorney General has determined and certified to Congress satisfies section 2523.

(3)

(a) Except as provided in paragraph (b) of this subsection, a person or entity providing an electronic communication service to the public shall not intentionally divulge the contents of any communication (other than one to such person or entity, or an agent thereof) while in transmission on that service to any person or entity other than an addressee or intended recipient of such communication or an agent of such addressee or intended recipient.

(b) A person or entity providing electronic communication service to the public may divulge the contents of any such communication—

(i) as otherwise authorized in section 2511(2)(a) or 2517 of this title;

(ii) with the lawful consent of the originator or any addressee or intended recipient of such communication;

(iii) to a person employed or authorized, or whose facilities are used, to forward such communication to its destination; or

(iv) which were inadvertently obtained by the service provider and which appear to pertain to the commission of a crime, if such divulgence is made to a law enforcement agency.

(4)

(a) Except as provided in paragraph (b) of this subsection or in subsection (5), whoever violates subsection (1) of this section shall be fined under this title or imprisoned not more than five years, or both.

(b) Conduct otherwise an offense under this subsection that consists of or relates to the interception of a satellite transmission that is not encrypted or scrambled and that is transmitted—

(i) to a broadcasting station for purposes of retransmission to the general public; or

(ii) as an audio subcarrier intended for redistribution to facilities open to the public, but not including data transmissions or telephone calls, is not an offense under this subsection unless the conduct is for the purposes of direct or indirect commercial advantage or private financial gain.

[(c) Redesignated (b)]

(5)

(a)

(i) If the communication is—

(A) a private satellite video communication that is not scrambled or encrypted and the conduct in violation of this chapter is the private viewing of that communication and is not for a tortious or illegal purpose or for purposes of direct or indirect commercial advantage or private commercial gain; or

(B) a radio communication that is transmitted on frequencies allocated under subpart D of part 74 of the rules of the Federal Communications Commission that is not scrambled or encrypted and the conduct in violation of this chapter is not for a tortious or illegal purpose or for purposes of direct or indirect commercial advantage or private commercial gain, then the person who engages in such conduct shall be subject to suit by the Federal Government in a court of competent jurisdiction.

(ii) In an action under this subsection—

(A) if the violation of this chapter is a first offense for the person under paragraph (a) of subsection (4) and such person has not been found liable in a civil action under section 2520 of this title, the Federal Government shall be entitled to appropriate injunctive relief; and

(B) if the violation of this chapter is a second or subsequent offense under paragraph (a) of subsection (4) or such person has been found liable in any prior civil action under section 2520, the person shall be subject to a mandatory $500 civil fine.

(b) The court may use any means within its authority to enforce an injunction issued under paragraph (ii)(A), and shall impose a civil fine of not less than $500 for each violation of such an injunction.

§2515. Prohibition of use as evidence of intercepted wire or oral communications

Whenever any wire or oral communication has been intercepted, no part of the contents of such communication and no evidence derived therefrom may be received in evidence in any trial, hearing, or other proceeding in or before any court, grand jury, department, officer, agency, regulatory body, legislative committee, or other authority of the United States, a State, or a political subdivision thereof if the disclosure of that information would be in violation of this chapter.

Index

F

I

J